THEOLOGY
of the
NEW TESTAMENT

THEOLOGY
of the
NEW TESTAMENT

by

Karl Hermann Schelkle

English Version by

William A. Jurgens

II
SALVATION HISTORY--
REVELATION

THE LITURGICAL PRESS

Collegeville,   *Minnesota*

THEOLOGY OF THE NEW TESTAMENT

Volume One: CREATION: World — Time — Man

Volume Two: SALVATION HISTORY — REVELATION

Volume Three: MORALITY

Volume Four: THE RULE OF GOD — CHURCH —
ESCHATOLOGY

THEOLOGY OF THE NEW TESTAMENT — II SALVATION HISTORY — REVELATION — is the
authorized translation of *Theologie des Neuen Testaments — 2 Gott war in Christus* by Karl Hermann Schelkle, copyright © 1973 Patmos-Verlag, Düsseldorf,
Germany.

Nihil obstat: William G. Heidt, O.S.B., S.T.D., *Censor deputatus. Imprimatur*:
† George H. Speltz, D.D., Bishop of St. Cloud.

Printed by the North Central Publishing Company, St. Paul, Minnesota.

Copyright © 1976 *by* The Order of St. Benedict, Inc., Collegeville, Minnesota.

FOREWORD

The first part of our *Theology of the New Testament* appeared in 1968, with the English version following in 1971, under the title *Creation (World — Time — Man)*. The third part was published in 1970, English version in 1973, entitled *Morality*. The fourth and final part, which will treat of the Rule of God, of the Church, and of Eschatology, is soon to follow.

Interest in the Bible, a thing which ten and twenty years ago was great indeed, has by this time, or so it seems to us, passed its zenith. Perhaps the reasons for this are to be found in the unfortunate contempt in which history is held in our times. For the words of Scripture, whose function it is to illuminate and shape the present while pointing the way to the future, come to us from out of the past. Like every spiritual movement, however, the Church too will return again and again to her sources, in which her history is asserted in undisturbed purity and in concentrated depth. And in the numerous and difficult problems which beset the Church in this present age, the Bible and the New Testament in particular will have to be the charter as it were, the primitive herald of Christian faith and life, the primary norm of illumination and assistance to the renewal and deepening of our congregations. Valid even now, therefore, is the prayerful aspiration of the Apostle: "May the word of God dwell abundantly in your midst" (Col. 3:16).

A remark of Karl Jaspers is worthy of some consideration: "All the prospects of the Churches lie in the Bible, if only they might again today find spontaneous expression in the consciousness of our being at a turning point in history."

— *Karl Hermann Schelkle*

CONTENTS

III. SPIRIT OF GOD

IV. BELIEF IN GOD AND DOCTRINE ABOUT GOD

INTRODUCTION

In the biblical exposition of history the creation of the world is followed by its being spoiled through human guilt. But through God's own operation, creation becomes a new creation. A systematic theology of the New Testament will describe, therefore, first of all the biblical doctrine of creation, and afterwards the salvation event and redemption.[1] In such an arrangement what must be treated first of all is revelation, its apex and goal, achieved in Jesus Christ (§§ 1-4 of the present volume of our *Theology of the New Testament*).

Salvation becomes a real event in Christ. His person and his works show themselves in his words, his deeds, his miracles, in his death and resurrection (§§ 5-10).

Since the theology of the incarnation is so intimately bound up with the New Testament proclamation of Christ, it seems logical enough to treat next of this kerygmatic aspect (§ 11).

Biblical Christology starts from history and time and proceeds from there to reflection upon the eternal pre-existence of him who, in the incarnation, enters into history. A New Testament theology of revelation and of redemption is essentially a Christology. Revelation and salvation are brought about in the Spirit (§ 12).

In the history of salvation the eternal God is plainly manifested. In a New Testament theology this is the place for the doctrine about God (§§ 13-21).

From the foregoing remarks we can see what is the actual methodological distinction between biblical theology and dogmatic theology; for the latter traditionally begins with the doctrine on God and develops its system of dogmas therefrom.

THEOLOGY
of the
NEW TESTAMENT

I

REVELATION

§ 1. CONCEPTUALITY AND NOTION OF
BIBLICAL REVELATION

To man, God is the one who is distant and hidden, full of mystery. When men speak of the Godhead, they suppose that the Hidden One has become manifest or has been revealed to them. Revelation in some form or other is surely a concept of primary consideration in all religions. Certainly this is true of the institutional religions, which trace themselves back to a founder who was a bestower of revelation (as is the case with Judaism, Christianity and Islam). But there can also be a philosophical religious sentiment, which achieves its knowledge of God through philosophical conclusions, which conclusions can refer even to their own insights as revelation.[2]

1. Words and Concepts

Biblical religion understands revelation as God's gratuitous disclosure of himself. Man can know about God only because God reveals himself, and only insofar as God reveals himself. The Greek Bible, Old Testament and New, speaks of God's revelation, mostly with the terms ἀποκαλύπτειν (ἀποκάλυψις) (unveiling), γνωρίζειν (to let something be known, to give knowledge), σηλοῦν (to make public), ψανεροῦν (ψανέρωσις) (to make manifest), ἐπιψαίνεσθαι (ἐπιψάνεια) to make an appearance, to appear).

In describing revelation the Bible has at its disposal a rich vocabulary; and the abundance of terms is indicative of the fullness and depth of the object itself. The terms mentioned occur also in profane Greek. In profane literature they have mostly the sense of making something

3

public. Only later in a post-biblical era — seldom enough even then, and perhaps under the influence of the Bible — are they used in a religious context. Even in the Old Testament Greek Bible the profane linguistic usage of these terms is more frequent than their sacred usage; and in the New Testament their profane usage is at least still known.

Some characteristic examples are the following:

a) Old Testament

The word ἀποκαλύπτειν *i.e.*, to unveil, to reveal, is found in its religious significance in the following contexts, by no means exhaustive: God "revealed himself to the house of Israel in Egypt" (1 Sam. 2:27). Certainly this took place in words addressed to Moses, but still more through God's powerful deeds. God "unveils his arm" (Is. 52:10; 53:1), "his mercies" (Is. 56:1), "his justice and his salvation" (Ps. 98:2f.). Here revelation means God's operation in history. To the prophets God reveals "his instructions" (Amos 3:7), "his secrets" (Dan. 2:27-30, 47). It is here that the revelation of hidden truth takes place. "To whom has the root of wisdom been revealed?" (Sir. 1:6). Revelation brings about knowledge.

The terms γνωρίζειν (to make known the otherwise inaccessible) and δηλοῦν (to make public what was unknown) are used in regard to God's giving an experiential knowledge of his power and favor. Thus in Jer. 16:21, "I will make them aware of my hand and allow them to know my power; and they shall know that my name is the Lord." God makes publicly known his name (Exod. 3:14), his plans (Exod. 33:12f.), his secrets (Ps. 50:8), the ways of life (Ps. 15:11), his requirements (3 Kings 8:36; 2 Chron. 6:27), his will (Ps. 24:4; Ezech 20:11).

The term ἐπιφάνεια signifies in the religious language of the Greek Bible (as well as in its pagan milieu) the benevolent manifestation of the otherwise hidden Godhead. God reveals himself in history in his marvelous deeds, and in an abiding way in worship. In the Septuagint the God who intercedes for the people is experienced as the Lord actually present (ἐπιφανής) (Judg. 13:6; 2 Sam. 7:23; Hab. 1:7; Mal. 1:14; 3:22). The day of judgment will be an epiphany (Joel 2:11; 3:4). In the books of Maccabees, written under a Hellenistic influence, the powerful intervention of God is designated an epiphany; thus in 2 Macc. 3:24; 14:15; *et passim*.

The word ψανερόω (to make manifest, to exhibit), a word of only late and infrequent occurrence in profane Greek literature, is found in the Old Testament in Jer. 40:6, "I will make clear to them the granting of their requests."

b) New Testament

In the New Testament the words used most frequently in this regard are ἀποκαλύπτειν (ἀποκάλυψις) and ψανεροῦν (ψανέρωσις).Of less frequent occurrence is δηλοῦν.

Revelation (ἀποκάλυψις) takes place in the gracious operations of God (Matthew 11:25; 16:17; Rom. 3:21; Eph. 1:17) and of his Christ (Matthew 11:27; Luke 2:32; John 17:6; Gal. 1:12; 1 John 4:9; Apoc. 1:1), and through the Spirit (1 Cor. 2:10; 12:7; Eph. 3:5; Heb. 9:8). Revelation takes place now in the messianic age both as salvation (John 9:3; Rom. 1:17; Eph. 3:5) and as judgment (Rom. 1:18).

Revelation took place and does yet take place in the Church. It was given to the apostles so that they might pass it on to others (thus with Paul, Gal. 1:16 and 2 Cor. 12:1), as well as to the apostles and prophets. "The mystery of Christ was revealed to the holy apostles and prophets" (Eph. 3:5). Revelation is imparted also to the individual. "When you gather together each one has a psalm, an instruction, a revelation, a speaking in tongues" (1 Cor. 14:26). "If on some point you are minded otherwise, this also will God reveal to you" (Phil. 3:15). Revelation will be completed in the eschatological unveiling (Luke 17:30; Rom. 8:19; 1 Cor. 1:7; 2 Thess. 1:7; 2:3; 1 Peter 1:5 and 1:13).

In the centuries before the New Testament an extensive apocalyptic literature had arisen in Judaism, in which literature the names of the holy men of past ages were assumed in order to put into their mouths particularized details about the world beyond as well as about the future messianic times and the eschatology. Some of these apocalypses were accepted into the canon (Daniel, Isaiah chap. 24–27).

In the New Testament there are several great apocalyptic texts (Mark 13; 1 Thess. 4:13-17; 2 Thess. 2:1-12; 2 Peter 3:10-13), as well as the Apocalypse of John. This latter is "the revelation of Jesus Christ, which God gave him." Its purpose is to unveil the events of the judgment and of salvation in the approaching endtime (Apoc. 1:1).

Of very frequent usage in the New Testament is the term ψανεροῦν, though its derivative ψανέρωσις is of somewhat less frequent occurrence. Paul interchanges ψανεροῦν and ἀποκαλύπτειν as synonyms: thus, in Rom. 1:17, "The justice of God is unveiled"; and in Rom. 3:21, "The justice of God is revealed." In the Christ-event the justification of believers is now a reality. Revelation is carried further in the proclamation as made by the Apostle (2 Cor. 2:14; 11:6), and indeed, in his very existence (2 Cor. 4:10).

In the deutero-Pauline Epistles the term ψανεροῦν contrasts what was formerly hidden with what is now revealed (Col. 1:26f.; Rom. 16:25–27 — surely a post-Pauline addition — and in a freer form in 1 Tim. 3:16; 2 Tim. 1:10; 1 Peter 1:18-20).

The term, moreover, is of frequent occurrence in the Johannine literature. Jesus unveils the divine reality. He reveals God's name (John 17:6) and God's works (John 3:21; 9:3). In the Johannine Epistles too, the activity of Jesus is designated as revelation (1 John 3:5-8). His activity reveals the love of God (1 John 4:9). The whole revelation can be conceived as life (1 John 1:2).

While in the New Testament revelation mostly designates the impending event of unveiling and of making publicly known, later texts look back upon revelation as something past and closed (1 Tim. 3:16; 1 Peter 1:20; and Rom. 16:26).

In the New Testament the term γνωρίζειν occurs not infrequently in its ordinary profane meaning. In its religious usage it signifies God's allowing his power, his majesty, and his salvation to be perceived; thus in Rom. 9:22f; Luke 2:15; Acts 2:28. God reveals his plan of salvation. "He made known to us the secret resolution of his will" (Eph. 1:9). According to Eph. 1:7 this resolution is God's grace. In the Gospel of John it is Jesus who reveals. "All that I heard from my Father I have made known to you" (John 15:15; 17:26).

In the religious history of Greece the concept and word epiphany (ἐπιψάνεια) are richly significant. The divinity is, if you will, epiphanized in mythical tales, in worship, and even in prominent and influential persons. In the cult of the ruler, the ruler bears the title Epiphanes. Such is the case with the Egyptian and Hellenistic princes. Even Caius Julius Caesar is called, in an inscription at Ephesus, "the epiphanic god and common savior of human life" (W. Dittenberger, *Sylloge inscriptionum graecarum*, Vol. 2, no. 760, 4th edition, Hildesheim 1960). The word epiphany occurs often enough in the later writings of the New Testament, attuned as they are to their Greek milieu. It designates the apocalyptic epiphany of the Antichrist as well as that of the Lord Jesus Christ at the end of the ages (2 Thess. 2:1-12; 2 Tim. 4:8). But even the visible earthly appearance of Jesus Christ as savior was already an epiphany (2 Tim. 1:10), a matter which will be treated at greater length below, in § 10, 2b.

The concept of revelation, in the New Testament in particular, can be descriptively stated in summary fashion: In revelation God displays himself through word and deed. The fullness of revelation is Jesus Christ. The recipients and witnesses of revelation are the apostles, prophets, as well as the whole Church. Revelation is completed as the eschatological fulfillment of redemption; and this revelation of redemption pertains both to Christ and to the sons of God: to Christ in an active way, he being the giver; and to us in a passive way, we being the recipients.

In the concept of revelation Catholic dogmatics emphasizes the revealed word as instruction. It usually understands revelation as the *"locutio Dei (attestans)*, that is, 'God speaking out of the treasury of his own understanding, communicating to men truths which would otherwise be attainable by them only with difficulty or not at all.'"[3] In the new covenant the recipients of revelation — according to scholastic theology — are the apostles. With the death of the last apostle the process of revelation is closed. Revelation designates, besides the process, also the sum total of the knowledge and certitude of belief, derived from that process, about God and salvation history. This knowledge can finally be explained in theses and in systematic teaching.

Let it be noted, however, that there is a conspicuous difference between the biblical and the dogmatic concept of revelation. According to the New Testament the recipients and witnesses of revelation are, in addition to the apostles, the prophets; in addition, therefore, to the official, there is the charismatic (Eph. 3:5). Indeed, the whole Church and each Christian receives revelation (1 Cor. 14:26; Phil. 3:15). In this wise, then, the process of revelation is not closed, but continues on and on.

2. First and Second Vatican Councils

On the concept, nature, and content of revelation, both the First and the Second Vatican Councils declared themselves expressly and in detail. The First Vatican Council emphasized the character of revelation as knowledge. Through revelation all are able to know the truth with certitude (Schönmetzer's Denzinger, *Enchiridion symbolorum*, Freiburg im Br., 32nd edition, 1963, no. 3005). The Council also determined: "God has revealed himself and the eternal decrees of his will" (*ibid.*, no. 3004). Revelation, accordingly, is God's giving knowledge of himself, not an imparting of abstract truths. If the decrees of God's will are named as subject of revelation, this too emphasizes the imparting of a knowledge of God's interventions; and again, it is not a question of abstract truths but of revelation in history. In this way an extravagantly intellectual concept of revelation is warded off. Revelation happened to the apostles, from whom it comes down to us in the Holy Scriptures as well as by oral tradition (*ibid.*, 3006).

The Second Vatican Council declared in its Constitution on Divine Revelation (*Dei verbum* 1, 2): "It pleased God, in his goodness and wisdom, to reveal himself and to make known the mystery of his will." If this new formulation, in contrast to that of the First Vatican Council, designates as content of revelation not the decrees of God's will but the mystery of his will, perhaps a legalistic interpretation, which would regard revelation as the decreeing of commands, should be avoided, instead of which it should be made clear that revelation effects salvation after the manner of a mystery. The term sacrament may here be substituted as a synonym for mystery (Eph. 1:9). The same Constitution in the same article also states: "This economy of Revelation is realized by deeds and words, which are intrinsically bound up with each other." It is clear that the constitution rejects a one-sidedly intellectual understanding of revelation.

3. Revelation in History, in Word, in Scripture

The formulation "revelation by deeds and words" involves a number of questions. The deeds which are a medium of God's revelation are encountered in his dealings with his elect community, but also with all peoples. Israel came to know God's salvation in the election of her fathers and of the people, in the institution of the covenants, and especially in the leading of the people out of Egypt and into the promised land. Salvation history unfolding in God's judgment and favor was perceived by the prophets in the course of historical events.

The New Testament recognizes the feature of salvation history when it understands its own era as the messianic fulfillment of the Old Testament promise. God will guide history on to its eschatological completion. Things may take place in such a way that they may seem to be explicable as simply a natural course of events. The prophet, however, recognizes God's salvational activity; and he explains and proclaims it, just as the faith which accepts his proclamation recognizes that salvational activity. That the Bible interprets time on the plane of salvational history cannot be disputed. To modern theology the recognition of the historicity of revelation is of essential importance. It is not easy for it, however, to ratify the old presentations of salvation, since it wants to avoid having to concretize God's dealings in the history of the world. The biblical testimony about the historical dealings of God must in any case be interpreted with faith as starting point.

Faith recognizes God's dealings in particular instances in extraordinary and wonderful deeds. The biblical concept of the miraculous will be treated in the context of the reports of the miracles of Jesus (§ 6). The miracle does not produce faith; rather, the faith which is already present perceives the miracle. This is true enough even of the revelation of Jesus Christ himself. In appearance he is but a man, indeed, a man crucified; but the gospel says that God operates and is made manifest in him. The scandal of the deprivation, yes, of the powerlessness of God, is ever present in the proof of God's might.

The other manner of revelation is revelation in words.[4] Many passages of both Old and New Testaments speak of the word of God which has been promulgated to men. Still, God's word cannot issue forth like the word which passes between men. God's words are reported to us in the Scriptures. But here they are reproduced either in Hebrew or in Greek. No man has ever heard the language of God. God has neither mouth nor speech such as men have. If he were to speak, no man could stand firm at the sound of his voice. When the Bible speaks of God's word and when we speak of God's word, it is always only by analogy.

The original word of God is not an external word, but always an internal word, which is perceived by the prophet or by the sacred writer or by the faith in general. It is perceptible only there where faith stands in God's presence and lives in responsibility to him. Nevertheless, the assertion that God's word issued forth frequently becomes quite formalized; thus in many legal texts of the Pentateuch, when these are introduced with the statement: "The Lord spoke with Moses and said . . . ."

The spoken word of God is set down in writing in the Holy Scriptures.[5] The Scriptures themselves are termed word of God.[6] Further, however, Scripture is a report or tidings, not a literally spoken word, which at all events must be drawn forth from the report. All the books, and indeed every sentence and every word of the Sacred Scriptures, are in some way marked by the historical circumstances of the times in which they were composed. And if they are God's word, they are, nevertheless, man's word also. It is the task of scientific exegesis as well as that of the community of the faith to perceive or to make perceptible within the ephemeral words of men the abiding message of God.

If we call the Holy Scriptures the word of God we do so on this account: because, since they are inspired, they are the speech of the divine Spirit. In the Old Testament, the prophet is God's mouth (Num. 24:2-4; Is. 6:8f.; Jer. 20:7-18). The Spirit fills up the prophets (Is. 61:1; Ezech. 11:5; Hos. 9:7; Zech. 7:12). The Qumran community, which made zealous study of the Bible a duty, is convinced that the prophets received God's revelation through his Holy Spirit (1) (QS 8:16; *Damascus Document* 2:12f.). Awe of the Holy Scriptures increases more and more. The *Fourth Book of Esdras* (14:22-26) describes the canonical books and the apocalyptic writings which supplement them as the work of God and of the divine Spirit.

The rabbis shared and strengthened the conviction that the Holy Scriptures are given by the Spirit and that he speaks in them. The words of the Torah are quoted as words of the Holy Spirit himself. In view of the undeniable problems and unignorable stylistic defects of the Scriptures one could the more easily accept the opinion that many passages therein were not spoken by the Spirit but by men, and that they are in the sacred text only as quotations of a human statement.[7]

The New Testament recognizes David's words as coming from the Spirit (Mark 12:36; Acts 1:16; 4:25; Heb. 3:7; see also Acts 28:25; Heb.

9:8; 10:15). The prophets announced the word of God (Heb. 1:1; 2 Peter 1:21). Just as Paul works in the Spirit, so too he decides in the Spirit what he will speak and write (1 Cor. 7:40; 2 Cor. 6:6). Even the author of the Apocalypse speaks in the Spirit (Apoc. 1:10).[8]

The New Testament already says that the Scriptures (meaning first of all the Old Testament) are "breathed out by God", "inspired" (2 Tim. 3:16; 2 Peter 1:21). In so stating, it is ultimately a profane terminology that is adopted. Hellenistic Judaism explained the Old Testament's being filled with the Spirit as ecstatic enthusiasm, thereby making use of Greek expositions (Philo, *De specialibus legibus* 1, 65; 4, 49; *Quis rerum divinarum heres sit* 263-265; Josephus, *Against Apion*, 1, 37-39). According to Greek soothsaying the oracles of the Pythian priestess at Delphi, like those of the Sibyl of Cumae, are "breathed out by God."[9] That the conceptualization of a foreign religious sentiment stands as the source of certain New Testament and Christian linguistic usages is not without its problems.

The doctrine of the inspiration of Sacred Scripture, nevertheless, does not mean simply that the Spirit collaborated in what was written down. Inspiration is not just a declaration in regard to a past origin of the Scriptures. Inspiration means that the Scriptures are filled with the Spirit and remain filled with the Spirit; that the Spirit speaks out of the Scriptures, operates through them, and that he will and must become effective through them again in their proclamation in the Church.

The New Testament is aware of the problematic which has its origin in the historicity of the Scriptures. According to a statement of Jesus, Moses permitted the bill of divorce as a concession to the hardness of men's hearts (Mark 10:5f.). The bill of divorce or written notice of dismissal is a departure from the original will of God, who from creation itself established and willed that marriage be a lasting bond (Gen. 1:27; 2:24). The bill of divorce, nevertheless, is given in Deut. 24:1 as a covenant statute. In what sense, then, is this statement of the Bible God's word?

For Paul, every problem can be decided by Scripture (γραψή — Rom. 4:3; 9:17; Gal. 3:8). But Scripture can also be worthless; indeed, a death-dealing alphabetic symbol (γράμμα) and a deadly law. "The letter kills, but the Spirit gives life" (2 Cor. 3:6). Paul is able to refer to the decalogue written by God as a "ministry of death, which was engraved

in letters on stone" (2 Cor. 3:7). The empty written law is an antiquated
and outmoded thing. Now there is the new covenant in the newness
of the Spirit (Rom. 7:6). This new covenant is a turning from the letter
to the Spirit (2 Cor. 3:14-16). Finally, the new covenant lives not by
the writing but by the Spirit.

Dogmatics and magisterium have deduced from inspiration the inerrancy of the Bible. The Second Vatican Council also concerned itself
with the problems that inerrancy raises. It explains in its Constitution
on Divine Revelation (*Dei verbum* 3, 11), "Since, therefore, all that
the inspired authors, or sacred writers affirm should be regarded as
affirmed by the Holy Spirit, we must acknowledge that the books of
Scripture, firmly, faithfully and without error, teach that truth which
God, for the sake of our salvation, wished to see confided to the Sacred
Scriptures." The text requires interpretation in the light of the history
of doctrine; and with certain texts different explanations do arise. The
Sacred Scriptures must be taken as a whole. As a totality, they are the
testimony of God, who reveals himself to men in word and in deed.
He makes himself known through the long succession of generations.
The Scriptures are the history of God's call and rejection; God's giving
and establishing, but also his re-working, laying aside, and creating
anew. In this their final totality the Sacred Scriptures are to be interpreted.[10]

4. Protestant Theology

Protestant theology emphasizes the hiddenness of God even in his
revelation. God never reveals himself directly in his essence, but only
in his deed and in his word. The revealed God, then, is always at the
same time the hidden God. This takes place in the highest and most
profound way on the Cross, where the grace of God conceals itself
under his judgment.

Even the testimony of revelation, which testimony is set down in
the Scriptures, is dimmed. The word of God is concealed under the
words of men. Bible and word of God are not identical. The Bible declares the promulgated word, and tells it to the docile listener. The
word is revealed ever in the form of a servant; and this whether the

Word made flesh or the word in the book. God's revelation is never a complete and perfect unveiling.

The theology of Protestantism emphasizes the difference and opposition between man's own recognition of God and revelation. Revelation takes place in opposition to man's intellection and volition, and particularly in opposition to the natural religion constructed by man for himself. This latter is ever man's vain endeavor, to make himself God's master. Natural religion is not a gateway to revelation but at most its negative presupposition, so that man, frustrated in his natural religious sentiment, can come to know revelation. Karl Barth,[11] in his consistently radical way, says that Christian revelation is the dissolution of all religion, insofar as religion is a system, founded in human self-assertion, of the relationships between God and man. Revelation, understood as God's dealings, puts an end to this self-aggrandizement and chutzpah of men.

Existential interpretation refers biblical revelation essentially to man. In the New Testament concept of revelation it is not a question of the plurality of the "what" of revelation; rather, it is a question only of the "that there is" of revelation. That is to say, it is not a question of a plurality of revelational content, but only of the fact that revelation has been made. Revelation is not an announcement about many and varied things. In revelation man is understood in his non-self, that is, in his sin; and in his reality, which is faith. Faith is not philosophical illumination of existence, since it grasps a historical event externally: the fact that Jesus Christ exists. Only now is the new understanding of self which comes from faith possible. Revelation, therefore, is nothing other than the reality of Jesus Christ.

§ 2. REVELATION IN CREATION

Theological terminology distinguishes between natural and supernatural revelation and between natural and supernatural theology.[12] Natural revelation is the revelation of God in the world of nature and in the nature of man; natural theology concerns the recognition of God through nature. This knowledge, moreover, is achieved by the natural light of purely human reason. Since, however, for the Bible the world is not simply nature, but creation and, as creation, history, it is appropriate to speak not of natural revelation and theology, but of the revelation and theology of creation. But certainly we can speak of general revelation (in creation) and of special revelation (in salvation history).

1. OLD TESTAMENT AND GREEK PHILOSOPHY

The notion of a recognition of God on the basis of creation is forcefully expressed in the New Testament. The roots on which this notion grows reach far back in time; for it is an idea the source of which can be discerned in the Old Testament and in Greek philosophy.

That God's majesty, power, and goodness is manifested in creation itself is indicated by the priestly creation narrative in its repeated refrain: "God saw that it was good" (Gen. 1:4, 12, 18, 21, 25, 31). The world is the mirror in which God's goodness is reflected. In the world which he created as a good thing and which he pronounced a good thing, history now commences; in history the meaning of creation will be fulfilled. The creation Psalms (Ps. 8; 19, 104; 148) are vocalized on the note: "The heavens tell the glory of God; the firmament declares the work of his creation" (Ps. 19:2).

Greek philosophy developed the cosmological proof of God's existence, which concludes from the world itself to the creating divinity. The beginnings of such a consideration are to be found already in the Ionian philosophy of nature. Through a severe criticism of the myths about the gods, there arises a refined religious sentiment. The visible and knowable world is not a senseless thing; rather, it permits one to catch a glimpse of its divine primordial basis. Thales already said: "Everything is full of the gods." According to Heraclitus, the Logos is embodied in everything; with Anaxagoras, it is the Nous; and for Plato, things participate in Ideas. The highest is the divine Idea of the Good (*Republic* 7, 517 B.C.).

Plato concludes from the existence of the world to its Author, from its beauty to a creating Artist thereof. "To discover the Creator and

Father of all things is certainly difficult; and having discovered him, to declare him to all men were quite impossible" (*Timaeus* 28 C).

Aristotle, who accepts the eternity of the world, nevertheless concludes from movement to a prime mover. In a pseudo-Aristotelian work of the first century before Christ, a work entitled *On the World*, there is a formulation in chapter six which reads: "Certainly God is invisible to every mortal nature; but he is perceived in his works."

Cicero too realizes how God is to be recognized through the grandeur and order of the world, and even from the spiritual inclinations of man (*Tusculan Disputations* 1, 68-70).

Natural theology is one of the great and imperishable discoveries and creations of the Greek spirit.

Biblical tradition and Greek thought not infrequently unite themselves, and so here too in Hellenistic Judaism. Through this union the biblical concept of creation and the philosophical concept of nature came to be understood as identical. Jewish wisdom now teaches: "From the grandeur and beauty of the creature, right reason permits a glimpse of the creator" (Wis. 13:5). "All men, therefore, are fools, who cannot, from the perfections of his visible works, grasp the truth of him who is" (Wis. 13:1; see also 13:24f.; chs. 13–15; Job 12:7-9). Even from early Judaism there are statements which declare that man can attain to a natural recognition of God, and that the disavowal of God is therefore culpable.

Because of its resemblances to Romans 1:18-32 (see below), let us quote a passage from the *Testaments of the Twelve Patriarchs*: "The Gentiles, who have gone astray and have abandoned the Lord, have changed their orientation and follow after stones and wood; for they succumbed to the spirits of seduction. But do you not so, my children, who have looked upon the firmament and the earth and the sea and upon all the works of the Lord who made all these things, so that you do not become like Sodom, which overturned the order of nature" (*Nephtali* 3, 3f.).

In a similar fashion Philo says: "No work of art originates of itself. But the finest work of art and that most full of wisdom is our world; · it must therefore have been constructed by a very knowledgeable and thoroughly perfected master builder. In this way we come to a conviction of God's existence" (*De specialibus legibus*, 1, 35).

2. NEW TESTAMENT

The New Testament joins ranks with the foregoing.[13]

The question itself of natural theology is not posited in the Synoptics. Certainly Jesus recognizes in creation the rule of his heavenly Father: in the beauty of the lily and in the divine concern for the beast (Matthew 6:26-28). Nevertheless, this is directed not so much to a conclusion on God's existence, but beyond that, to the fact that the truth of God is secure in the faith, and to the fact that God, already revealed, is seen here in his works. Only those who seek the kingdom of God come to know this God who cares for all creation as for his own.

Paul, however, joins himself to Hellenistic-Jewish theology. The most important text, perhaps, is Romans 1:18-32.[14] Certainly God is the one who is full of mystery. "His decisions are inscrutable and his ways undiscoverable. Who has known the mind of the Lord?" (Rom. 11:33-34). Nevertheless, he has also something about him that is recognizable, something which reason is able to perceive. There is the fact of God's divinity and man's creature status. The world is characterized as creation; and man can recognize the Creator through his creation, if only man consent to recognize him (Rom. 1:19f.).

Nevertheless, Paul does not say that God is simply and obviously recognizable through nature and by dint of nature. Even here God is at work. He is inferable to man because he himself desired and does yet desire it. "God himself makes it plain to them" (Rom. 1:19). Here Paul gives a salvation history interpretation to the notion of a philosophy of nature. This possible knowledge of God is not mere theoretical possibility; for this possibility is such that it involves an obligation. Failure to realize this possibility is culpable. This, then, is certainly the actual status of natural religion. Mankind, through sin, has frustrated this possibility. And this possibility or opportunity not taken advantage of becomes itself an offense chargeable against men "so that they have no excuse" (Rom. 1:20).

The nature of the religion of the pagans is such, then, that it is not really a primitive stage of religion, nor is it an innocent tragedy of early mankind's ignorance; rather, it is a lapse and a culpable one. Its culpability called forth the anger of God. Paganism itself was turned into a judgment. God left the pagans to their religious aberrations. "They exchanged the glory of the incorruptible God for an image in the shape of corruptible men and of birds, of four-legged beasts and of reptiles" (Rom. 1:23). And God abandoned the pagans to their perverted immorality (Rom. 1:28-32).

Paul recognizes another hallmark of God in the fact of man's conscience (Rom. 2:15).[15] Here too Paul is in touch with Greek philosophy. Like Paul, Greek anthropology perceives in the conscience of man the voice of the eternal law. Paul accepts both the term and the concept of conscience from general Greek ethics. Socrates and his followers speak of the accusing and absolving voice of conscience. The conviction of a divine law implanted in the soul belongs to the Stoics. Hellenistic-Jewish wisdom describes a bad conscience: "Malice passes judgment on itself; oppressed by conscience, it always expects the worst" (Wis. 17:10). Philo (*De decalogo* 87) describes the operation of conscience in a clear and analytical way: "It accuses, points the way; admonishes to repentance; and when it is successful in persuading one, then it is gladdened and at peace." Paul says the same thing, that God reveals himself in the conscience of every man, even the Gentiles or pagans, as legislator of morality. "They show that the command of the Law is written in their hearts. Their conscience appears as witness, when their thoughts are in conflict, whether to accuse or to defend them" (Rom. 2:15). Conscience shows itself as tied to a higher norm, which norm has not been set by man himself, but is decreed by God (Rom. 2:14).

Again the recognition of conscience is not merely a possibility but a moral obligation. The Gentiles are able to fulfill and do fulfill the command of the law inscribed in their hearts. If they do not heed this command, they are guilty of their vices (Rom. 1:32). In this way, to be sure, paganism has become addicted to sin (Gal. 2:15).

Here Paul passes judgment on ancient religion and ethics in hard terms indeed. Is his judgment justified? He speaks of a mythology of the gods in its most primitive and repulsive forms. In the images of an Apollo, a Dionysus, an Aphrodite, he does not see the higher form of polytheism. Nor does Paul think of the profound and serious Greek philosophy of religion. Occasionally the familiar ring of perceptions and formulations of Greek ethics is heard in his own exhortations. Did Paul see nothing of the beauty and grandeur of the ancient culture which surrounded him? In Paul, it is the zeal of orthodox Jewish monotheism that speaks. Paul speaks as the prophet, who measures everything against the highest eternal values, God and God's service, faith and morality. Against such a yardstick everything else is worthless and of no account. Moreover, in view of this, the theme of the Epistle to the Romans becomes entirely understandable: namely, that Jews and Gentiles alike are lacking of justification. The Apostle wants to affirm the end of all individual justification, even of religion (Rom. 3:20).

The Paul of the Acts of the Apostles also speaks of God's being revealed in nature. At Lystra he and Barnabas admonish the pagans to turn away from their empty idols to the Creator, the living God. "He certainly did not leave himself untestified to, as the Bestower of good things; for he gave you rain from heaven and fruits in their proper season, and he filled you with nourishing food and your hearts with joy" (Acts 14:15-17). In the sermon there are thoughts reminiscent of Stoic-Cynic philosophy; yet it is the biblical God who is proclaimed, he that is Creator and Sustainer of all.

Even more detailed is Paul's celebrated address before the Areopagus (Acts 17:19-33). Paul takes notice of the religious spirit of the Athenians. Men are supposed to seek for God; yet, he is not far from any one of us. Indeed, Paul even quotes a passage from Aratus, which declares that we have our origins from God: "We are of his stock." In contrast to Romans 1, his judgment on paganism is much milder, much more positive.

Luke uses many words and concepts which were current also in the contemporaneous Hellenistic philosophy and religion. He speaks of the ignorance of the Gentiles, which God disregards. Certainly Paul too speaks of God's forbearance (Rom. 3:25); but first of all, of his angry judgment upon the sins of the pagans (Rom. 1:18-32).

Neither does Luke, however, offer proof after the fashion of a philosopher; rather, as a prophet, he proclaims the fulfillment of the quest (Acts 17:23), and as a missionary, he demands repentance (Acts 17: 30).[16]

Even the Prologue to St. John's Gospel speaks of the fact that God has ever borne witness to himself in the world. All life in the world has its beginning as well as its continued existence in the Logos of God, Christ. He is the agent of creation. "Whatever was made, it was in him that it had life; and the life was the light of men" (John 1:4). In this light man sees not only the world round about himself, but he understands himself and his life in this world. Without this illumination, life is not really life, but anxiety and gloom. Light is the salvific remedy. Life and light are not simply within the range of human possibilities, but with the Logos they are a divine gift. God's being revealed in the world is not something dissociated from God, but is effected by him. Certainly the world has not recognized nor has it accepted the Logos (John 1:1-11). On this point the declaration of the Gospel is in general agreement with Romans (1:18-21).

3. First Vatican Council

The doctrine of the revelation of God in creation was subsequently expounded systematically, was further developed and consolidated, as natural theology. Accordingly the First Vatican Council declared: "The one true God, our Creator and Lord, can be known with certitude by reason of creation itself, by the natural light of human reason" (Schönmetzer's Denzinger, *Enchiridion symbolorum*, 32nd edition, Freiburg 1963, no. 3026). The oath against the errors of modernism added to it: ". . . be known with certitude and be demonstrated . . ." (*ibid.*, no. 3538). Dogmatic theology has interpreted the declaration of the Council in such a way as to actually modify it, as if the Vatican Council were speaking of a theoretical ideal, according to which the perfected reason might recognize God. In reality the light of reason is surely clouded by sin, and the recognition of God is never accomplished except with the assistance of grace.

Modern Catholic theology will not dispute the difficulty of the cosmological proof of God. Nature, as it is found in consequence of sin, is disturbed; and it is in no way a faithful mirror of God's majesty. It is not a simple and casual matter for philosophy and theology to take the step from finite to infinite, from time to eternity, from the world to God, in the *analogia entis*. Nevertheless, Catholic theology has a great interest in natural theology; for it is therein that one finds the basis for the theology of natural law, which is of such great importance in the proclamations of the ecclesiastical magisterium.

4. PROTESTANT THEOLOGY

Protestant theology perceives the problematics of all natural theology as very difficult. Through sin, world and man are completely spoiled. God's presence in creation is darkened. Human reason is so weakened, indeed, perverted, that in general it can no longer achieve anything good and cannot even any longer recognize God through creation. Romans 1 and 2 are therefore interpreted in part, and with manifest violence, contrary to the genuine sense thereof. While in Romans 1:18-21 Paul speaks of the universal and natural revelation of God in creation and in history, Protestant theology did and does yet understand from this passage especially, that God's anger is revealed through the preaching of the gospel and in particular of the Cross as of a judgment on sin. God can be recognized in creation only now that the revelation in Christ has taken place, and those who have been addressed by Christ have been bound to the truth. Accordingly, the Gentiles referred to in Rom. 2:14f. were Gentile Christians. It is not just any man but the man convicted in consequence of the preaching of the gospel who hears the voice of conscience.[17] Nevertheless, in Romans 1 and 2 Paul is speaking as a missionary to the pagans and about them; primarily, therefore, of man as he is to be found in his natural state.

§ 3. THE OLD TESTAMENT IN THE NEW

It is not within the scope of a theology of the New Testament to offer an exposition of the development of Old Testament revelation in all its ramifications, but only in respect to its admission into the New Testament. Let us begin with two preliminary observations.[18]

FIRST PRELIMINARY OBSERVATION:
OLD TESTAMENT JEWISH AND NEW TESTAMENT INTERPRETATION
OF SCRIPTURE

With its manifold use of Sacred Scripture, the New Testament continues the practice of the Old Testament and of intertestamental Judaism.

Interpretation of Scripture begins already in the Old Testament itself. The Pentateuch is a redaction, and by that very fact a new interpretation, of older traditions, asserted orally or in writing. Later texts and writings take up the earlier and carry them on. To a considerable extent this is the case with Deuteronomy, which presents anew large parts of the books of the Law; likewise with Chronicles, which expounds anew traditions from the era of the kings.

The books of the prophets themselves show that the original sayings of the prophets were subsequently expanded. Chapters 10–12 and 16–19 of the Book of Wisdom constitute a midrash on the Old Testament history from Adam to Moses.

In early Judaism a canon of admitted books took shape. The canonical Scriptures were read in the divine service and explained in preaching. In the "houses of learning" an intensive explanation of the Scriptures was practiced, by means of which strict hermeneutic rules were formed. Typology and allegory pertain thereto, as is pointed out even in the New Testament (1 Cor. 10:6; Gal. 4:24).

When the Hebrew language ceased to be functional as a vernacular tongue, translations became a necessity. The Septuagint presents a Greek translation, while the Targumim are translations in Aramaic, the everyday spoken language throughout the Fertile Crescent. That every translation is itself an interpretation holds good in great measure even for these translations.

The Septuagint not infrequently fills the old text with a new, Greek spirit. The New Testament betrays for the most part its utilization of the Septuagint text or otherwise of another Greek translation; direct translation from the Hebrew is undoubtedly quite rare. The historical narratives were explained and embellished in midrash. The New Testament occasionally takes over Jewish midrash (thus in the speech of Stephen in Acts 7; probably also now and then in the Pauline Epistles; see below, p. 38ff.). Some facets of the Moses midrash influenced the infancy narrative of the Gospels.

In the Qumran community[19] the Scriptures were highly treasured. This brotherhood lived with and by the Book. The excavations have brought to light a scriptorium or writing room. The community had an important library, of which large parts have been recovered. In the Qumran writings the most frequently quoted — and, it may be inferred, the books most frequently read in the community — were the Pentateuch, the Prophets, and the Psalms. Writings which were not accepted into the Jewish canon, like the *Testaments of the Twelve Patriarchs*, the *Book of Henoch*, and the *Book of Jubilees* have also been found there.

One seeking entry into the community had to swear to abide by the Torah of Moses and to observe it as it was understood in Qumran (1 QS 5:8-10). Scripture is full of secrets, which become clear to one who seeks. Research is incumbent upon the priest. Even the great teacher of Qumran, the "Teacher of Righteousness", shares in this duty (*Damascus Document* 6:7). The Law must be read and studied constantly. In each group of ten men there is not to be lacking "one who constantly, by day and by night, enquires into the Torah. . . . The general members of the community are to remain awake during a third part of all the nights of the year, in order to read in the Book and to enquire after what is right" (1 QS 6:6f.). Knowledge must be realized in the community (1 QS 9:13). Accordingly many quotations from the Scriptures are encountered in the Qumran scrolls. Often they are introduced with an "as it is written" (1 QS 5:15; 8:14; *Damascus Document* 1:13; 5:1f.).

Extensive parts of a continuous commentary on the Book of Habakkuk have been found; and also fragments of a commentary on the Book of Nahum and on Psalm 37. Such running commentaries on the Scriptures were not previously known.

The interpretation relates the texts forcefully to contemporary conditions and to the actual circumstances of the community: it is, therefore, an existential interpretation. The community is persecuted. Verses of the Book of Habakkuk which speak of the persecution of the prophet are understood as fulfilled in the community. The enemies of the prophet are explained in part as referring to the priests in Jerusalem (1 QpHab 8:8-13), and in part as referring to the Kittïyîm or Kittaeans, i.e., the Romans (1 QpHab 2; 3; 6).

There are important texts in reference to the Messiah and the messianic era. Among the Qumran scrolls a collection of messianic quotations (4 Q Testimonia) was found, and a florilegium of eschatological texts (4 Q Forilegium). The conviction that they are living in the end-time in which the prophecies have to be fulfilled prompts Qumran (1 QpHab 2:5f.; 7:1f.) just as it does the New Testament (1 Cor. 10–11) to refer the biblical texts to the community in its present status. Like Qumran, Jesus himself goes back to the Scriptures, and both reject the Pharisaic tradition of interpretation. Both take a radical view of the Torah (Matthew 5:7-48; Mark 7:13).

Nevertheless, Qumran's teaching of the Law remains in the realm of juridic regulations and of ritualized piety. Association with the sinners outside the community is severely prohibited. Inasmuch as Jesus associates with tax-collectors and sinners, he disregards legality for the sake of that which is essential, *i.e.*, love (Mark 12:31). In Qumran, on the basis of a rigid interpretation of the Torah, a new and narrower concern for the Law is required. With Paul, faith justifies in view of the salvational deed of Christ; this is crystal clear in a comparison of the difference in interpretation of Hab. 2:4 as found in 1 QpHab 7:17-8:2 and in Rom. 1:17 (*Theology of the New Testament*, Vol. 3, p. 85).

The New Testament continues the Old Testament Jewish interpretation of Scripture in respect to the form thereof, and not infrequently, even in respect to the content itself. We are often constrained to ask whether, with this or that citation or interpretation of the Old Testament, the New Testament is not following the exegesis practiced by the rabbis. This is true especially in the case of Old Testament texts of a messianic import. The pro's and con's of the question have been repeatedly debated, whether or not the New Testament already employed Christian florilegia of the Old, or whether it perhaps accepted rabbinic florilegia. Now that two florilegia have been recovered at Qumran, so much more must we reckon with the possibility of the utilization of such collections in the New Testament.

SECONDARY PRELIMINARY OBSERVATION:
OLD TESTAMENT IN THE BIBLE

The Church's Bible consists of the Old Testament and the New. The Church of the New Testament quarreled with the Synagogue over possession and interpretation of the Old Testament. Both appealed to it, and both wanted to use it to verify their position (John 5:45f.); (Acts 21:21). This situation has remained the same even to the present day. A tension between Old Testament and New is perceptible in the Church from the very beginning. Jesus criticizes the Old Testament as a Law inadequate from the beginning, and then further spoiled by men (Matthew 5:17-48; Mark 10:3-9). Paul once calls it straightforwardly a "ministration of death" (2 Cor. 3:7). There remained a tension between the Old Testament as a demanding Law and the New Testament as a remitting gospel. The New could and did accomplish its purpose of forgiving sin; the Old could not.

A man who must be accounted a sincere witness of the gospel, Marcion by name, thought that the opposition between Old Testament and New was such as to make them irreconcilable. He considered that creation was the mark of a wicked God, who bears witness to himself in the Old Testament as the God of revengeful righteousness. The Father of Jesus Christ, the God of the gospel, is, on the other hand, pure goodness.

For Origen the opposition between the Old Testament and New is seen in terms of the Pauline formula (2 Cor. 3:6), as opposition between the death-dealing letter and the life-giving spirit, an opposition which becomes for Origen a hermeneutic principle. The Old Testament literally understood is deadly; but its allegorical-spiritual understanding begets life. The problem of literalness and the literal meaning of the Scriptures, a problem so much pondered by the Fathers, confronts the interpretation of Scripture in every age. Even today and to ourselves the Old Testament posits serious questions. The ecclesiastical interpretation of Scripture had and does yet have to take up the labors, methods, and results of the critical-historical investigation of the Old Testament, an investigation which binds it uncompromisingly to truthfulness. The theological questions are not easy. How can the doctrine of Jewish national salvation be valid in the new covenant? What about the Old Testament notion of God? What about Old Testament morality? The problem of the Old Testament is intensified — or adulterated — through racial opposition to Judaism.

Nevertheless the Old Testament is an unrelinquishable part of the Bible. The Old Testament is the Book of Creation, which is always God's institution, even if creation has been spoiled through sin. Overt or underground dualist movements in the Church did in the past and do ever again and again attempt to contemn creation, its good things and its products. The testimony of the Old Testament on behalf of creation must be expressed over and over again, louder and louder.

The use of the Old Testament by Jesus and therefore by the New Testament can be summarized under three headings: the Old Testament as witness to salvation history, as Law, and as promise.

1. OLD TESTAMENT AS WITNESS TO SALVATION HISTORY

Jesus lived amid the religious traditions of Israel. He found in the Sacred Scriptures a witness to God's dealings with men and in respect to men. He was so much imbued with this history and so much did he live in it, that it imparted to him the form and content of his address. He made reference to the historical events of the Old Testament such as the creation of the world and of man (Mark 10:6; 13:19), the murder of Abel (Matthew 23:35), the history of Noah and the deluge (Matthew 24:37-39), the destruction of Sodom (Matthew 10:15; 11:23f.), the wife of Lot (Luke 17:32), the history of the patriarchs (Mark 12:26), the character and works of Moses (Mark 10:3; John 3:14; 5:46; 6:32), David's kingship (Mark 12:35-37), Solomon's glory (Matthew 12:39-41); and finally, the murder of Zechariah between the temple and the altar (Matthew 23:35).

In his parables Jesus pours out a flood of Old Testament reminiscences, as in the parable of the vine-dressers (Mark 12:1-9), where the vineyard is described after the fashion of that in Isaiah 5:1-7, or in the graphic representation of the good shepherd (John 10:1-16), into which numerous Old Testament reminiscences are woven (Ps. 23; Jer. 23:1-4; Ezech. 34:11-31). The Savior's calling of others to himself (Matthew 11:28-30) is clothed in a form and conceptualization that belongs originally to Wisdom and her summons (Sir. 6:24-30; 51:23-27). Just as the prophets once reproached the house of Israel (Is. 6:9f.; Jer. 5:21; Ezech. 12:2), so too does Jesus reproach his people, that they have eyes and do not see, ears and do not hear (Matthew 13:14f.).

In times of deepest distress Jesus declares himself with the experiences and sentiments of the righteous men of the Old Testament. Such is the case when he awaits betrayal (Mark 14:18 and Ps. 41:10); when he foretells the flight of his followers (Mark 14:27 and Zech. 13:7); when he calls them to prayer in Gethsemani (Mark 14:34 and Ps. 42:6); and finally, his words on the Cross (Mark 15:34 and Ps. 22:2; Luke 23:46 and Ps. 31:6). A more extensive treatment will be found below, in §3, 3.

It is as a Jew, and more than that, as a rabbi, that Paul understands the history of the time and the place of God's dealings with men. Salvation history takes place within history. However thoroughly Paul understands that man, in sin and justification, has a fully personal responsibility, he nevertheless sees man at the same time as member in a superimposed collectivity. Each individual human life is co-determined through the universal history and historical relevance. Paul knows and calls forth from out the long past ages towering figures, while at the same time he exposes their typical significance. Adam is the beginning of mankind and at the same time the type of him who renews it, the Messiah (Rom. 5:12-19; 1 Cor. 15:45); Abraham is recipient of the promise and the father of all who believe (Rom. 4:1-22; Gal. 3:6-9); Moses, the chosen friend of God (2 Cor. 3:7), witness to his word (Rom. 9:15; 10:5), giver of the Law (2 Cor. 3:15; Gal. 3:19) and leader of Israel (1 Cor. 10:2-4); David, the ancestor of the Messiah (Rom. 1:3).

For Paul the history of Israel is a pressing question. This is the people of election, and therefore Paul is proud: proud to be a Jew, and proud to be able to authenticate his pure lineage (Rom. 11:1; 2 Cor. 11:22; Phil. 3:5). The destiny of Israel, which has received from God promises that cannot fail (Rom. 9:6; 11:29), which has for so many generations endured unending troubles for the sake of the Law (Rom. 10:2) and which seems now to be failing to achieve messianic-eschatological salvation (Rom. 9:31), is a heavy burden for Paul (Rom. 9:3).

Brooding over the history of Israel and praying on it, Paul finds the answer. God's promise never constitutes an irrevocably assured guarantee of the possession of salvation. To belong to the Israelite people merely in the sense of pertaining to the fleshly community and to enjoy what is primarily only a natural sonship from Abraham does not at all constitute being a true Hebrew. This is demonstrated even by the history of the immediate sons of Abraham. Ismael was passed over and Isaac, born later, was chosen. The history of the twin sons of Isaac indicates the same thing again. Esau was passed over and Jacob was chosen. God is just; surely he owes no accounting for how he dispenses his grace (Rom. 9:6-29).

The true sonship from Abraham is that of faith and of the spirit (Rom. 4:1-25). Nevertheless, it was revealed to Paul in view of his great ongoing concern, that finally Israel too is to be saved (Rom. 11:25-32).

In the whole of history God reveals himself as the one "who gives life to the dead and who calls what does not exist so that it does exist" (Rom. 4:17). The Church, already now and ultimately in its perfection, is the true Israel of God (Gal. 6:16).

Paul's thought had its formation in the Jewish school of doctrine, and all his life his exegesis betrayed the formal schooling of the scribe. The piling up of quotation upon quotation (as in Rom. 3:10-18; 11:8-10) was an exercise in the rabbinic schools. Paul employs rabbinic formulas in quoting and rabbinic principles of hermeneutics. Not infrequently Paul quotes otherwise than we are accustomed to do. He does not always quote in a manner that is in literal accord with the text. Certainly Paul realized that he was obligated to a strictest fidelity to the Sacred Books. If he departs from the letter in quoting them, he is in no way conscious of any inexactness nor certainly of putting any incorrect construction upon a text. His attention is to something else, to what seems essential to him, the salvation-historical thrust, the sense, the spirit of the passage.

Paul believes that the Old Testament already contains the doctrine of the new justification through faith and love. Our modern exegesis is able to concur in his method at least to this extent, which also it confirms, that the Old Testament leads ever more and more away from the work of man and to the grace of God. Certainly not with the impulsive freshness that Jesus displays in the Gospels; but in his own way, Paul too makes the Scriptures pertinent and living. This takes place through the Spirit. "The letter kills, but the Spirit gives life" (2 Cor. 3:6). Understanding proceeds from Christ. "If anyone turn to the Lord, the veil is taken away. The Lord, however, is the Spirit" (2 Cor. 3:16-17). Thus do the old parchments become a constantly growing and bottomless treasure of insight and divine wisdom. Compared to the rabbis, Paul achieves a new form of Scripture interpretation which we can designate as existential, since the Scriptures are always explained "for our sakes" (Rom. 4:24; 15:4; 1 Cor. 9:10; 10:11).

2. Old Testament as Law

The Law is in part ritual or ceremonial law, and in part moral law.

a) The part that is ceremonial law regulated the solemnization of worship in Israel, the celebration of the Sabbath and of feasts, the priestly service, and sacrifice. It gave Israel her sacred orientation and form. Out of the conflict between priest and prophet which broke forth again and again, the prophets already leveled their severe criticism against a discharge of worship that was formalized and empty of meaning; see Hos. 6:6; Amos 5:21-27; Is. 1:10-15; Jer. 6:20; Micah 6:6f.

Both in word and in deed Jesus manifests his great regard for temple and altar.[20] He is zealous for the temple and purifies it of every desecration (Mark 11:15-17). His action was interpreted according to his own citation from Isaiah: "My house shall be called a house of prayer for all peoples" (Is. 56:7). Opened also for the Gentiles, the temple would cease to be a purely intra-Jewish institution. It is a house of prayer, for which very reason it is open to Gentiles as well. Prayer is indicative of the will to put one's whole trust and reliance on God rather than in the performance of any particular action. In this way law and legality are surmounted.

Jesus recognizes in principle the temple tax, even if the king's sons are not obligated to pay it (Matthew 17:24-27).[21] According to John's Gospel, Jesus repeatedly made the journey to Jerusalem for the celebration of feasts (2:13; 5:1; 7:10). Worship, moreover, imposes the obligation of a certain morality. "If you bring your offering to the altar and there you remember that your brother has something against you, leave your offering there before the altar and first go back and be reconciled with your brother and then come to present your offering" (Matthew 5:23-24). Seemingly the saying treats worship in an idealized way as it had been in the idealized past. The time when an Israelite might lay his offering on the altar was long gone.

Jesus criticizes the deliberate evasions by which the obligations of an oath sworn by the temple or by the altar were supposed not to bind, whereas oaths sworn by the gold of the temple or by the gift on the altar were regarded as binding. Similar casuistry is actually evidenced in the rabbinic writings. Jesus refutes their too-clever distinctions. It is the temple itself that sanctifies the gold, and the altar which makes holy the gift thereon (Matthew 23:16-21). As his last meal before his death, Jesus celebrated the Passover meal with his disciples; and with the elements thereof he instituted the meal of the new covenant (Luke 22:15-20).

At the same time, Jesus certainly criticizes ritual law. His words constitute ultimately a rejection of the levitical laws of purification and prescriptions in regard to eating. Jesus defends his disciples, who did not wash their hands before eating, against the charge made by the Pharisees. And he states it as a principle that it is not food that makes a man unclean, but the wicked thoughts in his heart (Mark 7:2-6; 14-23). Jesus proceeds also to keep the Sabbath truly holy through his work of salvific healing (Mark 3:4), humaneness being the general import of the Sabbath (Mark 2:27f.; *Theology of the New Testament*, Vol. 3, pp. 214, 287–291).

In the tradition of the prophets (Micah 3:12; Jer. 7:12-15; 26:6, 18) Jesus speaks a threatening word against the temple, that it will have not one stone remaining on another (Mark 13:2). In the face of sacrificial worship Jesus quotes the word of Hosea: "I desire mercy and not sacrifice" (Hos. 6:6; Matthew 9:13; 12:7). Worship and temple are becoming unessential. "The hour is coming when you will worship the Father neither on this mountain nor in Jerusalem. The hour is coming — indeed, it is already here — when the true worshipper will worship the Father in Spirit and in Truth" (John 4:21-23). Here Spirit and Truth are not to be understood as philosophical concepts; rather, the Spirit is the divine Spirit which creates men anew, and the Truth is the revelation of the Father in Christ. True worship takes place in the new congregation. The most profound basis for the end of former religion is declared as a statement of Jesus: "Here there is One who is greater than the temple" (Matthew 12:6). The new community of God's people is no longer formed about the old temple, but about a new center, Christ.[22]

Paul saw in the retention or in the reintroduction of the ceremonial Law in the Christian community an acute danger for the gospel. If through the efforts of the Judaizers the Galatians have been brought again to the "scrupulous observance of days and months and seasons and years" they do thereby turn themselves "back again to the weak and beggarly elements" (Gal. 4:9-10). Elements are the basic components of the world matter. The whole Torah with all its statutes pertains to these elements (Gal. 4:3-5). If one imagines that salvation is dependent upon the regular observance of fast days and feast days, then one is surrendering the freedom of the children of God and is again serving the powers of nature. Paul recognizes — and it is a fact perfectly verified by the history of religions — that these holy days are taboo through an anxiety before astral and cosmic powers who supposedly are operative on such days, and that it is they who are served by anyone who observes those days. For these, religion becomes a legalistic, yes, a superstitious observance; it is not a moral determination.[23]

But Paul's accusation is that those who want to force circumcision upon Christians actually do not themselves keep the Law, but want only to be able to boast of having imposed such a fleshly observance on others (Gal. 6:13). Undoubtedly Paul means to say that these Judaizers keep well enough the external prescriptions of the Law, but pay no attention to what is essential, *i.e.*, Christian faith and love. They seek only for the triumph of the Jewish nation over the true people of God. The only thing worth boasting of, however, is the Cross of Christ (Gal. 6:14). There is one justification and one only, and that is the justification granted by means of the Cross. Anyone who presumes that he can achieve still more through his own works achieves nothing and loses all (Gal. 5:2-12).

The Epistle to the Colossians too is obliged to combat a false zeal for ritual statutes, which zeal is exhibited especially in the keeping of fast days and festivals. "Of course there is the appearance of wisdom in self-willed worship and mortification and severe subjugation of the body; but there is no honor in it and it but serves for the gratification of the flesh" (Col. 2:23). Here the letter seems to be quoting the catchwords of its opponents in a polemical and ironic fashion. They honor and worship the elements and powers of the world. Their asceticism seeks their own honor and not that of God. The divine service is a willful and self-seeking worship. What passes for a merciless mortification of the body is really only gratification of the flesh, because its goal is only glorification of self and gratification of one's own will (*Theology of the New Testament*, Vol. 3, p. 168).

After its release from temple worship the New Testament can still place a typological value on the old laws of worship as "shadows of the future" (Col. 2:17; Heb. 10:1).[24] Certainly such a descriptive terminology was current; it is found both in Philo and in Josephus. According to Colossians 2:17, Christ is the only reality, whereas the things that foreshadowed him have become meaningless and their worship senseless. Hebrews 10:1 has it that the Law is but a shadow of the heavenly reality, and is therefore powerless to make perfect.

b) The Law of the old covenant is also moral law.[25] It has its basic source in the decalogue. Jesus too recognizes it as the ordering of life in accord with God's will (Mark 10:19; *Theology of the New Testament*, Vol. 3, p. 32). Jesus quotes in an approving manner the commandment of the love of God and of neighbor in accord with the Old Testament (Mark 12:29-31, after Deut. 6:4 and Lev. 19:18; see also the present work, Vol. 3, pp. 121–136). Whoever does not want to come to the place of torment must listen to Moses and the prophets (Luke 16:27-31). Certainly Jesus reinterprets the Law authoritatively. To follow the letter of the Law no longer suffices. What is demanded is the totality of the way of thinking which Jesus exhibits in reference to the prohibition of murder, adultery, and perjured testimony (Matthew 5:21-37). Jesus insists upon the sense and the heart of the Law, which is love (Matthew 22:37-40; see also the present work Vol. 3, pp. 124–128).

Nevertheless, Jesus criticizes not only the interpretation and the observance of the Law as practiced in his times, but he actually criticizes the Law itself. He rejects the bill of divorce, which, according to Deut. 24:1 had divine approval, and criticizes it as being a law of Moses, *i.e.*, a law of human origin. The original law of God was given in the ordering of creation, in accord with Gen. 1:27 and 2:24 (Mark 10:2-9; *Theology of the New Testament*, Vol. 3, pp. 243–247). Jesus demands not only that which the Old Testament demands, fidelity to one's oaths, but he proscribes the oath altogether (Matthew 5:33-37; see the present work, Vol. 3, pp. 280–286). In place of the Old Testament commandment of talion he substitutes the commandment of the love of one's enemy (Matthew 5:38-48; the present work, Vol. 3, pp. 121–124).

Inasmuch as Jesus turns aside from those who were unimpeachable and righteous under the Law and calls sinners, he rejects the legal religiousness which trusts in its own works (Luke 18:9-14). In the parable of the workers in the vineyard, it is not lengthy toil which receives the reward; rather, God gives with a sovereign goodness (Matthew 20:1-16).

The opposition between Jesus and legalistic religion is exposed with extraordinary sharpness in Matthew 23. The chapter is a striking composition of statements put together by the evangelist. And it poses the question of how far it is Jesus who speaks therein, and to what extent it is Church and Synagogue, after the fall of Jerusalem, as two different religions in inimical confrontation with each other. Whatever the case, the opposition between the old and new righteousness is exposed, certainly in part with the words of Jesus, and in its totality in the spirit of Jesus. Jesus sets himself in opposition not to a system of unbelief, but of a religion, not against immorality but against a morality. Pharisaic zeal for the Law is an error because it is lacking in truth and love and because it puts its trust in the self-justification of man and not in the freely bestowed grace of God won by the Cross of Christ.

The relationship of Jesus to the Old Testament Law and thereby to law in general is dialectical. The law cannot be simply approved nor can it be simply disavowed. The true law is divine order. But this must not become a formalized state of legality. A man's free determination remains essential in revealed religion.

For the primitive Christian community the status of Old Testament Law was a difficult and complicated question. Christians whose origins were in Israel recognized and heeded the Law as the ordering of each individual life as well as the ordering of the community and as the fundamental law of the land. Israel was indebted to the Law for her pure belief in God and for her high moral tone; and for that Israel was all the more thankful and took a great deal of pride in it, when she looked about her and saw the abominations of paganism on every side. Did not lawlessness mean licentiousness and a complete disruption of community? Even the pagans were impressed by the Law of Israel, and sometimes became "God-fearing", at least in a broad relationship to Israel. Some entered all the way into the community of the Mosaic religion. Moreover, the Law was plainly God's command. Could a man then dare to disengage himself from it?

The problem became even more acute with the extension of the mission beyond Palestine and to the Gentiles. Already in antiquity there was a strong opposition to Judaism, of the sort that we today call anti-Semitism. The Law forbade Jews to participate in pagan worship, and made any marriage or domestic sociability between Jew and Gentile impossible. The Jews, therefore, were despised as godless and inhospitable. Many of their religious practices, like circumcision and keeping the Sabbath, were ridiculed. Could one oblige the Christian convert from paganism to take upon himself this Jewish Law?

The New Testament bears considerable testimony to a difficult and long-lasting wrestling with these problems. Sometimes the sources are not easy for us to understand. The situations and events were quite variable between cities and countries. There were progressive and reactionary movements. An important source, the Acts of the Apostles, undoubtedly presents these matters in part from the vantage point of a certain hindsight, after freedom from the Law had already been won. In Acts 10:9-23 Peter is instructed in a vision about the abrogation of the levitical laws in regard to purification and food. In Acts 15:5-31 freedom from the Law for Christian converts from paganism is recognized as having been in possession since the time of Peter's vision. Jewish Christians undoubtedly attempted again and again and for a long time, sometimes in a lesser way and sometimes with extreme demands, to oblige Gentile Christians to the Law.

Christian freedom from the Law was probably first won in practice by Jewish Christianity among the Jews of the diaspora. They lived, to be sure, in a looser sort of union with Jerusalem and its temple, the center of Judaism, and were at the same time in a greater proximity to Greek culture and to the Roman government.

A remarkable indication of this is found in the account of the trial and death of the protomartyr Stephen in Acts, chs. 6 and 7.[26] Stephen was a Hellenistic Jew of the diaspora. In his speech of defense delivered before the High court or Sanhedrin, undoubtedly a Lukan composition but employing material from the Jewish Christian polemics against the Law, Stephen levels a severe criticism against Israel. Israel always was a stiff-necked nation. The true Israelites, like Joseph, Moses, and the prophets, were consistently persecuted by their own countrymen, who now have spurned the Messiah as well. Stephen even criticizes the temple in Jerusalem. God does not dwell in buildings wrought by human hands.

It was Paul, another Jew of the diaspora, who carried the struggle for freedom even further and clinched it. Since he was himself under the Law and lived by the Law, in the altercation with Judaism he is basically on the same ground with Judaism; and indeed, in his argumentation, he appeals again and again to the Old Testament as the infallible word of God. Paul shares the Jew's pride in the Law. The distinction that Israel has through the Law is among her titles to honor

(Rom. 9:4). "The Jew has much in every respect. The oracles of God are entrusted to him" (Rom. 3:1-2). Many years after his conversion on the road to Damascus Paul says of himself and of Peter: "We are of the house of the Jews and are not sinners from the world of the Gentiles" (Gal. 2:15). Paul holds firm: "The Law is holy and the commandment is holy and just and good" (Rom. 7:12). "The Law is filled with the Spirit" (Rom. 7:14). The Law leads to justification and to life (Rom. 7:10; Gal. 3:12).

Paul acknowledges Jewish zeal for the Law. "I bear them witness that they have zeal for God" (Rom. 10:2). If a man like Paul can say this of a people, it is certainly not a matter to be taken lightly. With all her zeal, however, Israel is not seeking God's honor but her own. "They know not the justice of God and seek to establish their own. They do not submit to the justice of God" (Rom. 10:3). The zealots, therefore, resist the Cross. The Cross signifies the justification that God gives. And to accept God's justice means to admit one's own status as a sinner. This sinfully self-sufficient attitude finds its highest expression in man's self-adulation. In his self-glory man forgets that all he has, he has received (1 Cor. 4:7). In itself the Law is simply a false path because it can never arrive at the goal. Salvation is from the Cross of Christ and only from the Cross of Christ.

Paul had to contend with the charge that he was subverting and abolishing the Law (Acts 21:21). It is quite understandable that the Jews would accuse him of such. Yet, Paul himself certainly has no consciousness of obviating the Law. "Do we destroy the Law? Far be it! On the contrary, we confirm the Law" (Rom. 3:31). And if the Law must be fulfilled afterwards even as before, certainly Paul gives assurance that now is the first time that it can in fact be fulfilled. The essential objective of the Law is supernatural love. "The fulfillment of the Law is love" (Rom. 13:10; Gal. 5:14). Now "the requirements of the Law are fulfilled in us, we who walk not according to the flesh but according to the spirit" (Rom. 8:4). The "Israel according to the flesh" could not fulfill the Law (1 Cor. 10:18). They, then, who fulfill the Law are the true Israel of God (Gal. 6:16).

If in the old covenant the Law could of itself never sanctify, what then was the purpose of the Law in Old Testament revelation? To this question which has ultimately to be posed, Paul answers that the Old

Testament Law was intended only to bring about the recognition of sin, in order to make man aware of his hopeless situation and to lead him to grace (Rom. 3:20). The real situation is this: "There is no one who does right, none, not a single one" (Rom. 3:12). The Law served even to increase transgression (Rom. 5:20). It brings about God's anger (Rom. 4:15), it is under a curse (Gal. 3:10, 13), and it leads to death (Rom. 7:10f.). "No man is made just by the works of the Law" (Gal. 2:16). "But where sin increased, grace became even more abundant" (Rom. 5:20).

This is presented again and more comprehensively in Romans, chapter 7.[27] "The commandment which was supposed to serve me unto life delivered me up to death" (Rom. 7:10). "The Law of the Spirit of the life in Christ Jesus" rescues us from this situation (Rom. 8:2). The Law is either a wrong way, or it is the way to the Cross of Christ. "Christ is the goal of the Law" (Rom. 10:4).

What Paul is pursuing in great detail and with strong and repeated sorties is not some ancient quarrel of a Jewish renegade with his former co-religionists. They are present matters, because the question of the Law is an ever-present question. Only he that knows the sterile way of the Law can understand what Catholic faith means as the only way of salvation. In order to be certain of itself, our faith needs to be constantly reminded about the other alternative, the Law, and that the way of the Law is clearly ineffective. Only thus can one understand what it means, that where the Law founders, there grace begins. Faith is constantly in danger of succumbing to the temptation of the Law, in one form or another. Faith contains the way of the Law as subdued permanently in itself; and thus it becomes faith in freely bestowed justification through the Blood of the Cross.

What Paul says of the Law holds good not only for the Old Testament Law, but for moral law and lawfulness in general. The admonition of the Apostle holds good even now for the Church, her order and her law. Her law would be turned about and become an abuse, if it were to be prescribed and enforced as an external decree without the thorough conviction of its thereby being of service to faith, to love, and to the spirit. The law would be changed into an ominous legalism, were the external prescriptions to become more important than its internal content. Paul's statement about the impotence of the Law is equally valid when it is applied to that law which man casually accepts again and again in the law of his moral and religious ideas and ideals. Paul would say that not by his most strenuous efforts can a man find his way out of that from which there is no exit, nor can he open for himself the door to salvation. Paul says that for man there is but one justification, the justification which God himself bestows freely (Rom. 3:24, 28).

3. Old Testament as Promise

The Old Testament contains no small number of declarations directed toward the future. Such are the threats about approaching judgment, as well as the promises about the future messianic era of salvation. At the same time, however, it is not just such texts as these that are understood in the New Testament as prophecy, but the whole Book, even in its historical accounts and in its temporally limited statements, can be explained as alluding to the future.

It would be extremely difficult for us to follow completely such an exposition of the Old Testament and its consequent interpretation. This conception of the Old Testament is temporally limited. In some measure the New Testament continues contemporaneous Judaism's estimate of the Old Testament. It was considered that prophecy had become extinct in Israel. The rabbis restricted prophecy to an idealized antiquity. The lament of Ps. 74:9, perhaps itself quite old, was heard even now: "No longer is there a prophet here; no one among us knows how long."

The books of the Old Testament were the depository of prophecy. The writings recognized as legitimate were regarded as imparted by the Spirit, filled with the Spirit, and consequently as prophecy (see above, § 1, 2). In that way the concept of the prophetic was restricted.

Originally prophecy was simply "announcement", proclamation. Certainly, an essential part of the proclamation always took the form of a threat or a promise in reference to the messianic-eschatological era. Accordingly, prophecy came gradually to be understood as a foretelling of the future. In later texts of the Old Testament, as afterwards in the New, it was already said that earlier prophetic sayings "must be fulfilled." According to 3 Kings 2:27, a threat in 1 Sam. 2:30-36, being "the word of Yahweh, must be fulfilled." According to 2 Chron. 36:21, "the word of Yahweh to Jeremiah (25:11; 27:7; 29:10) must be fulfilled."

After prophecy related temporally to the future began as a matter of course to contain also elements of apocalyptic motifs, this type of prophecy was taken up and continued by the early Jewish apocalyptics. Following the pattern of ancient prophecy, in the apocalyptic books, which had their inception with the Book of Daniel, predictions about the present and about the endtime were put into the mouths of the great men of antiquity. These books were avidly read even in Christian circles, as is demonstrated by the Christian interpolations in these Jewish writings.

The commentary on the Prophet Habakkuk, which was found at Qumran, serves as an example of how the Old Testament was understood as prophecy of the then present. Line by line the old text is related to the times of the Qumran community. The expositor recognizes himself as commissioned by God and enlightened by him, "to explain all the words of his servants, the prophets, through whom God has announced everything that is to happen to his people and his land" (1 QpHab. 2:8-10).

Like its own times and milieu, the New Testament too understands the Old Testament as prophecy which God is now fulfilling at the end of time. "God has fulfilled that which he announced beforehand by the mouth of all the prophets, namely, that his Christ would suffer" (Acts 3:18). The prophetic word is treated like a measure, which at one time is partially filled and now at last is completely filled up. God's word must be fulfilled to its total capacity, in fullest measure. "My word, which comes forth from my mouth, does not return to me void; it does what I determine it to do, and it accomplishes that for which I sent it" (Is. 55:11).

If it is scarcely possible, therefore, for us to accept this basic conception of the Old Testament as prophecy, we shall have also to decline, often enough, to accept the exegesis of individual passages which accompanies this conception. Jewish-rabbinic exegesis, and in accord with it, the New Testament, separates phrases, even words, from their context · in the Old Testament, and explains them without reference at all to their historical and literary continuity. Our modern exegesis, however, is obliged to attend to these matters, and takes considerable pains with

them in order to arrive at the real sense of a passage. Very often it finds
that a passage is concerned with its own time and place, while the old
exegesis heard therein a declaration about distant times and foreign
places.

We can mention some examples. In Jer. 31:15 Rachel, the mother of
Joseph and Benjamin, is lamenting because the two tribes so named
have sunk into oblivion in the captivity. Matthew 2:18 refers the
lament to the children murdered in Bethlehem, probably for the reason
that Rachel's tomb, then as now, was honored at Bethlehem. According
to Matthew 2:23, Jesus' being called a "Nazarene" has its basis "in the
word of the prophet". We are not able to tell what prophetic saying is
intended. Deutero-Isaiah announces the glad tidings of the return of the
exiles from out of Babylon, who have made their way back home
through the desert (40:3). Matthew 3:3 understands the passage as referring to John the Baptist, who preached in the desert. The community
of Qumran, living in the desert as it did, referred the saying to itself
(1 QM 1:2). Perhaps a common tradition of interpretation is discernible, which fixed itself on the term "desert". Psalm 19:5, the song of the
sky's glory, which song can be heard everywhere, is understood by Paul
in Rom. 10:18 as indicating the proclamation of the gospel through the
whole world.

The New Testament, like Jewish exegesis before it, often arrives at
such interpretation through the straightforward use of the allegorical
method, according to which the text "says something other" (ἄλλο
ἀγορεύει) than the words themselves would naturally indicate. In this
way there sweeps into the New Testament explanation of Scripture
from the ancient world surrounding it a hermeneutic method very
much determined by its times.

Even the epics of Homer and of Hesiod were explained allegorically.
Zeus, accordingly, is perhaps the heavens, Hera is the earth. The mythical alliance of the gods signifies the fructification of the earth by means
of the rain. This allegorization passes over into Hellenistic Judaism,
where Philo, among others, fosters a similar kind of explanation.

Occasionally Paul seems to explain Old Testament texts in an allegorical manner with a haggadah to be found also in Philo (1 Cor. 5:6-8;
10:4; 15:45). In Gal. 4:24 Paul offers an explanation of the history of
Hagar and Sarah, which explanation Paul himself designates as alle-

gorical, and the basis and meaning of which is obscure to us. In 1 Cor. 9:9, he understands the prescription of Deut. 25:4, "Thou shalt not muzzle the ox that treads out the grain", in respect to the missionary, who can lay claim to his support from the congregation. If Paul contests the original literal meaning of the Old Testament saying with the question, "Is God concerned about oxen?", exegesis is bound to reply that the God of Israel, as Creator and merciful Father, most certainly does concern himself with all creatures. That and that alone is the reason for the statement in Deut. 25:4. A further example of allegorical exegesis is to be found in Eph. 5:31f., when the Epistle recalls the ancient statement that the spouses in a marriage shall become one (Gen. 2:24); marital union has become a "great mystery", according to the Epistle, because it reflects the unity of Christ and his Church. The Epistle to the Hebrews offers, with an artistically developed methodology, an extended theology of Scripture that is imbued throughout with allegorical and typological interpretation.

The question is whether the Old Testament cannot be understood as promise in such a way that it is subject to New Testament application, elevation and perfection, and can thereupon be disclosed as such in interpretation. This method ought not be designated then as allegory, but as typology (after 1 Cor. 10:11). The old is prefiguration of the new. This relationship between old and new has its basis in the fact that it is one and the same God who operates in the old as well as in the new. The one, therefore, can be made to cover the other. This can be recognized in the panorama of salvation history. In 2 Cor. 4:6 there is an example of Pauline typology: "God, who said, 'Out of darkness let light shine', has shone in our hearts, to give a light of understanding about the glory of God, shining in the face of Christ." God is revealed at all times as the one and the same, as he who gives light and who is light. Just as he was made manifest in the beginning in the creation of light, so now he is revealed in the glory of Christ, and so will he evermore be revealed, in the illumination of his existence in the faith of men. Whereever there is light, there God is; and wherever God is there is light. God's words and deeds let him be known as the same always, in the past, in the present, and in the future.

As salvation history thematics which point across from the old era to the new we might perhaps mention the old and new covenant (Jer.

31:31-34); Ezech. 37:26-28 = Luke 22:20; Heb. 8:8-12; the new Jerusalem and its holiness (Ezech. 40–48 = Apoc. 21f.); worship and morality (Hos. 6:6 = Matthew 9:13; 12:7); the word of God (according to Isaiah, Jeremiah, and Paul); Israel's being filled with the Spirit, and the messianic community (Joel 3:1-5 = Acts 2:16-21); eschatological hope and fulfillment; justification as gift to the believers (Gen. 15:6 = Rom. 4:3); of works unto grace (Hab. 2:4 = Rom. 1:17); the Messiah as eschatological bringer of salvation; the Son of Man; the messianic king; Deutero-Isaiah's servant of Yahweh; the righteous one who suffers (in the Psalms and in the Passion of Jesus); incarnation as goal of God's taking up of human nature; finally, belief in God and doctrine about God.

This typology certainly does not mean that the prophet saw beforehand and foretold much later events, but that the later spectator recognizes the inner continuities. Thus Origen (PG 12, 1516 C), commenting on Psalm 69 and seeing the New Testament history of Christ's Passion fulfilled therein, can say: "The whole Old Testament preaches Christ crucified." Augustine's often quoted words (PL 34, 623) are validated in the same way: "In the Old Testament the New lies hidden, and in the New the Old is made manifest." Understood in such a way, if we may consider but another example, even the twist given to Jer. 31:15 in Matthew 2:18 might extract from it a possible meaning. The mothers of Israel had often to lament their children struck down in feuds and wars. The measure of sorrow has now been filled with the tears of the mothers of Bethlehem.

Understood in this way the relationship between the Old and the New Testament would certainly, in the final analysis, be similar to a relationship in which each idea and each ideal is open to a deeper understanding and to a fuller realization. Such an interpretation of the Old Testament would be a specially formed case of symbolic explanation. This is how art and poetry perceive the world. In this context one thinks of expressionism and surrealism, such as first became understandable in the work of Marc Chagall and Paul Klee through a subtle analysis of their symbolism. According to the "*Art poétique*" of Paul Claudel, "Poetry is possible and remains possible so long as nature and world are symbol and likeness of a hidden majesty."

After these fundamental considerations, that which is factually historical can now be pondered.

In the Gospels the Old Testament is already understood so thoroughly as promise, that all the Old Testament titles of honor that are conferred upon the expected Redeemer are accorded to Jesus: Messiah, Son of Man, Son of David, Son (of God). Jesus matches the picture of the servant of Yahweh drawn in the righteous man of the Old Testament. In the Gospels Jesus very often makes reference to the Old Testament, and he often speaks with its words and images.

At the same time the New Testament is thoroughly aware that the proof from prophecy cannot be adduced, nor made clear and apparent, in a manner that is logically compelling. The Old Testament prophecy can be fulfilled in such a way that it runs contrary to human expectations. In Luke 7:22f. we see that Is. 29:18f., 35:5f. and 61:1 are applied the work of Jesus: "Go and report to John what you have seen and heard: the blind see, the lame walk, lepers are cleansed, the deaf hear, the dead are raised up, and to the poor salvation is announced. And blessed is he that is not scandalized in me." This air of salvational healing is not heard so articulately in prophecy. It must first be extracted from various prophetic texts. And one can be scandalized by the realization of prophecy and refuse belief. Hence the beatitude of believing. The proof from prophecy is available only to one who is willing to believe.

In regard to Jesus' use of the Old Testament, exegesis ponders over a universal question. Is it always the historical Jesus who is speaking here, or has the community perhaps put its theology of Scripture into the mouth of Jesus? In Acts 17:11 the conduct of the community is described: "They studied the Scriptures daily to see whether these things were so." According to Luke 24:26-27 and 24:44-46, the resurrected Jesus explained the whole of the Scriptures to his disciples: "Whatever was written about me in the Law of Moses and in the Prophets and Psalms must be fulfilled." This suggests first of all that the Scriptures were now being examined for an explanation of the resurrection, which undoubtedly was the case (see John 2:22; 12:16). But it also shows that from Easter on the community must already have been in possession of an entirely Christological explanation of the Scriptures, an explanation, indeed, which it received as the teaching of Jesus. This simply leaps

over the concept of a community expending its efforts for a long period
of time in order to arrive at a new understanding of Scripture.

The New Testament explanation of Scripture not infrequently lets us
in on quarrels as to what was the proper interpretation. Here exegesis
asks whether Scripture debates between Israel and the community or
even within the community itself have not been carried back and inter-
posed into the history of Jesus. Such perhaps is the case with Mark
10:4-12, in the quarrel over marriage legislation (*Theology of the New
Testament*, Vol. 3, pp. 245–247); or with Mark 12:35-37 in the altercation over sonship from David (§ 10, 1c) or even with the interpretation
of the decalogue in the Sermon on the Mount (Matthew 5:17-48).

With such questions, however, it must also be borne in mind that if
Jesus' use of the Sacred Scriptures is abundant, it is also original and
autonomous. If Jesus, like any pious Jew, hears in the Scriptures the
word of God, he nevertheless differs greatly from the customary usage
of Scripture as applied by the scribes of his own time. For the latter the
Bible is the lawbook, which requires learned men for its interpretation.
Rabbinic exegesis likes to appeal to a long list of learned predecessors.
Often it permits itself a large measure of capriciousness with both the
literal meaning and the contextual meaning of a passage. Its ever-
recurring theme is Israel's performance and righteousness up to now,
and Israel's present and future priority among the nations. Jesus finds
the goodness, love, and life of God immediately in and behind the
words of the Old Testament. He himself gives expression to their dissimilarity when the learned, with a quotation from Deut. 25:5f., tried to
catch him up with the positing of a bizarre problem: "You err, because
you know neither the Scriptures nor the power of God" (Mark 12:24).
Even his contemporaries noted the newness of his approach: "He talks
like one who has authority, and not like the scribes" (Matthew 7:29).

The interpretation of the Old Testament as the Book of promise is
continued in the Church of the apostles. The Church knows herself as
the true Israel. Old Testament prophecy in its fulfillment, therefore,
belongs to the Church. The Church takes the Old Testament with her
out of the synagogue and makes it her own Book especially by the fact
that she discovers and discloses more and more how it is verified in the
life of Jesus the Messiah and in the history of the Church. The community recognizes the Old Testament predictions as prophecy about

Jesus (Acts 3:22 in accord with Deut. 18:15, 19); about the rejection of Jesus by Jews and Gentiles alike (Acts 4:25-28 in accord with Ps. 2:1f.); about the crucifixion of Jesus (Acts 8:32f. in accord with Is. 53:7f.); burial and being raised up again (Acts 2:25-28 in accord with Ps. 16:8-11; and Acts 2:34f. in accord with Ps. 110:1; Acts 4:11 in accord with Ps. 118:22); the ruination of Judas and the election of Matthias (Acts 1:20 in accord with Ps. 69:26 and 109:8); and finally, the pouring out of the Spirit (Acts 2:17-21, in accord with Joel 3:1-5).

Evidence of the study of the Scriptures in the community of the disciples is to be found also in the Gospels. The Evangelist Matthew demonstrates the fulfillment of the Scriptures in his striking observations about the fulfillment of prophecy (see Matthew 1:22; 2:15, 23; 4:14; 8:17; 12:17; 13:35; 21:4; 26:56; 27:9). The quotations, for the most part, can scarcely have, in their Old Testament context, the directly prophetic meaning attributed to them by Matthew. Matthew wants to use them in such a way as to point up the history of Jesus as having been foretold in the Old Testament. In that way it will be proved that he is the Messiah. In form and in content the citations are of a uniformly Christological interpretation of Scripture, which has its place of origin in the Jewish Christian community.

Even in John's Gospel Old Testament citations probably report the community's familiarity with Scripture. The position which it emphasizes is the hatred which Jesus experienced, and his agonizing death (John 2:17; 3:14; 12:38-40; 13:18; 15:25; 19:24,28-30,36-38). The account of Jesus' sufferings in all four Gospels is presented not simply as history but as prophecy fulfilled. The Psalms (especially Ps. 22 and 69) are interwoven into the account of his crucifixion. The blending is so fine and yet so deep that occasionally the Old Testament citations can only with difficulty any longer be discerned (thus in Mark 15:24,29,34,36; Matthew 27:43; Luke 23:46,49).

It was not the evangelist but the community who first, in its contemplation of the events, read prophecy and fulfillment into each other. Paul hands down as the main content of the gospel message, "that Christ died for our sins in accord with the Scriptures, and that he was, buried, and that on the third day, in accord with the Scriptures, he rose again" (1 Cor. 15:3f.). The statement is formalized, and was already handed on to Paul (§ 9a,c). To anterior tradition belong also the Scriptural evidence for the saving death and resurrection of Jesus. Here again it is also quite clear that the Scriptural evidence was already known and proclaimed by the primitive community.

The Church had great interest in the evidence of prophecy and developed it further and further. The reasons are easily perceived. Such evidence served to edify. Faith is strengthened and the congregation is edified when the fulfillment of promise is recognized. The evidence of prophecy served also in the work of apologetics and in the mission to Jews and Gentiles. Jesus did not simply fall helpless victim to cruel violence if his life and Passion were predetermined long before. If in his Passion he himself fulfilled the prophecies, then he was not the Messiah in spite of the Cross but because of the Cross.

Paul too is convinced that Old Testament revelation leads on to Christ and achieves its meaning and fulfillment in him. He is the highest and the definitive revelation of God. The gospel was announced beforehand by the prophets in the Sacred Scriptures (Rom. 1:2f.). Pauline conceptions are taken up in the probably post-Pauline passage appended to Romans: the gospel of Paul and the preaching of Jesus Christ, according to the revelation of the mystery which, though silent from all eternity, was nevertheless made known to all nations through prophetic writings, is now proclaimed at God's command (Rom. 16:25-26). After the writings of the Old Testament (and the apocalyptics) have alluded to the secret of God, now it has been entirely disclosed through Christ. The preaching of the Apostle is the present gospel of Christ.

Again according to Paul's conviction, the prophetic explanations offered beforehand by the Old Testament are thorough; they cover the long and the short of God's mystery. The history of salvation as well as that of damnation begins with Adam. He, however, is a type of the one who is to come, that is, of Christ (Rom. 5:14). The first and the last Adam stand in a peculiar relationship to each other (1 Cor. 15:45). Over all history there is a great all-embracing arch which spans the gap from Adam to Christ. If Christ can be likened to any other, it is not Moses, the leader of Israel, nor David, the king, but none other in fact than Adam.

Adam is the father of mankind, Christ is the father of the new humanity. In the sin of Adam misfortune had its beginning, not simply by way of a mechanically transmitted inherited sin, but in such a way that with Adam there was begun and established that colossal disaster in the guilt of which all his offspring come into the world (Rom. 5:12; *Theology of the New Testament*, Vol. 1, pp. 114–126).

Abraham (Rom. 4:3; Gal. 3:6), Ismael and Isaac, Essau and Jacob, are types of election and rejection, of belief and disbelief (Rom. 9:7-13). In the history of Israel Paul recognizes prefigurative symbols for the Church. Christ is the true Paschal Lamb (1 Cor. 5:7). The passage through the Red Sea is a prototype of baptism; the manna and the water flowing from the rock are prototypes of the Lord's Eucharistic banquet. Death in the wilderness is a warning for the present. The water from the rock reveals the presence of Christ in the old covenant (1 Cor. 10:1-12). Paul finds the reason for these correspondences in the fact that "the end of the ages has come upon us" (1 Cor. 10:11). In the salvation historical plan beginning and end correspond to each other.

An outstanding reflection on the Old Testament as prophecy is developed in 1 Peter 1:10-12. The Spirit of the pre-existing Christ abiding in the prophets made them aware of Christ's suffering and majesty, which is by now accomplished fact. It is in that same Holy Spirit that the apostles now proclaim the message. Prophecy and gospel correspond to each other. It is Christ who in the Old Testament is termed the cornerstone in Sion, on whom the spiritual house of the Church is built, and against which the lost stumble and meet their ruin (1 Peter 2:4-8, in accord with Is. 8:14f. and 28:16). Israel's titles belong now to the Church, "the chosen race, the royal priesthood, the holy people, the people particularly acquired" (1 Peter 2:9, in accord with Exod. 19:6).

The author of the Epistle to the Hebrews has the charism of Scripture interpretation. With outstanding clarity the letter portrays Melchizedek as the prototype of the High Priest, Christ (Heb. 7), and the great Day of Atonement as prefiguring the work of atonement which Christ as heavenly High Priest has now perfected at the end of the ages (Heb. 9). "The Law is a shadowy prefiguring of the good things to come" (Heb. 10:1). In the martyrs and righteous men of the old covenant the Christian has "a cloud of witnesses" around him (Heb. 11:1–12:1). Moses represents Christ. He already bore the "humiliation of Christ". The Old Testament and the New Testament people of God are one. What they endure is the one Passion of Christ (Heb. 11:26). The martyrs "sing the song of Moses, the servant of God, and the song of the

Lamb" (Apoc. 15:3). The exodus from Egypt is a prefigure of redemption, which is an exodus from the dominion of evil. The former leader, Moses, is a prefigure of the present Redeemer. Prototype and fulfillment, present and endtime are in harmonious accord.

§ 4. REVELATION IN THE NEW TESTAMENT

After John the Baptist, Jesus came forward with the message: "The time is fulfilled and the kingdom of God is at hand" (Mark 1:15). God wants to come forth from his former secrecy to let his reign begin and to introduce the promised era of salvation (the concept of "the kingdom of God" will be taken up in the fourth volume of our present *Theology of the New Testament*). The word revelation itself is lacking; but it is just as clearly stated here that now it is, in fact, the advanced time of revelation.[28] The eras in the history of revelation are to be marked off in this way: "The Law and the Prophets extend up to John. From there on the kingdom of God is proclaimed" (Luke 16:16). The eschatological zenith of the times has now commenced.

That now is the time of the great revelation is declared also in Jesus' cry of jubilation: "I praise You, Father, Lord of heaven and of earth, because you have kept this hidden from the wise and prudent, and have revealed it to the little ones. Yes, Father, such was your good pleasure" (Matthew 11:25-26 = Luke 10:21).

The Father reveals himself only to his own. But the revelation takes place also through the Son: "Everything has been given me by my Father. No one knows the Son except the Father, and no one knows the Father except the Son, and him to whom the Son wants to give revelation" (Matthew 11:27 = Luke 10:22).

There is but one agent of revelation, the one Son; and he is incomparably different from all other agents, who in the old covenant are the prophets and in the new, the apostles. The Son lives in an exclusive unity with the Father, from whom he receives all knowledge. This knowledge is an eternal one. The agency of the Son does not exclude directness between God and the believer, but actually produces it. Matthew 11:25-27 combines two logia of different form and probably of different origin. Matthew 11:25-26 is a prayer of thanksgiving to the Father, while Matthew 11:27 is Jesus' testimony to himself. The two sayings are bound together by the catchwords *Father* and *revelation*. And the two sayings are united also in Luke 10:21-22. Consequently they can be assigned to Source Q, and pertain to a relatively older tradition.

Furthermore, exegesis is virtually unanimous in accepting the first saying in Matthew 11:25-26 as a tradition from the Jewish Christian community and moreover as an original saying of Jesus.[29] The saying bears the characteristic signs of Old Testament Jewish language and conception; for the sake of comparison there are the thanksgiving prayers in Dan. 2:20-23 and Sir. 51:1,10-12.

The second saying, in Matthew 11:27, is appended to the first, probably editorially, as explanation and foundation thereof. As a "Johannine passage in the Synoptics", Matthew 11:27 was often characterized as a saying of Hellenistic mysticism, where the mutual knowledge between God and the religious man is similarly expressed. In more recent times, nevertheless, reference is made also to Old Testament Jewish texts in explanation of its origins.[30] The addressing of God as "(Father), Lord of heaven and of earth" bears witness to an Old Testament belief in creation. That all things are confided to the Son is reminiscent of Matthew 28:18; and it exhibits an apocalyptic conceptual content, since in Matthew 28:18 power has already been transferred to the glorified Christ. Knowledge is an essentially biblical concept, just as the notion that it establishes an intimate communion. God knows, because he chooses (Exod. 33:12; Ps. 37:18; Hos. 13:4f.; Jer. 1:5).

The association of election, knowledge of God, and revelation is typical also of Qumran. God "instructs the righteous in highest knowledge and in the truth of the sons of heaven; and he makes wise those who are perfect in their deeds. For God has chosen them for his eternal covenant" (1 QS 4:22; see also 1 QS 11:15-18; 1 QH 2:13). In praying one gives thanks and says: "I praise you, Lord! You have instructed me in your truth and have given me knowledge of your wonderful secrets" (1 QH 7:26f.).

Moreover, Jesus' testimony to himself in regard to his Sonship ought to be compared with various other declarations (Mark 1:11; 12:6; 13:32; see also below, § 11, 3). According to Matthew 11:25, revelation is hidden from the wise and prudent; and in the context of Jesus' saying, these are the scribes in Israel. The little ones who receive revelation are the same as the poor in spirit (Matthew 5:3; *Theology of the New Testament*, Vol. 3, pp. 305-306) and the children who are a model for the disciples (Matthew 18:3; *Theol. of the N. T.*, Vol. 3, pp 325-327).

It is from this latter point that the saying draws its peculiarity, a peculiarity which marks it through and through. In the Old Testament God reveals himself to the great ones among the people: to Abraham (Gen. 12–24); to Jacob (Gen. 35); Moses (Exod. 3); Samuel (1 Sam. 3); to the prophets (Amos 3:7; Is. 22:14; Dan. 2:19-30); and finally, to pious people in general (Ps. 25:14). They who received God's word were for the most part those who might be expected to proclaim it further and with power. Alongside Jesus' cry of jubilation it is possible to adduce passages like that of Ps. 119:130, which make the word of God understandable to the simple, and those in which, like Wis. 10:21 and Sir. 3:19f., wisdom is imparted to the little ones.

In Qumran God is called a "Father to all the sons of truth" (1 QH 9:35). "The wise and those who make haste to contemplate knowledge" are invited to listen (1 QH 1:35). The pious are known as "the simple ones of Judah" (1 QpHab 12:4). To the humble God proclaims his truth and his goodness (1 QH 18:14). Nevertheless, in its wholeheartedness Matthew 11:25 is something new in the history of revelation. Here it is the little ones, those who have no position in the community, who are the recipients of revelation. God's revealing love devotes itself to them for their own sake alone.[31]

In the realities of those times, Jesus actually associated with the poor, sinners before the Law. Inasmuch as revelation remains hidden in respect to the wise, it is made apparent that man cannot achieve this knowledge by his own efforts, but that it must be imparted to him as gift and grace. In this respect Matthew 11:27 is of similar import to Matthew 16:17, "Blessed are you, for flesh and blood has not revealed this to you, but my Father in heaven." This knowledge does not have its origins in human capability, for that can err. In both logia the Father reveals; revelation and knowledge are referred to the Son; and the one who receives the revelation is pronounced blessed.

In Matthew 11:27 knowledge of the Son is derived through the

Father, and the Son imparts knowledge of the Father to the elect. In accord with the structure of early Christology the operation of the Father has a priority. The Son does not reveal himself, but the Father. The Son and his work are referred totally to a relationship with the Father.

The elect or chosen ones receive this revelation, but to the rest it remains hidden. "To you is given the secret ($\mu\nu\sigma\tau\acute{\eta}\rho\iota\sigma\nu$) of the kingdom of God. To the others, who are outside, everything is conveyed in parables" (Mark 4:11). The use of the passive suggests, as so often in biblical language, the veiled operation of God. It is God who gives revelation. It is a "mysterium" even after it is given. If revelation is designated here as a mysterium, it is not to be understood in accord with the religious language of the Greek mysteries, but in accord with Jewish apocalyptics. Even here the knowledge of the secret is a gift (Dan. 2:19, 28; Wis. 2:22; 6:22; 7:15, 22).

The secret referred to in this saying of Jesus is the dawning kingdom of God. A parable, however, or so it is stated in Mark 4:11, is supposed to veil something. Nevertheless, this is not the original meaning or purpose of a parable; rather, by its clarity, it is supposed to render something more easily comprehensible. The saying is hardly a saying of Jesus, but is an apologetic reflection of the community, which seeks to explain for itself Israel's disbelief. Mark 4:12, quoting Is. 6:9f., adds that Israel's stubbornness is God's will. The quotation is offered, with the same end in view, also in John 12:40 and Acts 28:26. It belongs to the congregation's proof of prophecy. Moreover, the veil theory is a vehicle of presentation employed in the Gospel of Mark. The secret of Jesus is hidden to the world, but it is manifest in the community, that is, to those with faith (Mark 4:34; 7:36; 9:28, 33; 10:10; 13:3; see below, § 11, 1).

The Son, through his word and his work, is the revelation of God (Matthew 11:27). He has full authority to speak in God's place. The prophets were God's messengers, and they delivered God's word. That is why they introduced their announcements with the phrase: thus says the Lord. But Christ proclaims: I say unto you. Thus in the antitheses in the Sermon on the Mount: "You have heard that it was said to the ancients: 'Thou shalt not kill' . . . but I say to you . . ." (Matthew 5:21-48). Jesus draws attention to the proclamation of the ten com-

mandments. He contrasts his own word to the Law of God revealed on
Sinai. His word is of the same dignity as the Law. One who can so
speak is not a mere messenger of God, but God's very mouth. In his
word God's word is revealed and heard.

In the activity of Jesus God's operation is revealed. Jesus points out
to the messengers of the Baptist that the blind see, the lame walk, and
he thereby declares that prophecy (Is. 35:5f.) has been fulfilled (Matthew 11:5). Actually, the prophet did not say that these things would
one day be done by the Messiah, but that God himself would do them.
"God himself will come to you and will save you. Then will the eyes
of the blind be opened . . ." God's healing work of salvation takes
place in the healing salvational activity of Jesus.

Christ acts in God's place as the one who forgives sin. This is represented in Luke 15:1-32. Jesus is surrounded by tax collectors and sinners. His opponents are grumbling because he welcomes sinners and
forgives them their sins. This is, to be sure, a right that belongs to God
alone. Addressing himself to this setting, Luke narrates the parables
of the lost sheep, of the lost drachma, of the prodigal son. These parables justify the action of Jesus. Like the Father, here Jesus too welcomes back the lost sinners; indeed, because Jesus welcomes sinners,
the Father welcomes them. Jesus maintains that he is carrying out the
work of the Father. God's purpose and action is revealed and realized
in the purpose and action of the Son.

Revelation, nevertheless, is as yet in an intermediate state. It is still
veiled while it yearns for completion. This will be achieved "on the
day when the Son of Man is revealed" (Luke 17:30).

Critical interpretation will now ask whether revelation ever takes
place as a real communication of God to men, or whether what is
termed revelation is really only the reflection of religious men. The
question as to the truth of the claim of revelation, for faith and theology at any rate, will find its end and its answer in the words of Jesus,
as in Matthew 11:25-27 or Matthew 5:21-48 and Luke 15:3-32.

The primitive community understands the history of Christ as the
overwhelming revelation of God in history. Revelation is the word of
Christ, which is proclaimed further and further; revelation is also the
person and life of Christ, which are likewise to be proclaimed. The
preaching of Peter provides a summation of this revelation: "God sent

his word to the sons of Israel, so that he might have peace proclaimed through Jesus Christ." This original word of Jesus must be spread further and further. Also to be announced, however, is "the thing that has happened in Judea. . . . Jesus of Nazareth, who went about doing good and healing those who were overcome by the power of the devil . . . — they killed him, but on the third day God raised him up. He is appointed Judge of the living and the dead" (Acts 10:34-43). Now the revelation of God is furthered by the operation of the Spirit. It is in the power of the Spirit that the gospel is proclaimed (Acts 2:4; 4:31) and the service of the community is performed (Acts 6:3; 9:31; 20:28). Revelation, accordingly, is not only doctrine but also an event in the Church.

It is Paul's gospel too, that Christ is the definitive revelation of God. True enough, Paul may hesitate to say of the earthly Jesus that he is the revelation of God. Here the form of God was veiled in the form of the servant. The unveiling took place in the resurrection and in the exaltation of Christ to the glory of God (Phil. 2:7-11). A credal formula in the Epistle to the Romans (1:3-4) is composed in much the same conceptual frame: "The Son of God was born of the seed of David according to the flesh; he was shown to be the Son of God in power according to the spirit of holiness in consequence of the resurrection from the dead" (see below, § 9e; the "spirit of holiness" is not the divine and personal Spirit).

That the revelation of God was all but hidden in the earthly Christ is stated by Paul in a mythological presentation in 1 Cor. 2:8. The demons, who have mastery over the world, did not know God's plans for salvation. Even the glory of Christ was hidden from them. So they nailed him to the Cross unto their own destruction. The Cross is the salvation of the world, and by the Cross, moreover, the power of the demons came to an end. The divine glory of Christ is hidden under the Cross for disbelief as well as for belief.

The Gospels agree with Paul, for they too indicate that in his earthly life Jesus' glory was hidden. In the Gospel of Mark, Jesus commands the conquered demons (1:25; 3:12) as well as those persons whom he healed (1:44; 5:43; 7:36; 8:26) to be silent. His teaching and his works as well are misunderstood even by his disciples (Mark 4:13; 6:52; 7:18; 8:17-21). His disciples are not permitted to speak of his glory revealed in the transfiguration until after the Son of Man will have risen from the dead (Mark 9:9). The earthly life of Jesus was moving on towards the Cross. The resurrection first unveiled fully his divine Sonship.

In the Gospel of John, Jesus reveals himself as the Son through eternal self-testimony and through most powerful miracles, so that disbelief is inexcusable (John 15:22-24). Nevertheless, Jesus does not openly declare before the Jews that he is the Messiah (John 10:24f.). Even for his disciples his speech is "veiled" (John 16:25). The evangelist himself says that the mystery of Christ is first disclosed through his resurrection (John 2:22; 12:16) and the mission of the Spirit (John 14:26). Only faith can understand it (John 10:25).

At the same time, however, Paul speaks also of the revelation of God in the historical appearance of Christ. "God, who said, 'Out of darkness let light shine', is lighted up in our hearts to bring us the bright light of the knowledge of the glory of God shining on the face of Christ" (2 Cor. 4:6). Paul himself experienced this revelation. He received the gospel "through a revelation of Jesus Christ" (Gal. 1:12). Here Christ himself is named as the one revealing. However, God can likewise be designated as the revealer: "It was God's pleasure to reveal his Son in me" (Gal. 1:15-16). Here Paul is speaking of his conversion on the road to Damascus. Perhaps even 2 Cor. 4:6 is enveloped in this personal recollection. God's revelation turned Paul from the Law to grace.

The whole Church is the recipient of revelation. Paul says in this regard, "God has revealed it to us through the Spirit." Nothing is hidden from the divine Spirit; he "plumbs the depths of God" (1 Cor. 2:10). Knowledge is given the believer through the Spirit. Even now Christ is present as the Spirit in the world and in the Church. "The Lord is the Spirit" (2 Cor. 3:17). In this capacity, Christ discloses the meaning too of revelation. "If anyone turn to the Lord, the veil will be taken away" (2 Cor. 3:16 in accord with Exod. 34:34). Probably 1 Cor. 2:9 is also to be understood of the fullness of revelation, in which the wisdom of God is disclosed: "What no eye has seen and no ear has heard, and what no human heart has conceived, all this is what God has prepared for those who love him."

In his Church it is always God who is the revealer. "If on some point you are minded otherwise, this too God will reveal to you" (Phil. 3:15).

Certainly this applies not just to the community in Philippi, but for every community in the Church and forever. God gives revelation to his Church directly. Thus Paul describes the divine service in Corinth: "When you are gathered together, each one has a hymn, a teaching, a revelation, a speaking in tongues, an interpretation" (1 Cor. 14:26). The community is extraordinarily distinguished by the richness of its spiritual gifts. And with these gifts, revelations too pertain to the individual members of the Church.

The deutero-Pauline writings bespeak the same conviction. The mystery that was hidden for ages and generations "has now been revealed to the saints" (Col. 1:26), that is to say, to the Church. The Epistle to the Ephesians prays: "May God grant you the Spirit of wisdom and revelation in knowledge" (Eph. 1:17). Here too it is the whole Church who is the receiver of revelation, which is brought about in the Spirit. The same Epistle can speak also of "that mystery which in other generations was not made known to the sons of men, as it has now been revealed to the apostles and prophets in the Spirit" (Eph. 3:5). Revelation is made in an extremely narrow circle, to the representatives of the Church; it is, however, intended for all men. The agent is the Spirit. The Church is represented by the apostles and prophets, therefore by those who occupy official positions and also by the charismatics. Both are commissioned with the further dissemination of revelation.

An outline of the economy of revelation is discernible, the first traces of which are found already in Paul (1 Cor. 2:7-9), and which is afterwards broadened and confirmed (Col. 1:26; Rom. 16:25f.; 2 Tim. 1:9f.; Titus 1:2f.). According to this schema: God's mystery was determined from all eternity, but was hidden; from now on, however, it is unveiled. The revelation takes place through the manifestation of Jesus Christ (2 Tim. 1:10), is advanced through the word (Titus 1:3) and is further manifested through the Spirit (1 Cor. 2:10; Eph. 1:17; 3:5). The codicil, certainly post-Pauline, to the Epistle to the Romans (16:25f.) reflects on this revelation. God's mystery, hidden from time eternal, is now made manifest through the coming of Jesus Christ, and is evermore revealed in the proclamation of the Gospel to all nations.[32]

Like the Gospels (Matthew 11:25-27; 16:17), the Epistles too declare that the revelation is not available to men in such a way that it might be grasped by anyone who would want it. It must be given by God. "The word of the Cross is foolishness to those who are perishing; but to those who are saved it is the power of God" (1 Cor. 1:18). If God's grace does not open the meaning that the Cross has for the gospel, then the Cross appears to be foolishness and its meaning is not grasped. In a picturesque statement Paul says of himself as the messenger of the gospel that he is "the fragrance of Christ for God among those who are saved as also among those who are going to perdition; for the latter an odor of death that leads to death, for the former an odor of life that leads to life" (2 Cor. 2:15f.). Men decide for themselves and, with eyes upon the gospel, choose between life and death. The decision is surely made in accord with men's freedom of choice. But in this decision a decision made by God also comes to pass. Undoubtedly the New Testament is certain that God's eternal decision in regard to a man is never made without that man's having so decided for himself.

Although divine revelation took place abundantly and continues to broaden itself, it is not yet completed. It pushes on toward its perfection. Christians "await the revelation of our Lord Jesus Christ" (1 Cor. 1:7). This future and complete revelation of Jesus Christ is to take place with his parousia. It is described thus: "The Lord Jesus will appear from heaven with his mighty angels in flaming fire" (2 Thess. 1:7-8). This revelation will be made for everyone. "Now we see distortedly in a mirror, but then we shall see face to face. Now I know only partially; but then I will know even as I have been known" (1 Cor. 13:12). Faith does not now behold the divine Truth itself, but it knows and beholds only an incomplete image. Hope, however, expects the full revelation in the future personal encounter with God. This hope has its basis in the fact that God already knows man and sustains him. God's care is such that he will not abandon man.

The whole of creation will share in the eschatological revelation. At present creation is afflicted with misery and filled with a yearning for deliverance. It is the old biblical expectation that in the messianic era of salvation the world will be renewed. This is the prophetic promise: "I am going to create a new heaven and a new earth (Is. 65:17). The Apocalypse of John (21:1-4) depicts in glowing colors the new heavens and the new earth, which is free of sickness, sorrow, and death. Now Paul too says that when the children of God attain their eschatological glory, all creation along with them "will be freed from the servitude

of corruptibility into the freedom of the glory of the sons of God"
(Rom. 8:19-22). The misery of the world is but the birth pangs of its
restoration. Man is not ransomed from the world, but along with it.

Revelation is one and the same in the old era and in the new. "After
having spoken to our ancestors at many times and in many ways in
the prophets, God has in these last days spoken to us" (Heb. 1:1f.). All
revelation known to the Bible has its one source in the one God. In a
backward glance to the Old Testament the Epistle confirms as characteristic of former revelation that there was in the old covenant in
the great number of prophets a multiplicity of the bearers of revelation
just as in general there was a multiplicity in the ways in which revelation was conveyed (the word of God, but also messages brought by
angels, then there were various events, and even dreams and visions).

This multiplicity, however, did not signify richness and fullness, but
because there were so many revelations, they were dispersed; and individually they were provisional, partial, unfinished and incomplete.
Now, however, revelation has taken place in the Son. In this revelation
everything is brought together in definitive unity and perfection. As
the Son, this bearer of revelation comes forth from the innermost communion of divine life, and therefore surpasses in an incomparable
measure all the other and earlier bearers of revelation.

In the Son the world was created, and in him it is now perfected
(Heb. 1:2). The Son embraces and holds all. In him revelation has its
goal as it achieves its perfection. The goal is achieved, moreover, because now it is "the end of the days" (Heb. 1:2). The eschatological
expectation of the Epistle to the Hebrews continues even yet. If it has
not yet been fulfilled, the essential apprehension of its declaration remains valid even yet for the faith. Christ is the perfection of revelation.
If other passages of the New Testament (1 Cor. 14:26; Phil. 3:15; John
14:26) state that revelation takes place in the Church in an ongoing
way, one will have to balance these declarations with the explanation
that the continuing revelation takes place within the definitive revelation that came with Christ, and that it therefore contains nothing new
as to content, but is compatible with the one revelation and sheds light
upon it.

The Apocalypse of John refers to itself as "the revelation of Jesus
Christ, which God gave him" (Apoc. 1:1). The revealer is God, but

here too it is Christ who is the chief agent of revelation. As the Lamb, he opens the book with the seven seals. When he breaks the seal what was under the seal comes forth (Apoc. 6). Christ finally emerges as the Word of God, and he conquers the last enemy, the antichrist (Apoc. 19:13). The orientation of the revelation is toward the future. Creation is suffering the labor pains of the new world. The Church of the martyrs prays for the revelation of the kingdom of God with the cry: "Come, Lord Jesus!" (Apoc. 22:20).

The Gospel of John made the assertion of the perfect and definitive revelation of God in the manifestation of Christ the central point of its exposition. It expresses this through Christ's own designation of himself as "the Son". Jesus is simply the Son, while God is the Father. Certainly as the Son he is subordinated to the Father: "The Father is greater than I" (John 14:28). But at the same time he stands in a relationship to God such as is enjoyed by none other: "The Father and I are one" (John 10:30). As this Son, Christ brings the full revelation of God. Since the unbelievers (the Jews) deny the one revealing, neither do they know the Father, from whence Jesus comes. And since they do not know the Father, neither do they know the origin of the Son. "You do not know him who sent me. But I know him, because I am from him and he has sent me" (John 7:28f.; see also John 8:55).

The world is in an even greater state of ignorance. "Just Father, the world has not known you; but I have known you, and these have known that you sent me" (John 17:25). The recognition of belief in the Father by the disciples has the basis of its being made possible in the Son's being recognized as God; and belief in the Father always includes along with it belief in the Son as the one who reveals. It is God himself who speaks in the words of the one sent by God. "He whom God has sent speaks the words of God" (John 3:34). The words do not just impart knowledge; rather, the word is also the deed. "The words which I have spoken to you are Spirit and Life" (John 6:63).

The Spirit of God is always a creationally mighty and amazing power. Faith, which hears the word of Jesus and accepts it, will experience this. Revelation through the word is completed through "works" (John 4:34). Deeds are signs. The multiplication of the loaves signifies that Christ is and gives the bread of life (John 6:32-35); the cure of the man born blind signifies that Jesus is the light of the world

(John 9:5); the raising of Lazarus signifies that Jesus is the resurrection and the life (John 11:25f.).

The Johannine Christ is more than just the vehicle of God's revelation. He is revelation in his own person, since the Father is present in him. Whoever sees and recognizes him will also recognize the Father, indeed, has already seen and recognized him (John 14:7-9). Present, future, and consummation are inextricably interwoven in these passages. The constantly bestowed possibility must be constantly realized anew. To the faith, which ratifies this decision in confrontation with the Revealer, everything is given that can be given at this time. Revelation continues onward. "The Advocate, the Holy Spirit, whom the Father will send in my name — he will teach you all things and will recall to you everything that I have said to you" (John 14:26).

Revelation is not at an end with the departure of Jesus; rather, through the Spirit, it will be bestowed upon the community again and again as eschatological gift. Here gift signifies the re-minder of the word of Jesus as realization thereof in faith and in life. That Jesus is in general the Revealer is expressed ultimately throughout the Gospel by its application to Christ. He is plainly and simply the Word of God to the world. In him this Word is not merely spoken, but has become Man (John 1:1-14; 1 John 1:1f.).

From the universality of immediate revelation in relation to that belief, there follows the immediacy of the relationship to God. The texts are seldom enough invoked in exegesis and application, but they must not on that account be overlooked. Thus in 1 Thess. 4:9, "You have no need of our writing to you about brotherly love; for you have been taught by God himself to love one another." This can hardly be intended to say that the teaching has been accomplished through the word of God in the Scriptures (perhaps Lev. 19:18 = Mark 12:31); it is in fact accomplished in the immediacy of God and of the believing man.

Further, there is John 6:45, "It is written in the Prophets: They will all be taught by God. Everyone who has listened to the Father comes to me." The believer is taught by God. He hears the Father himself. The evangelist cites no particular passage of the Prophets, but says that this is the common conviction of all. As illustrations we might mention Is. 54:13, according to which in the new Jerusalem all the children will be pupils of God; Jer. 31:33 (from the promise of the new covenant); Joel 3:1f. = Acts 2:16-21; in Heb. 8:8-12 the text quotes Jer. 31:31-34, "I will put my law into their mind. None shall have to teach his neighbor, none his brother, and say to him, 'Know the Lord.' For they all shall know me." [33] God himself teaches. None other is needed, no human teacher is required.

Jesus' departing address in the Gospel of John says again and again that Jesus has made known to his disciples all that he heard from the Father (15:15; 17:26), and that the Spirit will be given to the community, and the community will learn the truth (14:17; 15:26; 16:13). To be sure, the disciples to whom he is speaking in the first instance are the twelve apostles. But his pledges and promises are valid for the whole Church.

Finally we might mention 1 John 2:20-27, "You possess the anointing from the Holy One, and are altogether knowledgeable. You know the Truth and have no need of anyone to teach you." The anointing probably signifies the bestowal of the Spirit (by word and sacrament?). But is the Holy One to be understood as God or as Christ? The Truth spoken of is not philosophical truth, but revealed divine reality. In the context of such a remark, external teaching authority is unimportant; the inner instruction gives knowledge and certitude of Truth. The whole Church has a prophetic endowment and duty (Acts 2:17f.; Rom. 12:6; 1 Cor. 12:10, 28; 14:1, 24; Eph. 4:11; 1 Thess. 5:20). The whole Church has a priestly character (1 Peter 2:5, 9; Apoc. 1:6; 5:10).

II
REDEMPTION AND SALVATION

§ 5. WORD OF CHRIST — CHRIST THE WORD

One of the most decisive impressions that the Gospels convey about Jesus is that he was a teacher with great power.[34] He teaches on the streets and in the squares, at the seashore and from a boat, as well as in the synagogue.

In the world at that time a teacher was nothing extraordinary. In the cities one might easily come upon philosophers teaching and engaging in argumentation. In Israel the rabbis taught the Law out in the open, in schoolhouses, and in the synagogues.

Jesus uses the customary instructional forms of admonitions and warnings, of proverbs and parables, and handles the spoken word with great mastery.[35] Like a rabbi, Jesus gathered his students around himself. People turned to him for a decision in disputed questions, just as they turned to a celebrated rabbi. We have the examples of the question about divorce (Mark 10:2-9), of resurrection (Mark 12:18-27), and even of a dispute over an inheritance (Luke 12:13f.). Like a rabbi, Jesus was accustomed to explain the Scripture in the synagogue (Mark 1:39; Luke 4:16). Jesus accepts the title rabbi. He is addressed as such by the disciples (Mark 9:5; 11:21). Judas greets him as "Rabbi" (Mark 14:45). This title of address is frequently accorded Jesus in the Gospel of John: by his disciples (1:38; 4:31; *et passim*); by Nicodemus (3:2); by the crowd (6:25). The longer form, rabbuni (Mark 10:51; John 20:16), signifies the same thing, *my teacher*, or *my master* (see the article ῥαββί of E. Lohse in the *Theol. Dict. N. T.*, Vol. 6 [1968], p. 962, text and note 14, for the forms rabboni, rabbani, and rabbuni).

In other respects Jesus differs from the rabbis. Jesus is never seen in argumentation or in a common search for learning with his disciples; rather, he teaches with incontestable authority. He never appeals to other teachers or to the authority of tradition, as the rabbis liked to do, but he simply announces on his own authority: "I, however, tell you . . ." (Matthew 5:21-48). The disciples of Jesus never want to strive, as do the students of the rabbis, to become rabbis themselves; rather, they remain always the students of Jesus. Whereas the rabbis decline to instruct women, Jesus has women too for disciples (Luke 8:2f.; 10:38-42). His association with tax-collectors, prostitutes and sinners must have seemed to be most extraordinarily strange for a rabbi (Matthew 11:19).

The difference between Jesus and the rabbis does not escape the attention of the masses of the people. They are startled by his teaching. For he teaches them as one who possesses authority, not like the scribes (Matthew 7:28f.; 13:54). In place of the term *rabbi*, the Gospels employ the translations διδάσκαλος = teacher (Mark 4:38, *et passim*; John 1:38) or ἐπιστάτης = master (Luke 5:5; 9:33, *et passim*).[36] The word rabbi would have had a foreign sound to the Greco-Roman world. On the lips of the disciples Matthew regularly replaces the Markan title of address, rabbi, with the term Lord (κύριε; Matthew 8:25; 17:4; 20:33). The title rabbi no longer suffices for the use of the community of disciples. If John employs the title rabbi for emphasis, this simply indicates in the mentality of his Gospel the paradox that this Rabbi is God's Son.

Jesus speaks of himself as a teacher and refers to his own teaching. According to the Gospel of Mark, on the first day of his healings he went apart by himself in the evening in order to pray. Simon and the others went out looking for him, in order to bring him back with them. Jesus replied to them: "We must go to the other villages so that I can preach in them too. That was my purpose in going away."

Teaching, then, is Jesus' essential task. Here his miracles seem to be subordinate to the word. The miracle can be understood only in view of the word. For the miracle is ambiguous. One can attribute it to evil (Mark 3:22). In the parable of the sower (Mark 4:3-9) Christ is certainly speaking ultimately of himself. He sows the seed of the word in the fields of the world.

A saying of the Lord states flatly: "The pupil is not greater than the teacher, and the slave is not greater than his master" (Matthew 10:24). A primarily profane imagery from relationships in the world comes from the mouth of Jesus. It has, however, overtones of something deeper. This teacher is more than a teacher; he is the Master. The disciple in this relationship is less than a disciple; he is a slave.[37] Therefore the word of Jesus also imparts something other than mere instruction. His word works life and salvific healing, inasmuch as it expels the demons (Mark 1:25) and heals and redeems the whole man (Mark 1:14f.), yes, even calls the dead back to life (Mark 5:41; Luke 7:14; John 11:43).

Jesus also went into the synagogue as a teacher (Matthew 9:35; Mark 1:39; 6:2). Luke (4:16-30) creates (from Mark 6:1f.) the impressive scene of Jesus' first sermon in his native city of Nazareth. Already at Jesus' first appearance it is made manifest (which can scarcely be chronologically correct) that the Messiah is being rejected by Israel and the gospel is going to go to the Gentiles, just as Elijah went to the widow in Zarephath and Elisha healed the leper Naaman. This is the way the gospel will take, which Luke will describe in the Acts of the Apostles. Similarities to the songs of the servant of Yahweh (Is. 58:6 and 61:1) mark Jesus as the messianic teacher. He works in the power of the Spirit. He is anointed (ἔχρισέν με is suggestive of the title Christ), to announce the gospel to the poor, to free those who are imprisoned (by the demons), to heal the sick and to proclaim the era of salvation.

In two accounts similar to each other, from the last days of Jesus, it is told how he sent two disciples, either to find the ass for his entry into Jerusalem (Mark 11:1-3), or to prepare the upper room for the Last Supper (Mark 14:12-16). The disciples are supposed to say: "The Lord has need of it" (*i.e.*, of the beast; Mark 11:3) and: "The teacher says, 'Where is my room where I will eat the Passover supper with my disciples?'" (Mark 14:14). In a marvelous way Jesus knows his destiny in advance. He assents to it, inasmuch as he himself makes preparations for it. In his Passion he is not overcome by crude force, but goes to it voluntarily. Jesus is plainly the Teacher and the Lord.

In a sharp altercation with the Pharisees and scribes the teaching of Jesus on the rabbinate is preserved: "You must not be called 'rabbi'; for one only is your Teacher, whereas you are all brothers. You must not call anyone here on earth 'father', for you have one only Father,

he that is in heaven. Neither shall you allow anyone to call you 'master';
for you have one only Master, the Christ" (Matthew 23:8-10).

The quarrel between Church and synagogue, who stood opposed to
each other as differing religions by the end of the first century, finds
expression in the indictment of Pharisaism in Matthew 23. Matthew
23:1-10, moreover, already presumes an institutional community, in
which designations of office and titles in accord with the example of
the synagogue are beginning to be used or have already come into use.
In the time of Jesus and in his presence his disciples can hardly have
been striving, like rabbis, to have themselves called 'father' or 'teacher'.
Finally, Jesus claims plainly and simply to be the Christ. Here it is the
Faith that recognizes Jesus as the Teacher of the Church.

The teaching of Jesus is shown also by the title 'prophet', which is
accorded Jesus in the New Testament. The prophets of the old covenant are recognized and celebrated in Israel as teachers, miracle workers,
and martyrs. In a backward glance at this threefold test Jesus too turns
out to have been a prophet: through his teaching (Matthew 23:34;
Luke 24:19), through his miracles (Luke 7:16; John 6:14) and through
his suffering (Matthew 23:29, 37).

Did Jesus claim for himself the task and title of a prophet? Rejected
in Nazareth, Jesus says: "A prophet is not held in contempt except in
his home town and by his relatives and in his own house" (Mark 6:4).
Using a proverb, Jesus compares his destiny to that of a prophet; but he
does not thereby precisely call himself a prophet.

When the Pharisees warn Jesus about Herod, he replies to them:
"Go there and tell that fox, 'Behold, I cast out demons and work cures
today and tomorrow, and on the third day I will be finished. Indeed,
today and tomorrow and a third day I must be on my way, for it is
not right that a prophet should perish outside Jerusalem" (Luke 13:31-
33). The account contains biographical elements. Here the Pharisees
are friends of Jesus, not like later when they are plainly and simply his
opponents. It even preserves a recollection of Jesus' relationship to his
ruler. That is probably how the original saying of Jesus came to be
interpreted afterwards as a prophetic announcement about his own
Passion and resurrection. The lament over the murder of the prophets
is repeated: "Jerusalem, Jerusalem, you that kill the prophets and stone
those who are sent to you, how often have I wanted to gather your

children together" (Luke 13:34). In such statements Jesus ranks him-self with the prophets.

The accusation, however, that Israel is guilty of the murder of nu-merous prophets, poses a problem.[38] Certainly the Old Testament treats of the persecution of such prophets as Amos, Elijah, and Jeremiah, but only exceptionally of the murdering of prophets (Jer. 26:20-23; 2 Chron. 24:21). Israel herself, nevertheless, blames herself for the persecution of the prophets (2 Chron. 36:16) and even for their murder (3 Kings 19:10; Neh. 9:26). The work called the *Ascension of Isaiah* includes the *Martyrdom of Isaiah*, a writing of Jewish origin, in which the prophet's death is recounted in 5:1-14. Martyrdoms of the prophets were collected in the early Jewish writing, *Lives of the Prophets*, dat-ing probably from between the years 50 and 100 A.D. Israel herself, in severe and even overly severe self-judgment, declares herself guilty of the murder of the prophets. The accusation is repeated in summary fashion in the New Testament (Matthew 5:12; 23:31-37; Acts 7:52; 1 Thess. 2:15f.; James 5:10; Heb. 11:36f.). We might ask: Did Jesus himself share in the repetition of this accusation, or are we dealing with the early Church's polemic against Judaism (such as may be taken, and not without reason, as the basis for Matthew 23)? A saying about the persecution of the prophets, which, in Luke 11:49 is quoted as proverbial wisdom, is placed in the mouth of Jesus in Matthew 23:34. Is it right for Christian preachers to affirm this accusation and to repeat it?

Other sayings of the Lord signify that Jesus is more than a prophet. Jesus hears the conjectures that he is John the Baptist resurrected, that he is Elijah or some one of the prophets returned. Peter speaks for the disciples when he says that Jesus is more than the messianic prophet; he is the messianic King (Mark 8:28f.).[39]

Did Jesus himself ever claim to be a prophet? The texts provide no certain answer to the question. It seems unlikely, however, if Jesus was convinced that the era of the prophets was closed with John the Baptist: "The Law and the prophets continue until John"; now God's kingdom has begun (Luke 16:16). Elijah, the last herald of the messianic era of salvation, has come in the person of John the Baptist. Jesus is the one who is announced by the last prophet as the Messiah himself (Mark 9:12f.). In the parable of the wicked vine-dressers Christ is, in the succession of the prophets, "the one beloved son" (Mark 12:1-11; for interpretation of the parable see below, § 11, 3).

The disciples see and hear that which was longed for by the proclaimers of the promise, the prophets, and by the bearers of the promise, the kings. Now is the time of the messianic fulfillment (Matthew 13:16f.). He that this era brings with it is more than the prophets and kings, since he redeems their promise. Finally there are the point-blank sayings of the Lord: "Here there is something greater than the temple" (Matthew 12:6). Jesus is more than the presence of God in the temple, which is to be erected anew in the messianic era (Ezech. 40–48). "Here there is something greater than Jonah" (Matthew 12:41). "Here there is something greater than Solomon" (Matthew 12:42). This is surely meant to be understood as saying: "Here is the high-priestly Messiah! Here is the prophetic Messiah! Here is the royal Messiah!"

In Israel it was believed that prophecy had died out generations earlier. "There is no sign given us; no longer is there any prophet here" (Ps. 74:9). In the time of the Messiah, however, it was supposed that prophets would be raised up again (Joel 3:1). This, so one might suppose, had now come to pass. In the judgment of the people John the Baptist and Jesus are prophets. The Baptist was proclaimed a prophet already by his father Zechariah (Luke 1:76). The people recognized him as such (Mark 11:32). Herod was afraid to kill John; "for they regarded him as a prophet" (Matthew 14:5).

Jesus too recognized John as a prophet; indeed, he is more than a prophet; he is the last prophet before the Messiah himself (Matthew 11:9f.). Therefore signs are demanded of Jesus, like the signs worked by the Old Testament prophets (Mark 8:11f.; Luke 11:29; John 6:30). Jesus works miracles just as did the great prophets of old. He feeds the people miraculously, like Moses (Exod. 16:4; 11-17) and Elisha (4 Kings 4:42-44). The crowd responds: "He is in truth the prophet who is to come into the world" (John 6:14). Jesus raises a dead person, just as Elijah (3 Kings 17:17-24) and Elisha did (4 Kings 4:32-37). The spectators accordingly acknowledge: "A great prophet has risen up in our midst" (Luke 7:16).

In the Gospel of John the prophetic office of Jesus is referred to again and again (John 4:19; 7:52; 9:17). In the temple in Jerusalem Jesus is greeted as "the prophet, Jesus of Nazareth in Galilee" (Matthew 21:11). His opponents do not dare, and primarily because of this popularity, to lay hands on his person. "They feared the masses of the people, who regarded him as a prophet" (Matthew 21:46). Certainly the evangelist knows that Jesus is more; he is the messianic Lord (Matthew 21:4f.).

That Jesus is more than a prophet is made clear in John, when he calls him *the* prophet (John 6:14; 7:40; see also 1:21, 25). The departing Moses had promised Israel, that the prophetic office would remain forever in Israel. "The Lord your God will raise up for you a prophet who will be like me. Him shall you hear" (Deut. 18:15). By this statement it was henceforth understood that in the messianic era prophets would be raised up again, and then would arise the greatest prophet of all. This expectation is attested to in 1 Macc. 4:44-46, and 14:41, according to which decisions are postponed "until a true prophet will arise"; and in Joel 3:1f., according to which the Spirit will again be poured out over Israel, and "all will prophesy".

The Qumran scrolls make it clear anew how lively was this expectation there. Deut. 18:15-18 is to be found in the messianic florilegium, 4 Q Testimonia 5-7. The statute is prescribed: "The men of the community are to live modestly until the prophet and the anointed one of Aaron and of Israel shall come" (1 QS 9:11). In Qumran the great teacher of the community, called "the teacher of righteousness", is surely regarded as the expected prophet, now actually come. God has made known to this teacher "all the secrets of the words of his servants, the prophets" (1 QpHab 7:4f.).[40]

In the account of the transfiguration of Jesus the voice of God himself presents Jesus as the expected prophet. His voice is heard: "This is my beloved Son. Hear him" (Mark 9:7). The attestation to the Son in accord with Ps. 2:7 is tied in with the promise of the prophet in accord with Deut. 18:15. The Son fulfills the promise beyond all expectations, for the Son is indeed more than the greatest prophet.

The first preaching of the apostles designated Jesus as a true prophet. In his sermon in the temple area Peter says that in Christ the word of Moses (Deut. 18:15) has been fulfilled. "Moses said, 'The Lord God will raise up for you from among your brethren a prophet like me.'"

Jesus, however, is more than a prophet, for he is the Son (Acts 3:22-26). Stephen likewise says that the promise of Moses refers to Jesus Christ (Acts 7:37).

The New Testament compares and contrasts Moses and Christ with each other in such a way that Christ, as the new Moses, far surpasses the earlier one. The historical facts of Jesus' infancy are presented by Matthew after the model of the history of Moses in the Book of Exodus and in the late Jewish Haggadah (§ 10, 2). In the Sermon on the Mount Jesus delivers the new Torah; in so doing, however, he speaks with quite another authority than Moses possessed: "To the ancients it was said . . .; I, however, say to you . . ." (Matthew 5:21-48). Moses revealed the Law, Christ revealed Grace and Truth (John 1:17). He surpasses the miracles of Moses during the wandering in the desert: he dispenses the living water (John 4:14). He gives something more than manna, for he is himself the Bread of Life come down from heaven (John 6:31-35). The passage through the sea with Moses, the feeding by means of manna and the drinking from the rock are prototypes of baptism and of the Lord's Supper. "The rock was Christ" (1 Cor. 10:1-4). "With the fathers God spoke by means of the prophets; now at the end of days he has spoken with us through his Son" (Heb. 1:1f.). Moses was a servant in the house of God; as the Son, Christ is Lord over that house (Heb. 3:2-6). The redeemed sing the song of Moses and of the Lamb (Apoc. 15:3). The salvational works of both are drawn together and viewed as a single entity.[41]

As teacher and revealer Jesus is a historical figure. His history is interpreted and deepened in the New Testament. Jesus is elevated beyond all human learning. The truth of his word is guaranteed by his divine Sonship. "All things are given over to me by my Father, and no one knows the Son except the Father, nor does anyone know the Father except the Son, and him to whom the Son chooses to give a revelation" (Matthew 11:27; on the interpretation of the saying, see below § 10, 3). The Christ of the Gospel of St. John says this repeatedly: "My teaching is not mine, but belongs to him who sent me" (John 7:16; again in 8:28 and 8:38).

Jesus never says in the gospel that he has to transmit the word of God, in the way that the prophets asserted this. Nor do the Gospels say of him that he proclaimed the word, a thing that is very frequently said of the apostles. Such a declaration would be seen as inappropriate for the Christ. The deepest basis for both of these observations is the fact that he is himself the Word of God (John 1:14).

Outside of the Gospels and the Acts of the Apostles, in the New Testament Jesus is called neither teacher nor prophet. That the titles are lacking in Paul is not to be wondered at. Certainly Paul knows about the distinctive importance of the sayings of the Lord (1 Cor. 7:10; 9:14), but it is rare that he alludes to such sayings. This but points up that Jesus is not presented by Paul as a teacher. Moreover, to accord to Christ the title teacher would not have sufficed for a declaration of what Paul wanted to declare about him. After the Cross and resurrection Jesus is now the exalted Lord.

St. Ignatius of Antioch (*Letter to the Ephesians* 15, 1) calls Jesus, in terms that are reminiscent of Matthew 23:8, "the one teacher who but spoke and so it happened." The apologetes of the second century, who understood the Christian religion as "the true philosophy", refer to Christ as the one teacher (St. Justin the Martyr, *First Apology* 4, 7; his *Dialogue with Trypho the Jew* 108, 2). As eternal Word Christ was in the Jewish prophets as also in the pagan philosophers (St. Justin the Martyr, *First Apology* 62, 3; *Second Apology* 13, 2). For the Fathers who, like St. Irenaeus and St. Clement of Alexandria, were engaged in altercation with the Gnostics, Christ is the true and universal Teacher and Educator of men.[42]

Christ's title of teacher lives on, finally, in the dogmatics of the Church, which, under the influence of the Old Testament hierarchical orders as well as of the New Testament and the Fathers of the Church, teaches the threefold office of Christ as Prophet, Priest, and King.[43] The Enlightenment and the liberal theology of the nineteenth and twentieth centuries thought of Christ as a wise teacher and the founder of a religion; and at the same time, through a one-sided use of biblical sources, they curtailed other Christological predications. Inasmuch as modern biblical and dogmatic theology again speaks emphatically of the salvational power of the Word, it once again presents Christ more emphatically as Teacher.

§ 6. CHRIST'S MIRACLES AND WONDERS

Not just Jesus' words but his works as well pertain to his image, in the way that works are peculiar to any prophet (Luke 7:16; 24:19).[44]

In designating extraordinary and miraculous deeds the New Testament generally uses the terms δύναμις, σημεῖον, and τέρας. The Synoptic Gospels most frequently designate Jesus' miracles as δυνάμεις, whereas the Gospel of John refers to them as σημεῖα or simply as ἔργα. The word δύναμις characterizes the deed of Jesus as personally worked by him; σημεῖον views the deed in its capacity as a portent of the messianic and eschatological. In the mouth of Jesus, τέρατα designates only the false wonders of the pseudo-messiahs (Mark 13:22) or the miracles demanded out of disbelief (John 4:48).

The Acts of the Apostles (2:19; 5:12; 6:8; 15:12; *et passim*) and Paul (Rom. 15:19; 2 Cor. 12:12) designate the deeds of the apostles as δυνάμεις and as τέρατα καὶ σημεῖα. In this they follow profane linguistic usage as also the linguistic usage of the Septuagint. To the New Testament the term τέρας by itself seems to be inappropriate when it wants to speak of salvific deeds. Probably the term lays too much stress on the miracle as prodigy.

The experience of the marvelous is brought to mind occasionally in the word group θαυμάζειν, θαῦμα, θαυμάσιον. It is by use of these terms that the Septuagint frequently refers to the astonishment accompanying faith when confronted with the marvelous in God's revelation (Exod. 34:10; Ps. 44:5; Sir. 36:5). In the New Testament certainly this meaning is sometimes suggested; but mostly the terms of this word group are intended to convey an entirely profane sense, stressing the wonderment itself. The Old Testament sense of the term is preserved in a citation from Ps. 118:22, which the Gospel of Mark refers to the exaltation of Christ: "By God has this been done, and it is wonderful in our eyes" (Mark 12:11). The wonder of Jesus' works is acknowledged: "And he healed them; so that the people marvelled . . . and they praised the God of Israel" (Matthew 15:30-31). "The disciples marvelled" when they saw how the fig tree, upon being cursed, withered up (Matthew 21:20). "All were astounded at the great power of God. They marvelled at all the things that Jesus was doing" (Luke 9:43). The deeds of Jesus are designated as "wonders": "The High Priests and the scribes saw the wonderful things that he had done" (Matthew 21:15).

1. Biblical Concept of Wonder

According to our modern philosophical and theological way of thinking, a wonder or miracle is something which is beyond the laws of nature. The biblical understanding of the world knows no nature and no laws of nature as a self-sufficient world alongside God and his creation. God is the primordial origin of the world. It is his work, and he is everywhere and at all times engaged in his work. Man looks in astonishment at the inconceivable grandeur of this work. For man, creation is wonderful, and he constantly experiences wonder. The creating of the heavens and the earth are wonders (Ps. 136:4-9), as well as the preservation of creation (Ps. 104). The preparation of man is also wonderful (Ps. 139:14). The salvific deeds of God for the redemption of his people are wonders (Ps. 114; 135; Neh. 9:6-33). God's assistance and aid for the redemption of the pious man are wonders, for which the pious man gives thanks to him in prayer (Ps. 40:6; 71:7; 107:8). God's wonders are to be perfected in the messianic-eschatological age, in which powerful apocalyptic events will be unfurled (Is. 65:17-25). In the meantime we "wonder" over that great final wonder of the world's definitive redemption. Thus for the biblical world-outlook it is possible, indeed, it is fitting, that wonders take place always and everywhere.[45]

We must not force the Bible into our mentality. It can only lead to misunderstanding and error, if we, without being aware of it, employ the same term wonder in an entirely different outlook upon the world and the events which transpire therein. A different understanding adopts different ways of explaining. The biblical narrators do not make use of our ways of reporting on history and natural science. They are able to state what they want to say just as well or even better in stories and myths, poems and hymns. All these means of expression are suitable for bearing witness to the living God.

The New Testament has the very broad terminology and concept of wonder which belongs to its time. Nevertheless, it does not demand a belief in wonders, nor that this or that specific event was a wonder. The New Testament demands belief in the God of whose works the wonders are a sign. As the Creator and Lord of the ages, he guides them on to their goal.

Not only do the disciples of Jesus work wonders, but they are performed also outside the community. Jesus himself is able to compare himself to contemporary exorcists: "If I cast out demons by Beelzebul, by whom do your sons cast them out?" (Matthew 12:27). "False messiahs and false prophets work signs and wonders" (Mark 13:22). The coming of the antichrist "takes place through the working of Satan and with all power and signs and lying wonders" (2 Thess. 2:9). The New Testament is aware, therefore, that wonders are ambiguous. They are nct in themselves a proof that God is in the work.

Paul is convinced that, as an Apostle, signs and wonders are at his disposal. "The credentials proper to an apostle I have presented to you in all patience: signs, wonders, miracles" (2 Cor. 12:12; see also Rom. 15:19). The Apostle, however, does not base faith on such miracles: "While the Jews require signs and the Greeks wisdom, we preach Christ crucified" (1 Cor. 1:22-23). The Apostle works no exhibition wonders. He employs the word, which is no miracle, but a passing breath. This word, however, is the preaching of the crucified Christ, of an event and a figure, therefore, of external weakness and of the revelation of the foolishness of God. Paul has no magical powers at his disposal. He tells of the illness of Epaphroditus, who was at the point of death. "But God had mercy on him, and not only on him but on me also, that I might not have sorrow upon sorrow" (Phil. 2:27). Paul does not presume to be able to cure a sick man marvelously. The healing is left to God. The Apostle tells of his own illness: "Three times I prayed the Lord that the angel of Satan might leave me. And he answered me: 'My grace is sufficient for you'" (2 Cor. 12:8-9).

If Paul is certain of the possibility of wonders, it is apparent nonetheless that his notion of a wonder is something quite other than that which we understand by our concept of wonder or miracle. For him, the charism of preaching and of pastoral care is a wonder.

The Church of the apostles too, according to its conviction, has marvelous powers at her disposal. Upon being sent out, the disciples are given a commission and the ability to fulfill it: "Heal the sick, raise the dead, cleanse the lepers, drive out demons" (Matthew 10:8; it may be significant, if Luke 9:1-2 has this verse in mind, that his account does not mention raising the dead).

Paul mentions as extraordinary gifts of the community "charisms of healing" and "power to work miracles" (1 Cor. 12:9-10). The mission of the Church is assisted by divine helps. The Acts of the Apostles tells of manifold wonders: healings (3:4-9; 5:15; 9:32-35; 14:8-10; 19:11f.; 28:8f.); raisings of the dead (9:36-41); marvelous punishments (5:5-10; 12:23; 13:11; 19:14-16); marvels of deliverance (4:31; 5:17-25; 12:3-12; 16:26); prophecies (11:28; 21:11); marvels of the apostles (5:12); of Peter (3:4-9; 5:1-11; 5:15; 9:32-41); of Stephen (6:8); of Philip (8:7f.); of Paul (14:9f.; 19:11f.; 28:8f.).

Probably the themes of Hellenistic tales of marvels and the beginnings of Christian legends of the saints have in some degree already penetrated the Acts of the Apostles. The Epistle to the Hebrews also tells of the wonders that attend the mission work: "God bore witness by signs and wonders and many kinds of miracles, and by impartings of the Holy Spirit in accord with his will" (Heb. 2:4). In the conclusion of the Gospel of Mark (which conclusion could be dated about the year 200 A.D.), the wonderful powers of the mission Church are thus described: to cast out demons, to impose hands on the sick, to speak in new tongues, to take up serpents, to drink deadly poison without harm (Mark 16:17-18).[46]

2. MIRACLES (WONDERS) OF JESUS

The evidences of Jesus' power which are recounted in the Gospels are in part narratives of the driving out of demons and healings of the sick, and in part miracles in respect to nature. The former have an internal similarity, since sickness can be regarded as caused by the demons (Luke 13:16). A saying of Jesus himself unites these aspects of his power thus: "Behold, I cast out demons and perform cures" (Luke 13:32).

a) Expulsions of Demons and Cures

Belief in demons was common to the whole ancient world, the Greco-Roman as well as the Biblical-Jewish.[47] If the Old Testament repressed

belief in demons with its prohibition of witchcraft and the conjuring up
of spirits (Deut. 18:10f.), it but resulted in this belief's being pursued
all the more in the postcanonical writings and among the rabbis. At the
time of the New Testament it was really quite universal.

A new example of this has been found in the Qumran writings. God
created the world as well as two opposed spirits, one of truth and the
other of error. Between heaven and earth there is now a kingdom in
opposition to the divine, one referred to as that of Belial, the lord of
demons. Man is situated between the good and the evil spirits and must
choose between them (1 QS 3:13–4:26). He tries to restrain the demons
by the use of maledictions (1 QM 13:4f.; 1 QS 2:4-10). In the endtime
the sons of light will conquer the sons of darkness in a mighty war
(1 QM).

Throughout the whole of the ancient world magicians, priests, and
physicians concerned themselves with the exorcism and expulsion of
demons.[48] The New Testament itself provides evidence that exorcism
of demons was widely practiced, even outside the community of disciples (Mark 9:38; Acts 19:13).

For the driving out of demons a schema took shape. The wonderworker threatens the demon, touches the person possessed; the demon resists, but finally he must yield. Upon emerging the demon
proves his reality with a show of his destructive powers. The person
healed declares his gratitude. The cure makes a great impression on all
the bystanders. An excellent example of these themes is found even in
the history of the possessed man of Gerasa, in Mark 5:1-19.

The arrangement of subject matter and a certain quality that can be
called typical can generally be noted also in the accounts of wonderful
cures. For comparison there exist rabbinic histories, as well as accounts
of marvelous deeds from the ancient world, and further there are the
inscriptions about cures in the sanctuary of Asclepius at Epidaurus. The
rabbinic accounts about the driving out of demons and healing of the
sick, nevertheless, are not numerous, and such as we do have originate
nearly all from the period after the year 70 A.D. Among them are marvelous rains that have no counterparts in the gospel.

These stories tell of wonderful responses to prayer which were vouchsafed to the rabbis. In the Gospels the wonders are not granted by reason
of the prayer of Jesus, but he works them by his own power. Marvelous

deeds do not belong to the image of the rabbi. They cannot have been attached to the history of Jesus simply through his having been regarded as a rabbi.

Critics have discussed whether the Gospel miracles might perhaps have come from the Hellenistic milieu. Were the accounts about Jesus, prior to their being written down, shaped in any measure by such influences? Many of the histories of wonders presuppose Jewish situations, like the cures worked on the Sabbath (Mark 3:1-6; Luke 13:10-17). In Hellenistic accounts of wonders there are miracles to be found of such a kind as would be scarcely conceivable in the Gospels. In Epidaurus a woman is made to deliver after a five year pregnancy; the new-born child immediately begins to jump about. Or there is the case of the god who causes a bald-headed man to grow hair, in order to protect him from ridicule. Before the gates of Rome, Apollonius of Tyana raises a girl from the dead. The witnesses present him with fifteen thousand drachmas, which the wonderworker then gives the girl for her dowry (Philostratus, *Apollonius* 4, 45). The *Life of Apollonius*, who lived in the first century of the Christian era, was written down by Philostratus about the year 220 A.D. The disparity of time between the events and their being written down is therefore markedly greater than in the case of the Gospels.

That which is most characteristic of the wonders of Jesus is their moral aspect. They are granted in view of belief. The disbelief which sets itself against Jesus receives nothing. Jesus can work no wonders in Nazareth because faith is lacking there (Mark 6:5). From faith and only from faith does he really have every ability and every power (Mark 9:22-23). The wonders of Jesus are not sorcery and magic which the person concerned can seize upon and use without his knowledge, or indeed, even against his will. His wonders have the healing of body and of soul for their purpose. They are a salvific offer from God, an invitation to repentance, belief, peace and love. "Daughter, your faith has saved you. Go in peace" (Mark 5:34; similarly, Luke 7:50; 17:19).

Jesus shared in the outlooks of his time and in the beliefs of his people. He expected wonders like all the rest. But he expresses reservations. He says that wonders are ambiguous. They prove nothing. They can come from the power of evil. "False messiahs and false prophets will arise, and they will do signs and wonders in order, if possible, to lead even the elect astray" (Mark 13:22). It is possible to ignore wonders. They are not compelling. "He began to reproach the cities in which his wonders had been worked, because they had not repented. Woe to you, Chorazin! Woe to you, Bethsaida! If these wonders had been done in Tyre and Sidon they would have done penance in sackcloth and ashes" (Matthew 11:20-21). The Gospels tell nothing of any wonders done by Jesus in Chorazin and Bethsaida. This is in itself an indication in favor of the historicity of the saying. The narrative of the parable of the rich reveler and poor Lazarus emphasizes the truth which is finally vocalized by Abraham: "If they do not listen to Moses and the prophets neither will they let themselves be convinced if someone rises from the dead" (Luke 16:31). Is this perhaps an allusion to the disbelief even in the face of the resurrection of Jesus?

Matthew 7:22f is a criticism of the faith that is based on wonders: "On that day many will say to me, 'Lord, Lord, did we not prophesy in your name and perform many miracles in your name?' And I will assure them, 'I never knew you!'" The passage in this form undoubtedly belongs to a later tradition. The name of Christ is already a confession and an efficacious power. Christ is the Judge who is accorded the title Lord (see below, §11, 5). Missionary work is presumed as historical fact, already in existence (just as it is in the later text of Mark 16:17f). In point of fact, prophetic-charismatic speech and the working of wonders like the expulsion of demons and miraculous cures had not yet been given to the genuine group of disciples.

The demand for wonders and signs does not advance the honor of God, but may be only malice and disbelief. For that reason Jesus refuses miracles. "This generation is an evil generation. It seeks a sign, and no sign will be given it except the sign of Jonah" (Luke 11:29). The disbelief which expects nothing of Christ also receives nothing from Him. Jesus does not accede to the demand for a miracle, though certainly he grants the prayer of faith when it seeks help.

Mark often attaches to the accounts of the working of wonders a command to be silent about them (Mark 1:44; 3:12; 5:43; 7:36). In the final analysis this command may have been attached simply as a part of the schematization of the accounts (see below, §11, 1). But it will have preserved at least the historical circumstance that Jesus wanted to avoid

that kind of propaganda which would not have been unwelcome to a
worker of showy miracles.

To the question of his being the Messiah, Jesus sends an answer to
John the Baptist: "The blind see, the lame walk; lepers are cleansed,
the deaf hear, the dead rise, and the poor have the gospel preached to
them. Blessed is he that is not scandalized in Me" (Matthew 11:4f).
Testimony to his being the Messiah is still covered in this saying. It
still calls for the ever individual judgment of faith, the decision to believe. This saying, then, may go back to a very early time. On the other
hand, however, the messianic work is described in those details, by
means of which it is interpreted in terms of prophecy (Is. 35:5; 61:1).
The message is already called the *evangelium*. This may be an elucidation
drawn after the events. In its total mentality the saying reflects a correct
evaluation of wonders. External wonders are mentioned along with the
preaching of the gospel and the gift of salvific healing to the poor. This
preaching is just as valuable as the wonders, indeed, perhaps even counting for more, if the enumeration is meant to be in an ascending order.
The wonders stand in need of the word that explains them.

Finally the appeal settles everything on faith, which is demanded
without any security or proof having been offered. "Blessed is he that
is not scandalized in Me." Jesus expects the working of miracles and
accepts it. But there is something much more essential: "You ought not
rejoice because spirits are subject to you; but much more should you
rejoice because your names are written in heaven" (Luke 10:20).

The wonders performed by Jesus must be understood as part of his
messianic work. The gospel sees in these wonders the fulfillment of the
image of the servant of Yahweh: "He took our infirmities on himself
and bore our illnesses" (Is. 53:4 in Matthew 8:17). God is the Creator
and Lord of all life. Sickness and death which disturb and destroy life
cannot stem directly from this God. They are contrary to what is divine.
Destructive and Satanic power is operative in them. Therefore Jesus
says of the crippled woman whom he heals, that Satan has bound her
(Luke 13:10-17). Now, however, Jesus announces the approach of the
kingdom of God. It begins already in him. God's kingdom is creation
restored. If Jesus addresses the inimical, Satanic power in illness and
conquers it in the healing power of God, it is because he sees the moral
distress behind the physical. He designates evil as the cause from which

ruin comes forth. He says that behind nature there are other powers, wholesome and unwholesome, which hold sway. The wonderful cures worked by Jesus are indication, promise, and assurance of the dawning of God's kingdom.

The sick whom Jesus heals are, according to the Gospel accounts, not infrequently the possessed and the lepers. Both classes were excluded by contemporary society. Sick persons, who provided an image of ruin and destruction, passed as demoniacally possessed. Jesus took this human misery to himself. He did not shrink before the evil spirits nor before human condemnation. Even in the conquest of evil spirits the kingdom of God is made manifest. The lepers were set apart from human companionship by strict legal prohibitions. In accord with the opinion of the scribes, leprosy was regarded as a punishment from God.[49] To all this Jesus paid no heed at all, but cultivated association with the lepers and brought them back cured into the community.[50]

According to some current writing the frequently posited question about the historicity of the miraculous cures of Jesus is to be answered to the effect that Jesus conquered illnesses with what was, according to the judgment of the gospel, incomparable divine power, working these cures at first quietly and in the background but later quite openly.[51]

For the Gospels the wonderful deeds of Jesus are the essential revelation of his being the Messiah. Individual accounts are frequently supplemented by attaching to them collective summations of the cures worked by Jesus (Mark 1:32; 3:7-12; 6:55f.; also Matthew 9:35; 14:14; 19:2; 21:14). The powerful cures worked by Jesus have the same function in the preaching of the message of Christ in the Acts of the Apostles. Peter announces on Pentecost: "Jesus of Nazareth was approved by God among you by miracles, wonders, and signs" (Acts 2:22). Peter preaches in a similar fashion to the Gentile Christians in Caesarea (Acts 10:38).

The content of Paul's Epistles, however, is certainly not the wonders done by Jesus. Paul never suggests that Jesus is proved to be God's Son by reason of his miracles. If Paul can take it as self-evident that apostles are able to work miracles, signs, and wonders (Rom. 15:19; 2 Cor. 12:12; see above), then the wonders done by Jesus cannot prove that he is Lord and Son of God. Neither do the Catholic Epistles nor the Apocalypse of John speak of the wonders performed by Jesus.

b) Wonders in the Gospel of John

In the Gospel of John the wonders of Jesus are accentuated. The changing of water into wine (2:1-11) is an unequivocal marvel of nature. The son of the royal official is healed at a distance (4:46-53). The lame man at the pool lay ill for thirty-eight years (5:1-9). The blind man was born blind (9:1-38). Lazarus was already four days in his grave (11:1-44). Perhaps the Gospel took the miracles from a source which already numbered them (2:11; 4:54). The fourth Gospel counts seven wonders, which probably signifies their abundance. The totality of Jesus' operation is an effecting of signs (20:30). The wonders reveal the majesty of Jesus (2:11).

The external wonders, however, must be understood as signs of more profound truth and reality. The multiplication of the loaves signifies that Jesus gives and is himself the bread of life (6:27, 35); the cure of the blind man, that he is the light of the world (9:5); the raising of Lazarus, that he is the resurrection and the life (11:25).

Faith on the basis of wonders was not a genuine faith. Jesus therefore refuses to comply with the demand for signs (2:18; 4:48; 6:30). One can see a miracle and still withhold faith (12:37), or one can misuse miracles in a profane way. They want to make Jesus king (6:14f.). They are seeking earthly nourishment and advantages (6:26). John recounts mighty wonders, which he probably receives from tradition. But he requires that they be understood by faith. Faith can in general forego miracles: "Blessed are they who do not see but believe anyway" (20:29).

With this latter saying, finally, at the end of the Gospel, the accounts of miracles are after all assigned a secondary value. It is not belief in miracles that is demanded, but belief in the Revealer and in his words and in his works. The miracles are understood only when they are regularly conceived as requiring faith and renewal. They make available the possibility of life in faith.[52]

The recollection of the wonders performed by Christ is condensed and impressed in more than one of his titles of majesty or titles of office. Soon Christ received the title *Physician* (ἰατρός; see St. Ignatius of Antioch, *Letter to the Ephesians* 7, 2 [in Jurgens, *The Faith of the Early Fathers* no. 39]; St. Clement of Alexandria, *Who is the Rich Man that is Saved?* 29; Origen, *Against Celsus* 2, 67). The salvific or healing deeds of Jesus are at all events frequently described as a σῴζειν. The title σωτήρ pertains to this verb, though it probably has other origins also (§11, 4). Even in the term *Savior* [German *Heiland*, Latin *Salvator*, Greek σωτήρ], there is the suggested ring of the terms *to heal* [German *heilen*, Latin *salvare*, Greek σῴζειν] and *healing* [German *Heilung*, Latin *salus*, Greek σωτηρία]. More profoundly and more comprehensively, this title, which might refer to the physical curing of the ill, is used in reference to the gift of eternal salvation through the Redeemer.

The tradition of the wonders worked by Jesus became very important for the Church's image of Christ. The miracle narratives in the Gospels were and are yet among their most widely known and remembered texts. Already at a very early time they were impressively portrayed in works of art. As examples we might mention the mosaics of the Church of S. Apollinare Nuovo in Ravenna, as well as the frescoes, probably of the tenth century, at Oberzell on the Reichenau. In the arrangement of the liturgical pericopes, too, the Gospel accounts of the miracles for a thousand years and more were read regularly and with a certain emphasis, and were then expounded upon in the sermon. This esteem bespeaks in a penetrating way a hope in healing and salvation through Christ. The testimony of the Gospels is of great significance insofar as the work of healing is continued in the Church's care of souls in regard to the sick.

3. SPECIFIC TEXTS

We shall now discuss some specific questions and cases.

a) The possessed man in the land of the Gerasenes (Mark 5:1-20) [53] presents a picture of complete human ruin. No one is able to restrain him. Fetters and chains he rips apart. He bruises himself on the rocks and dwells in impure tombs, being himself possessed by a legion of unclean spirits. The demons recognize in Jesus their conqueror and attempt to resist. Jesus grants their request and allows them to enter into a herd of swine. The swine hurl themselves down the mountainside and drown in the lake.

The story proves, according to the conviction of tradition, the mighty power of Jesus over the demons. At the end the possessed man sits there clothed and healed. Belief and unbelief go their separate ways. "They began to entreat him to go away from their area." The man who was healed, however, wants to stay with Jesus. Jesus does not allow this, but bids him, "Go back to your home and to your relatives, and tell them what God has done for you."

What follows at the very end of the account is an instruction on the right way of following Jesus. The narrative is entirely in the gospel mentality. Nevertheless, it is not easy for us to accredit it as a legitimate historical account. Occasionally it is characterized as a burlesque or as a farce about a cheating or cheated devil. Do the demons deceive the owner of the beasts which they hurl into the lake, or are they themselves deceived, when they drown in the lake? That the demons instinctively recognize the One who restrains them, and that he questions and commands them belongs to the themes then current in the matter of healing the possessed. The spirits defend themselves, but still they must obey. In comparable narratives the demon demonstrates his reality by upsetting a water basin or by damaging a statue.[54] For a Jew the swine are unclean beasts, forbidden and scorned; and a herd of swine is for him an abomination (Deut. 14:8; Lev. 11:7). Swine, therefore, are the appropriate place for demons. That the huge herd drowns is a thing that a Jew might well relate with amused delight.

Comparison of the Synoptics shows that Matthew and Luke both provide a shorter wording than does Mark. It is Mark alone who mentions the number of the swine as two thousand. Two explanations are possible. Since Matthew and Luke have probably both read Mark, but have no collaboration between themselves, they may have come to the conclusion independently of each other that the narrative contained elements that could be shortened. In this way Matthew and Luke would have exercised a literary judgment over the account of Mark.

The other possibility is that Matthew and Luke were not yet able to read our detailed Markan account, but a shorter Ur-Mark. This original or primitive Mark would then have been expanded later. An Old Testament stylization can be perceived in many of the New Testament accounts of wonders (quieting of the storm on the lake, multiplication of the loaves, raisings of the dead). In the healing of the possessed man of Gerasa it is occasionally conjectured that the account has been portrayed in accord with Ps. 67:7, in the Septuagint version: "God settles solitaries in a house, leading forth to strength those bound in fetters;

and likewise with the rebellious ones who dwell in tombs." Perhaps it has something of the flavor too of Is. 65:1-5.

b) In three Gospel accounts the power of Jesus to heal is advanced even to the conquering of death. These accounts tell of the raising of the daughter of Jairus (Mark 5:22-43 and parallels), of the raising of the young man outside the city gates of Naim (Luke 7:11-17), and the raising of Lazarus in Bethany (John 11:1-46; above, § 6, 2 b).

There exist exegetes who call the historicity of these accounts more or less into question. Besides some general considerations there are observations to be made in regard to the individual histories, as well as comparisons from the history of religion.

The three raisings of the dead told of in the Gospels seem to be told in an order of intensification. The daughter of Jairus lies at the point of death when Jesus is called; she dies by the time he arrives (Mark 5:23, 25). The young man of Naim is being carried to his grave, and Jesus meets the funeral procession (Luke 7:12). Lazarus is already four days in the tomb (John 11:17). Two of these extraordinary wonders, the raising of the young man of Naim and the raising of Lazarus, are attested each in only one of the Gospels.

Jewish and non-Jewish narratives as well know of people being raised from the dead. The biblical narratives employ typical themes. Thus in the raising of the daughter of Jairus, unbelievers and scoffers laugh at the wonderworker (Mark 5:40). The idle curious are kept at a distance (Mark 5:40; see 3 Kings 17:19; 4 Kings 4:33). The restoration takes place with gesture and word (Mark 5:41). Mysterious formulas in foreign languages are occasionally found in the accounts of such wonders (Mark 5:41). The restoration is manifest to all and is acknowledged by the spectators (Mark 5:42).[55]

The narrative of the raising of the young man of Naim (Luke 7:11-17)[56] is a heightening of the immediately preceding story (Luke 7:2-10), where the cure of the dying servant of the centurion is told. The raising from the dead in Luke is reminiscent of certain Old Testament narratives. Elijah raises a dead boy (3 King 17:17-24). That this story was in the mind of the evangelist or in that of the tradition before him is clear when in Luke 7:15 we find a direct citation from 3 Kings 17:23 — καὶ ἔδωκεν αὐτὸν τῇ μητρὶ αὐτοῦ. Elisha raises the son of a Sunamitess (4 Kings 4:32-37). Naim is situated in the neighborhood of Sunam. It may seem that a typical theme of a miraculous restoration is the chance encounter along the road (as is the case too in Luke 7:12).[57]

Whatever critics may say about the historicity of these accounts, their meaning is nevertheless quite evident. The generative power of God is revealed in Christ, a generative power which is more effective than the hard reality of death, and which annuls the latter. It is bestowed in view of faith (Mark 5:36). It is a challenge to faith, and should lead to faith. In Christ is the resurrection and the life (John 11:25). In Christ life has been brought to light (2 Tim. 1:10). It is God who makes the dead to live, and calls forth that which before did not exist (Rom. 4:17).

c) Connected locally and thematically are three accounts of marvelous epiphanies of Jesus on the Lake of Gennesaret: the accounts of the quieting of the storm (Mark 4:35-41 and parallels), of his walking on the water (Mark 6:45-52 and parallels), and of the marvelous catch of fish (Luke 5:1-11 and John 21:1-14).

Some critics see the quieting of the storm as stylized with Old Testament themes. The introduction and conclusion (rising of the storm and the coming of calm) are portrayed in accord with Jonah 1:4f. and 1:15f. The storm and the depths of the sea are images of temptations against faith (Ps. 18:17; 69:2, 15). At God's bidding the waters must retreat (Ps. 104:7). The occurrence of the storm seems to be portrayed in accord with Ps. 107:25-31, "He caused the wind to arise, and the storm churned the waves. The waves mounted up to the heavens, and descended down to the depths, so that the souls of those who went out upon the sea were despondent and miserable. They cried out to the Lord in their misery. He stilled the storm to a gentle breeze, and the waves of the sea abated. He led them to the port they yearned for. Let them give thanks to the Lord for his goodness, and for his wondrous deeds on behalf of the children of men."

The picturesque language of 1 QH 6:22-25 is comparable: "I was like a sailor in a ship caught in a raging sea. Its breakers and all its waves beat against me. It was a typhoon with nothing for the comforting of my soul. My soul approached nigh to the gates of death. And I was like one who comes into a fortified city. And I rejoiced because of your truth, O my God!"

Old Testament texts are inextricably interwoven in the Gospels in the story of the calming of the storm. This is the work of a more lengthy tradition of reading and meditating upon the Old Testament in its relation to Christ. The divine epiphanic wonder of the Psalms is translated to Christ. His word, his work, his person are the revelation of the might and of the solicitude of God. When the community and the gospel relate this history, they are not telling of something past, but of something everpresent. Christ is the Lord and Helper of his own in their every need.

In the Gospel of Matthew (8:23-27) the story seems to have taken shape with some deliberation. It appears in a new context. Prefaced to the account are some remarks in Matthew 8:19-22 on the following of Jesus. The key-word about such following leads into Matthew 8:23 and the story of the storm. The cry for help is a prayer: Lord, save us! (Matthew 8:25). Jesus reproves the disciples' lack of faith, in Matthew a typical disciple situation. At the conclusion it is not just the disciples as in Mark, but men, full of astonishment, who ask: Who is he? (Matthew 8:27). This is the response of the world to the proclamation of the gospel. In Matthew the account is example and announcement of the misery as well as of the majesty of the following of Jesus. Is the little boat already a symbol of the little boat that is the Church?[58] That the history of religion is able to exhibit comparable narratives is not remarkable. Men have often prayed when in danger on the seas and have experienced help.[59]

Connected with the accounts in the gospels of the calming of the storm is the narrative of Jesus' walking on the water (Mark 6:45-52 with Matthew 14:22-33; John 6:16-21). In the narrative Jesus comes to the disciples, who are caught up in a storm on the sea at night. In the Old Testament the sea is a metaphorical term for death and the abyss (2 Sam. 22:5f.). The one praying supposes he is about to sink into the watery depths, and he calls out for rescue at the hands of God from on high (Ps. 18:5, 17; 69:2-4, 15; 144:7). Yahweh strides across the waters (Ps. 77:20; Is. 43:16; Job 9:8; Sir. 24:5). According to the *Odes of Solomon* (39:5-7) the waters of death separate this side from the beyond. "Those, however, who stride across in faith are not terrified."

In the narrative of Jesus' walking on the waters, Jesus at first is about to pass the disciples by, and the disciples do not recognize him. The Lord is nearby to the congregation, but always hidden in mystery. Jesus addresses the disciples with the words: "It is I." These are the words by which God reveals himself in the old covenant (Is. 43:10f.), and in the new as well. The Lord gets into the boat and the storm ceases. "They were quite beside themselves with astonishment." When God steps into reality, man is terrified. Through belief, however, he finds peace. (In regard to this narration as an instruction on faith, see *Theology of the New Testament*, Vol. 3, pp. 86-87). The Christ who came striding over the sea to rescue the disciples from danger becomes a demonstration of the might of the Savior both at a particular time and always. For his Church, his epiphany takes place constantly.

The two narratives of the marvelous catch of fish in Luke 5:1-11 and John 21:1-11 are undoubtedly interconnected.[60] The account of the abundant catch of fish is shaped by Luke to serve in a vocation framework, and it is repeated by the post-Johannine author of John 21 as a manifestation narrative. The story probably borrowed themes also from the Easter manifestations in Galilee and at the Lake of Gennesaret. In the stories of the manifestations of Christ at the Lake of Gennesaret there is a mutual penetration and uniting of recollections of the pre-paschal companionship of the disciples there, with their experiences of the resurrected Savior in that same place.

d) In regard to the miracle of the multiplication of the loaves (Mark 6:33-44 and parallels; doublet in Mark 8:1-9 and parallels),[61] there are comparable stories available from the Old Testament. In the desert the nation is wonderfully fed with manna (Exod. 16:14f.). John 6 enters into some detail in expressly comparing the miracle of the manna with the multiplication of the loaves. Christ is and gives the true bread of heaven. At God's word, delivered by Elijah, the flour and oil of the widow of Zarephath (3 Kings 17:8-16) are not used up. Elisha works a miracle in multiplying oil for the widow of a prophet who was his disciple (4 Kings 4:1-7). With twenty barley loaves Elisha feeds a hundred men (4 Kings 4:42-44). This last story comes closest to the New Testament narrative of the multiplication of the loaves. Indeed, it is quoted more or less directly by Mark: "And they ate, and there was still some left over" (Mark 6:42 = 4 Kings 4:44).

The gospel narrative about the multiplication involves clear reference to the Last Supper of Jesus, and therefore to the Eucharist, which renews that Supper. Mark 6:41 and 14:22 correspond one to the other: And Jesus took the loaves . . . blessed them and broke them and gave them to his disciples. Multiplication of the loaves and the Eucharist are seen as one. The wonder of the multiplication of the loaves is more veiled than manifest. Did the thousands for the most part grasp what had happened? No praise of God is heard. Recollections of historical meals of Jesus along with his disciples have found entry into the accounts of the multiplication of the loaves. In these stories the hidden but nonetheless real epiphany of the exalted Lord is celebrated. He gathers his congregation in the wilderness of the world and feeds them with his word and his supper. Even the eschatological supper is anticipated therein. These experiences of the Church are exhibited in the historical life of Jesus.

e) The story of the temple tax in Matthew 17:24-27 is unique.[62] Requested to pay the tax, Jesus bids Peter: "Go to the sea, throw out a hook; take the first fish which you draw in and open its mouth, and you will find a stater. Take that and give it to them for me and for you." The narrative makes use of an old folk-theme about a precious object in the mouth of a fish. It appears in the story of Polycrates' ring (Herodotus 3, 40-42) as well as among the rabbis in narratives about Jews who, as a reward for virtue, find precious pearls in fish which they have bought.

The meaning of the story is explained in Matthew 17:24-26. The question of the temple tax is solved with Jesus' affirmation that sons do not have to pay taxes. Matthew 17:27 seems to be a secondary addition. The legend employed here, that of the treasure in the mouth of the fish, is only half-formed. Only the assignment to catch the fish is recounted, and not the actual fulfillment of what is expected. Moreover, this would be the only miracle in the Gospels, in which Jesus would be using his power to his own advantage.

f) The narrative of the cursing of the fig tree in Mark 11:12-14, 20f. parallel in Matthew 21:18f.) is not easy to explain. On the way to Jerusalem Jesus looks for fruit on a fig tree. When he finds none, he curses the tree, even though, as the evangelist remarks, it was not yet the time for figs. "Never again forever shall anyone eat fruit of you." On the following morning the disciples see that the tree has withered up from the roots. The narrative is notably the only cursing marvel or miracle of punishment in the Gospels. And it is all the more astonishing in itself, inasmuch as it was not even the right season for figs.

The fact is, Mark uses the foregoing account to frame in the narrative of the cleansing of the temple (Mark 11:15-19). Here Jesus announces, even if in veiled terms, an end to the temple and to Israel as the chosen people. Now the true house of God will be built for all nations. The cursing of the fig tree probably indicates symbolically the nation of Israel, which bears no fruit. There are sayings of the prophets (Jer. 8:13; Joel 1:7; Micah 7:1) which bewail the fruitlessness of Israel in an imagery of barren vines and fig trees. Accordingly the story of the cursing of the fig tree is perhaps to be understood as a historicization of a prophetic threat uttered by Jesus. Was this moreover called forth by a conspicuously withered fig tree, for which a reason was sought? Luke (13:6-9) narrates a parable about a fig tree which had been without fruit for three years. If it continues to bear no fruit, it is to be cut down. Is it perhaps such a parable as this that has been turned about into a historical account in the narrative of Mark as well as of Matthew?

In antiquity Greek rationalism represented by men like Celsus and Porphyry applied its criticism to the biblical accounts of miracles. The apologetics of the Fathers of the Church defended the accounts; and Fathers and writers like Origen and Augustine said that the constant wonder of the world's being sustained by God is greater than individual wonderful happenings.

The biblical accounts of miracles were never seriously doubted in the Church, not in antiquity nor in the middle ages, nor by the Protestant reformers. This changed about the middle of the seventeenth century, with the Enlightenment. A purely natural-scientific and empirical explanation of the world was undertaken, and its religion was Deism. For the Deist the world is a wisely ordered and disposed totality. The laws of the world are of divine establishment. Miracles would be the destruction of divine order and therefore impious; to accept miracles would constitute disbelief!

Historical criticism then came to the aid of natural science, turned its attention also to the biblical accounts of miracles, and called them into question. It seemed that the actual event could no longer be recognized with security. In general, however, it validated in principle the impossibility of basing eternal religious truth on a historical contingency. Protestantism brought to this question the basic theological principle of radical, pure faith, the *sola fides*. That faith which seeks the assurance of the miraculous is not this pure faith.

These principles have a broad influence upon modern Protestant theology. There is only one wonder: the God-given revelation of forgiveness and grace. The accounts of wonders are miracles, which require existential interpretations. These can perhaps be attempted somewhat in this fashion: Our age is living in deep dissension. Progress in the natural sciences and technology can lead man astray into pride. The world exists in accord with its inherent laws. A Creator is forced farther and farther into the background. Nevertheless, our age lives in anxiety because of the destructiveness that technology, should it be unleashed, is capable of working.

The biblical tradition of the wonders worked by God attests, on the contrary, that the Christian belief in God is not pantheism or monism, which identify God with the world, but that biblical faith knows and recognizes God as the Lord and Father who does not forsake the world nor the man in it. Faith is related to future promise, but it is not without experience in the present time. The multiplex questionableness of the biblical accounts of wonders but reveals the whole paradoxicalness of God's becoming man. Thus the skeptics of our age.[63]

§ 7. THE PASSION OF CHRIST — HISTORY AND MEANING

An essential and crucial part of the life and work of Jesus is his Passion and death.[64] In the New Testament, belief and doctrine concerning his death is developed in great depth and breadth. In the present chapter and in the next it will be our task to gather first of all the general themes of the theology of the Passion (§ 7); and then the New Testament doctrine of the pardoning of sins accomplished by the death of Christ, of atonement and of redemption, will be presented separately and in detail (§ 8).

About the year 54 or 53 B.C., Cicero had to defend in the Roman Forum a certain C. Rabirius Postumus, who was accused of having had Roman citizens in the provinces crucified. Crucifixion could be inflicted on slaves as a punishment in most extreme cases. It was a horrible mockery if Roman political rebels, who made their appearance as freedom fighters, were made to die the death of slaves. If Rabirius had let citizens be crucified, his action in so doing, Cicero says, would be indefensible. "The idea of the cross must be far removed not only from the bodies of Roman citizens, but from their thoughts, their eyes, their ears as well" (Cicero, *Pro Rabirio Postumo* 5, 16). One ought not even speak of so shameful a death in the presence of decent men.

In that same Roman Forum and throughout the whole empire of which the Forum was the center, only a hundred years later the gospel of the crucified Christ was announced. A third century scribbling on a wall of the Palatine, a scrawl which undoubtedly has reference to the Christian Cross, shows how that gospel was received. It is a cross drawn in ridicule. The figure on the cross is of a man with the head of an ass. Beside the cross there is a figure standing; and the inscription reads: "Alexamenos worships [his] God."

The Cross of Christ could never be reported simply as history and nothing more. It had to be interpreted from the very beginning, and be explained in the light of the resurrection. From the very beginning the historical fact of the Cross had need of a theology of the Cross. Under the pressure of internal and external necessities, a theology of the Cross developed as an apologetics of the same. Reasons for this apologetic development were present even within the Church. The Cross was immediately conceived as the sum and center of faith and life. The Cross manifests the nature of the biblical God as the one who, through death, sets free unto life. Paul, therefore, wants to proclaim nothing other than the Crucified (1 Cor. 2:2). The Cross is the point of separation between the Church on the one hand, Judaism and paganism on the other; that is to say, between belief and disbelief (1 Cor. 1:18, 23f.).

If the Cross has become an out and out symbol, one can ask whether it does not thereby correspond to a primordial human presentiment. In the *Republic* (360E–361A), Plato contrasts the utterly unjust with the truly righteous man. The righteous man cannot defend himself against the unjust. He undergoes a frightful end: "The just man will be scourged, tortured, put in chains and will be blinded in both eyes; and finally, after every extremity of suffering, he will be lifted up on a stake and thus he will learn his lesson that not to be just but only to seem so is what ought to be desired" (Plato, *Republic* 361E–362A). Plato writes this in remembrance of the death of Socrates, who, nevertheless, died a much more humane death. Yet, in Plato's description the spotlight of prophetic vision seems to have fallen for a moment upon the stake, the cross, as the summation of the injustice which is suffered by the highest representative of human righteousness, purity, and holiness.[65]

That the account of the Cross of Christ was never historical fact alone, but was always theology too, is verified by the accounts of the four Gospels. They are full of apologetic, dogmatic, and hortatory themes. What the Gospels declare after the fashion of historical account is illuminated and confirmed by the preaching of the apostles in kerygmatic and dogmatic passages.

The themes included in the New Testament theology of the Cross can perhaps be analyzed and accentuated in the following schematization: *a*) light brought to bear by the resurrection; *b*) the Passion of the Messiah; *c*) fulfillment of the Old Testament; *d*) the willingness and innocence of Jesus; *e*) Jesus as the just and holy martyr; *f*) the Passion of Christ as content and basis of preaching and worship; *g*) the passion of Christ as prototype and model of Christian life; *h*) the salvific fruits of the Cross (§ 8).

a) Light Brought to Bear by the Resurrection

The Gospels in their totality and in their every line recount not the history of Jesus, a man who lived many years ago; rather, they proclaim him always, who is now the exalted Lord. The Gospels constantly presuppose the resurrection, and whatever they proclaim, it is with the resurrection in mind. This is true also and even primarily in the case of the Passion narratives. The Cross is transfigured from the very beginning by the resurrection. There never was an account of the Passion of Christ without the account of the resurrection, and it never could have been possible for the former to exist without the latter. Otherwise the death of Jesus would have been only the history of a catastrophe beyond all compare, but which the memory of the human race would not have retained.

Even before the narratives of the Passion, the Gospels, in the predictions of the Passion, point to the conquest of death in the resurrection. All these predictions begin with the Passion and end with the resurrection (Mark 8:31; 9:31; 10:33-34; with synoptic parallels; for an analysis of the predictions of the Passion, see below § 7d). In the Passion narrative itself one was able to read the announcement of the resurrection and of the new communion with the glorified Lord in the familiar surroundings of Galilee (Mark 14:28) as well as of the return of him who was, in his Passion, powerless, as the Ruler of the Kingdom (Mark 14:62; Luke 23:42).

In the oldest formulas of faith, death and resurrection are united: "Christ died, and rose again" (1 Cor. 15:3f.; § 9a). Humiliation even to death on the Cross and exaltation over all are united by way of contrast already in the pre-Pauline hymn in Phil. 2:5-11 (§ 10, 1e). If the Apostle's preaching is exclusively the tidings of the Cross (1 Cor. 1:18), then the Crucified can be proclaimed meaningfully only as the Resurrected: "Jesus Christ is the one who dies, or rather the one who was raised again and who is at the right of God" (Rom. 8:34; 2 Cor. 5:15; 13:4).

The resurrection is the interpretation of the Cross by God himself. By raising him up God acknowledged the Crucified and manifested him as Messiah. An ancient formulation is able to say: made him Messiah (Acts 2:36; 5:31).

Without the resurrection, preaching and faith would be senseless (1 Cor. 15:17). In the Gospel of John (12:23; 13:31), Cross and exaltation are understood as a unit. Elevation on the Cross is already exaltation in majesty (John 3:14; 8:28; 12:32, 34).[66] Nevertheless, the resurrection does not annul the death of Christ, in such a way that now one were no longer able to speak of his death. The Glorified is ever the Crucified. The Cross remains a fact; and it is at one and the same time the scandal of the proclamation and the way of salvation through death into life (1 1:18–2:9; 2 Cor. 12:7-10). The Cross is ever the hallmark of apostolic service and of the life of discipleship (2 Cor. 4:7-11).

b) The Passion of the Messiah

Jesus is revealed as the Messiah also or even especially by the fact of his suffering and crucifixion. It is a peculiarity of Mark's Gospel that the Messiahship and divine Sonship of Jesus remains temporarily in the background. Jesus forbids that any public acknowledgement or confession of himself as Messiah be made (Mark 1:34; 9:9; § 11, 1). Nevertheless, in his Passion the secret is disclosed. Jesus replies affirmatively to the question of the high priest as to whether or not he is the Son of God (Mark 14:61f.; in regard to the question, see below, § 11, 3).

Even before Pilate, Jesus affirms that he is the King of the Jews (Mark 15:2). Pilate repeats the title (Mark 15:9). The soldiers use it in a mocking way (Mark 15:18). According to the Gospels Jesus is made manifest as messianic King in the superscription on the Cross, "King of the Jews" (Mark 15:26). Since the Christian community did not make use of the name King of the Jews as a Christological title, the inscription on the Cross is not to be regarded as a Christian construction. While the Jews are ridiculing their Messiah, a pagan finally understands and declares that the Crucified is truly God's Son (Mark 15:39). If, however, the Messiahship of Jesus is now finally made manifest, it is made clear at the same time that his Messiahship can be rightly understood only if it is comprehended together with his servitude and humiliation, his suffering and death.

In the later Gospels there is an increase of the explicit declarations that Jesus, in his sufferings, is the Christ. These acknowledgements are quoted from the mouths of his opponents (Matthew 26:68; 27:43; Luke 23:39); the Christian community is highlighting its reflections.

c) Fulfillment of the Old Testament

The history and theology of the Passion is a multiplex example and proof of the verification of the Old Testament in the New (§ 3). The oldest history of the Passion is that of Mark. It is already stamped by the proof from prophecy. About the casting of lots for his clothes, the account says: "And they divided his garments, casting lots for them" (Mark 15:24). The account is apparently pure history, but narrated in accord with Ps. 22:19, "They divided my garments among themselves and cast lots for my robe." John (19:23f.) recognizes the correspondence to the Old Testament.

Also to be compared: the announcement of impending betrayal in Mark 14:18 with Ps. 41:10; the end of Judas in Matthew 26:15 and 27:3-10 with Zech. 11:12; the deriding of Jesus in Mark 14:65 with Is. 50:5f.; the acting in unison of Pilate and Herod in Luke 23:6-12 with Ps. 2:1f.; the drink of vinegar in Mark 15:36 with Ps. 69:22; the ridicule offered by those standing around, in Matthew 27:29, 43 and Mark 15:29, with Ps. 22:8f; the prayer of Jesus in Luke 23:46 with Ps. 31:6.

Psalms 22 and 69 in particular served as a means for the descriptive representation of the Cross. Besides these, Isaiah 53 is important for the theology of the Passion.[67] Exegesis is divided in its explanation of the New Testament evidence. Some are of a mind that Jesus himself explained his service in terms of the image of the Servant of Yahweh; others, however, are of the opinion that it was the theology developed in the community which first portrayed Jesus as the suffering Servant of Yahweh. According to Luke 22:37 Jesus himself had referred Is. 53:12 to his own destiny: "The word that was written, 'And he was reckoned with the lawless', must be fulfilled in me." In Luke the saying is included in Jesus' parting discourse with his disciples (22:24-38), for which the evangelist makes use of special traditions, which in many respects sound as if their origins are pre-Lukan.[68]

References to the hymns of the Servant of Yahweh are probably to be understood even elsewhere as sayings put into the mouth of Jesus; *e.g.,* Mark 8:31; 10:45; 14:24. Acts 8:32-34 provides evidence of the community's Christological interpretation of Is. 53:7f.

Rabbinic exegesis in part understood the hymns of the Servant of Yahweh as spoken collectively about Israel (and this, no doubt, was the understanding of the Qumran community); but in part also as referring to the person of the Messiah (thus already in the Septuagint, and then in the Apocalypses of Henoch, of Esdras, and of Baruch). Jewish exegesis, however, completely ignored the declarations about the suffering of the servant, and took into account only the sayings about his glorification. Likewise for the Christian community, it was in no way obvious or self-evident that the Passion of Christ is to be explained with reference to Isaiah 53. On the contrary, this was a new and creative interpretation. It has to have originated with someone. Should this not have been Jesus himself? If he was reckoning with his terrible death, he will certainly have sought an explanation for it.

Paul too in his preaching pointed out the fulfillment of prophecy. He borrowed the scriptural proof from the primitive community. "I delivered to you what I too received, namely, that Christ died for our sins according to the Scriptures" (1 Cor. 15:3). In Rom. 4:25 Paul is possibly using a formula which was shaped in accord with Is. 53:4-12. Paul develops the scriptural proof further. The condemned criminal was suspended on a stake as an object lesson to others. Hence the saying: "Accursed is he that hangs on the tree" (Deut. 21:23). And the sinless, holy Christ (2 Cor. 5:21) hung on the Cross. Like a blasphemer against

the Law, he was thrust out of Israel. He bore the curse for others, for us
(Gal. 3:13). Paul is interpreting the Cross in Old Testament words and
ideas when he refers to its salvific fruit as reconciliation (2 Cor. 5:18f.;
cf. 2 Macc. 1:5; 7:33) and as propitiation (Rom. 3:24f.; *cf.* Lev. 16:12-16).

The evidence of prophecy is drawn forth broadly in the Epistle to the
Hebrews (7–9), when the Cross is described with the concepts of Old
Testament worship. As the true High Priest, Christ has entered into
the heavenly tabernacle and has offered the ever-worthy sacrifice. In 1
Peter 2:22 the Passion is described in terms of Is. 53:9, "He did no sin,
nor was any deceit found in his mouth."

The meaning and value of the evidence from prophecy are not difficult to assess. Only in the language of Scripture can it be suitably declared that what took place in the Passion of Jesus was a sacred event.
If the Old Testament is fulfilled in the Passion of Jesus, then it is seen
that the Cross has its place in God's eternal plan of salvation. The Passion, then, says nothing against the Messiahship and divine Sonship of
Jesus; rather, it but evidences them the more. Then "the Son of Man
must suffer much" (Mark 8:31). The divine imperative of suffering
was fulfilled in accord with prophecy. "The Lamb has been slain even
from the foundation of the world" (Apoc. 13:8).

d) The Willingness and Innocence of Jesus

Jesus' prophecies of his Passion long beforetime on the road to Jerusalem attest to his willingness (Mark 8:31f.; 9:31; 10:33f.; also Mark
9:12; Luke 13:33; 17:25; Matthew 26:2). The three great prophecies of
the Passion are dispersed through the account by the Evangelist Mark
with editorial care. They are shaped in accord with Old Testament
prophecy, which makes suffering an imperative demand. Like the
righteous man, Christ must "be rejected" (Ps. 118:22); like the Servant
of Yahweh, he must "be delivered up" (Is. 53:12). The individual events
of the Passion from the betrayal until the resurrection on the third day
(especially in Matthew 20:18f.; Mark 10:33f.) are elucidated in a knowledge of the history of those events. Even if the detailed prophecies of
the Passion were formulated after and in accord with the events, it does
not at all indicate that Jesus had not considered nor spoken of the possibility of a terrible death.

Jesus heard the accusations of blasphemy against God (Mark 2:7) and of Sabbath-breaking (Mark 2:24; Luke 13:14). This contempt for the Law was threatened with death (Mark 3:6). Jesus saw himself in the ranks of the prophets and martyrs of Israel (Matthew 23:35; Luke 13:33). He interprets his service after the image of the Servant of Yahweh in the Deutero-Isaiah, which servant is delivered up on behalf of the many (§ 3, 3). Jesus knew how the destiny of John the Baptist was completed. He announced persecution and suffering to his disciples (Mark 8:34f.; 9:1; 10:38f.; Matthew 10:28, 36). Can he then have exempted himself? Jesus reckoned with the possibility of a like destiny, so he must have sought a meaning for it, such we find in Mark 10:45 and 14:22-25. Can one really dismiss the whole report as a secondary theologizing of the community? Would one not then be robbing the gospel of an essential feature of its Christ image?

In the history itself of the Passion we find the predictions of the betrayal by Judas (Mark 14:18), of the flight of the disciples (Mark 14:27), and of Peter's denial (Mark 14:30). Jesus enters into his suffering with clear knowledge and willingly. He surrenders himself, inasmuch as he forbids the disciples to offer armed resistance (Matthew 26:52). Luke (22:51), who has a special preference for exhibiting Jesus as the healer of the sick, recounts that Jesus healed the servant whose ear had been cut off.

The theme of Jesus' willingness is enhanced by John. All the attempts of his enemies to seize Jesus fail, so long as his hour has not yet come (John 7:30, 44; 8:20, 59; 10:39). He has the power to lay down his life and to take it up again (John 10:18). On the Mount of Olives Jesus faces his captors. They fall to the ground, and he must invite them to take him. He himself releases his disciples (John 18:4-9). The historical events are interlarded with proverbial phraseology. In the face of the appearance of the divinity or of a heavenly being men sink to the ground (Ezech. 1:28; 44:4; Dan. 10:9; 2 Macc. 3:27; Acts 9:4; Apoc. 1:17; 19:10; 22:8). Before the divinely protected righteous man his enemies must fall back and make way (Ps. 27:2; 35:4). At his coming the Messiah will strike the godless and destroy them (Is. 11:4; 2 Thess. 2:8; *4 Esdras* 13:3-11). Before Pilate Jesus asserts: "You would have no power over me if it were not given you from above" (John 19:11). Tradition was seeking to defend Jesus against such accusations as that to which Celsus gives expression (in Origen, *Against Celsus* 2, 9): "How could we be expected to regard him as a God, who, when we had convicted and condemned him and wanted to punish him, hid himself and tried to escape and was captured in a shameful way and was betrayed even by those whom he called his disciples?"

The innocence of Jesus had to be acknowledged even by the courts, nonetheless hostile to him. Pilate condemns Jesus unwillingly and only when forced to it (Luke 23:25). Pilate's wife attests the righteousness of Jesus (Matthew 27:19). Pilate washes his hands of the matter, in the symbolic gesture that has made the phrase a commonplace, thereby professing both the innocence of Jesus and his own innocence in regard to what must follow (Matthew 27:24f.). In the narrative of the Passion in Luke, Pilate repeatedly asserts the innocence of Jesus (Luke 23:4, 14, 20, 22). Even Herod affirms it (Luke 23:15). According to John (18:29–19:16) Pilate expended himself in a lengthy negotiation for the release of Jesus. Granting that proverbial themes have played a part in all this, it still remains a fact that the community of disciples had certitude that Jesus, though crucified, was innocent; and it was incumbent upon them to bring this fact to the knowledge of others. He suffered for the guilt of the world. Perhaps there is a concurrent purpose operative here also, to prove to the Roman empire at large and to the Roman authorities the political loyalty of Christ (and of Christians).[69]

e) Jesus as the Just and Holy Martyr

The senseless horror of the death on the Cross could be made more understandable by comforting themes, by which Christ was presented as a holy martyr. The oldest of the Gospels, that of Mark, recounts only one word from the Cross: "My God, my God, why hast thou forsaken me?" (Mark 15:34). By itself, without the supplementation read in the other Gospels, this account is distressingly difficult. The accounts of the later Gospels have a different character. Luke and John pass over the cry of abandonment, and each tells of three other words from the Cross.

Luke recounts Jesus' prayer for his enemies (23:43a),[70] the word of promise to the good thief (23:43), and Jesus' prayer in dying, "Father, into thy hands I commend my spirit" (23:46). The crucified is not the forsaken God. He is Son and Savior, and he is moreover the model for love of enemy.

Again, three other words from the Cross are recounted by John. In grieving love Jesus takes leave of his Mother and of his beloved disciple (John 19:26f.). The complaint "I thirst" fulfills the Scripture (John 19:28). With a cry of conquest, "It is finished!" (John 19:30) Jesus gives up his life. He is the King, on the throne of the Cross.

The different expositions of the Gospels are each one valid in itself. Can one be allowed to join them with each other in a single concurrent history?

In Matthew and Mark the Gethsemane accounts point to a sorrowing Christ in deepest distress. While the older Gospels portray how Jesus falls to the ground and struggles three times in prayer (Mark 14:34-41), Luke tells how Jesus prayed once on bended knee (22:41). Through the appearance of an angel — mentioned only in Luke 22:43 — it is made known that God is with him as he prays.[71] In John's Gospel one finds no Gethsemane scene; at most, John 12:27 seems to be a recollection thereof.

The Crucified is made (Matthew 27:43) to bear ridicule like the righteous man of the Old Testament. He too was taunted: If the just man is God's Son, God will defend him and rescue him from the hands of his enemies (Wis. 2:13-20).

Processions to martyrdoms have emotional scenes and conversions of the participants. Along the way of the Cross, for the last time as prophet, Jesus speaks in prophecy and comforts the people, especially the weeping women (Luke 23:27-31). It is the good thief who, in his last moments, receives his salvation as the firstfruits of the Cross (Luke 23:39-43). The centurion and the soldiers acknowledge the divine Sonship of the dying Jesus (Matthew 27:54). The bystanders went back home frightened (Luke 23:48). Marvelous signs at the death of Jesus (Mark 15:33, 38) attest the sympathy and sorrow of creation. In popular traditions the number and power of the wonders of Mark increase beyond what is found in Matthew (27:51-53) and Luke (23:44f.) until they reach the proportions in which they are found in the apocryphal accounts (*Gospel of the Nazarenes*, fragment 21; *Gospel of Peter* 5[15]; 6[2-22]; see also Melito of Sardes, *Homily on the Passion* 97f.). We should not miss the wonderful symbolism in that the temple curtain, which veiled the Holy of Holies, was torn from top to bottom (Mark 15:38). The sanctuary of Israel is abolished and laid waste; in the death of Christ the entrance to the Holy City is opened to all (Heb. 10:19f.).[72]

f) The Passion of Christ as Content and Basis of Preaching and Worship

The Cross of Christ is the sum total of preaching. "I was determined not to know anything among you, except Jesus Christ and him crucified" (1 Cor. 2:2). "Christ was depicted before your eyes as the crucified" (Gal. 3:1). All proclamation is the presentation of the message of the Cross.

In the earliest hymns of worship the Passion is celebrated. An example of this and a testimonial to it is seen in Phil. 2:6-11 (§ 10, 1e). In the First Epistle of Peter there are three texts conspicuous for their paradoxical contrasts (1:18-21; 2:21-24; 3:18-22), which, by reason both of their form and their content, can be recognized as constituting a Christological hymn. The passage in 2:21-24 treats of the Passion of Christ; 3:18-22, of his descent into the lower regions in the time between his death and resurrection.[73]

The Apocalypse of John in its visions gazes upon the celebration of the heavenly liturgy. It is the liturgy of the Lamb that was slain. "Worthy is the Lamb, who was slain and who by his blood has acquired for God the redeemed from among all nations, to receive honor and glory and power for all eternity" (Apoc. 5:6-14). The Apocalypse portrays the heavenly liturgy after the model of the liturgy which was carried out in (synagogue and) church. The liturgy of the Church was the celebration of the Cross and of its glory.

The salvation event of the death of Jesus has now taken place once and once for all. "Henceforth Christ dies no more" (Rom. 6:9f.). The sacrifice, offered once only, of Christ, the one High Priest, has brought about eternal redemption and sanctification (Heb. 9:12; 9:25-28; 10:10). All worship has achieved its perfection and its goal. For the future, worship in the Church can be only a memorial representation of the Cross. Thus the Lord's Supper represents the submission of Christ in death, wherein the new covenant has its basis (1 Cor. 11:23-26; Mark 14:22-24).

In Paul (Rom. 6:3-8; likewise Col. 2:12), baptism is referred to the death of Christ. Paul makes reference to the knowledge which the community has (Rom. 6:3). Is he drawing on an already accepted interpretation? Is the basis thereof the idea that salvation is anchored in the Cross of Christ, and that baptism is the reception in faith of salvation, and therefore entry into the sphere of Christ's death?[74]

Blood and water stream forth from the side of the Crucified, pierced by a lance (John 19:34). From the time of the Fathers of the Church even to the present, exegesis, in interpreting this after the fashion of a wonder or sign, has understood that the two sacraments of baptism and Eucharist take their grace and actuality from the redemptive death of Christ. "Jesus Christ came through water and blood and Spirit" (1 John 5:6 *var.*). This is an allusion to the baptism and the death of Christ, which become really present now through the Spirit.

g) *The Passion of Christ as Prototype and Model of Christian Life*

The decision to become followers of Christ must be made radically in view of the Cross. This is required by the saying of the Lord: "If anyone wishes to follow after me, he must deny himself and take up his cross" (Mark 8:34; *Theology of the New Testament*, Vol. 3, p. 163f.). Perhaps the disciple's following of the Cross is pointed to in the history of the Passion, when it speaks of Simon of Cyrene after the fashion of a prototype: "They laid the Cross on him, to carry it after Jesus" (Luke 23:26). Certainly individual scenes were recounted from the history of the Passion as implicit admonitions and warnings: thus with the betrayal at the hands of Judas; the denial by Peter; and the flight of the disciples. Gethsemane likewise was understood as the ever-present temptation endangering the faith. It is true always: "The spirit is willing, but the flesh is weak" (Mark 14:38).

In the Gospel of John the way of Christ in the Passion is an example of resignation and love. At the beginning of the Passion the Gospel says: "He loved them to the end" (John 13:1). The washing of the disciples' feet is an example of service that continues even to the sacrifice of his life (John 13:12-17). And Christ himself says: "This is my commandment, that you love one another as I have loved you. Greater love than this no man has, that one lay down his life for his friends" (John 15:12-13).

Also in the letters of the apostles the Passion of Christ is pointed out as model and example. "He died for all, so that they who are alive may live no longer for themselves, but for him who died and was raised up again for them" (2 Cor. 5:15). The love of Christ, who died for all and came to life again, obliges all to live and to die for all (Rom. 14:7-10). When Paul admonishes not to seek after one's own interests but to serve each other, it is Christ who is the model, who did not cling to his being equal to God, but was obedient even unto death (Phil. 2:4-11). The Christian is admonished to let himself be crucified with Christ and to acknowledge the Crucified as Lord; therefore, to surrender his former understanding of himself and to gain a new one in Christ. "They who belong to Christ Jesus have crucified their flesh with its passions and desires" (Gal. 5:24).

The Cross is the overthrowing of the world. In the Cross the former attachment and union between the world and myself is severed, and freedom is gained. "I will glory only in the Cross of our Lord Jesus Christ, through which the world is crucified to me and I to the world" (Gal. 6:14). The Apostle's own life is one of exemplary submission to the Lord's death on the Cross. "I bear the marks of Jesus in my body" (Gal. 6:17). In patient suffering the very Passion of Christ takes place. "We carry about always in our body the dying of Jesus, so that the life also of Jesus may be made manifest in our body" (2 Cor. 4:10). With the death of the Lord the life of the resurrection too becomes forevermore a new actuality.

"He was crucified through weakness, but he lives through the power of God. We too are weak in him, but we shall live with him through the power of God for you" (2 Cor. 13:4). Christian living is "being in Christ". This means, to share in his death agony; but it also means, out of God's bounty, to share already now and for the future in the life and strength of the glorified Christ.

In the New Testament the weakness and the power of Christ are frequently mentioned together as mutually complementary antitheses (1 Cor. 4:10; Rom. 8:34; Mark 16:6; Acts 2:23f.). This is probably indicative of a very early formalized confession that includes the death and resurrection of Jesus. Ultimately it is the goal of life "to know him and the power of his resurrection and the fellowship of his suffering, so that I may be conformed to his death, in the hope that I might attain to the resurrection from the dead" (Phil. 3:10f.).

The Cross of Christ stood outside the city. For men of antiquity the city was the embodiment of the cultural and governmental society. The crucified was expelled, despised, stripped of honor. The Christian too must be prepared for such an existence. "Jesus suffered outside the gate.

Let us therefore go forth to him outside the camp and bear his shame along with him" (Heb. 13:12f.).

In one instance in particular (1 Peter 2:18-25) the slaves are reminded of Christ as the prototype of innocent suffering (the New Testament is frequently obliged to wrestle with the difficult problem of the slaves in the congregation). The passage cited validates the slave's consciousness of the fact that he must bear injustice. But the letter requires of the slave that he bear it patiently, while gazing upon the suffering Christ. "Christ also has suffered for you, leaving you a model so that you might follow in his steps." If Christ suffered for others, he was himself innocent. In the Passion narratives his innocence is portrayed in detail, after the image of the Servant of Yahweh in Isaiah 53:4, 9 (1 Peter 2:22-25). The suffering of the slave, a thing about which scarcely anyone cares, is compared and related to the greatest suffering that is known in the community, the suffering of the Redeemer.

Ultimately the Passion of Christ is the inner form of the martyrdoms of all times: of the present, of primitive times, and of the endtime. Moreover, the Cross of Christ, already erected, shapes the tradition of the words of Jesus in the Church. The particularized details of the sufferings of the disciples in imitation of the Passion of Jesus Christ clearly presupposes that that Passion has already taken place: "I will send you prophets and wise men and scribes. Some of them you will put to death and crucify and scourge in your synagogues" (Matthew 23:34). Peter will follow his Lord in death on a cross. At first it is said to him: "You will follow later" (John 13:36). Afterwards quite clearly: "When you are old, you will stretch forth your hands and another will gird you and lead you where you would not want to go" (John 21:18). It presupposes already the tradition that Peter, like Jesus, died on a cross.

In Acts 6:8–8:2, the account of the first martyrdom in the Church, that of Stephen, follows the model of the Passion of Jesus (Luke 22:63–23:49). False witnesses come forward against Stephen (Acts 6:14) as they did against Christ. The testimony to the glory of the exalted Son of Man is in both instances denied and taken as blasphemy (Acts 7:56 and Luke 22:70f.). Like Christ, Stephen is thrust out of the city (Acts 7:58 and Luke 23:26, 33). Like Jesus, Stephen prays for his murderers (Acts 7:59 and Luke 23:34); and finally the dying man exclaims, "Lord

Jesus, receive my spirit" (Acts 7:58 and Luke 23:46). Devout men bury Stephen (Acts 8:2 and Luke 23:50-53).

According to the Apocalypse of John (1:5; 3:14), Christ is the proto-martyr. In a vision of the Apocalypse (11:3-14) the two witnesses, Elijah and Moses, are killed by the beast from the abyss. Their corpses lie "in the streets of the great city which in a mystical sense is called Sodom and Egypt, where their Lord also was crucified." Sodom is the place where the righteous were molested; Egypt, where the chosen people of God were oppressed and persecuted. Sodom and Egypt are places of abomination and disbelief (Wis. 19:13f.). Jerusalem, the place of Jesus' crucifixion, is a type of all places of martyrdoms. The perfected martyrs "sing the song of Moses, the servant of God, and of the Lamb". (Apoc. 15:3). The passion of Moses, of Christ, and of the disciples, form a sal-vation-historical unit. The primitive Church regarded the martyrs as the perfected disciples of Christ. "Christ we worship as the Son of God; but the martyrs we love as disciples and imitators of the Lord; and rightly so, because of their unsurpassable devotion to their own King and Teacher" (*The Martyrdom of Saint Polycarp* 17, 3; in Jurgens, *The Faith of the Early Fathers* [hereinafter cited as Jurgens], no. 81).

The Cross of Christ finally discloses its deep meaning where its salvific fruit is recognized and appreciated (§ 8).

The Church of the apostles within one or two generations produced the theology of the Cross for all time. This is an incomparable achieve-ment. The historian would be hard put to account for it, if one were to suppose that the community and the apostles had created the theology of the Passion entirely by themselves, without Jesus' having himself re-vealed its basic content.[75]

§ 8. REDEMPTION AND ATONEMENT

According to the words of Jesus and the judgment of the New Testa-ment, mankind is lost in sin and has fallen victim to death. At the report that Roman soldiers (in the temple at Jerusalem?) were killing Gali-lean pilgrims and mixing their blood with the blood of the sacrificial beasts, and the further report that a tower at the pool of Siloam had collapsed and killed eighteen men, Jesus answered: "They were not greater sinners than the other inhabitants of Jerusalem. I tell you, if you do not repent you will all likewise perish" (Luke 13:1-5). Men have fallen victim to death (*Theology of the New Testament*, Vol. 3, pp. 52-59). The New Testament, however, says that Jesus rescues and frees men from their ruined estate, inasmuch as he takes upon himself their sin and guilt.[76]

1. GOSPELS

The Gospels portray the redemption as fruit of the Cross, while they tell of the word and work of Jesus. Jesus goes about in the company of sinners. He absolves them of their sins, which he thereby takes upon himself. In declarations about himself he explains his ministry and offers his forgiveness to all.

a) Jesus Goes About in the Company of Sinners

It is genuinely historical that Jesus was the friend of sinners. This was an important reason for the opposition between himself and the Pharisees; it was they who defended law, justice, and morality against him. According to the schema of Deuteronomy and the two Books of Chronicles, the man faithful to the Law is rewarded by God, while lawlessness is punished. The righteous man even brings salvation upon the nation, whereas the sinner brings disaster. The sinner is the enemy of the people. The righteous reject Jesus, because he visits with sinners and tax-collectors and is their companion. Jesus counters that it is not the healthy who need a physician but the sick, and that he has not come to call the righteous but sinners (Mark 2:16f.).

That which is a point of opposition between Jesus and the Pharisees is also an essential difference between Jesus and the community at Qumran. The members of the covenant there must "love all the sons of light, each according to his lot in the council meeting of God; but all the sons of darkness they must hate, each according to his guilt in the vengeance of God" (1 QS 1:9-11; see also 1:4). The pious man cherishes against sinners "eternal hatred with a will to keep apart from all men of perdition" (1 QS 9:29f.). Enemies of the community are God's enemies. In the eschatological war punishment will befall them. The pious man keeps himself far away from the sinner. Jesus, however, calls even the latter.

Nevertheless, Jesus is the friend of sinners not in such a way that he regards their sin with indifference, but with the purpose in mind of bringing about an awareness of sin as godlessness and guilt before God. Jesus begins his proclamation of the gospel with a call to repentance (Mark 1:15). The disciples are directed always to pray: "Forgive us our debt" (Matthew 6:12).

b) Jesus Absolves Sinners

In the narration of the healing of the paralytic (Mark 2:1-12), Jesus first speaks amazing words to the sick man: "Son, your sins are forgiven!" Then he says to the poor cripple, "Stand up!" — and he stood up. All praised God and said: "We have never seen the like of this before." [77] Illness and sin are connected. Removal of guilt and settlement of the past are the prerequisite of healing. This is a thoroughly Jewish outlook, even if Jesus declines to conclude to the personal guilt of the sick man.

Jesus grants forgiveness. The passive, "Your sins are forgiven you", indicates, in accord with biblical style, the workings of God. At the same time, the fully authoritative power of Jesus is made manifest. For now the kingdom of God is breaking into the open, and this is the hour for the forgiveness of sins. With the word of forgiveness, entry to the kingdom of God is opened to the sick man.

It is contrary to every Jewish notion for Jesus to declare forgiveness without any action on the part of the sinner to compensate for his guilt. Elsewhere it is fulfillment of the Law, alms-giving, votive offerings, sacrifice that is required. This whole system is annulled. The High Priest can grant forgiveness to Israel on the Day of Atonement, on the basis of the divinely established ordinance of atonement (Lev. 16). Otherwise Israel awaits forgiveness of guilt in the messianic era of salvation. The Messiah will sanctify his people (*Psalms of Solomon* 17:28f.). Jesus acts like a High Priest of the messianic time. This draws forth the antagonism of his opponents. Their judgment is that Jesus blasphemes. He claims authoritative powers which he does not have. In the ensuing argument Jesus asks them about what is easier and what more difficult. In his view (and that of the evangelist) to forgive sins is the more difficult; in the view of the audience it is the visible and verifiable cure. It is true of the forgiving of sins as well as of the healing, that here God is acting in Christ.

Jesus forgives sins also according to the narrative telling of his being anointed by the sinful woman (Luke 7:36-50).[78] Jesus is called a "glutton and wine-bibber and companion of sinners" (Luke 7:34). This is then illustrated in Luke 7:36-50. Jesus participates in a banquet and is anointed by a sinful woman. It is not stated, and is in no way certain, that the sinful woman is a prostitute. She can also be a sinner as the wife of a man who lives lawlessly. She receives forgiveness: "Your many sins are forgiven you." The passive again points to the operation of God. Jesus, however, expressly grants her forgiveness: "And he said to her: 'Your sins are forgiven you.'" Jesus accepts the woman's redeeming faith as a basis for her being forgiven. But he proclaims the operation of God and executes it authoritatively himself. Those who are reclining at table with him so understand it, and quite rightly, when they ask: "Who is this, who even forgives sins?" Jesus grants the woman peace. She is received into the redeeming salvation of God. The pious and righteous, however, take umbrage at Jesus' action, and keep aloof from one who guarantees and assures forgiveness of sins.

c) In Parables Jesus Vindicates His Forgiving of Sins

In a composition which unites editorially three similar examples of a theme, Luke 15 recounts the three parables about lost things: the parable of the lost sheep, of the lost coin, and that of the lost or prodigal son. According to Luke's exposition Jesus relates these parables in order to vindicate himself before the Pharisees, to justify the fact that he associates with sinners and accepts sinners (Luke 15:2).

Jesus relates the story of the father who goes out to meet his lost son and welcomes him back (Luke 15:3-10). It is a vindication of Jesus' own actions. He does as that father does, but even more: since Jesus welcomes sinners, God himself, the Father, likewise welcomes them. Christ acts in the place of the Father, and the Father acts through him. The Pharisees are standing by, silent or muttering, like the son who had remained at home. When Jesus tells in the parable of the stony silence of the older son, he is pointing to the reaction of the Pharisees. They are silent because they deny the forgiveness of sins by Jesus.

Jesus knows that his activity, which makes the goodness and forgiveness of God visible and operative, will be at last the occasion and the basis for the Pharisees to hate him with a deadly hatred. The shadow of the Cross falls over the narration of the parable. God's love for sinners becomes real through Christ, now, when he welcomes sinners, just as finally it will become real by reason of the Cross. Here in this parable Christ takes the sins of men upon himself, just as he will finally do so upon the Cross.

d) Jesus Speaks Expressly of His Redemptive Ministry

"The Son of Man has not come to be served, but to serve, and to give his life as a ransom for the many" (Mark 10:45).[79] Jesus speaks of the surrendering and giving up of his life, which is now taking place in the service of proclamation and of healing, but which is finally to take place in his death. This latter is not so much an undergoing of death as a yielding up of life.

Some scholars debate the question as to what extent the saying in Mark 10:45 (= Matthew 20:28) can be regarded as a saying of Jesus. In a similar remark, Luke 22:27 lacks the predicate "Son of Man", as well as the entire second half of the passage: ". . . and to give his life as a ransom for the many." These words appear to be structured in accord with Is. 53:10-12; and some critics doubt whether or not Jesus understood his ministry in accord with the figure of the Servant of Yahweh. Moreover, such an explicitly declared soteriology in a saying of the Lord seems to be a source of surprise in certain quarters.

The question is not an easy one to decide. The parallel in Luke 22:24-27 is not evidently more primitive than Mark 10:45. In Luke, in fact, the saying of the Lord seems to be a Hellenistic-Christian formulation.[80] Mark 10:45 has Old Testament Jewish overtones. According to Exodus 21:30 the guilty must pay a ransom (λύτρον) for his life. In the Greek Bible just as in Judaism of the same period, λύτρον is a familiar word. According to the Jewish notion, however, atonement is accomplished again and again; and for the Gentile nations there is no ransom. In Mark 10:45 redemption takes place for all in this eschatological hour. The saying declares something quite new. Who would have presumed to assert this, or who would have been able to get by with it? Could it reasonably be anyone else but Jesus?

Mark 10:45 is not entirely unique in the Synoptic tradition; rather, it is supplemented by the Last Supper tradition (Mark 14:22-25 with Synoptic parallels, and 1 Cor. 11:23-25). These accounts are solemnly stylized; they probably already reflect the liturgy of the Eucharist. The oldest text is presumably that of the First Epistle to the Corinthians. It is the earliest written down. The formulas for the bread and wine are not yet shaped so perfectly parallel as in the Synoptics. The texts of the Last Supper tradition are full of Semitisms and therefore go back to the primitive community in Palestine. The formulations allow us to catch a glimpse of important Old Testament terminology (Exod. 24:8; Is. 53:12; Jer. 31:31). If the Sinai covenant was in blood, as in Exod. 24:8, so too is the new covenant instituted in blood, the covenant prophetically promised in Jer. 31:31.[81]

Sayings like Mark 10:45 and 14:22-25 are not incomprehensible in the Judaism of their time. However the songs of the Suffering Servant in Deutero-Isaiah were understood by Jewish exegesis, whether collectively of the nation or of an individual, they tell of the surrender of the Servant for the sake of others (Is. 53:13–53:12). Experience teaches the terrible death of the righteous (Wis. 2:20). In the not long past era of the Maccabees the righteous not infrequently paid with their lives for their adherence to the Law. Israel understood their deaths as atonement for the sins of the nation (2 Macc. 7:18, 37.; *4 Macc.* 6:28f.; 17:22).[82]

The community at Qumran knows that it has itself "been chosen by God's good pleasure to atone for the land and to requite the godless for their iniquitous deeds" (1 QS 8:6-10). The ordinances of the covenant must be fulfilled "to absolve the guilt of transgressions and of sinful deeds, so that the divine good pleasure may be upon the land" (1 QS 9:4; *cf.* 1 QS 5:6; 1 QSa 1:3).

Mark 10:45 and 14:22-24 are understandable in the light of Old Testament Jewish thought. They can probably be taken as formulated by the primitive Palestinian community. The pre-Pauline formula in 1 Cor. 15:3; "died for our sins according to the Scriptures" points back to the same primitive community. According to numerous declarations of the Gospels, Jesus was not unaware of what awaited him in his messianic mission (see § 7d above). If that is the case, then he would also have been conscious of its meaning. Passages like Mark 10:45 and 14:25 are certainly not impossible as sayings of Jesus, at least in their basic content, even if the reshaping of their details by the post-paschal New Testament Christology must be taken into account.

As with many sayings of the Lord, so too with that handed down in Mark 10:45 and Luke 22:27, we do not know the exact occasion or the precise time when the saying was originally spoken. The Gospels (or the evangelists) often enough indicate such by the context in which they place a saying. In the present instance too this is significant. Luke puts it in the farewell address of Jesus on the evening before his mortal agony, and thereby interprets it in accord with this context. When Mark speaks expressly of the surrender of life as a ransom, is it merely the formulation of what is implied in Luke? The ministry performed by Jesus is consumated in his death, which brings salvation. Thus the thought and content of the words of Jesus are authoritatively and authentically exalted by the Gospels themselves.

2. Preaching of the Apostles

The doctrine of the saving death of Christ, the foundation of which is set down in the Synoptics, is developed and given a greater dogmatic depth in the preaching of the apostles.

The meaning that Jesus' death has for salvation is most frequently given vocal expression by the use of the prepositions "for" and "because of", expressive of a relationship. In the Greek New Testament it is the following terms of relationship that are found:

ἀντί with the genitive = *for, in place of*; (as a proxy, expressive of vicariousness, in Mark 10:45). *For* or *in place of* the forfeited life of the sinner, Jesus lays down his own.

διά with the genitive = *because of*. This term is found in 1 Cor. 8:11 with specification of a personal object: "the brother *for* [or *because of* or *on account of*] whom Christ died"; with a neuter object in Rom. 3:25 and 4:25, "*for* [or *because of* or *on account of*] our sins."

περί with the genitive = *for* (in the sense of *in favor of* or *for the benefit of*); in 1 Thess. 5:10, with a personal object: Jesus Christ died *for* us, *i.e.*, to benefit us; likewise in Matthew 26:28. The preposition can also take a neuter object: *"for* sins" (Rom. 8:3; 1 Peter 3:18; 1 John 2:2).

ὑπέρ   with the genitive = *for* in the sense of *for the benefit of* is of quite frequent usage. See Mark 14:24; *"for* the many"; Rom. 5:8, *"for* us"; Rom. 8:32, *"for* all"; and numerous other examples might be adduced.[83]

In Mark 10:45 the death of Jesus is conceived as ransom (λύτρον). This conception of the event is contained also in the word ἀπολύτρωσις, by which the redemption is designated as fruit of the Cross (Rom. 3:24; 1 Cor. 1:30; Eph. 1:7; Heb. 9:15). Even verbs significant of redemption or of loosing are used in describing the operational effect of the death of Jesus; thus with λυτρόω (1 Peter 1:18); λύω (Apoc. 1:5). The notion of ransoming is closely related to that of purchasing freedom or of buying oneself or someone else off for a price; and in this case it is Christ's death that is the price to be paid (1 Cor. 6:20; Gal. 3:13; 4:5; Apoc. 5:9).

The work of salvation is also described in the terminology of worship, which occasionally makes use even of a juridic conceptualization. Such is the case with the term justification. Romans 3:25f. is especially important in this context: "God has publicily exhibited him as a sacrifice of atonement (propitiation) through faith in his blood, in order to show forth his justice, since, in the patience of God, previously committed sins had been passed over; and in order also to show his justice in the present time, inasmuch as it is he that is just and who justifies through faith in Jesus." [84] The difficult dogmatic language, employing terms some of which are otherwise foreign to Paul, permits us to make the conjecture that in this place the Apostle is making use of an already traditional formula of faith. Perhaps he interprets it through a concept especially important to him, the concept of faith. The formula makes use of Old Testament ideas. In the community of Yahweh nothing that was in need of atonement dared remain unatoned for. Guilt forfeited life. Atonement required blood because life resides in blood (Lev. 17:11).

The New Testament work of atonement is "publicly exhibited" by God himself; therefore, it is instituted by God. God is not a raging demon who might be appeased by atonement; rather, he is ever gracious. The cosmic and soteriological publicness and objectivity of the work is always apprehended in faith, through which the eternal event becomes salvation for men. Up to now God's patience has passed over sin. But since guilt of its very nature demands atonement, were God to continue to ignore sin, the justice which is of God's very nature could thereby become obscured. God's keeping to himself until now was possible only with a view of Christ's propitiatory death. Now God has set up the propitiatory sacrifice in order to disclose his justice. Christ was able to intercede for sin because he had become a member of the human race. All mankind is included in him as in the new Adam (Rom. 5:14f.). He bears the curse of sin for all (2 Cor. 5:21; Gal. 3:13). If atonement is made through the Cross of Christ, then justification too is worked for all. When God grants justice in view of faith, he reveals himself as the one who is just and who makes men just. God's properties are always overflowing, bestowing and creative, so that just as he is life, so also he gives life.

The concept of the propitiatory sacrifice used in Rom. 3:25 appears also in passages like 1 John 2:2 and 4:10, "God sent his Son as propitiation for our sins"; like Heb. 2:17 and 5:7-10, wherein as High Priest Jesus atones for the sins of the people.

A related concept is that of reconciliation (καταλλαγή), which Paul applies to the redemptive work of Christ: "Everything is from God, who has reconciled us to himself through Christ and has charged us with the ministry of reconciliation" (2 Cor. 5:18). Paul uses the term reconciliation also in Rom. 5:10 and 11:15, in describing the operation of the Cross. Paul, and he alone, thereby describes the Old Testament concept of atonement with a word which was not yet available to the Greek Old Testament, first appearing in 2 Macc. 1:5 and 7:33, and then in Josephus. Again it is stated that in the work of reconciliation God is not appeased; rather, a transformation takes place in the man. It is God who is active. He reconciles the world to himself (2 Cor. 5:19). "When we were sinners, we were reconciled with God" (Rom. 5:10). The sinner takes hold of the reconciliation extended to him by God. "Let yourselves be reconciled to God" (2 Cor. 5:20). The Church is charged with the ministry of reconciliation in the proclamation of the gospel. The "message of reconciliation" (2 Cor. 5:19) effects what is declares. For "the word is vital and creative" (Heb. 4:12).

Ultimately the death of Jesus can be understood as sacrifice.[85] This is intimated when, prior to his Passion, Jesus says: "For them I sanctify myself" (John 17:19). *Sanctify* is used in the sense of *offer sacrificially* (as in Exod. 13:2; Deut. 15:19). Christ is "the Lamb of God, who takes away the sins of the world" (John 1:29). The metaphor can unite several ranges of ideas. The Servant of Yahweh, who carries away our sins (Is. 53:4), is like a lamb that is led to the slaughter (Is. 53:7). In the temple the sacrificial lambs are offered daily (Num. 28:3-8). Christ is the Paschal Lamb. In the Gospel of John (19:14), Jesus begins the way of the Cross at about the sixth hour on Preparation Day — at the very time, therefore, when one would be preparing to bring the paschal lambs to the temple to be slaughtred. A typification of the paschal lamb, of which no bone dare be broken, is fulfilled in the death of Jesus (John 19:36).

Paul declares: "Christ, our Passover, has been sacrificed" (1 Cor. 5:7). The work of Jesus *is* offering and sacrifice of deepest love. "He delivered himself up for us, an offering and sacrifice to God, like sweet-smelling incense" (Eph. 5:2).

According to the Epistle to the Hebrews, Christ is the true High Priest. The principal ministry of the High Priest is to offer sacrifice (Heb. 8:3). The sacrifice of Christ is prefigured in the blood-offering of Moses on Horeb (Heb. 9:18-20) as also in the yearly sacrifice on the Day of Atonement, Yom Kippur (Heb. 9:1-10, 18). Christ's death is his high-priestly offering of himself (Heb. 7:27; 9:14). His death is also the sacrifice of the true and everlasting covenant (Heb. 13:20).

In the Apocalypse (5:6 *et passim*) Christ comes forward as the slain lamb. Christ is the one true sacrificial lamb, who does away with the previous multiplicity of offerings, and whose atonement suffices for the sins of the whole world.

Old Testament sacrificial terminology is being used when the New Testament, as it so often does, speaks of the blood of Christ in an abbreviated formulation of the gospel proclamation (Mark 14:24; Rom. 5:9; 1 Cor. 10:16; Col. 1:20; 1 John 1:7; 1 Peter 1:2; Heb. 9:12; 10:19; 12:24).[86] In the New Testament the single term "Blood of Christ" means many different things. The blood of Christ is the antitype of the Old Testament blood offering. The term, therefore points first of all to the fulfillment of the Old Testament. Blood of Christ expresses the historical event of the Cross, as well as the reality of the death of Jesus in the ceremony of worship (1 Cor. 10:16) and the present salvational reality of his redeeming death, "for we are now justified in his blood" (Rom. 5:9). "The blood of Jesus cleanses us from every sin" (1 John 1:7).

The salvational fruit of the Cross is also explained as "justice, sanctification, and redemption" (1 Cor. 1:30; Eph. 5:25f.; Heb. 10:10), as peace (Eph. 2:14-16; Col. 1:20); as salvation (Eph. 2:5-8; 1 Thess. 5:9f.; Heb. 5:9). All these benefits of redemption are also the expectation of Old Testament messianic promise. The saving death of Christ is thereby united even closer with the conceptions of the Old Testament.

If faith and theology have to reckon with the possibility that the explicitly developed meaning of the death of Jesus as sacrifice, redemption and reconciliation, and as salvational operation of God has its expression in the formulations of the primitive community, clearly seen after the exaltation of Christ, and that such is the work of that community, all this must be understood in the sense that it is God and his spirit who have empowered and authorized the community and its faith. to arrive at this formulation and to make this proclamation; an understanding and a preaching, therefore, which is valid forever.

Behind all its varying terms, themes, and concepts, the New Testament theology of the Cross seeks after the reason for the event itself. Certainly the Cross is a judgment on sin (Rom. 3:25; 1 Cor. 15:3; 2 Cor. 5:21; 1 Peter 3:18; 1 John 2:2). Nevertheless, the faith recognizes as ultimate motivation the love of Christ, the love of God. The most extreme ministry of Christ's love is his surrendering of self to death (Mark 10:45). Paul says with utmost candor: "I live in faith in the Son of God, who loved me and gave himself up for me" (Gal. 2:20; see also Gal. 1:40.

The ultimate motivation for the Cross is God's love. In John (3:16) Christ himself expressly declares: "God so loved the world that he gave (up) his only Son, so that anyone who believes in him may not perish, but may have life everlasting." Here the Gospel speaks of the incarnation in general of the Son, as proof of God's love. Still, the propitiatory death of Jesus is the highest expression thereof. By that death the world, alienated from God, became a redeemed world. Meditation on the faith says the same: "He loved us and sent his Son to be propitiation for our sins" (1 John 4:10). By his nature, God is love (1 John 4:8). What always was and is, now was made manifest in the mission of the Son, since the love of God thereby appeared among men. Thus did the Son reveal the Father. "God demonstrated his love to us by the fact that while we were still sinners Christ died for us" (Rom. 5:8). The love of God came to men beforehand, through the Cross. The sinner was not worthy of being loved. But God made him worth loving by justification and grace. And the creative action of love will make a present of itself forever more. "Will he, then, who did not begrudge us his own Son, but delivered him up for us all, not give us also everything else along with him?" (Rom. 8:32).

Our deliberations on history and on New Testament doctrine attempt to understand the proposition that Christ died for us and for sin. Jesus puts his claim to authority, the authority of his word and of his works, above that of Moses and of the Old Testament Divine Law. He reveals God as the One who makes his sovereign law of grace rule over righteous and sinner alike. His God is quite otherwise than the God of the statutes of Law and worship in Israel. His proclamation was opposed to all the traditions of Israel, since he proclaimed the kingdom as the hope of those who were outcasts of the Law and justice.

Jesus speaks and acts also in a manner contrary to the expectation of the apocalyptics which were so powerful in the New Testament era. For Jewish orthodoxy, his teaching was blasphemy against God. The opposition which was manifested against Jesus from the very beginning was ultimately a mortal enmity. The Law, which Jesus called radically into question, was turned against him and killed him (John 19:7). He died as one "who was reckoned among the lawless" (Mark 15:28). His death was the consummation of the curse of the Law (Gal. 3:13). His death in lonely abandonment (Mark 15:34) was the apparent triumph of the Law. This death of one abandoned by God appeared to be also the refutation of Jesus' confident trust in the communion between himself as Son and the Father.

It was by the staggering event of the resurrection that God acknowledged this outcast as his own. The resurrection of Jesus was understood as the beginning of the eschatological resurrection of the dead. That very outcast was to be "the firstborn of the resurrection" (Col. 1:18). This resurrection was the refutation of the Law, and its termination (Rom. 10:4). But since Jesus was crucified by the Romans, and that as a rebel against them, his exaltation was also the abrogation of the politics and of the gods of the state. This finally comes to light in the opposition which the Apocalypse recognizes between Christ and the Emperor, between the Church and Imperial Rome.

The God of Israel is the God too of the new covenant. But since he is now and forevermore to be proclaimed and to be believed to be the One who raised Jesus from the dead (Rom. 4:24; 10:9), he is no longer the God of the Law that kills, but the God of the grace that dispenses life (Rom. 4:17). The Cross puts an end to all reckoning with one's own righteousness; it crosses out the whole Law of works and of self-glory (Gal. 6:14). Moreover, all Christian preaching and theology treats not merely of the Cross, but must ever be concerned with condemnation by the Cross (1 Cor. 1:19f.).

The notion and belief that the event of the Cross and resurrection of Jesus, taking place only once, is the decisive factor for all generations and times before him and after him, is not an easy one for our mental abilities to grasp and accept. But is it not here that concrete realities are revealed, which are not to be measured by our minds, but by which our minds are to be measured? Here it is disclosed what sin and abandonment of man are. Sin is not merely a state and suppression of human self-awareness, such that a man need only be issued a summons to forget the sin and to vanquish it. It is not merely the consciousness of guilt but the guilt itself which is to be removed. Sin is a reality beyond human disposition. Forgiveness must come, must take place, from a source beyond human capabilities. Forgiveness is not something self-evident, but something unprecedented, something that the full authority of God alone can grant. The biblical doctrine of redemption tells us that in our being lost and in our being saved, no one is alone. That is a condemnation of all; but it also bespeaks mercy and confidence for all.

§ 9. RESURRECTION AND EXALTATION: HISTORY AND MEANING

The New Testament witness to the resurrection of Christ is a report so unprecedented that it is not surprising if it was not simply accepted, but from the very beginning inspired questions and doubts.[87] The resurrection was doubted even within the very circle of the Lord's disciples (Matthew 28:17; Luke 24:11, 41; John 20:24f.; Mark 16:14). The disbelief of Israel (Matthew 28:15; Luke 16:31; Acts 26:23) and of the Gentiles too (Acts 26:8) fixes upon the resurrection. The questions are no less difficult for us. They were very much discussed even and especially in earliest times by exegesis and dogmatics. Critical analysis asks what the first experience and primitive testimony in the New Testament in regard to the resurrection are, and how these are explained further upon investigation.

It may be well to recall right here the undisputed truth that there is never such a thing as naked observation; that which is observed is invariably explained by what is already known.

Perhaps the development of the kerygma can be set forth as follows: The primitive experience is attested to as (*a*) an appearance of Jesus in circumstances in which, since it is described by use of the term ὤφθη (1 Cor. 15:3-8 and elsewhere), (*b*) this appearance is explained as a divine theophany. Another interpretation by means of apocalyptics says: (*c*) He was raised up, he is risen. (*d*) The former terminology emphasizes the work of God in the event, the latter, the proper action of Christ. (*e*) Further inspection designates the raising up as exaltation. The Gospel accounts of the resurrection depict (*f*) encounters with the risen Christ (*g*) in the face of the evidence of the empty tomb. (*h*) The corporeality of the risen Christ is made more and more certain by experientially demonstrative evidence. (*i*) The exaltation is graphically portrayed in the account of the ascension into heaven. (*j*) The three days of resting in the grave are first computed (*k*) and then, by theological reflection, are filled up with activities. (*m*) Preaching expounds upon the meaning that Christ's resurrection has for salvation.

a) 1 Cor. 15:3-9

In many of its aspects the account given by the Apostle Paul in 1 Cor. 15:3-9 is to be esteemed as the oldest testimony.[88] The First Epistle to the Corinthians was written in Ephesus about the year 55 or 56 A.D., a decade, therefore, before the Gospels.

Here Paul makes use, at least in part, of a formula of faith already handed down to him by tradition. He states expressly that he is passing on a tradition (15:3a). Probably it includes primarily 15:3b-5, that is, the clauses introduced by "that" or ὅτι. These verses constitute a formula complete in themselves, which stands out in the text because of its style, its un-Pauline linguistic usages,[89] as well as because of its intensity. Nevertheless, 15:6f. will also contain older tradition, alluded to in any case by Paul's remark inserted in 6b, to the effect that many of these witnesses are still alive. Paul concludes with a recollection of the manifestation of the resurrected Christ that was granted to himself (15:8).

The account is especially valuable in that it does not simply repeat accounts of the experiences of others, as do the resurrection narratives of the Gospels, but is the personal testimony of Paul to his own experience.

In Cor. 15:8 Paul has in mind the manifestation of the exalted Lord that was granted to him on the road to Damascus. He speaks of the same event in 1 Cor. 9:1, "Have I not seen Jesus, our Lord?" This seeing was possible only because the One seen allowed himself to be seen. Again in Gal. 1:16 Paul says: "It pleased God . . . to reveal his Son in me." It was God who was operative, who unveiled the divine Truth and Reality. Furthermore, the statement in 2 Cor. 4:6 may be a reference to the vision of the exalted Christ: "God, who said, 'Out of darkness let the light shine', shone in our hearts to give enlightenment about the knowledge of the glory of God on the face of Christ." In the Acts of the Apostles the manifestation on the road to Damascus is depicted in detail three times (9:1-22; 22:3-21; 26:9-20). After the fashion of a legend about a vision, what for Paul was an interior event is described here as an external transaction.

b) Appearances

In 1 Cor. 15:3-8 Paul characterizes the appearances with the term ὤφθη. In profane as well as in biblical Greek the word signifies in the passive, *he was seen*, and in the middle voice, *he let himself be seen, he appeared*. Paul accepts the term with the formula handed down by tradition, in which it is used also to designate the manifestations of the risen Christ in Luke 24:34; Acts 9:17; 13:31; and 26:16. This is also, however, the term with which the revelation of God is described in the Septuagint. The "angel of the Lord," by way of representing God himself, appeared to Moses in the burning bush (Exod. 3:2, 16). God's own statement is: "I appeared to Abraham, to Isaac, and to Jacob" (Exod. 6:3). The glory of the Lord appeared in the cloud (Exod. 16:7, 10). In the era of salvation "the glory of the Lord will appear" (Is. 40:5). With the passive verb forms ὤφθη and ὀφθήσεται, as occasionally with similar biblical passives, it is the active operation of God that is described (thus in Matthew 5:4, 6). It means, strictly speaking, that such and such a one was caused to see: God appeared to him = God brought him to see God. The glory of God is made to appear by God himself. The word appearance designates the revelation of God.[90]

The description of the appearances of the transfigured Lord, employing the term ὤφθη, is therefore not just an account but already an interpretation. Further themes, interpretative in themselves, which certainly belong to the already traditional formula of 1 Cor. 15:3f., are the declarations that Christ "died for sins", that he "was raised up on the third day", and that his death and resurrection took place "according to the Scriptures".

Paul lists together the appearances of the resurrected Christ to Cephas, to the Twelve, and further on, the one which he himself experienced on the road to Damascus. He describes all of them with the same term ὤφθη. While the Acts of the Apostles (1:3) restricts the appearances to forty days between the resurrection and the ascension, in Paul they are spread out for years, since the appearance on the road to Damascus certainly took place years after the resurrection. For Paul, therefore, the interval of forty days and the ascension does not exist. According to the perception underlying 1 Cor. 15:3-8, the resurrected Christ would seem to have stepped out of the grave into heaven and to have then made his appearances from there; whereas, according to the representation of the Acts of the Apostles he would seem to have delayed first for forty days on earth, and then to have returned to heaven.

The special and invariable characteristic of the appearances of the resurrected Christ consists in the fact that they are never appearances in the night, while sleeping, or through dreams. They are different, thereby, from the revelations in Matthew 1 and 2, as also from other appearances of Christ which are recounted in the Acts of the Apostles (18:9; 23:11), and from other stories told therein (Acts 9:10, 12; 16:9; 27:23). This makes those appearances of the resurrected Christ unique.

In 2 Cor. 12:1 Paul speaks of the "visions and revelations of the Lord", of which he himself could boast. But Paul does not include with these the well-known Damascus experience. The genitive "of the Lord" in

2 Cor. 12:1 is probably the genitive of origin and not an objective genitive, since in the verses following 2 Cor. 12:1, there is no mention of any seeing of the Lord. The appearance on the road to Damascus called Paul to be an Apostle and made him a herald of the gospel. To this he testifies before the Church (Gal. 1:15f.; Acts 9:20). The other visions and revelations were given to Paul when he was already án Apostle. It was not needful to tell of these in the Church, and they had no part in the content of a preaching intended to shape the community (2 Cor. 11:17; 12:1). According to the personal testimony of Paul the appearance on the road to Damascus was of an interior kind, perhaps it might be said, of a mystical kind, whereas the others were of an ecstatic-visionary sort. If the former had its basis in a coming down of the exalted Christ, these others are represented by a mounting up and an enrapturement of the Apostle (2 Cor. 12:2-4). For Paul the revelation of the transfigured Lord on the road to Damascus is unique.

c) Universal Resurrection of the Dead

Succeeding interpretations of the appearances of the resurrected Jesus are expressed in the declarations "He was raised up" and "He is risen". Here the event is understood and interpreted in the light of the apocalyptic expectation, current in the Judaism of that time, of the universal raising up of the dead. It had been developing since the times of later prophecy (Is. 26:19; Ezech. 37; Dan. 12:1-3). At first only the resurrection of the just was expected, while the wicked should remain in death (2 Macc. 7:14; Wis. 3:9-11). Late Jewish apocalyptics went on to the acceptance of the universal resurrection of the dead (*Testaments of the Twelve Patriarchs: Judah* 25:3f.; *Zebulon* 10:1-3; also the *Ethiopic Henoch* 92:3-5).

In the Qumran scrolls certainly at least a belief in the resurrection of the just is attested. "Out of the dust of the worm you raise up the dead man to eternal assembly . . . that he may advance to the place before you with the everlasting host" (1 QH 11:12f.). In the crisis of the endtime the sons of truth will awake to do battle against wickedness (1 QH 6:29-34).

At the time of the New Testament the belief in the resurrection of the dead, even if still contested by some, like the Sadducees (Mark 12:18-

27), was accepted, nevertheless, in the authoritative Pharisaic circles and no doubt quite broadly beyond (Acts 24:15, 21).[91]

In accord with this eschatological expectation, when Christ appeared to the disciples as living, it was inferred that he was raised from the dead. This is clear from 1 Cor. 15:13, "If there is no resurrection of the dead, then neither has Christ been raised." The presupposition is the universal resurrection of the dead. It is on this level that Christ's resurrection is understood. His being raised up, then, was the beginning of the universal resurrection of the dead, accordingly expected as something soon to follow: "Christ was raised up from the dead as firstborn of those who have fallen asleep" (1 Cor. 15:20).

If the resurrection of Christ took place "according to the Scriptures" (1 Cor. 15:4), this refers back to the Old Testament Jewish conceptions. The New Testament enables us to see how this Scripture proof was brought to the fore. An example is the appeal to Ps. 16:8-11, "You will not leave my soul in Hades, nor will you allow your holy one to see corruption." Since this Scripture proof appears both in the preaching of Peter (Acts 2:27) and in that of Paul (Acts 13:35), it must be acknowledged that the community's interpretation of the Scripture passage was broadly disseminated. A further proof is adduced in Acts 13:32-33 with the appeal to Ps. 2:7, "In raising up Jesus, God has fulfilled for our children the promise he made to our fathers, even as it is written in the first Psalm [according to the Jewish numbering current at that time, in which our Psalms 1 and 2 were combined in one], 'You are my Son, this day I have begotten you.'"[92] Raising up is installation into Sonship in exaltation.

The universal resurrection, nevertheless, and as Paul particularly emphasizes, is not a return to the former corporeality. Everything will be quite otherwise than it is now: "What is sown in mortality is raised up in immortality; . . . what is sown a natural [psychic] body is raised up a spiritual [pneumatic] body" (1 Cor. 15:42-44). In our resurrection body we will have, as it were, "a dwelling-place of God, a house not made by hands, existing eternally in heaven" (2 Cor. 5:1). If the resurrection body is a creation of God and is now already prepared in heaven, pushed to the extreme, it might be concluded that Paul's notion is that the dead body remains in the grave and a transfigured corporeality is given by God. It must also be kept in mind that elsewhere Paul speaks

of the sleep of the dead (1 Thess. 4:14f.). Can the figure be understood
in such a way that the dead are resuscitated, raised up to life in personal
existence, similarly to the way in which this happens with one who has
been sleeping?

Paul is a Jew. Jewish anthropology does not, like Greek anthropology,
divide man into body and soul; rather, for the Jew, man is a single living unity. Accordingly, one must assume that the raising up of the dead
restores this integral man. This makes it all the more impossible to understand those writers who raise the question of whether or not Paul
took it that the tomb of the resurrected Christ was empty, as the Gospels
say. Indeed, Paul does not speak of an empty tomb. But what does
that prove?

d) Raising Up and Resurrection

The resurrection of Christ is proclaimed with the formulas: "God
raised him up from the dead" (ἀνέστησεν or ἤγειρεν; Acts 2:24; 3:15;
10:40; Rom. 4:24; 8:11; 10:9; 2 Cor. 4:14; Gal. 1:1; Col. 2:12; 1 Thess.
1:10; 1 Peter 1:21); "He was raised up" (1 Cor. 15:14; Acts 17:31); "He
rose up" (ἀνέστη; 1 Thess. 4:14).

"He was raised" emphasizes the action of God. This is especially clear
in an ancient formulation of the first Apostolic preaching: "But God,
having loosed the anguish of death, raised him up" (Acts 2:24). "He
rose up" bespeaks the action of Christ's own power. Thus, between the
former and the latter formulations, a progress in Christology may perhaps be discerned if certain texts are conveniently ignored. Nevertheless, in the earliest of his extant letters Paul already makes use of the active predication: "If we believe that Jesus died and rose . . ." (1 Thess.
4:14). Paul seems to be making use in a general way of an already established formula of faith.

e) Exaltation

The kerygma of the raising up of Jesus from the dead, under the constant impetus of the faith's logical reflection upon itself, continues its
development with the admittance of the resurrected Jesus into divine,
heavenly glory.[93] The resurrection is completed in the exaltation and
enthronement of Jesus. This conviction finds expression in formulas of
archaic Christology which are used in the Apostolic preaching reported

in the Acts of the Apostles (2:24, 36; 3:15; 4:10). They declare that Jesus was indeed man in his lowliness, but that after the resurrection henceforth "God has made him Lord and Messiah" (Acts 2:36). Messiahship and divine Sonship is first declared not of the earthly but of the exalted Christ.

A similar old Christology is hinted at even in Paul, inasmuch as he makes use of traditional formulas in his Epistles. The formulation of a creed in the process of taking shape can be discerned in the passage: "The gospel treats of the Son of God, born of the seed of David according to the flesh, constituted as Son of God in power according to holiness of spirit on the basis of resurrection from the dead, Jesus Christ our Lord"(Rom. 1:3-4). It is suggestive already of the Apostles' Creed. Its formalized character is apparent in its being structured of sharply antithetical clauses as well as in its content, which maintains an older, properly un-Pauline, two-stage Christology.[94]

To the human and earthly manner of Christ's existence in the flesh, the passage adds another manner of existence, following after and by reason of his resurrection. In this latter manner of existence he was exalted to divinity and was constituted Son of God. This took place "according to the spirit of holiness" or "according to [his] holy spirit". This spirit is not the third divine Person; rather, what is referred to is the divine nature of the Son. God is the primordial Holy One (Is. 6:3), and God is spirit (John 4:24). This nature was long hidden, but now it came forth in power and brought about this new existence. The Christology of Paul progressed in a way opposed to that of the older Rom. 1:3-4. For Paul, Christ is the Son of God from all eternity (Rom. 8:3; Phil. 2:6). That is why Paul prefixes this title to the formula in Rom. 1:3-4.

A further and likewise pre-Pauline testimony to such a Christology is the hymn on the incarnation and glorification of Christ, which Paul receives into his Epistle to the Philippians (2:5-11). "God has exalted him above all." From the humiliation of the form of a slave and finally even that of death on the Cross, God has exalted Jesus Christ to the position of Lord, with universal dominion (on this hymn, see below, § 10, 1e).

The exaltation of Christ is proposed in 1 Tim. 3:16, again in a credal hymn: He was

> Revealed in the flesh,
> Vindicated in the spirit;
>
> Made visible to the angels,
> Announced among the Gentiles;
>
> Believed in the world,
> Taken up into glory.

From the earthly-fleshy sphere Christ is raised up to the heavenly-spiritual sphere. His dominion is acknowledged by the Gentiles and by the world, when the super-terrestrial powers are made subject to it. He is taken up into divine glory (on the hymn, see § 10, 2a).

The manner of viewing the exaltation of Christ and the message about it were shaped by means of the Old Testament Scriptures. The kerygma declares: "Christ is lifted up to the right hand of God." Psalm 16:8-11 was read as a prophecy of the resurrection and exaltation: "I see the Lord ever before me. He is at my right hand, lest I might waver." Peter quotes the Psalm in his Pentecost sermon and interprets it as a saying of David about his future son, the Messiah (Acts 2:25-31).

In the preaching of the resurrection in the Acts of the Apostles the theme of the exaltation of the Messiah at the right hand of God is likewise drawn from Ps. 110:1.[95] The preaching of Peter goes on to explain: "God has raised him up from the dead. . . . He is exalted at the right hand of God. . . . David says of him: 'The Lord said to my Lord, "Sit thou at my right hand"'" (Ps. 110:1). The glorification is described as progressing in two steps: raising up from the dead, and exaltation. In an act of his power, God exalted Jesus with his right hand; and Jesus now sits at the right hand of God (Acts 2:33-36).

In another place the Psalm is continued: "Him God exalted to his right hand as Leader and Savior" (Acts 5:31). In the Christological evidence of the Synoptics, Jesus himself refers to Ps. 110:1, in order to show that the Messiah is not merely David's son, but David's Lord also (Mark 12:36). In the judicial process before the Sanhedrin Jesus awards the seat at the right hand of God to the Son of Man (Mark 14:62). That Psalm verse re-echoes even when it is said — with the distinction of the two stages — that the resurrected Christ is now at the right hand of God: "It is Christ who died, or rather, who was raised up, and who is at the right hand of God!" (Rom. 8:34). The reminiscence is evident, when in 1 Cor. 15:25 Paul draws upon Ps. 110:1 to add: "He must rule as King, until he has put all his enemies under his feet."

The Epistle to the Hebrews makes rich use of Ps. 110. It describes the heavenly enthronement of Christ in terms of Ps. 110:1, "He took his place at the right hand of the majesty on high" (Heb. 1:3). In other places it testifies with Psalm 110:4 to the eternal priesthood of Christ (Heb. 5:6; 6:20; 7:21). The Epistle depicts the exaltation of Christ at the right hand of God under the image of entry of the high priest into the Holy of Holies (Heb. 4:14; 6:19f.; 9:11f.). Christ entered into the heavenly sanctuary with his own blood. Cross and exaltation of Christ are a present unity. The exaltation of Christ at the right hand of God is further declared in Acts 7:55; Eph. 1:20; and 1 Peter 3:22. The reception of the seat at the right hand of God is finally described as an event of past occurrence in the very late text of Mark 16:19.

Even the term "exaltation" is drawn from the Psalms. In Eph. 4:8, Ps. 68:19 is quoted: "Indeed, it says, 'mounting on high, he led captivity captive'". If the Psalm speaks of the triumphal ascent of Yahweh to the mountain of God after the victory over his enemies, who are taken along as captives, the Epistle to the Ephesians speaks of Christ, who at his ascent leads captive the satanical powers dwelling in the zephyrs between earth and heaven. Here the kerygma of the ascension is proclaimed by means of a Gnostic view of the world. Col. 2:15 will also be indicative of this, if the triumphal procession, in which Christ carries along the Principalities and Powers, is likewise his ascent into heaven.

Behind the individual texts there is the broader Old Testament expectation and promise that God humbles the proud and exalts the lowly. This was promised the pious in the Psalms (75:8, 11; 113:7; 149:4) as well as with the prophets (Ezech. 17:24; see also 1 Sam. 2:7). It is especially applicable, however, to the Servant of Yahweh: "My servant will be exalted and glorified" (Is. 52:13). Perhaps it is also recalled in the prayer of the Qumran hymn: ". . . in order to lift up the dead from the dust of the worm, that he may advance to the place before you with the everlasting host" (1 QH 11:12f.). In the raising up of the dead, man is lifted up to God. It is in such terms and concepts as these that the Christological declarations of the New Testament have their advance preparation.

The Gospel of John uses the phrase about the exaltation or lifting up of the Son of Man in a special way.[96] The lifting up on the Cross is a lifting up in glory. "As Moses lifted up the serpent in the desert, so must the Son of Man be lifted up" (John 3:14; see also 8:28; 12:32, 34). The evangelist makes a typological use of the narrative about the bronze serpent in Numbers 21:8f. The Old Testament itself (Wis. 16:6f.) and the rabbis had already concerned themselves with that narrative. In primitive Christian tradition the Johannine interpretation is encountered repeatedly (*Letter of Barnabas* 12:5-7; St. Justin the Martyr, *First Apology* 60; and his *Dialogue with Trypho the Jew* 91, 94, and 112). It is an open question whether John shared in an even older Christian tradition, or whether the tradition goes back to John.

Whereas in the rest of New Testament theology the exaltation or lifting up is consequent upon the humiliation of the Cross, for John the Cross is already the exaltation or lifting up. It is, however, the return to the glory which the Son always possessed beside the Father and the revelation forevermore of that glory (John 17:5).

The New Testament declaration of the exaltation of Christ describes in a graphically vivid way the consummation of God's dealings with his Christ as the eventful beginning, the lasting continuance, and the awaited fulfillment of the dominion of Christ over Church and world.

f) Encounters

The resurrection accounts in the Gospels (Mark 16:1-8; Matthew 28:1-10; Luke 24:1-11; John 20:1-29) portray the discovery of the empty tomb and afterwards in Matthew, Luke, and John, the appearance of the resurrected Christ to the women who in Galilee had belonged to Jesus' circle (Mark 15:40f.), and to others among the disciples. The texts offer the exegete numerous and difficult questions. Difficult to explain is Mark's short account, closing abruptly with the remark: "They said nothing to anyone, because they were afraid" (Mark 16:8). The canonical conclusion, Mark 16:9-20, is an addition from the second century, drawing upon the three other Gospels. It seems probable that the Gospel did not in the process lose some other conclusion originating with Mark, but that from the very beginning this Gospel simply closed with 16:8, however enigmatic that concluding line may be. How did the manifestation which took place in the women's presence become known, so that its having occurred could be handed down, if the women said nothing about it to anyone? Was this said in order to emphasize the fact that the gospel account of the resurrection does not depend upon (unreliable?) women, but upon the Apostles as reliable witnesses of the apparitions? [97]

The persons mentioned in the Gospels as those to whom the resurrected Christ appeared do not seemingly correspond with those enumerated in the oldest account, 1 Cor. 15:3-8. Only the appearance to Peter is mentioned in 1 Cor. 15:5, as in Luke 24:34. While in the Gospels of Matthew, Luke, and John the women are important as witnesses to the empty tomb and to the appearances made by the resurrected Christ, the women are not mentioned in Paul's account. This can scarcely find a satisfactory explanation in the fact that according to the Jewish nation women were untrustworthy or in any case were not to be relied upon as witnesses before the court, when one considers how very much Paul treasured women in the service of the Church (Rom. 16:1-16).

Mark 16:7 and Matthew 28:7, 16-20 tell only of appearances of the resurrected Christ in Galilee, Luke only of such in Jerusalem; and John 20 of appearances in Jerusalem, while the supplementary chapter, John 21, tells of appearances in Galilee. The variations of place are to be explained theologically. Galilee, by reason of the preaching and wonders of Jesus, is a land made holy. Jesus and his disciples return there. The disciples are now united around him, far removed from unbelieving Israel (Mark 16:7; Matthew 28:16). For Luke, on the other hand, Jerusalem is the place of fulfillment (Luke 9:31; 18:31). It is here that the Church has her beginning, from here that she goes forth (Luke 24:47, 49; Acts 1:4, 8). Therefore the manifestations of the resurrected Christ must take place in Jerusalem, as fulfillment and as establishment of the Church. In Luke 24:49 and Acts 1:4 the disciples are directed to remain in Jerusalem, awaiting the pouring out of the Spirit.[98]

According to Mark 16:1 (and the Synoptic parallels) Mary Magdalene is with the women to whom Jesus appears on Easter morning; according to John 20:1 she goes alone out to the tomb on Easter morning. The apparition experienced in each case is described quite differently in various details. Even the reasons for which the women went to the tomb are explained in quite different ways by the evangelists. The Gospels shape tradition very freely in accord with their differing purposes. Did tradition itself no longer have precise recollections of all details at its disposal?

If among the pericopes of the Gospels a constant stream cannot be discovered, this too can certainly be an expression of something of essential significance: that the resurrected Christ did not enter into the constant stream of history. Abstracting from space and time, he can be present everywhere and always in the community. His own saying shows it: "Do not hold me fast" (John 20:17).

Angels are encountered as the agents of God's tidings (Mark 16:5; Matthew 28:5f.; Luke 24:5-7; John 20:12). Are they forthrightly historical figures, or is it really more likely that they are the characteristic apocalyptic angels of explanation and of revelation (Luke 2:9-14; Apoc. 5:2; 7:1; 14:6-20)? The angels and the encounter with them are portrayed in a way that is traditional in epiphanies. Men are terrified upon seeing them, so the first word from the angel is: "Fear not!" (Mark 16:6). The message seems to be a tenet of Christian belief: the One who was crucified is the one who has arisen (Mark 16:6). Each of the evangelists shapes the words of the angel according to the purpose of his own particular narrative. The miraculous portrayal grows. Matthew (28:2) relates: "And behold, a great earthquake occurred. An angel of the Lord came down from heaven, drew near, rolled the stone back and sat down on it." The external appearance of the angels is described. Their countenance is like lightening, and their garments white as snow (Matthew 28:3; Luke 24:4), which makes apparent the swiftness and the majesty of the messengers of God. The angels cause earthquakes, just as in general they shake up the apocalyptic world (Apoc. 8:5; 16:8).

The apocryphal *Gospel of Peter* (9-10 [34-42]) infringes upon the boundaries set by the canonical Gospels, when it depicts the resurrection of Jesus in a fantastic way. The soldiers on watch saw the angels come down from heaven. Then they saw "three men come forth from the tomb and two of them supported the other one, and a cross followed behind them, and the heads of the two reached up to the heavens, but the head of the one whom they led by the hand extended above the heavens. And they heard a voice cry out from the heavens: 'You have preached to those who sleep in death'; and the answer was heard from the cross: 'Yes!'"

g) Empty Tomb

The evidence of the empty tomb appears in the context of the resurrection narratives. The oldest account of the apparitions, 1 Cor. 15:3-7, makes no mention of this. Is the story, as some critics propose, consequent upon the understanding of the resurrection as a solid, corporeal raising up from the dead, and perhaps an apologetic legend? The tendency of apologetic legends is usually easy to recognize. Here any such tendency were very well hidden. First of all, the empty tomb is ambiguous in its presentation; filled with terror, the women flee away from the tomb (Mark 16:8). In our texts the disciples never appeal to the discovery of the empty tomb, whether to strengthen the faith of the Church or to refute and convince her opponents. The tradition is closely bound up with Jerusalem. A lively interest in the matter existed there. If the tradition of the empty grave is regarded by some as legend, there is nevertheless a weighty number of exegetes who affirm it as historical.[99]

h) Corporeality of the Resurrection

The development of the narrative aims at assuring the reality of the resurrection. Paul too, no doubt, by his enumerating the witnesses (1 Cor. 15:5-8), wants to confirm the historical occurrence of the resurrection. When he emphasizes that many of the witnesses are still alive, certainly he is referring to them as guarantors. The true, tangible corporeality of the resurrection must be made evident. The resurrected Christ is not a spirit (Luke 24:37). Jesus comes repeatedly into the midst of his disciples. He shows them his transfigured wounds and has his disciples touch them (Luke 24:39; John 20:27). He has long conversations with them (Luke 24:17-29; Acts 1:3, 6-8). He is with them at table (Luke 24:29f.; Acts 10:41; John 21:12f.; Mark 16:14). As proof of corporeality he eats a broiled fish before the very eyes of the disciples (Luke 24:36-43). The resurrected Christ passes in and out through a closed door (John 20:19, 26). Thomas puts his finger into the wounds of the resurrected Christ and acknowledges: "My Lord and my God!" (John 20:24-29). Nevertheless, it is always clear that the corporeality of the resurrected Christ is immaterial. Nowhere in the Gospels is it suggested that he simply returned into his human existence. Do his conversations follow the usual human manner? The truth of the manifestations is assured while the doubts of the disciples are overcome again and again (Matthew 28:17; Luke 24:11, 37-41; John 20:25, 27; Mark 16:11, 13f.). Doubt conquered is proof secured.

Matthew alone appropriates connected traditions which tell of the sealing and guarding of the tomb (Matthew 27:62-66), of the watchmen being overwhelmed (Matthew 28:4), and of the deception practiced by the Jews (Matthew 28:11-15). An apologetic interest is obvious. The resurrection and the empty tomb ought to be attested to even by the opponents of Jesus. The purpose of the narrative is stated in the text itself: So that the rumor circulated by the Jews and at that time still current, to the effect that the disciples of Jesus had stolen his remains might be refuted (Matthew 28:15).[100]

The Gospel of John, which contains the most remarkable accounts of wonders (§ 6, 2b), likewise contains — probably in accord with a tradition handed down to it — especially impressive stories of the resurrection. More important than any imposing miracle, however, is the personal address of the resurrected Christ and the certitude of recognition which faith prompts in the response (John 20:16). And ultimately the importance of every miraculous event is set aside when they are declared blessed, who do not see but nevertheless believe (John 20:29).

The proof from prophecy also serves as a basis for the preaching of the resurrection. Reflection on the Old Testament Scriptures is of considerable significance for the presentation of the resurrection. The oldest kerygma states that Christ's death and resurrection took place "according to the Scriptures" (1 Cor. 15:3f.; § 9c), *i.e.*, "in accord with the Scriptures". The aspect of exaltation has its basis in the Scriptures (§ 9e). According to the Acts of the Apostles (17:3), in the synagogue at Thessalonica Paul showed the Jews and explained to them "by means of the Scriptures, that the Messiah had to suffer and rise from the dead, and that this Jesus is the Messiah." According to Luke 24:26-27, 46 the resurrected Christ himself disclosed the prophetic statements of the Old Testament leading to the Passion and resurrection. This shows that the community read the Old Testament in the light of Christ's resurrection. John 2:22 states as much: "When he had risen from the dead, the disciples remembered that he had said this, and they believed the Scriptures and the word of Jesus" (John 12:16 and 20:9 indicate the same).

i) Ascension into Heaven

The Gospels agree that the resurrected Christ, before his entry into heaven, delayed for some time on earth. The length of time is not specified in Matthew and Mark, but is limited nonetheless by his appearing only once to his disciples in Galilee (Mark 16:7; Matthew 28:16-20); in John the period lasts for at least eight days (John 20:26); and in the Acts of the Apostles, for forty days (Acts 1:3). Significantly, the corporeal appearances of Jesus are brought to a conclusion with an especially meaningful one, after which he returns to heaven.[101] In this way the earlier declarations of the exaltation of Christ, which exaltation took place outside of space and time and without any human eyewitnesses, was visualized in story and historically concretized. The conclusion of the Gospel of Matthew (28:16-20) permits at least the suspicion of this. It recounts only one story of an appearance. The disciples are gathered about their Lord for the last time on a mountain in Galilee. "When they saw him, they fell to their knees; but others doubted." The faith of the Church lives between worship and doubt. The word of the Lord and his guidance will always have to overcome the disbelief encountered within the Church. The appearance closes with the great missionary command and the promise of perpetually enduring support for the Church. The departure and going home of the Lord is not described, but contemplation of the scene makes it clear enough in any case.

In the twin Lukan writings the exaltation of Christ is visually represented in the narratives of the ascension (Luke 24:50f.; Acts 1:1-11). The short notice in Luke 24:50 could be so understood that Jesus went back to heaven already on the evening of the resurrection. In the detailed narrative in Acts 1:1-11, the resurrected Christ ascends to heaven after having appeared among the disciples through a period of forty days. An explanation of the difference was sought in the supposition that Acts 1:1-11 was a later post-Lukan interpolation, an opinion, however, which is refuted by the positive Lukan peculiarities of style in the passage; or it was suggested that the tradition of a delaying on earth for forty days first came to Luke's attention in the period between his writing of the Gospel and his authoring of the Acts of the Apostles. It is more likely, however, that Luke ignored the external scope of time and presented only an internal passage of time, in order that with the mention of the

ascension the Gospel might arrive at a striking conclusion. The assertion of the forty days would have introduced an anticlimactic element
into the conclusion of the Gospel. In general, this period is the beginning of the Church, and therefore it does not belong to the Gospel. Occasionally Luke ignores differences in time quite unhesitatingly (Luke
9:57-61; 13:1-5).

In the Bible, Old and New Testaments alike, forty is a period of days
that is holy, a period of days blessed by God. After forty days the rains
of the deluge cease (Gen. 7:17). On the fortieth day after the ark came
to rest Noah opened its window (Gen. 8:6). The spies sent to scout out
the land were forty days in Canaan (Num. 13:26). Moses remained forty
days and forty nights on the mountain of revelation (Exod. 24:18; 34:28).
The wandering of Israel in the desert, of salvational-historical significance, lasted for forty years (Exod. 16:35). Elijah wandered forty days
and forty nights before he came to Horeb, the mountain of God (3 Kings
19:8). Jesus himself spent forty days praying in the wilderness (Luke
4:2).

Thus, the forty days of the Lukan story of the ascension of Christ into
heaven ought to be understood as a symbolic number, indicative of a
period of blessings for the disciples. In the story of the ascension there
are features of the notion of enrapturement employed, even if the en-
rapturements were properly told of living persons enraptured without
passing through death. Thus Henoch was seen no more, "because he
was taken away by God" (Gen. 5:24). Elijah rose up to heaven (4 Kings
2:11). The idea of the enrapturement of the righteous is frequently encountered in later tradition (Wis. 4:10f.; Sir. 44:16; 48:9; 49:14; 1 Macc.
2:58) and likewise in the apocrypha.

Other themes in the Lukan account of the ascension pertain to the
stories of epiphanies. A cloud carries Jesus away (Acts 1:9). The cloud
is a sign of the presence of God in ancient times (Exod. 13:21f.; 24:15-18;
40:34-38), as also in the history of Jesus (Mark 9:7) and in apocalyptic
works (Apoc. 1:7; 11:12; 14:14). Even angels to explain matters belong
to the apocalyptic scenario (Dan. 7:16; Matthew 24:31; Apoc. 5:2; 14:6-
20).

Other elements in the account in the Acts of the Apostles permit us to
recognize therein the style of Luke. The presence of two angels in shining garments at the ascension (Acts 1:10; *cf.* Luke 24:4), the cloud

which takes Jesus up (Acts 1:9; *cf.* Luke 9:34f.), the mountain as the place of the revelation of God (Acts 1:12; *cf.* Luke 19:37; 21:37) are used repeatedly by Luke as a narrative vehicle of epiphanies as well as of apocalyptics. To what extent Luke (24:50-52 and Acts 1:9-12) could have employed tradition in his narrative of the ascension is a question difficult to answer. From Matthew 28:16-20 one is able to conclude that that passage is shaped by such traditions. But certainly the Lukan narratives are shaped in both a theological and in a literary way for the most part as the creation of the evangelist.

j) Third Day

In the chronological ordering of events the resurrection is placed "on the third day" (1 Cor. 15:4). The prophecies of the Passion (Mark 8:31; 9:31; 10:34), details of which, it cannot be contested, were formulated after the events, say "after three days". The counting up of three full days is manifestly inexact. Nevertheless, of importance in all the formulas is the use of the significant number three. Although the old tradition did not in any case maintain that witnesses were standing by at the resurrection of Jesus, it was nevertheless fixed at the third day. Counting from the death of Jesus, this third day might have been the day of his first appearance (Luke 24:34; John 20:19), or the day on which the empty tomb was discovered (Mark 16:1). Now, the formula of faith says that Jesus "was raised up on the third day according to the Scriptures" (1 Cor. 15:4). Is it only the raising from the dead that is indicated in advance in the Scriptures (as Acts 2:25-28 and 13:35 find this foretold in Ps. 16:8-11; see above, § 9e), or is the third day also prophetically indicated? In the event that scriptural evidence for such were sought, Hosea 6:2 might be quoted ("He will raise us up on the third day, that we may live in his presence"), or the story of Jonah, who, according to Jonah 2:1, was "three days and three nights in the belly of the fish." Reference to the latter appears in Matthew 12:40 as a prophecy of the resurrection, in a saying of the Lord. Yet this saying, found only in Matthew, is manifestly a later interpretation of the obscure statement about the sign of Jonah (Matthew 12:39). The statement is contradictory to the history of Jesus, who was at most three days but only two nights in the bosom of the earth.[102]

k) Descent into Hell

Theological reflection came to grips finally with the question of the tarrying of Jesus during the time between his death and his resurrection.[103] Christ promised the contrite thief: "Truly, I tell you, today you shall be with me in paradise" (Luke 23:43). According to that statement Jesus too will be in paradise after his death. According to late Jewish apocalyptics (and 2 Cor. 12:4 as well), paradise is the abode of the souls of the elect, the pious and righteous ones of Israel's past and present. If, in accord with the promise to the thief, blessedness after death is communion with Christ, then all the speculation and fantasy developed in the apocalyptics, about the paradise beyond and its joys, is unessential. The dying Christ commends his spirit into the hands of the Father (Luke 23:46, following Ps. 31:6). Even in this hour God is the Father of Jesus, to whose faithful hands he submits his spirit, his life, until the restoration. The words themselves express the certitude of life in death.

There are also declarations to be found, according to which the living spirit of Christ tarried in the underworld while his body rested in the tomb. This was in accord with the usual notion that the dead go down to the underworld and to the fathers. The descent of Jesus into hell is probably assumed at first without reflection; thus in the sermon of Peter in Acts 2:27. An indication of this is probably to be found also in a passage in which Paul (Rom. 10:6-8) makes use of Deut. 30:12f., "Do not say in your heart, 'Who shall ascend into heaven?' — which means to bring Christ down; or, 'Who shall descend into the abyss?' — which means to bring Christ up from the realm of the dead." Christ and salvation are present realities; they do not have to be first laboriously procured. Heaven and the realm of the dead probably do not signify merely a polarity of distances; rather, Paul is calling to mind the tradition according to which Christ made a descent into hell and an ascent into heaven. A similar tradition is probably presupposed also by the use of Ps. 68:19 in Eph. 4:8-10, "He ascended to the heights and took captives. . . . Now this, 'He ascended', what does it mean but that he also descended into the lower regions of the earth?" [104]

The tradition of Christ's descent into hell is expressed unambiguously in Heb. 13:20, "The God of peace has brought the great Shepherd of the sheep forth from the dead, in virtue of the blood of an eternal covenant." The eternal covenant of God with mankind is established in the blood of Christ poured out on the Cross. For the sake of that covenant in blood God raised Christ from the dead, so that Christ can be the exalted Shepherd and Lord.

A developed doctrine of a journey into the beyond made by the spirit of Jesus while his body lay in the tomb is attested to in 1 Peter 3:18-20.[105] Christ was "put to death in the flesh, but made to live in the spirit, in which he went and preached to the spirits in prison, who once were disobedient, when, in the days of Noah, God's patience waited while the ark was being built." In his visible human nature Christ was vanquished by mortality. But in the existence of the spirit he was alive from divine eternity on (1 Peter 1:11), and this spirit cannot die. From that spirit, Christ was made to live again in the resurrection. In the time between death and resurrection Jesus tarried in the underworld. The Epistle can hardly mean the descent of Jesus to the righteous of limbo, as the Church's interpretation often understands it; more likely the text does in fact speak of the disobedient spirits.

Modern exegesis of the kind that relies heavily upon the history of religion explains that the spirits in prison are the sons of God of Gen. 6:1-4, who took to themselves the daughters of men and with them begot the giants. Later Judaism, even that of the New Testament era, busied itself with that myth. The outrageous sons of God were then understood as angels. The narrative is found in Genesis immediately before the story of Noah; for that reason, in 1 Peter it is transposed to the time of Noah.

In its midrashic manner of interpretation, 1 Peter 3:18-20 wants to say that the royal and redemptive power of Jesus is valid for all time, past, present, and future; and that it penetrates everywhere, even into the most abysmal depths of the underworld. It subdues and redeems even the heaviest guilt. In this way 1 Peter makes clear what is proposed to the faith by the mythical story of the descent of Christ into the underworld.

m) Meaning for Salvation

The New Testament kerygma states the salvational import of the tidings of the resurrection. The gospel of the resurrection of Christ conveys even the announcement: "If Christ has not been raised up, then vain is our preaching, vain too your faith. . . . For then you are still in your sins. For then those who have fallen asleep in Christ have perished" (1 Cor. 15:14-18). The resurrection of Christ is the guarantee of life. Indeed, Paul says in a penetrating way, that the Cross and death of Jesus signify and effect the forgiveness of sins. The Cross of Christ, therefore, is to be preached, but even more, his being raised up: "It is Christ Jesus, who died; yes, and what is more, who has been raised from the dead" (Rom. 8:34). For only through his being raised up is the death of Christ made manifest as the salvational work of God.

If the Cross cannot be proclaimed without the resurrection, neither can the resurrection be preached without the Cross. In Corinth, it would seem, there were fanatics who wanted to do just that, who were of a mind that their perfection was already realized and achieved in the resurrection. Paul, however, vigorously maintains that the Cross is not eliminated by the resurrection, but is erected specifically for the sake of the resurrection. Faith knows the resurrected Christ only as the crucified Christ (1 Cor. 1:23). There is no wisdom without the foolishness of the Cross, no glory without the Cross's renunciation (1 Cor. 1:18). Faith and life are human weakness and divine power joined in one (2 Cor. 13:4).

Since Christ conquered death, death in general is vanquished. Just as God raised up Christ, so too will he raise us up (1 Cor. 6:14; 2 Cor. 4:14). The resurrected Christ is the firstborn of the dead (Col. 1:18). Sin and death came forth from the first Adam; from the new Adam, life in every way: "As in Adam all die, so too in Christ all are made to live" (1 Cor. 15:22). The resurrected Christ is "the Author of life" (Acts 3:15; 5:31). The resurrection of Jesus guarantees the eschatological resurrection of those who believe in him. But the resurrection is even now a reality. Those who die sharing the death of Christ are partakers already in his life (Rom. 6:8). For "to this end did Christ die and come again to life, that he might be Lord both of the dead and of the living" (Rom. 14:9). "By baptism into his death we have been buried with him, so that just as Christ was raised from the dead by the glory of the Father, we too might walk in new life" (Rom. 6:4).

Co-resurrection, sharing in his resurrection, is no natural event; rather, it is to be accomplished in faith. Faith is dying and rising again with Christ (Rom. 6:11). Paul is obliged to embody the death and life of

Christ. The Apostle aims to attain to the resurrection from the dead by means of communion with Christ in suffering and death (Phil. 3:10f.). As the one who was raised up, Christ is the one who is alive, in order to make intercession for all (Heb. 7:25). The resurrection of Christ is what makes possible our rebirth and hope thereof (1 Peter 1:3).

In the Apocalypse, accordingly, the exalted Christ is celebrated as the mediator and guarantor of life: "I am the First and the Last, and he that lives. I was dead, and behold, I live unto ages of ages, and I have the keys of death and of the underworld" (Apoc. 1:17-18). By his resurrection, Christ both overcame death and gives the power to overcome death. Christ is "the resurrection and the life" (John 11:25). Whoever believes in him has already passed over from death to life (John 5:25). The eschatology is already present.

How the resurrection of the endtime can and will take place, however, surpasses all imaginational powers. We know only that everything will be otherwise than that which can now be experienced (1 Cor. 15:35-50). It is sufficient to know that the future life is existence with Christ (2 Cor. 5:7f.; Phil. 1:23; 1 Thess. 5:10).

Since Christ, the crucified and exalted One, is the Lord, Paul can say ultimately that the acknowledging of Christ effects man's salvation. "If with your mouth you confess Jesus as the Lord and with your heart believe that God raised him from the dead, you will be saved" (Rom. 10:9). Christian belief in God is belief in the God who raised Christ from the dead (Rom. 4:24). For God showed himself in that work as the one who is ever the Creator and Giver of life (Rom. 4:17). "He that raised Jesus from the dead" is directly the surname or, if you will, the nickname of the biblical God (Rom. 8:11; 2 Cor. 4:14; Gal. 1:1; Eph. 1:20; Col. 2:12).

By way of conclusion it were not out of place to note some considerations on modern questions and answers. Historical criticism is obliged to say that the historian can affirm only — or, at any rate, he can do little more than affirm — that the disciples shared the conviction that Christ had appeared to them alive after his death. This is indisputable. To themselves and to the Church the disciples explained his appearances on the level of their notions and expectations. With that in view, however, the gospel stories of the tomb and of the resurrection signify that the tomb found empty was an external sign of the resurrection of Jesus.

It was, to be sure, ambiguous from the very beginning and required interpretation by means of the word. The testimony of the empty tomb will not be able to be dismissed in a facile manner as legend. But neither will this tradition be able to be reckoned as certainly pertaining to the essentials of gospel belief.

Theological deliberations occasionally question whether the resurrection can be designated at all as historical event. That does not mean that nothing happened, but that what did happen bursts through the boundaries and classifications of history, is on the other side of it and stretches out beyond all history. The resurrection of Christ is to that extent not a subject at all for historical acknowledgement, but a summons to belief. The New Testament itself seems to say as much. "God raised Christ up on the third day and caused him to be visible not to all the people, but to the witnesses chosen by God beforehand" (Acts 10:40f.). Only faith could see and experience the resurrected one, not the "world". Such is the foundation for saying that the resurrected Christ was not a "historical" personality. The latter can be seen by everyone.

Nevertheless, according to the New Testament, it is a historical fact that after the death of Jesus on the Cross the disciples were without any hope; and they were overwhelmed by his appearances, events which ran contrary to all their expectations and dispositions. They responded to the first reports with doubts and disbelief. The appearances are not to be explained on the grounds of the secure faith of the disciples; rather, their faith is to be explained by reason of those appearances.

It is likewise historical that an incalculable influence on the history of mankind emanated from the gospel of the resurrection. Are we to suppose that the source of such great efficacy lay in deceit?

The resurrected Christ says to Thomas, "Because you have seen me, you believe. Blessed are they who do not see me, and believe anyway" (John 20:29). The experience of the corporeal reality of the resurrection, which was granted to Thomas, cannot any longer be the lot of future generations. Their faith does not believe in view of historical evidence; rather, it trusts itself to the word of the gospel, in spite of all criticism and apologetics.

More recent theological attempts to find the meaning of the resurrection could probably also be understood in accord with the above-described mentality. If we may be permitted to cite some of these:

Karl Barth in his *Der Römerbrief*, 2nd edition, Zürich 1921, p. 175, declares: "The raising up of Jesus from the dead is not an event of historical extension like the other events of his life and death; rather, it is the 'unhistorical' reference of his whole historical life to his origin in God."

The view of Rudolf Bultmann is frequently censured as being neither acceptance nor rejection. In the chapter entitled *"Das Verhältnis der urchristlichen Christusbotschaft zum historischen Jesus"* (*i.e.*, "The Relationship of the Primitive Christian Tidings about Christ to the Historical Jesus"), in *Exegetica*, Tübingen 1967, pp. 445–469, Bultmann says among else: "Frequently and mostly as a criticism it is said that according to my interpretation of the kerygma, Jesus rose from the dead within the kerygma. I accept this proposition. It is completely correct, provided that it is correctly understood." The resurrection of Jesus, therefore, is "the expression of the importance of the cross" (R. Bultmann, *"Neues Testament und Mythologie"*, in *Kerygma und Mythos*, Vol. 1, Hamburg 1948, p. 44f.).

Resurrection is truth, since faith and Church remain firm against every objection and contradiction, and confess that God did not abandon his Son in death. This faith and the Church itself are the creation of the Spirit. Renouncing the security and guarantee of historical, probative processes, this faith is the genuine "faith alone" (*sola fides*). The question which presents itself is evident. Did the resurrection take place only within the kerygma, or is a prior event interpreted in the kerygma and heralded as the operative word of God?

Karl Rahner, in the chapter *"Dogmatische Fragen zur Osterfrömmig-keit"*, in *Schriften zur Theologie*, Vol. 4, Einsiedeln 1960, pp. 157–172, makes the following formulation: "The resurrection of Christ is not another event after his passion and after his death; rather, it is the manifestation of that which took place in the death of Christ." Death and resurrection of Christ are "two aspects, received essentially in succession, of a strictly homogeneous event."

Karl Rahner debates whether it were possible "to extract from the experience alone that the faith has with the resurrection of Jesus, those theological perceptions which are already declared by the New Testa-

ment and then by the later confessions of the Church in her Christology."
It seems to be "conceivable that the resurrected Christ can already, by
means of the resurrection alone, be sufficiently recognized as the one
whom the orthodox Christological declarations of Christianity confess"
(K. Rahner, *"Bemerkungen zur Bedeutung der Geschichte Jesu"*, in
G. Bornkamm and K. Rahner, *Die Zeit Jesu. Festschrift H. Schlier*,
Freiburg 1970, pp. 273–283). The Christological titles of majesty, and
even the doctrine of the saving death of Jesus, show the extent of the
exaltation of Jesus.

§ 10. INCARNATION

1. PAUL

The oldest texts of the New Testament which make declarations on
the incarnation of Jesus Christ are to be found in the Epistles of Paul.
Especially notable are the passages in Rom. 1:3f.; 8:3; 2 Cor. 8:9; Gal.
4:4; and Phil. 2:6-11.[106] The more important places in the deutero-
Pauline writings are, above all, 1 Tim. 3:16; 2 Tim. 2:8; Titus 2:11; 3:4.
Almost all of these texts convey the impression of a formulary statement,
or betray at least the traces of such. In part they draw upon credal formulas (Rom. 1:3f.; 2 Tim. 2:8), and in part upon hymns (Phil. 2:6-11; 1
Tim. 3:16). The texts, therefore, extend back beyond the time at which
they were written down.

a) In respect to the time at which they were written, the earliest of
the texts on the incarnation of the Son of God is that in Gal. 4:4-5, "But
when the fullness of time came, God sent his Son, become of woman,
become subject to the Law, that he might redeem those who were under
the Law, that we might receive the adoption of sons." [107]

Paul is to be understood in the light of Jewish apocalyptic expectations.
God is the Lord of the ages. He has set their measure, and guides them
on to their goal. "He has weighed the age in the balance. He has gauged
the hours with a measure, and reckoned up the number of the times. He

does not disturb them nor does he stir them up until the announced measure is reached" (*4 Esdras* 4:36f.). The old era is now concluded in its fulfillment. In many passages the New Testament bespeaks the conviction that the old era, the time of expectation, has run out and the kingdom of God is at hand (Mark 1:15). It is not only the end of an epoch, but the end of earthly and human time and history in general, since God's eternal kingdom is now beginning.

We may perhaps understand the phrase about the fullness of time in respect to the development of mankind and its history, which in philosophy, culture, and religion, as well as in the political structure of the monolithic Roman Empire, were ripe for the coming of Christ. But Paul is speaking not of an unfolding of world history, but of the sovereign activity of God. The contribution of history, according to Romans 1–3, is not a natural preparation for the Gospel, but universal sin. The time did not reach its zenith and fullness through its historical evolution toward Christ; rather, the time is fulfilled through the Son's becoming man.

God sent his Son into world and time. This Son was previously already in real existence as the Son of God. The sending was accomplished in the incarnation. As man, he is the Son of God "become of woman". Paul does not say "born of woman" but "become of woman"; similarly in Rom. 1:3; "become of the seed of David"; and Phil. 2:7, "become in human form." This phraseology is not mere chance. Perhaps the language of it is already formalized. But birth signifies the passage from non-existence to existence. "Become of woman" characterizes the entry into historical existence of one who already existed.

When the Son of God took human existence, he entered also into human history. This means for him, his being made subject to the Law. According to Gal. 3:13; 4:5, it is an oppressive curse. The statement of Paul, therefore, is a declaration of austere humiliation. It was the goal and objective of the Son's incarnation to liberate those who were under the Law. Moreover, they are to receive sonship (Gal. 4:5). The eternal Sonship of the only Son is the basis for the sonship of others. Their sonship is not the ordinary human sonship arising out of nature, but is a sonship imparted by grace.

There is no argument either for or against the Virgin birth of Jesus to be extracted from Gal. 4:4f., although there were or are exegetes who have appealed to the passage in their attempts either to prove or disprove the same.[108] The Fathers, and even Luther and Calvin as well as a part of modern exegesis, interpret the text in reference to the Virgin birth. Certainly one cannot conclude that because Paul mentions no male parent, he is intimating the Virgin birth. But neither can one insist that Paul would have had to have said "born of a virgin", if he had intended to teach the Virgin birth. Paul intends only to attest the true incarnation and true humanity of the Son. Or can one perhaps hear an overtone in the passage, such that this complete incarnation and genuine taking on of humanity would have been abridged by a marvelous conception and birth?

b) "You know the grace of our Lord Jesus (Christ), how he, although he was rich, became poor for your sakes, so that by his poverty you might become rich" (2 Cor. 8:9). Paul is begging for contributions to the collection for the community in Jerusalem. He is bolstering his request with the reference to the example of Christ. The latter abandoned his divine glory beside the Father, which was proper to him as the Son, and chose the poverty of human existence so that he might bring the riches of redemption to the poverty and sinfulness of men. In a similar admonition not to consider one's own good but the good of others, New Testament hortatory form refers again and again to the example of Christ, who emptied himself in the incarnation (Rom. 15:3, 7; Phil. 2:5; Col. 3:13; Heb. 12:2).

In 2 Cor. 8:1-9 Paul recalls the threefold bestowal of blessing ($\chi\acute{\alpha}\rho\iota\varsigma$) which ought to urge the Corinthians on to excellence. He points out first of all the bestowal of grace upon the Church in Macedonia, "whose unfathomable poverty has resulted in a wealth of liberality" (8:1-2). The Corinthians excel in all other charisms; may they excel likewise in the grace of works of charity (8:7). Finally, the Corinthians should be moved by the example of the grace which was made visible in Christ (8:9). Grace, in the present context, is a strength of neighborly assistance bestowed out of God's bounty. Paul is promoting a collection, a most secularly realistic business. But 2 Cor. 8:9 opens its theological dimensions.

c) God's message of salvation treats "of his Son, who was born of David's seed according to the flesh, who was constituted as Son of God in power according to his holy spirit in consequence of the resurrection from the dead" (Rom. 1:3-4). Paul is probably quoting a formula of faith (§ 9e; § 11, 3). The formula combines declarations of lowliness and of majesty. Jesus Christ, who now is Lord, is, insofar as his human descent is concerned, of the progeny of David. Sonship from David does indeed pertain to Christological recognizance. The human existence of the Lord has its dignity in the fact that he was, as David's son, the Messiah.

A statement of the prophet Nathan had promised King David: "Your house and your kingdom shall be faithful to me forever. Your throne shall be firm forever" (2 Sam. 7:16). The promise is made repeatedly in the Old Testament. According to Ps. 18:51; 89:4f.; Is. 11:1; Jer. 23:5, it is expected that the Messiah will be Son of David.

In accord with this Davidic expectation, it was hoped in New Testament times — at least in broad circles — that the Messiah, as Son of David, would re-establish the glory of David's kingdom. In the first century before Christ this expectation is given emphatic expression in the *Psalms of Solomon* (17:4-32).

In the Qumran community besides the priestly Messiah of Aaron's line a royal Messiah of David's lineage was expected (". . . until the Prophet and the Messiahs of Aaron and Israel come" — 1 QS 9:11). A florilegium of Old Testament eschatological texts (4 Q florilegium 1:7-11) also quotes 2 Sam. 7:11-14.

In the New Testament Jesus is attested to as David's Son. But is this to be regarded even from the beginning as an historically understood assertion that Jesus was genealogically a descendant of David? On this question it were well to remember that the claim of belonging to the progeny of David was widespread in Israel; indeed, it was almost a universal claim and meant scarcely more than being an Israelite. Moreover, according to oriental and biblical linguistic usage, the title of son certainly did not signify only genealogical descent, but might be applied to relationship in a very broad sense. There are scholars who hold that our texts do not permit the conclusion that in the family of Jesus there was a living consciousness of belonging to the Davidic house. Did Jesus, then, in embarking on his messianic career, determine his being of David's offspring?

The question of Davidic sonship was broached by Jesus himself in the debate recounted in Mark 12:35-37. The conversation is candid, and

Jesus claims to surpass Davidic sonship when he appeals to Ps. 110:1, wherein David calls the Messiah his Lord. Therefore he is more than David's son. The remarks seem to conform to the rabbinic method of a harmonization of two apparently contradictory passages from Scripture. Modern exegetes ask in this instance also, as they do in similar discussions over the correct interpretation of the Old Testament, whether what we have here does not boil down to a dispute between the primitive Christian community and the Synagogue over the evidence of Scripture.[109]

In a Johannine passage (John 7:41f.) some Jews contend that Jesus, who comes from Nazareth, could not be the Messiah, since the latter must be of David's line and from Bethlehem. The Jewish dogma that the Messiah must be David's son presumably is known to the evangelist; but he makes no comment on the issue. Is the tradition of Jesus' birth as Son of David and in Bethlehem foreign to the evangelist? The "Jews" appeal to the testimony of Scripture (John 7:42). Is there a Christian-Jewish controversy over the interpretation of Scripture mirrored in the Gospel? In the *Epistle of Barnabas* (12:10; Jurgens, no. 35), the assertion of the Davidic origin of Jesus is rejected as an error. The question of the Davidic sonship of the Messiah, therefore, could well have continued as a subject of controversy between Church and Synagogue.

In the Synoptic Gospels Jesus is frequently greeted as Son of David (Mark 10:47 and progressively in Matthew 9:27; 12:23; 15:22; 20:30; 21:9, 15; 22:42, 45). Nevertheless, those who call him such can scarcely have a knowledge of Jesus' physical descent; rather, they want to declare their faith in his messianic dignity, and especially in his power to work wonders.

The earliest written certain evidence of a belief in the genealogical Davidic sonship of Jesus is in Rom. 1:3f. The old formula is repeated in 2 Tim. 2:8, "Remember Jesus Christ, raised from the dead, of David's seed." In Acts 2:25-36 the resurrection and exaltation of Jesus are understood as the promised enthronement of the royal Son of David. The Apocalypse proclaims the glory of the exalted Christ with titles of the promise, now fulfilled. Christ manages the key of David (Apoc. 3:7), he stems from the root of David (Apoc. 5:5). The genealogies of Christ (Matthew 1:1-17 and Luke 3:23-38) are intended to furnish the genealogical demonstration of Jesus' descent from the family of David (§ 10, 3c).

In Rom. 1:3f., the human existence of the Son of David is surpassed and absorbed into the divine-spiritual existence of him who now is Lord. This is brought about through his "spirit of holiness". Since God is the Holy One (Is. 6:1-7; see also *Theology of the New Testament*, Vol. 3, p. 171f.) and Spirit (John 4:24; § 19, 1), spirit of holiness signifies the divine power and glory. It was operative in the resurrection of Jesus and exalted him into the divine world.

A two-stage Christology lies at the basis of the old confession which Paul employs. The human Messiah was exalted to become Son of God. This Christology is indicated also in the oldest sermons of the Acts of the Apostles (2:22-24, 32-36; 3:13-15; 4:10-12). In the Acts of the Apostles Luke will conform to this Christology of an older tradition, which was maintained largely through the liturgy. His own Christology is much more highly developed. For him, Christ is the eternal Son of God come down from heaven (Luke 1:35). Even the Christology of Paul is other than was preserved in the traditional formula which he repeats. For Paul, Christ is the eternal Son of God, who became man (Rom. 8:3; Gal. 4:4; Phil. 2:6).

d) "God sent his Son in the likeness of sinful flesh, and on account of sin and he condemned sin in the flesh, so that the legal demands of the Law might be fulfilled in us" (Rom. 8:3-4). Even the Law of the old covenant condemns sin and wants man to be free of sin. But this Law was not able to achieve the condemnation of sin in such a total way as to conquer it and divest it of its rule. The Law was powerless against man's fleshly nature. The flesh is what keeps man remote from God, and makes man's existence useless. He could not, because of his flesh, fulfill the Law. Sin, on the contrary, was able to use the Law in order to kill men (Rom. 7:11). Then God himself worked the conquest of sin.

Paul stresses the magnitude of the difference. The Son of God comes out of God's world and, as man, enters into humanity. He came "in the likeness of sinful flesh." The body that he had was not merely the illusion of a body (which were, it may be supposed, like the appearance of the Spirit in the shape of a dove at the baptism of Jesus in Mark 1:10); on the contrary, he participated in the universal, absolute human nature. He was fully man, with human knowledge and will, and as man was subject even to human temptations. Christ came in the likeness of sinful flesh.[110] Paul does not say, and indeed he could not say, that Christ came in sinful flesh. For Paul it is quite certain that Jesus knew no sin. "For our sakes he made him to be sin, who knew no sin" (2 Cor. 5:21). Jesus entered into the continuum of the human race, but not into that of sin.

Nevertheless, the sinlessness of Jesus, since he was complete man, is to be referred not directly to his nature, but to his will. The obedience of Jesus vanquished sin. His becoming flesh has really the goal "of condemning sin" (Rom. 8:3). That terse statement has to be interpreted in the light of the whole body of Pauline doctrine. Paul is thinking of the death of Jesus on the Cross. Jesus took death upon himself on behalf of sinners who have deserved death, and thereby satisfies the legal claim of Law and sin. He is the propitiatory sacrifice, effecting reconciliation between God and man (Rom. 3:25). The power of sin, which holds sway over men, is entitively one. The flesh, in which all share, is entitively one. If that power is broken once, it is broken for all. If in Christ sin and flesh are condemned and made powerless, then they are made powerless in general and for all. The new era brings not only the conquest of sin, but the fulfillment of the Law's purpose as well (Rom. 8:4). Now the legal demand of the Law, *i.e.*, righteousness, which was striven after by means of the Law, is at last attained. "The fulfillment of the Law is love" (Rom. 13:10). Now the Law can be fulfilled by those "who walk not according to the flesh but according to the spirit" (Rom. 8:4). All Christian existence is an existence "according to the spirit" (Rom. 8:10).

e) Paul substantiates an exhortation to mutual service with a hymn to Christ, in the Epistle to the Philippians, 2:5-11. "Let the attitude which you have among yourselves be that (same attitude which was manifested) in Christ Jesus:

> "Though he subsisted in the form of God,
>   He did not think being like God a condition to be clung to;

> "Rather, he emptied himself and took the form of a servant,
>   Fashioned in the likeness of men;

"And recognized by outward appearance as a man,
He humbled himself and became obedient to death, even to
    death on the Cross.

"And for this reason God exalted him exceedingly
And gave him that name above every other name:

"So that at the name of Jesus every knee should bend,
Of those in the heavens, of those on the earth, and of
    those beneath the earth,

"And that every tongue should confess,
To the glory of God the Father, that

        " 'JESUS CHRIST IS LORD' " [111]

Phil. 2:6-11 sets itself apart from its context by its solemn and rhythmic style. The verses constitute a rationale for the admonition to humility. This could have been done with a brief calling to mind of the humility of Jesus. The text, however, which is quite cohesive in itself, constitutes a digression which goes far beyond its evident purpose. Moreover, the verses contain words and ideas which are otherwise foreign to Paul.[112] For the foregoing reasons, exegesis is rather thoroughly convinced that at this point in his letter Paul has introduced a traditional hymn, although in many places therein he adapts and interprets the song.[113]

The explanation of the song, especially in view of the terms found therein that occur elsewhere not at all or only rarely, is not entirely certain. The second half of verse 5 has no verb. The thought can be completed: which also was manifested in Christ Jesus. Christ, accordingly, were the model of humility.

Elsewhere in Paul, however, "in Christ" designates existence in Christ. If it means the same thing here, then Christians are not being admonished to live as Christ lived, but in accord with their existence which has its basis in Christ through faith and sacrament (thus in 1 Thess. 1:1). "Let this attitude be in you" can refer to the internal dispositions of Christians, but it can also be an admonition to the mutual service which is internal to the community.

Verse 6 is a declaration on the pre-existence of Christ. This teaching is attested also in other places in the New Testament (§10, 6). Here it is said that the Pre-existent "was in the form of God." [114] In relation to that what does "being like God" mean? Are the two declarations identical in their import? Exegesis proposes two different explanations. According to one view, being-like-God is a heightening and means full divine power and glory. The Pre-existent (it is imagined) might have had to withstand a temptation to usurp for himself full divinity (as the angels were tempted, according to Apoc. 12:7, and as Adam was tempted according to Gen. 3:5, in their pride, to strive after divinity). This would have been a prehistoric, mythical event. In a second view, in-the-form-of-God and being-like-God are synonymous in their meaning; and then the interpretation would be that Christ did not jealously hold fast to his being-like-God, but emptied himself thereof in his incarnation.

In verse 7b the Pre-existent enters, as the historical Jesus, into the life of man which has fallen into the ruin of death. With the term "form of a servant" human existence is characterized in its most extreme humiliation. As a slave he is made subject to men, to the forces of his environment and of the world, and ultimately even to the demoniacal powers. The deepest humiliation is death on the Cross. If "he emptied himself" describes what is really indescribable, a prehistoric event, then "he humbled himself" is said of the historical life of Jesus in his surrendering of himself to death. The rhythmically echoing refrain "even to death on the Cross" may have been subjoined by Paul. The announcement of the Cross is always for Paul his most important task (1 Cor. 1:17-23; 2:2; Gal. 3:1).

The great turning-point is found in verse 9. "God exalted him exceedingly." [115] The turning-point is indicated even grammatically by the change in subject. Until now the talk was of Christ, but here the subject is God. God takes hold and directs the action. And God's action exceeds all bounds. The glorification of Christ is designated as his exaltation (just as in Acts 2:33; 5:31; Eph. 1:20; Apoc. 19:16; see above, § 9e). "Exceedingly exalted" or "exaltation over all" is apparently a terminology dependent upon the ancient view of the world. Christ is exalted to the highest heaven. He receives a new name. According to ancient and biblical understanding, the name signifies the characteristic being of the man (just as today, it will be noted, in our own linguistic usage, the naming of a man to an office signifies his being invested with the powers thereof).

The name above all other names is the name "Lord", which in Old and New Testament language means God (§ 11, 5). As Lord, Christ is enthroned not only for the Church but for the world. The universe is made subject to him. In accord with the ancient conception, there is a distinction of locales; the heavenly, the earthly, and the subterranean. Does this indicate the angels of heaven, men on earth, and the departed in the realm of the dead? Or is it more likely a reference to the powers inimical to God, who are found everywhere and whom Christ, passing through their regions in his exaltation, has vanquished? (Thus in Rom. 8:38f.; Col. 1:20; 2:15; 1 Peter 3:22).

Verse 10 utilizes Is. 45:22-25. The word of Yahweh is promulgated to the people: "Turn to me and you shall be saved, you from the ends of the earth! For I am God, and there is no other. . . . Every knee shall be bent before me, and every tongue shall acknowledge (that I am) God. . . . In God shall all the seed of the sons of Israel be glorified." In Phil. 2:10f. the prophecy about God is transferred to Christ. Indeed, it is God who presents the Ruler of the world, but the world is to do homage to the One Presented. Christ takes the place of God. In Isaiah the judgment of God brings wrath upon the Gentiles and salvation upon Israel. In the song of the Epistle to the Philippians salvation comes to the whole world.

In verse 11, the confession is not "Our Lord", but simply "Lord". Christ is Lord of the world, which is to be acknowledged by "every tongue". Acclamation and genuflection together signify the recognition of the ruler. The glory made public before the world and acknowledged by the world is the honor that the Exalted One possesses in respect to his being the Pre-existing One.

"To the glory of God the Father" probably does not pertain to the acclamation, but is the elucidation offered by the author of the hymn, or it may perhaps be an addition made by Paul. In the New Testament God is the Father of Christ and the Father of men. Do we have here a simple declaration of both? Then the glory of Christ is directed to God. 1 Cor. 15:28 too speaks of this last aim of salvation history when it says: "That God may be all in all" (cf. 1 Cor. 3:23). The title itself, "God's Son", contains the implication of this orientation or classification of Christ in relation to God the Father.

Philippians 2:6-11 may well be the oldest of the Church's hymns to

Christ. And what it lauds is not the teaching nor the miracles of Jesus, nor even explicitly the redemption achieved through him, but his humility and obedience. So too in Rom. 5:19, "Just as through the disobedience of the one man all became sinners, so too through the obedience of the one all will be made just." The obedience of Christ is for the future the way of faith. Redemption is liberation to obedience with him who was himself obedient. "Set free from sin, you have become slaves of justice" (Rom. 6:18).

The Christology of pre-existence will be treated at greater length in its proper place (see below, § 10, 6).

In the theology of Paul the incarnation of the pre-existing Christ is understood as a humbling of himself. Like every man born of woman, Christ is made subject to history; and in a special way, to the burden of the Law (Gal. 4:4). His human existence is poverty (2 Cor. 8:9), in the likeness of sinful flesh (Rom. 8:3) leading to extreme humiliation, even to death on the Cross (Phil. 2:8). In his earthly existence Christ is loaded with the sins (2 Cor. 5:21) of the outcasts and the accursed (Gal. 3:13). His glory is veiled (1 Cor. 2:8). Cross and resurrection are the beginning and basis of salvation. Incarnation is humiliation and prerequisite for exaltation, which is the end of the work of salvation.

By way of comparison it may be recalled that even in the oldest of the Gospels, that of Mark, Christ is the hidden Messiah. His wonders must not be made public (Mark 1:34; 3:12), because his messiahship is not to be proclaimed prior to his resurrection (Mark 9:9; see also § 11, 1). By way of contrast it may also be recalled that Greek theology will later place the emphasis elsewhere. When the Logos takes flesh he brings his human nature into contact with his divinity. He divinizes the human nature which he takes, and with it, collective humanity. The incarnation is already the beginning of salvation, and is in fact the decisive salvific deed. Jesus Christ, "on account of his great love, became what we are, so that he might bring us to be what he himself is" (St. Irenaeus, *Against Heresies* 5, Pref.; Jurgens, no. 248). The Logos "became man so that we might be made God" (St. Athanasius, *Treatise on the Incarnation of the Word* 54, 3; Jurgens, no. 752). This is the Christology of the descent. More recently, dogmatic theology is attempting to bring once again to the fore a recognition of the theology of the ascent.

2. Deutero-Pauline Writings

a) In 1 Tim. 3:16 a song proclaims the incarnation: "All attest as if with one voice that great is the mystery of piety:

> "Who was revealed in the flesh,
>   Vindicated in the spirit;

> "Made visible to the angels,
>   Announced among the Gentiles;

> "Believed in the world,
>   Taken up into glory."

The form of a hymn is clearly recognizable.[116] The text sets itself apart from its surroundings by its rhythm. The song consists of six short lines with an internal parallelism. Each of the six begins with a verb in the passive, a mood which frequently, in the Old Testament and in the New, indicates the activity of God. Each pair of two lines describes in paradoxical opposition the earthly and the heavenly world. And the first line in each pair continues in the sphere in which the former ended, according to the schema ab / ba / ab; or earth-heaven / heaven-earth / earth-heaven. The text has been lifted in its entirety out of another context. The relative clause "Who was revealed in the flesh" is without antecedent and conclusion. Perhaps it is to be completed somewhat in this fashion: "Praise and honor is his due, who. . . ."

The introduction indicates that the text is a profession made by the Church. "All attest as if with one voice, that great is the mystery of piety." The community of the Church joins in one voice in the confession of faith given expression in this hymn. The great mystery pertains to the truth taught by the Church (3:15). This is what is designated a "mystery".[117]

In the Bible this ancient term of the Greek mystery religions achieves a new content. Its usage in the Septuagint and in Jewish Hellenism is the determining factor. From its use in the Book of Daniel onwards, the word carries with it an apocalyptic import. It signifies those secret things which are now hidden, but which will be made manifest in the endtime. In 1 Tim. 3:16 the revelation of Christ is designated and disclosed as just such a mystery, and it is unveiled in the present eschatological era.

In the New Testament "great" usually has its ordinary profane sense, but it also signifies divine grandeur and might. Such is the meaning of the term in Acts 19:28, "Great is Artemis of the Ephesians"; in Eph. 5:32, "This is a great mystery" (namely, that Gen. 2:24 is signified by the union of Christ and his Church).

"Piety", sometimes rendered "godliness" in English, is a word familiar to the Greek of early Jewish writings and of the New Testament, especially so in the Pastoral Epistles (see *Theology of the New Testament*, Vol. 3, p. 224f.). In 1 Tim. 3:16 the term suggests faith and living; probably "Christianity" or "our religion" could be substituted for it. What we have here, then, is a very old answer to the question posited again and again, as to the substance of Christianity. This substance is Christ; for 1 Tim. 3:16 is a hymn celebrating Christ.

The hymn explains the mystery of Christ. "He was revealed in the flesh." Paul speaks mostly of the revelation now taking place. In the gospel even today the righteousness of God (Rom. 1:17f.; 3:21) is revealed. God makes the knowledge of himself manifest through preaching (2 Cor. 2:14). The life of Christ must be made manifest in the life of the Apostle (2 Cor. 4:11).

Post-Pauline texts are more likely to speak of the revelation that has already taken place. "The mystery hidden for ages has now been revealed" (Col. 1:26). "The mystery wrapped in silence through the ages has now been revealed" (Rom. 16:25f.; Rom. 16:25-27 is, no doubt, post-Pauline). In the Pauline texts the revelation is taking place in the present time; in the deutero-Pauline writings, with the inclusion of 1 Tim. 3:16, it has already taken place, and the statements look back upon it. This is a technique peculiar to a later time. One looks back upon that which has already happened. In the present, revelation no longer takes place; it is the treasure of the faith (1 Tim. 6:20; 2 Tim. 1:14).

"Flesh" in St. Paul usually designates the state of the natural man, inimical to God (see *Theology of the New Testament*, Vol. 1, pp. 133-136); but here in 1 Tim. 3:16 it is simply body and life (as also in Rom. 1:3; 8:3; 9:5). John 1:14 describes the incarnation in a similar fashion: "The Word became flesh." Pre-existence is not the subject of discussion in 1 Tim. 3:16, but certainly it is nonetheless presumed. A time of concealment preceded the time of revelation.

He was "vindicated in the spirit." "Spirit", juxtaposed to "flesh", designates the divine world. Thus Christ is "David's son according to the flesh, Son of God according to the spirit of holiness" (Rom. 1:4). "Christ was put to death in the flesh, but brought to life in the spirit" (1 Peter 3:18). In the message of Paul, the sinner is justified in the sight of God (Rom. 3:24). This meaning of the word is not possible in 1 Tim. 3:16; for Christ was not a sinner. In the Gospel of John (16:10) the going of Jesus to the Father reveals the justice of Jesus before the world, since, exalted in the heavens, he is received by the Father. It is in this sense that 1 Tim. 3:16 is to be understood. Christ was justified by divine power, which power endorsed him before the world in his being raised up, just as it does now in the mission of the Church.

"Made visible to the angels." The angels may be, even as in current linguistic usage, the good and holy spirits. The exalted Lord was presented to them upon his entry into heavenly glory. On the other hand, it may be that "angels" signifies the spirit world in general, even evil spirits and satanic beings (as in Matthew 25:41; 2 Cor. 12:7; Apoc. 12:7-9). Christ triumphs over this spirit world at his heavenly enthronement as Conqueror, a notion like that attested to in Rom. 8:38f.; Phil. 2:10; Col. 1:20; 2:15; 1 Peter 3:22.

Christ was "announced among the Gentiles." The preaching of the gospel among the pagan nations is described as an event on earth in juxtaposition to the heavenly world. For the concept of preaching, the New Testament uses more than thirty words, among which "announced" or "proclaimed (κηρύσσειν) is one of the more important. Our modern poverty in regard to terms cannot but result in a certain impoverishment in conceptualization.

"Believed in the world." The result of the preaching of the gospel is faith. This faith, however, is situated "in the world". It is not something hidden in the heart, it is not something possessed only by the individual faithful, but it has and lays claim to a public acceptance. Faith assembles the Church. The world is not faith-ful; rather, it is indifferent or disbelieving. Faith, however, is in the midst of this world. Considering what was then the situation of the Church, this is a most extraordinary declaration. The Church consisted of a few small communities in the many and great cities of the ecumene. The world scarcely knew of its existence. But the faith knows and recognizes that the decision has been made. The gospel has been proclaimed among the Gentiles, it is believed in the world. The world is redeemed, it belongs to Christ. In just such an overwhelming consciousness of the mission of the Church, Paul declares along with Ps. 19:5, "Their call has gone out over the whole earth, their words have penetrated to the boundaries of the ecumene" (Rom. 10:18).

"Taken up into glory." In the New Testament narrative of the ascension into heaven the exaltation of Christ is likewise described: "He was taken away from them, up into heaven" (Acts 1:11). Nevertheless, such references and certainly the graphic narration of the ascension are found only in the two works of Luke (Luke 24:51; Acts 1:4-14). These narratives were shaped largely by Luke (§ 9i). The story of the ascension into heaven can hardly have been known, the critics presume, by the author of the First Epistle to Timothy. It would seem, therefore, that the Epistle refers in a general way to the exaltation, the establishing of Christ as Lord over Church and world, and the continuing reign of the Exalted One.

Exegesis questions whether in 1 Tim. 3:16 a sequential principle can be discerned. Some have attempted to find herein a chronological ordering of the life of Jesus. If the first mentioned revelation in the flesh refers to the incarnation, then the first thing to which attention is called is the beginning of the human life of Jesus. The last line can be understood in reference to Christ's ascension into heaven. One could attempt to find a chronological order in the rest of the declarations. Justification in the spirit has been referred to the baptism of Jesus, at which, through the appearance of the Spirit, he was shown to the world as Messiah. In Matthew 3:15, moreover, the baptism of Jesus is designated as "the fulfillment of all justice." The angels have been understood as those who, according to the Gospels, served the earthly Christ: in the infancy narrative (Luke 2:13); after the temptations in the desert (Mark 1:13); in the resurrection narratives (Matthew 28:2-7); and in general there were angels attending upon Christ (John 1:51). The next event mentioned, then, would be the proclamation of the gospel by the apostles, and the belief accorded the gospel, and finally the return of Jesus into heaven. In this way the hymn would be a presentation of the historical course of the life of Jesus. The epiphany of Christ would appear to be a unified process, even if depicted in stages, from his birth to his ascension.

Nevertheless, the above chronologically ordered interpretation is hardly the viewpoint of the hymn. It does not evolve any historically ordered sequence of events, but is proclamation of the epiphany and majestic rule of Christ. In its praise and glorification it announces as if already completed that which is now taking place and must yet take place on earth.[118]

b) The Pastoral Epistles (2 Tim. 1:10; Titus 2:11; 3:4) speak of the incarnation of Christ as his epiphany; and they include therein his whole life, from his becoming man until his death. "Grace is now revealed through the epiphany of our Savior, Christ Jesus" (2 Tim. 1:9f.). His epiphany effects the conquest of death and the winning of life. The manifestation and its efficacy are continued in the proclamation of the gospel, in which grace is bestowed.

In other places the epiphany is not postulated as that of Christ himself, but of the salvation effected through him. "The grace of God has appeared to all men unto salvation" (Titus 2:11). With this grace Christians must live temperately and justly and piously in the expectation of the Savior's definitive epiphany (Titus 2:13). "The goodness and kindness toward men of God our Savior has appeared" (Tit. 3:4).

The three aforementioned texts (2 Tim. 1:9-10; Titus 2:11-13, and 3:4) employ to a great extent the cultic language of their own time and world. Certainly this is true in the instance of the word and concept epiphany (ἐπιφάνεια).[119] The term signifies the appearance of the otherwise hidden divinity in an action of assistance or in some other sign. Greek poetic literature tells of many apparitions of the gods. Myths tell of establishments of cult through the apparitions of gods and of their appearances, bringing with them blessings anew, during cultic celebrations. In such an event god comes down from heaven into the congregation. For such an event, Hellenism shapes the term ἐπιφάνεια. Religious documents extol numerous divine epiphanies, rich in graces. Even in the civil ruler divine power is epiphanic. Rulers bear the epithet ἐπιφάνής (like Antiochus Epiphanes). The state visit of a potentate is celebrated as an epiphany.

The Old Testament knows of many wonderful divine appearances, especially at various turning-points in history; and it expects the definitive eschatological epiphany on the "Day of Yahweh." Written under a very strong Hellenistic influence, the Second and Third Books of Maccabees tell of the appearances of heavenly figures and for these concepts they employ the terminology of apparitions (2 Macc. 3:24; 5:4; 10:29; 11:8; *3 Macc.* 2:9; 5:51; 6:9). When the Pastoral Epistles describe the incarnation of Christ as an epiphany they are speaking in that style which had already been shaped for them by the Greek religion as well as by Hellenistically influenced Judaism.

There are other terms also in the texts we have cited from the Pastoral Epistles which pertain to the same area of religious language. Christ is designated as Savior (σωτήρ, 2 Tim. 1:10; Titus 3:4; σωτήριος θεός, Titus 2:11). Other divine redeemers are also called such (§ 11, 4). In the worship of Greek epiphanic gods, the term grace (χάρις) is used (*cf.* Titus 2:11). Kindness in regard to men (φιλανθρωπία and χρηστότης, Titus 3:4) are celebrated even as the virtues of a ruler. This religious terminology is employed also by the Septuagint (§ 20).

How very much the proclamation of the incarnation of Christ utilized the language of the times can also be seen from the celebrated inscription found at Priene about the year 1890, and which, on internal evidence, can be dated in the year 9 B.C.[120] It makes public the decision that for the future the year is to begin on the birthday of the Emperor Augustus, on September 23, and it is on this day that new officials are to take office. In this inscription we read:

> "The birthday of the most divine emperor has given to the whole world a new outlook. It would have fallen into ruin if the emperor had not appeared, as the common good fortune of all. For this reason all men rightly acknowledge the emperor's birthday as the beginning of life for themselves, and the beginning of their vital powers. At last the time is at an end when a man might have to regret having been born. It is impossible to give thanks in any appropriate way for the great benefactions which this day has brought. The providence which rules over our life in every detail has filled this man with such great gifts for the salvation of mankind, while it has sent him to us and to coming generations as savior. He has put an end to every war and has set all things nobly in order. In his epiphany the hopes of our ancestors are fulfilled. He has surpassed all earlier benefactors, and those of the future can never institute any greater welfare. The birthday of the god was, for the whole

world, the beginning of the gospels which are proclaimed about him. Let the reckoning of time begin from his birth onwards."

This is a language many terms of which remind us of the New Testament and especially of the infancy narrative about Jesus. The birthday of the emperor is a gospel, and indeed, the first gospel. Further gospels are tidings of his accession to the throne or decrees of clemency. The emperor bears the titles savior and god. Over Bethlehem the song of the angels resounded: "I announce to you the gospel of great joy! Today a savior is born to you!" (Luke 2:10f.). New Testament epiphanic terminology also names Christ Savior and God (Titus 3:4).

The birth of the emperor is the beginning of new life. Christ too is the life of the world (John 1:4; 6:51). The hopes of ancestors were fulfilled in the birth of the emperor. Christ too is the fulfillment of the expectations and hopes of Israel (Rom. 9:4) and of the Gentiles (2 Cor. 1:19f.). Thanks is to be given henceforth for the birth of the emperor. For the appearance of Christ in the world the great thanksgiving of the Eucharist is celebrated evermore.

Fragments of the Priene inscription were found at several places in Asia Minor. The inscription had been set up in many places, perhaps even in the very marketplaces where the Apostles proclaimed the Christian gospel. The political and religious language of the inscription was known everywhere and was everywhere understood. Therefore the New Testament speaks this same language. If it accepts this language, it is because it wants to oppose the many gospels with the one gospel; the gospel of the birthday of the emperor and the birthdays of many kinds of saviors with the gospel of the birthday of the one true Savior; the many gospels of renderings of mercy and favor with the gospel of the fullness of grace.

If the gospel speaks the language of its own time, this indicates also that it recognizes the hopes and yearnings of its time as legitimate. What it wants to say thereby is what Paul preached to the Areopagus: "What you are worshipping without knowing it, that do I proclaim to you!" (Acts 17:23). Paul was convinced that in times past God had not left even the pagans utterly in the dark (Rom. 1:18-32; 2:14). The Gentiles' hopes of salvation found expression in their myths. If mythological traits are made use of in the gospels, it should but indicate that Christ is the fulfillment even of the myths. "As many as are the promises of God, their 'Yes' is found in him" (2 Cor. 1:20).

The inscription of Priene states that for the future the year is to begin with the birthday of the god and savior, Augustus. Even this honor was transferred to Christ. For a long time the new year began with the liturgical birthday of Christ on December 25th. For practical reasons the beginning of the year was shifted to the beginning of the next month after the 25th of December, January 1st, which, moreover, was already serving in some areas in antiquity as the beginning of the year. If the gospel transferred to Christ the language which was being used in honoring the emperor, this signifies that One stronger than the emperor has come and has taken from him his power and his splendor — as is remarked by Adolf von Harnack.

3. Synoptic Gospels (Birth Narratives)

The Gospels of Matthew and of Luke contain detailed presentations of the prehistory, birth, and earliest infancy of Jesus. It is from these narratives that the theology of the incarnation is to be developed.[121]

a) Literary Genre and the Shaping of Tradition

The infancy narratives of the Gospels present special and rather difficult questions to historical research and exegesis. In their literary genre and in their utilization of tradition the narratives are of a special type. This must be kept in mind in any consideration of their historical and theological content.

Matthew and Luke agree in essential details (names of the parents of Jesus, conception through the Spirit and Virgin birth, birth in Bethlehem, youthful years in Nazareth), although their accounts are not directly coincident in any section, nor indeed, in any sentence. In part it is still uncertain how the accounts are related to each other temporally or to what extent they depend one upon the other.

After telling of the circumcision of Jesus and of his presentation in the temple on the fortieth day after his birth (Luke 2:21-38), the Gospel of Luke immediately remarks: "When they had done everything enjoined by the Law, they returned to Galilee" (Luke 2:39). The evangelist seems to have no knowledge of such events as the visit of the Magi, the murder of the innocents in Bethlehem, and the flight of Jesus' parents into Egypt (Matthew 2:1-21), which might have found a place between Luke 2:38 and 2:39. Matthew (2:22f.) seems to be unaware that the reason the parents of Jesus choose Nazareth as their dwelling place is that Nazareth was in fact their home before the birth of Jesus.

Both evangelists (Matthew 1:1-17; Luke 3:23-38) deem it advisable to record genealogies of Jesus. But their genealogies, when they depart from Old Testament lists from Abraham to David, differ entirely from each other; nor can their differences be reconciled in any absolutely convincing manner. The assertions about a census for tax purposes when Quirinius was governor (Luke 2:1f.) seem not to be in agreement with reports available from profane history.

The star in the narrative about the Magi (Matthew 2:2, 9) has been called a legendary theme, comparable to other accounts, according to which apparitions of light herald the birth and advent of great men, like the reports according to which pious heroes were guided by apparitions of light.[122]

The slaughter of the innocents at Bethlehem (Matthew 2:16) is not found in profane sources, or at any rate, there is no clear mention of it. Since it accords well with the brutal cruelty of Herod, it may be that some kind of tradition has found entry into the Gospel at this point.

Luke unites and intertwines in an artistic way the infancy narratives about John, later the Baptist, and Jesus, so that the often wonderful events in the history of John are surpassed now and then in the history of Jesus. The families of Jesus and of John were known to each other and were related (Luke 1:36-56); yet the Baptist later states that he did not know Jesus (John 1:33). Luke is probably making use of traditions gleaned from the disciples of the Baptist, the traces of whose community can sometimes be discovered in the New Testament (Mark 2:18; Luke 11:1; Acts 19:1-7).

In their respective Gospels the infancy stories of Matthew and Luke were probably written about the year 90 A.D. During this long period the remembrance of the story seems to have become in part uncertain. But also during this same long period the story would have become thoroughly pervaded by theological significance. Numerous appearances of angels are proper to both of the Gospels that deal with the infancy.

At the capture on the Mount of Olives Jesus says to Peter: "Do you not know that I can ask my Father and he will give me twelve legions of angels to stand at my side?" (Matthew 26:53). Yet Jesus declines to do so. The Gospels tell nothing of any actual intervention of angels in the life of Jesus. Mark 1:13 and Luke 22:43 are exceptions, in which, in the case of Luke 22:43-44, it is questionable, since the verses are found only in a portion of the manuscript evidence, whether they belong to the original text. Angels do not appear again until the account of the resurrection (Matthew 28:2-7). In the infancy narrative of Matthew (1:20; 2:13, 19) as well as that of Luke (1:11-20; 26-38; 2:9-14) angels make their entrances and exits as heavenly messengers sent to men. They announce the birth of John (Luke 1:11) and of Jesus (Matthew 1:20; Luke 1:26). Angels make an entrance in the capacity of heavenly heralds, to explain what has taken place (Luke 2:9-14). In apocalyptic passages angels appear before men as messengers and interpreters of revelation (Matthew 13:41; Apoc. 5:2; 7:2; 8:2; 15:1).

In a very similar way to that recounted in the story of Jesus' birth, heavenly messengers announce the birth and destiny of great personages of prehistory. Thus the message of an angel comes to Ishmael (Gen. 16:7-13); to Gideon (Judges 6:11-21), to Manoah and his wife, concerning Samson (Judges 13:3-24). Old and New Testament stories about angels and their announcements have common themes. The appearance of the angel terrifies men, and they must be put again at their ease (Judges 6:22f.; 13:23; Is. 6:5; Dan. 8:17; 10:11f.; and Luke 1:12f.; 1:29f.; 2:10). The proclamations of a birth sound almost alike (Gen. 16:11; Judges 13:3; and Luke 1:31). The importance of the child is revealed (Gen. 16:10-12; Judges 13:5; and Luke 1:15-17; 1:31-33). A sign is given (Gen. 15:8; Judges 6:36-40; 1 Sam. 10:2-7; 4 Kings 20:8f.; and Luke 1:18-20; 1:36; 2:12). It is incontestably clear that Luke's tableau of the annunciation is shaped in accord with Old Testament prototypes.

While ideas and teachings about angels are rather meager in the earlier times of Israel, the later Old Testament (Dan. 3:28; 7:10; 9:21; 12:1) and the Judaism subsequent thereto developed this doctrine quite broadly. In Luke 1:11 the angel is called "angel of the Lord" (ἄγγελος κυρίου), which is apparently a translation of *mal'akh Yahweh*. The *mal'akh Yahweh* is the product of ongoing theological reflection in

Israel (§ 21, 2). Whereas earlier one was able to say quite unabashedly that Yahweh spoke and dealt with men, later God retreats into the distance. Now angels enter as God's messengers to men.

In Luke 1:19 the Archangel Gabriel says to Zechariah: "I am Gabriel, who stands in the presence of God." This is manifestly human conceptualization and language, whereby the angels of God's household are at his throne. Moreover, the passage accepts contemporaneous notions, since Judaism too of that time speaks of those angels who are especially close to God as the "angels of the countenance", that is, the angels who are permitted to look upon God's face (*Testaments of the Twelve Patriarchs: Levi* 3:5; *Judah* 25:2; *Book of Jubilees* 31:24; and more recently at Qumran, 1 QH 6:13; 1 QSb 4:25f.; see also Matthew 18:10). In the angels, God's power and glory appears among men.

In the infancy narrative of Luke there are three songs: the Canticle of Mary (1:46-55), the Canticle of Zechariah (1:68-79), and the Canticle of Simeon (2:29-32). The infancy narrative in Luke's Gospel — if we may trust the indications of form and content — goes back to Jewish Christian tradition, whether this came to Luke orally or in writing. These Canticles stem also from this tradition. All three of them reflect the spirit of Old Testament poetry, and the Hellenist Luke himself can hardly have so constructed them. Modern critics are convinced that the Canticles are not historical testimonies, but pious reflections, liturgical choruses as it were.

b) Jesus, the Christ

In the Gospels the present glory of Christ is never absent from what is being asserted. The crucified Messiah, if the message is not to be meaningless, could only be proclaimed as the resurrected Christ. The infancy narratives already testify to Jesus as the Exalted One. It is the later confessions of faith and credal formulas that are being proclaimed. The Child Jesus is already presented as the new Moses, as Son of David, and true King David. He is the Messiah, Savior and Lord (Luke 2:10). He is conceived of the Spirit, and as Son of the Virgin he is God's Son (Luke 1:35). Here Jesus is, from the very beginning, accorded those high titles which, in the New Testament, are the results of a lengthy evolution of Christian faith and doctrine.

aa) The New Moses

The story of the birth of Jesus as told by Matthew is seen to have certain relationships with the story of Moses in the Book of Exodus and even more clearly with the later Haggadah about Moses.[123] The Pharaoh issues a command to kill the new-born Israelite boys. Herod searches for the infant Jesus and murders the infant boys in Bethlehem. Moses escapes the snares of the Pharaoh, Jesus those of Herod.

The evangelist himself lets it be understood that he is following the story of Moses. In Matthew 2:20f., he recounts as the word of the angel to Joseph: "Those who sought the life of the Child are dead." Consequently, "Joseph took the Child and his Mother and went into the land of Israel." In the Old Testament story of Moses, God speaks to Moses, who has fled into Midian: "Return to Egypt; for all those who sought your life are dead. And Moses took his wife and his sons and put them on an ass and returned to Egypt" (Exod. 4:19-20). Matthew is writing the story of the infancy of Jesus with the memory of the story of Moses as a prototype.

Other themes and references are in accord with the Haggadah about Moses, in particular as it is told by Josephus (*Antiquities of the Jews*, 2, 205-215). The Pharaoh learns from his astrologers about the imminent birth of Moses, the liberator of Israel. In Matthew 2:1f. Herod obtains information from astrologers about the birth of the Messiah-King. According to a legend about Moses, God announces to Moses' father in a dream both the endangering and the rescuing of the child (*cf.* Matthew 2:13). The Egyptians are terrified when the predictions concerning Moses become known (cf. Matthew 2:3). According to later legend (ca. 250 A.D.) the house was filled with light when Moses was born (*cf.* Matthew 2:2, 9).[124]

If the story of Moses has been impressed upon the story of the birth of Jesus, what is expressed thereby is that Christ is the new Moses. Originally the parting words of Moses were probably only a promise of the continuation of the prophetic office in Israel; but those same parting words came to be regarded as a prophetic reference to the Messiah: "The Lord your God will raise up for you out of the midst of your brothers a prophet like me" (Deut. 18:15 = Acts 3:22; see above § 5). A midrash says in reference to Moses and the Messiah: like the first redeemer, so too the last. The New Testament recognizes the fulfillment and confirms it. Moses gave the fathers in the desert bread from heaven; Christ not only gives but is the true Bread from Heaven (John 6:32-59). Christ is more than Moses. As the Son and Master of the house, which is the Church, Christ is superior to Moses, who was a servant in the house (Heb. 3:2-6).

Joined like a codicil to the story of Moses is the fact that the liberation of Israel from Egypt served as prototype for the New Testament redemption from the servitude of sin and of Satan. The typology probably begins already in the New Testament when it (Matthew 2:15) recognizes in the return of Jesus from Egypt the fulfillment of a prophecy: "Out of Egypt I have called my Son" (Hosea 11:1). The sacraments of baptism and of the Eucharist are prefigured in the passage through the sea and in the gift of manna (1 Cor. 10:1-4). Like the serpent elevated by Moses, so too does Christ save, elevated on the Cross (John 3:14). The redeemed sing the song of Moses and of the Lamb (Apoc. 15:3).

bb) The Son of David

The very first sentence of Matthew's Gospel (1:1) states that Jesus is the Son of David.[125] Jesus is born in Bethlehem, the city of David (Luke 2:4, 11). God will give him the throne of his father David (Luke 21:32). Joseph, the father of Jesus, is of David's lineage (Matthew 1:16; Luke 1:27; 3:31). The Gospels state quite unambiguously that Jesus is only the putative son of Joseph (Matthew 1:20; Luke 1:35). The breaking off of the physical sequence of generations (Matthew 1:16; Luke 3:23) is bridged over by Jewish law, according to which the acceptance of a child by the father validates the father-son relationship. A principle of rabbinic law declares: "If anyone says, 'This is my son', then it is his son."[126] Thus the inference drawn by some that the genealogies, since they lead to Joseph, depend upon a tradition according to which Joseph were the real father of Jesus, is not convincing.

By means of the genealogies (Matthew 1:1-17; Luke 3:23-28) the title Son of David is genealogically established. In their solicitude for the purity of Jewish blood, families in Israel prepared and preserved genealogical tables, as is attested by Josephus (*Autobiography* 1) as well as by the New Testament itself (Luke 2:36; Rom. 11:1; Phil. 3:5). The genealogical tables of Jesus in the Gospels are in agreement with each other from Abraham to David, where they go back to Old Testament genealogies (1 Chron. 2:1-15; Ruth 4:18-22). From David on the line continues in Matthew (1:6) with the main branch and Solomon; but in Luke (3:31) it follows a secondary branch with Nathan. The result is that two different fathers are named for Joseph (Matthew 1:16; Luke 3:23). Since the time of the Fathers of the Church exegesis has been at pains to reconcile the differences; the precise historical value of the tradition of the genealogical tables remains difficult to assess.

The genealogical tables are not intended, anyway — or at least it is not their primary purpose — to provide a historiography. This is as good as stated in the surprising summation: "All the generations from Abraham to David are fourteen generations, and from David to the deportation to Babylon fourteen generations; and from the deportation to Babylon to Christ fourteen generations" (Matthew 1:17).

Matthew finds a mysterious numerical schema operative in the genealogy of Jesus. We cannot say with certainty what Matthew intends the number fourteen to signify. Often the following explanation is accepted:

In Hebrew, letters have also a numerical value according to their position in the alphabet. In the three letters of the name David, DWD in Hebrew, D is 4, W is 6, and D again is 4. By adding the digital values of the letters of the name David, 4+6+4, we arrive at the sum total 14. When Matthew finds the number 14 three times in the genealogy of Jesus, probably what he wants to show thereby is that the genealogy of Jesus bears the portent of David in a threefold way, and indicates to anyone who understands the secrets of God, that Jesus, who appears at the end of the genealogical table, is the promised Son of David, the new King David, which is equivalent to saying, the messianic King.

The genealogical tables may have still another meaning. In the Old Testament long genealogical registers are found again and again. Such is the case with the Books of Genesis, Ruth, and Chronicles. For the Israelite nation and for the Bible, a genealogical table is a means of stating something. Genealogical lists attest to the special biblical image of God and of man. The biblical God is the personal God of history. He deals with all generations of men from the beginning until the end of time. He is not the God of the philosophers, but the God of Abraham, of Isaac, and of Jacob (Blaise Paschal). The continuing communion of operation and of visitation between God and men is finally completed, and certainly in a way far beyond anything that man could expect, in the gospel of God's becoming man in his Son. By the fact that the lists of generations go on in unbroken succession and necessarily arrive at Christ, it is asserted that all history leads to Christ. "Through him and unto him is everything created" (Col. 1:16). If in the genealogies Christ is pointed out as Son of Abraham and Son of David, what this expresses is that he closes and perfects the Law. "Christ is (the goal and) the end of the Law" (Rom. 10:4).

The meaning and import of Davidic sonship is explained in the words of the angel: "The Lord God will give him the throne of David his father. And he will be King over the house of Jacob forever" (Luke 1:32f.). The promise is taken up from 2 Sam. 7:12, 16 (see also Dan. 7:14). Now, however, the throne of David stands empty. Israel no longer has a divinely appointed king. The infant Messiah will possess this throne. Some Judaeo-Christians may have misunderstood Luke's source to mean primarily a messianic kingdom to be established in the here and now. The evangelist, however, and the listening Church understand the text in accord with their other eschatological expectations.

The earliest written testimony to Jesus' Davidic sonship is found in the formula of faith in Romans 1:3f. It was discussed along with the disputation recounted in Mark 12:35-37. On both texts, see above, § 10, lc.

c) Conception through the Spirit and Virgin Birth

First of all we must treat the question of the possible biblical meaning and import of the Virgin birth.[127]

Negative explanations are to be dismissed. The biblical meaning and the basis of the traditions cannot be found in the notion that Jesus, on account of his utter sinlessness, could not have come forth from marital procreation. Marriage is not to be charged with evil. Such may have occasionally been the intent of a mistaken moral theology; but it is certainly not the biblical understanding and teaching. To be sure, even some of the Fathers of the Church regarded the Virgin birth of Jesus as a necessity on account of his holiness. This conviction took shape along with the development of a doctrine according to which original sin were transmitted in the procreative act. This estimate of the Virgin birth seems to begin with St. Ambrose and is championed by St. Augustine in his fight against Pelagianism. It is voiced even by Pope Leo the Great (*Sermons* 22, 3) in a Christmas sermon: "Where no paternal seed was poured out, neither did any germ of sin penetrate. Mary's undiminished virginity knew nothing of sensual pleasure; it furnished, however, the womb. The Lord took of his Mother only his human nature; not, however, sin." This idea that Jesus, for the sake of his holiness, could not have come forth from a marital union, can be found operating in undercurrents even today.

There have been and are even yet attempts to derive the biblical Virgin birth from Egyptian mythology.[128] A certain affinity may have existed between Egyptian mythology and Jewish religion, since the Pharaoh was honored as divine king and Judaism awaited the Messiah as divine King. In the Egyptian myth of the miraculous conception and birth of the Pharaoh, the spirit-god Amun, in the form of the reigning king, copulated with the virgin queen and begot the new god-king. In Egypt the myth is traceable to the second century before Christ and was still current in the Hellenistic era. Writers of this school of thought are also minded to link the Egyptian myth with the Septuagint version of Is. 7:14, "Behold, the virgin (παρθένος) will be big with child and bear a son!" The myth may have been employed even by Philo (*De Cherubim* 40-52). He expounds upon a mysterious allegory, according to which the names of the wives of the patriarchs signify virtues. By their virtues they have become virgins again, and God has worked in them miraculous conceptions; for God traffics with none but virgins.

The biblical accounts, it should be apparent, are essentially of a different kind than the Egyptian myths. And Philo's allegory seems to be his own discovery. Neither can it be shown by what means or when the Egyptian myth could have penetrated into the prehistory of Matthew and Luke, since both histories bear the clear stamp of their Judaeo-Christian character. Would Jewish Christianity have been prepared to receive Egyptian mythology?

Another interpretation relying on the study of the history of religions seeks to establish a link between the biblical Virgin birth and Greek mythology. The latter contains many stories of "holy marriages" between gods and daughters of men, by which sons of the gods came to be. Indeed, it was said even of historical persons, such as Homer, Pythagoras, Plato, Alexander, and Augustus, that they were the offspring of a god and of a human mother. Nevertheless, there are also noteworthy dissimilarities between these parallels from the history of religion and the New Testament. When a god has relations with a virgin, the virgin thereby becomes a wife and as a wife she bears her child; contrariwise, Mary remains a Virgin. The mythological narratives are unequivocally erotic, a characteristic of which the biblical accounts are entirely free. The myths are repeated by the ancient accounts with a distinct aloofness, whereas the Gospels want to report accurately the belief of the community. And here too the question must be asked: how could such a mythology have penetrated into the New Testament? The man of antiquity recognized in extraordinary historical figures the appearance of divine power. He was able to accept the passage from man to God easier than the biblical intuition could, which was under the overwhelming influence of the uncompromising Old Testament monotheism.[129]

Another exegesis pondered whether the root of the legend of the Virgin birth of Jesus might be found in Is. 7:14. Whatever the original meaning of the saying of the prophet may be, and whatever the Septuagint wanted to express when it used the term virgin — παρθένος in its translation,[130] it is perfectly clear, as Matthew 1:23 demonstrates, that the New Testament interpretation understands the saying as a promise of the birth of the Messiah from the Virgin Mary. Rabbinic teachings on the Messiah, however, never supposed anything else than that the Messiah would be the son of earthly parents. Thus, rabbinic exegesis never understood Is. 7:14 as suggesting a Virgin birth for the Messiah. The Christian exegesis is something new. Belief in the Virgin birth, therefore, can scarcely be based on Is. 7:14. It must derive from other sources beforehand; then it discovers Is. 7:14 and uses it for verification. The quotation of Is. 7:14 in Matthew 1:23 seems only to be using the passage as confirmation of a tradition already formed.

One must attempt in another way to expose the biblical contextual signification of the Virgin birth. Jesus is God's Son. In the Old Testament all of Israel can be called Son of God. Israel is God's "firstborn Son" (Exod. 4:22). As representative of the nation the king is called Son of God in a special way.

David received for his successor on the throne the divine promise: "I will be a Father to him, and he shall be my son" (2 Sam. 7:14). Here the title does not signify physical begetting, but election and reception of the condition or place of a son. In the ritual of the accession to the throne, God says to the king: "You are my son, this day I have begotten you" (Ps. 2:7). "On the holy hill (*i.e.*, Zion), from the womb of your mother . . . I have begotten you" (Ps. 110:3). In accord with the Old Testament notion of acceptance into sonship, the faith would have recognized from the first that in the resurrection Jesus was exalted to the status of Son of God (Rom. 1:3f.). His divine Sonship was then moved back farther and farther. After the fact of the recognition of faith, Jesus showed himself as Son of God already in his performance as Prophet and Wonderworker (Mark 3:11). Election into Sonship was then set before his public works. It took place in his baptism, at which, indeed, God's voice was heard from the heavens: "You are my beloved Son. In you I am well-pleased" (Mark 1:11). And the faith takes still another step backward. Divine Sonship was attributed to Jesus from his very origins. He has no human father; rather, as creation of the divine Spirit, he is God's Son from the very beginning. The theologoumenon of the Son of God was presented as history in the birth narratives of the Gospels. The theologoumenon became a mythologoumenon.

Another line of investigation may lead from the biblical doctrine on the Spirit of God to the Virgin birth. The Spirit holds creative sway in the world (Gen. 1:2) and in the history of Israel. In the messianic-eschatological era of salvation he will renew Israel (Ezech. 36:25-27; Joel 3:1-5). The Messiah himself will be the bearer of the Spirit. "The Spirit of Yahweh rests on him" (Is. 11:2). The Servant of Yahweh too is gifted with the Spirit. "I lay my Spirit on him" (Is. 42:1). These declarations are enhanced in the history of Jesus. Without the intervention at all of a man, his life is entirely the creation of God. As Messiah, he is not only filled with the Spirit, but is begotten by the Spirit (§ 12, 2b).

The Old Testament tells betimes of great ancestors like Isaac (Gen. 18), Samuel (1 Sam. 1), and Samson (Judges 13), that they were conceived and born of a mother's womb which, by human estimation, was unfruitful. The same is said of John, the precursor of Jesus (Luke 1:7). The prophet (Jer. 1:5) and the Servant of Yahweh (Is. 49:5) are chosen by the Spirit before their birth. Paul explains the history of the sons of Abraham (Gal. 4:22-29). Ishmael, the son of Abraham and Hagar, was begotten "according to the flesh"; Isaac, however, the son of Abraham and Sarah, "by virtue of the promise" and "according to the Spirit." The explanation resembles the story of the annunciation as told by Luke (1:26-35), inasmuch as in both passages word and Spirit are essential.

Even the texts of Qumran may perhaps be quoted. The *Genesis apocryphon* (1:2) found there tells that Lamech, Noah's father, was in some doubt as to whether or not he was himself really the father of such an unusual child. But his wife swore to him: "This seed was from you, not from a stranger nor from a guarding angel (after Gen. 6:2), nor from the sons of heaven." The legend, therefore, regards the heavenly begetting of a child at least as a possibility.[131]

An idea which is in any case hinted at in the New Testament can perhaps be strengthened. The Virgin birth means that even in the manner of the physical generation of the Messiah it is signally proclaimed that here a new beginning is established for the race of mankind, which is entirely God's creative action and the demonstration of his might.

Thus by the Pauline declaration it can be understood that Christ is the new Adam, the beginning and head of a new mankind (Rom. 5:14-19). As a type of the one who was to come (*i.e.*, no doubt, the Messiah), Adam points in advance to Christ. If Christ is to be compared to one who came before, it cannot be to any of the great ones of Israel, like Abraham or Moses, but only Adam, as the origin, the head of mankind. The fulfillment of the type is accomplished in a matchless superabundance: the antitype is as much greater than the type as the grace of God is greater than the sins of men. "If by the sin of the one man the many died, how much more has the grace of God and the gift of grace of the new man, Jesus Christ, abounded, becoming the lot of the many!"

Even in the eschatological perfecting, which has already begun, Adam and Christ stand face to face (1 Cor. 15:45-49). Here Paul is probably using speculations, like those which Philo (*De allegoriis legum* 1:31f.) develops, according to which first (Gen. 1:26f.) a divine ideal man was created, and only afterwards (Gen. 2:7) the real Adam. Nevertheless, Paul modifies the idea. Adam was the first, the earthly man; the second man is Christ. He comes "down from heaven", he is "the last Adam, the life-giving spirit." If Adam embodied the earthly humanity, then Christ embodies the new humanity. As eschatological redeemer, Christ is the perfécter of creation. Perhaps these views share in the Gnostic myth of the primordial man, who comes into the world as revealer of the truth and as redeemer, and gathers the redeemed into a new creation.

Is it Luke's intention too, to suggest that Christ is the new Adam when he carries the genealogical table back to Adam, and beyond him to God? (Luke 3:38). In any case, it suggests that Jesus is the redeemer not just for Israel but for all mankind. Adam originates directly from God; and none other does so until Jesus (Luke 1:34f.). The genealogy of Jesus according to Luke contains seventy-seven names. Are they to be taken as eleven groups of seven? In the Bible, as in many religions, seven is a holy number. Is there a number symbolism here, declaring that the genealogy of Jesus is sanctified intensively? Jesus stands at the end of the eleventh group of seven. Apocalyptic writings reckoned with a schema of twelve periods in the world (*Syriac Apocalypse of Baruch* 53-72; *4 Esdras* 14:11; *Apocalypse of Abraham* 29:2). Does this mean that with the last period Christ ushers in the consummation?

Protestant theology, exegetic and systematic, explains the biblical tradition of the Virgin birth remotely as admissible symbol. We may quote Wolfhart Pannenberg, *Grundzüge der Christologie*, 2nd edition, Gütersloh 1966, pp. 148–149: "The narrative of the virgin birth bears all the marks of a legend which has been constructed out of etiological interest, namely, in order to illustrate the title 'Son of God'. . . . The idea of the virginal birth of Jesus has two functions, neither of which can be dogmatically surrendered; yet, it is better to do justice to them in another way than through the notion of the virgin birth. It involves, on the one hand, the anti-adoptionist idea, that from the very beginning Jesus was what He is, totally from God. . . . Just as unrelinquishable is the anti-docetist point of view in the expression '*ex Maria virgine*', that the origin of Jesus, His birth, was after all a truly human occurrence."

In this same regard Paul Tillich says, in his *Systematische Theologie*, Vol. 2, Stuttgart 1958, p. 173: "in the virginal birth what should be taken as expressed is that the divine Spirit, who made the man Jesus of Nazareth to be the Messiah, had already created Him previously as His vessel. For that reason the redeeming presence of the New Being is independent of historical contingencies and is dependent only on God. . . . But the story itself is a myth, the symbolic value of which must be seriously called into question. It leans in the direction of docetist and monophysite Christian thought."

Recently even Catholic exegesis and dogmatics are tending toward similar interpretations. The so-called *Dutch Catechism* (*De niewe kate-*

chismus translated under the title *A New Catechism*, New York 1972, p. 75 [the following, however, is our own translation and not the previously published English]) explains:

> "The deep meaning of the article of faith 'born of the Virgin' is: In the final analysis, mankind has no one else to thank for this Promised One but the Spirit of God. His origin is neither from blood nor from the will of the flesh, nor from the will of a man, but from God."

A Catholic Commission of Cardinals, convened by order of Roman Congregations, demanded that the Catechism should "teach in clear language the fact of the virginal conception of Jesus (*Report über den Holländischen Katechismus*, Freiburg 1969, p. 226). [*Translator's note*: The corrections requested were made; and for the passage quoted above and what immediately precedes it in the original edition, a lengthier wording was substituted, and can be found on pp. 538–540 of the English edition of 1972, published by Herder and Herder of New York. The new wording does contain what appears, at least on the surface, to be a franker admission of the virginal conception; but one still has the impression, in the total context of the newer wording, that its authors are doing considerable hedging, and are not willing to state plainly what they do believe.]

Piet Schoonenberg has repeatedly defended the new interpretation. In the *Report über den Holländischen Katechismus* (p. 81f.) he explains: "The New Testament as a whole gives the impression that the virginal birth is a poetic expression of the unique divine Sonship of Jesus." He questions whether the reality of the human nature of Jesus is not diminished by the doctrine of the Virginal birth. In his book *Verbond en schepping,* translated under the title *Covenant and Creation* [University of Notre Dame Press 1969], Schoonenberg has addressed himself to the question again. He says that the infancy narratives of Matthew and Luke have "a strongly legendary character." To what extent they contain a historical kernel is uncertain. The Old Testament legends of the miraculous conception of men of God like Isaac, Samson, and Samuel are similar. In the New Testament legends a legitimate development of the insight of faith is expressing itself and declaring that divine Sonship was inherent in Jesus Christ not just since his exaltation or since his baptism, but from the very beginning of his human existence. It is an

overwhelming probability that the Virgin birth is a theological interpretation presented in the form of a legend. The declaration of the creed,
"born of the Virgin Mary", can be understood as the rendering of a historical account as well as of a theological legend.

In a pamphlet entitled *Zweierlei Glaube oder Holland und Rom* [*i.e.*,
Faith of Two Different Kinds, or Holland and Rome], published at
Stuttgart in 1970, R. Pesch reports on the discussion over the *Dutch
Catechism*. In his explanation he agrees to this: that the Virgin birth is
not to be understood as a historical-biological event, but as a meaningful
expression of the fact that Christ is God's gift to mankind (pp. 16–20).[132]

In its dogmatic constitution on the Church, *Lumen gentium* or *Light
of Nations*, in the eighth chapter thereof, the Second Vatican Council
treats in the usual way of "*The Blessed Virgin Mary, Mother of God*"
(nos. 52–69). She is the model and exemplar of the Church, which, like
her, is Virgin and Mother (no. 63).

It will not be contested that the Gospels according to Matthew and
Luke, with creation by the Spirit and Virgin birth — a deeper significance notwithstanding — mean to recount historical-corporeal events. If
Catholic theology wants to understand this as a theologoumenon in the
form of a mythologoumenon, then the traditional doctrine of the inerrancy of the Bible, of the teaching office, and of the consciousness of
faith, as well as the dogmatic theological area of Mariology would have
to be newly explained and substantiated! [133]

4. APOCALYPSE OF JOHN, 12:1-5

The birth of Jesus Christ is represented with mythological images in
the Apocalypse, 12:1-5. "A great sign appeared in the sky, a woman
clothed with the sun, and the moon beneath her feet, and on her head
a crown of twelve stars. And she is bearing in her womb, and she cries
out in the pain and anguish of childbirth. And another sign appeared in
the sky, and behold, a great dragon, fiery red . . . And the dragon sta-
tioned himself before the woman who was about to give birth, so that
when she had delivered her child he might devour it. And she bore a
son, a male child, who is destined to shepherd all the Gentile nations

with an iron staff (Ps. 2:8-9). And her child was enraptured to God and to his throne." [134]

Since the dignity and power of the child is depicted in terms of Psalm 2:8-9 he is characterized as the Messiah. In accord with the oldest and most widespread interpretation of the rabbis, Psalm 2 speaks of the Messiah. In the ideal image of the Messiah in the *Psalms of Solomon* (17:26), carrying considerable authority in the messianic era, Psalm 2:8-9 is referred to the Messiah.

The Apocalypse of John, written no doubt about the year 100 A.D., refers in this vision not to some future Messiah, but to the Messiah who had already appeared in Jesus Christ. To whom is the woman to be referred?

The Old Testament, referring to Israel, makes use repeatedly of the image of a wife. Jerusalem is the daughter of Zion (Is. 1:8). Israel is seen as a mother giving birth (Is. 66:7) and as a mother rich in children (Is. 49:20; 54:1). After the political catastrophe of the year 70 A.D., Jerusalem is depicted in *4 Esdras* 9:38 — 10:24 as a grieving mother. The image is confided also to the New Testament. Paul (Gal. 4:22-31) applies the history of the two wives of Abraham to Israel and the Church. The present Jerusalem is in bondage. The Jerusalem above is a free-woman, our mother. The Church is represented as the bride of Christ (2 Cor. 11:2; Eph. 5:25). The woman of the Apocalypse could probably be regarded first of all as signifying Israel, who has brought forth the Messiah. But since Apoc. 12:17 says that the other children of the woman have the testimony of Jesus, the woman cannot be the former Israel; she is the Church, who, according to Gal. 6:16, is indeed the Israel of God. Perhaps the figure embraces the totality of the one people of God, whether of the Old Testament or of the New. In Apoc. 12:2 the pains of the woman are quite realistically portrayed. In the Old Testament the theme signifies extreme helplessness and affliction. It is an image of the nation under judgment (Is. 13:8; 26:17f.) and of painful recommencement (Jer. 4:31; Hosea 13:13; Micah 4:9f.).

In the psalms from Qumran (1 QH 3:6-18) the petitioner, in great misery, says: "They . . . made my soul like a ship on the stormy seas and like a fortified city in the face of the enemy. I was in distress like a woman bringing forth her firstborn; then do her pangs come quickly." The woman "gives birth to a male child . . . a wonder, a counsellor, a hero mighty" (Is. 9:5). The text is of uncertain interpretation. Is the child who is characterized in terms of Isaiah 9:5 the Messiah? Is the woman who is giving birth supposed to symbolize the terminal community which brings forth the Messiah? If so, the portrait drawn is not far from that of Apoc. 12:1-5.[135]

The dragon (Apoc. 12:3) is interpreted in verse 9 as "the ancient serpent, the devil and Satan." In late Judaism the serpent (Gen. 3:1) was regarded as synonymous with Satan (Wis. 2:24; *Ethiopic Henoch* 69:6). Satan cannot hinder the birth of the child. Before he can harm him, the child is "enraptured to God and to his throne" (Apoc. 12:5). The enrapturement or exaltation is depicted in the manner of Ps. 110:1 (see above, § 9e). The life of Christ is designated in Apoc. 12:1-5 only with its two limits, birth and exaltation. In the old hymn to Christ in Phil. 2:6-11, Christology is similarly condensed.

In the vision which it recounts in 12:1-5, the Apocalypse of John, as it does so often, employs old mythical tradition in order to represent with it the history of Christ and of the Church.

5. The Prologue of John's Gospel

The prologue of the Gospel of John (1:1-14) gives a presentation explaining the history of the incarnation.[136] The prologue is set apart from the rest of the Gospel by its rhythmic language. This is true, at any rate, of 1:1-5, 9-14, while the report about John the Baptist identifies itself as an insertion in prose.

Only in the prologue of the Gospel is Christ called Logos. Other words that are of importance in the prologue are developed in the Gospel itself; thus with the terms life, light, truth, glory, and world. The prologue is like an overture to the Gospel. Certainly it was prefixed to the Gospel after the rest of the Gospel was written. Exegesis finds it questionable, whether the prologue was produced by the evangelist or has perhaps some other origin. It could have originated in the Christian community, and have been accepted and at the same time interpreted by the evangelist.

It has also been conjectured occasionally that the prologue was originally a Gnostic hymn, perhaps composed in honor of John the Baptist by his community. This hypothesis was greeted with doubts for a long time, and more recently it has been rendered thoroughly questionable by the fact that exegesis — French exegesis above all — has pointed out the significance and influence of the wisdom literature for the prologue (see note 138).

John's Gospel does not explain the word or concept of Logos. It presumes a knowledge thereof. In point of fact the Logos of God is spoken of even outside the New Testament. The Old Testament describes God's powerful word of creation (Gen. 1:1–2:4; Ps. 33:6; Is. 48:13). The word of God accomplishes his will in history (Is. 55:11; Ps. 33:9; Ezech. 37:4; Wis. 18:15f.). The wisdom literature speaks, even if not of the word, nevertheless, of the personified Wisdom of God. This Wisdom is prehistoric and was present at the creation of the world and participated therein (Prov. 8:22-30). It sought and found an abode among men (Sir. 24:8-12).

Of various meanings, the word *logos* is a characteristic term in Greek philosophy and spirituality. From that source, it becomes an important influence on Philo. With Philo, the Logos is "God's firstborn Son" (*De agricultura Noë* 51), a "second God" (*De allegoriis legum* 2, 86). The Logos is the agent of creation. "The shadow of God is his Logos, whom he employs, as it were, as his instrument in the creation of the world. This shadow and this image, as one can call him, is in turn the archetype of other things" (*De allegoriis legum* 3, 96). The Logos guides the world (*De cherubim* 36; *De migratione Abrahami* 6) and maintains it in its existence (*Quis rerum divinarum heres sit* 188). The Logos is also the agent of revelation. He is the angel of God, who imparts divine gifts and benefactions to men (*De allegoriis legum* 3, 177; *De cherubim* 35; *De profugis* 67). The Logos grants the soul participation in the light (*De allegoriis legum* 3, 171); he is the well-spring of wisdom (*De profugis* 97) and the great teacher of the soul (*De somniis* 1, 68; *De migratione Abrahami* 174). Philo's Logos, however, as distinct from the Logos of John's Gospel, is certainly always just a power of God, and not completely a divine Person. Moreover, Philo could never say that the Logos became flesh, because for him the flesh is a principle inimical to God.

For the Gnosis, too, the term and concept Logos is recognized and important. The Logos is God's Word and God's Son. Through his Logos

God created the world. Man has his origins from the heavenly world. As God's revealer, the Logos teaches man about his heavenly homeland and opens for him the way back.[137]

The prologue of John's Gospel teaches that from eternity onwards Christ, in his own substance, was with God and was himself God, and therefore — since God is one — was in God's substance (John 1:1). In time, the Logos was the agent of creation. He is the life-creating power (1:3f.). He is the light of men. In him alone does man understand himself and find his way (1:4). While remaining what he was, the Logos revealed himself in the flesh as true man among men (1:14) — even to his *"Ecce, homo!"* (19:5). If the world closed itself to the light and the Logos (1:9-11), still, his own received him. To those who believe, is given the new existence of the children of God (1:12f.). In the Logos, who has become flesh, the presence of God dwells among men even as once God occupied his throne in the ark of the covenant (1:14). Belief is continually rewarded by him with grace and truth (1:16). The Church professes to have fellowship with the Father, through the Word of Life (1 John 1:1-3).

With themes from the Old Testament, but also with contemporaneous images and concepts, the Gospel of John describes the incarnation of Jesus as the revelation of God in the world. The turning of God toward mankind in Christ is made more generally known in the Gospel in the words of Jesus about the Father, and in his great wonders and signs.

6. Pre-existence

The notion of pre-existence is intimately bound up with the incarnation.[138] It is attested in the pre-Pauline hymn to Christ in Phil. 2:6-11 (§ 10, 1e). There is a further declaration of it in texts which say that the creation took place in Christ. "One God the Father, from whom is everything and we unto him; and one Lord Jesus Christ, through whom is everything and we through him" (1 Cor. 8:6). Christ is "the firstborn before all creation" (Col. 1:15). God has "created the ages in Christ" (Heb. 1:2; see *Theology of the New Testament*, Vol. 1, pp. 24-27).

Following Jewish speculation, Paul finds in the declarations about the rock from which Israel drank water in the wilderness (Exod. 17:6;

Num. 20:7-11), a revelation about the Christ, who, in his pre-existence, was already present in Israel's history (1 Cor. 10:4). In 1 Peter 1:11, it probably has to be understood that Christ, in his pneumatic pre-existence, filled the prophets and spoke through them.

The declarations of John's Gospels are unequivocal. Christ, the Logos, was with God in the very beginning (John 1:1f.). John the Baptist expresses the confession of Christian faith: "After me comes he, who has ever been before me. For as the First, he was before me" (John 1:30). Pertinent also are the self-declarations of the Johannine Christ. "Glorify me, Father, with glory that I had with you, before the world existed" (John 17:5; see also John 6:62; 8:58; 17:24).

The declaration of pre-existence proceeds from the end of the New Testament Christology. Faith recognizes Christ as the exalted one and Lord of the universe. He is the goal of creation and of history. It is from this point that reflection and faith reach backwards. Christ is "the first and the last" (Apoc. 1:17). From time immemorial this Christ belongs to God's plan of salvation. He that is now in the glory of God was eternally in the Unity with the Father. He was in divine pre-existence, came out of it, and returned into it.

Pre-existence and post-existence are posited in Christ's regard in Heb. 13:8, "Jesus Christ, yesterday and today the same, and in eternity." In the passage of generations and ages, and in the changing of offices and officers in the Church, the announcement and the conduct of the Church remain unchanged, because Christ remains her Lord. Her eternal continuance is expressed more profoundly in the schema of the three ages, which is applied originally to God (§ 20, 1).

Reflection employed notions and possibilities already at hand. They were provided by Old Testament Jewish tradition. The Old Testament wisdom speculation tended to make ready the pre-existence Christology. God's wisdom, which knows all, understands all, and directs all, belongs to his substance (Sir. 1:9). God's wisdom is occasionally represented as personified. She is the image of the grandeur of God (Wis. 7:25f.), she dwells in heaven (Sir. 24:4) and shares God's throne with him (Wis. 9:4). Wisdom participated and does yet participate in all that God did and is doing in the world. She was present at creation, examining (Prov. 8:27-30; Wis. 9:9), counseling (Wis. 8:4), as an artist

(Wis. 8:6). She herself can be called the "mother of all things" (Wis. 7:12).

The transfer of these notions to Christ is so much the more easily possible, when Christ can be called "the Power of God and the Wisdom of God" (1 Cor. 1:24). Christ is at one and the same time the Son of Man who is present, and the Wisdom who has appeared (Matthew 11:19).

Apocalyptic writings (Dan. 7:13f.) are aware of the pre-existing Son of Man. The idea was developed further after Daniel, as is shown by the picturesque language of the Ethiopic *Book of Henoch* (*Ethiopic Henoch* 48:3; see also *4 Esdras* 13:26). As the future bringer of salvation, the Son of Man possesses a real existence, hidden in God.

Rabbinic theology awarded pre-existence before the creation of the world to important figures and personages of salvation history. This may have been at first a pre-existence in the eternal thoughts and eternal plans of God, and not yet an independent existence outside the substance of God. But the idea evolved to the latter. According to the midrashim, there are seven things in existence before the creation of the world: Torah (*i.e.*, Wisdom), Repentance, Garden of Eden, Hell of Gehenna, Throne of Glory, Sanctuary, and Name of the Messiah.[139]

Also prepared before the creation of the world are the good things of the future world, which will be brought forth out of the place of concealment in the endtime (*cf.* Matthew 25:34).

Even the Qumran community was open to thoughts on pre-existence, inasmuch as every created thing is regarded as having been founded in the eternal thoughts of God. The generations of men perdure from eternity to eternity. "In your wisdom you have established generations unto eternity. And before you created them, you were acquainted with your works" (1 QH 1:7f.; see also 1 QS 3:15f.).

In Philo (*De specialibus legibus* 81; *De allegoriis legum* 3, 96), the Logos is the pre-existing divine likeness of God. Through him was the world created. In Philo (*De gigantibus* 12-15; *De somniis* 1, 138f.), in Josephus (*Jewish War* 2, 154f.), and among the rabbis, there can be detected even the idea of the pre-existence of the immortal soul, an idea deriving ultimately from Platonic philosophy.

Do extra-biblical speculations also play a part in this? According to Gnostic notions, the soul of a man, or at least the core of the soul, has fallen out of God's world of light and has sunk into matter. It seeks a way back. Individual destinies are condensed in the figure of the primordial man, who abandons his divine existence in order to assemble the individual men, to redeem them, and to lead them back to the divine world. Such is the mythological beauty in which this notion is depicted in the song of the king's son, who sets out to seek the precious pearl (*Acts of Thomas* 108-113). An enigmatic saying in the *Gospel of Philip* (57) is also to be explained in the light of the foregoing notions "Who exists before he came to be, blessed is he: for he exists, who was and who will be." The eternally true existence participates in God's existence.[140]

The assertion of pre-existence is not direct revelation, but the result of theological reasoning. Nevertheless, the faith traversed this path very quickly and very securely. It is attested already in the pre-Pauline hymn in Phil. 2:6-11, and then also in various texts of the New Testament that are certainly not mutually dependent one on another. If the development of the idea of pre-existence is presented rather strikingly therein, then the question must be asked whether this theological conclusion is valid and obligatory for the New Testament and consequently for the Church. Its value may have to be distinguished in accord with where one finds the prior model expression of the doctrine of pre-existence.

If the Christological doctrine of pre-existence is developed with ideas from the Old Testament and the connecting Judaism, the doctrine of faith has its source in the Bible and in revelation. If the notion of pre-existence were developed by means of extra-biblical notions (perhaps that of the Gnostic myth of the primordial man), then one could say that foreign myths penetrate the Christian faith. Naturally one would have to investigate further, to see whether a myth had been interwoven only formally or whether it constituted a substantial intrusion in view of its contents.

Catholic dogmatics maintains the New Testament Christological doctrine of pre-existence. Just as the Trinity, however, must not be misunderstood as a doctrine of three Gods, so too pre-existence is not to be taken as a mythical doctrine of two Gods. The pre-existing Son must not be thought of as separated from the Father; rather, he is with him in the eternal Unity of substance. It is doubtful that with the formula of pre-existence the divine eternity is based on human time and calculated therefrom. The salvation-historical phase is extended in a backwards direction and is stretched into the infinite. The pre-existing before-times and the salvation-historical time must neither be separated nor added; rather, they are present in each other. Christology and Trinitarian theology are a unity.

An abridgement of Christology is developed with pre-existence as its starting point, a procedure which, perhaps, in a broad way, the common conception of the faith and even scholastic dogmatic theology can be tempted to follow. Christology is then concentrated on the incarnation in the wonderful birth of Christ. The significance of the revelation of the historical way of Jesus is relegated to the background. The resurrection unveils the meaning of the birth event. The eschatological expectation of the return and consummation become unessential.[141]

Critical interpretations are reported on by Piet Schoonenberg in his work *A God of Men*, e.g., God's Word was present and operative in creation and in history as a living power. Independently of the man Jesus, however, and as a person pre-existing, God's Son is not brought into relation with the eternal Father, in order to be joined into a unity with the human nature of Jesus; rather, God's Son first becomes person in the man Jesus. In accord with the experience of the community of disciples, that God acted in Christ ("In him dwells the fullness of the Godhead bodily" [Vol. 2:9]), the biblical assertion about the pre-existence wants to attest that Christ represents God's presence for us.[142]

Recent Protestant theology has frequently proposed the dogma of the divinity of Christ in the wording of the ancient ecclesiastical formulations. The consequence of this too is a novel understanding of the old doctrine of the pre-existence of Christ. The divine Sonship originally attributed to Christ on the basis of his resurrection (Rom. 1:3f.), was, in view of his pre-existence, moved back into eternity. Accordingly, Jesus was worshiped as a pre-existing Divine Being come down from heaven. The assertion in regard to his existence, metaphysically formulated by dogmatics, is brought into question as a mythological representation.

In place of an essential pre-existence, dogmatics then accepts something of an ideal pre-existence of Christ in the counsel of God. A comparable ideal pre-existence were his election "before the foundation of the world" (Matthew 25:34; Rom. 8:30; Eph. 4:1f.).[143]

We may quote the considered theorizing of R. Bultmann, from the

sixth edition of his *Theologie des Neuen Testaments*, 1968, pp. 303–305;
"The passages on the pre-existence of Christ and his becoming man are
mythologizations . . . Nevertheless, in the context of the kerygma they
serve to give expression to a decisive fact, namely, that the person and
the destiny of Jesus do not have their origin and their meaning in the
context of what takes place in the world around us, but that God was
acting in them, and that this action of his took place 'when the fullness
of time was come' (Gal. 4:4), so that the eschatological deed is God's . . .
The fact that there is a proclamation authorized by God of the prevenient
grace and love of God finds its mythological expression in the talk of
the pre-existence of Christ."

§ 11. JESUS' TITLES OF MAJESTY

The New Testament declares its faith in the life, works, and person
of Jesus in the titles of dignity and majesty which it accords him.[144] The
primary and most significant of these titles and names are Messiah
(Christ), Son of Man, Son (Son of God), Savior, and Lord.[145] A basic
question to be asked is whether and how Jesus himself laid claim to
these titles, or even accepted them.

According to the evidence of the text he was reluctant at best to permit their use. They were altogether insufficient to express what his call,
his word, and his work wanted to state. As a definitive confession, the
titles of dignity belong to a later stage of New Testament Christology.
That is why in our own presentation of New Testament Christology
they must stand not at the beginning but at the end of our treatment.[146]

For the earthly Jesus and for the Resurrected One, the New Testament knows about fifty-five different names. The title Christ is used
about five hundred times. For the use of the name Lord (Kyrios) there
are about three hundred and fifty examples; for Son of Man, eighty; for
Son (Son of God), seventy-five; for Son of David, twenty examples.
Such, at any rate, is the count made by L. Sabourin and V. Taylor (see
footnote 146).

1. MESSIAH (CHRIST)

Israel's hope that God would in the end restore her splendid prosperity reaches back to ancient times.[147] Originally, however, the expectation is vested not so much in an individual bringer of prosperity, whom we are accustomed to call the Messiah; rather, it is God himself who will create prosperity. Israel awaits the Day of Yahweh, who on that day will raise up the kingdom. That day will be a day of judgment upon the Gentiles (Is. 2:9-22) and upon Israel herself (Amos 5:18-20); yet it will also bring prosperity, at least for the remnant of Israel (Joel 3:18). Yahweh himself will then be King forever and always (Exod. 15:18; Ps. 145:11-13). According to later notions, Yahweh will someday, enthroned in Jerusalem, rule over the whole world (Is. 24:23; Zech. 14:9, 16f.; Obed. 21).

A personal bringer of prosperity first enters into the expectations as a secondary element. In recollection of David's kingdom, he is expected as a king in the endtime, who will renew the ancient kingdom. The ruler will be a scion of the house of David. The hope rests on the promise in 2 Sam. 7:13, that David's dynasty will remain forever. David's son will be accepted by God as his Son. Thus in Isaiah 11:1 and Micah 5:2-4 it is someone of the line of David who is expected as king of prosperity. In Deutero-Isaiah (Is. 49–55) the bringer of prosperity is the ministering and suffering Servant of Yahweh; in Daniel (7:13), he is son of man. In Zechariah (4:11-14) two messianic figures appear, the king and the high priest. The eschatological bringer of prosperity precedes the kingdom of God. The dominion and effectiveness of the bringer of prosperity are temporally circumscribed.

In the Old Testament the expected Savior is never called Messiah. Messiah, in Hebrew *mashîaḥ*, and in later Hebrew *meshîḥa'*, means the "anointed one", the same as the Greek *christos*. In the old covenant priests (Exod. 28:41; Lev. 8:30) and kings (1 Sam. 10:1; 16:13; 2 Sam. 2:4; 5:3) and probably prophets too (3 Kings 19:16; implied in Is. 61:1) were anointed. The meaning of the external anointing is the inner permeation with the power of holiness, the quality of being set apart, and of being sealed. The Septuagint already translated *mashîaḥ* with *christos*. If in Is. 45:1 Cyrus is designated as Messiah, it is not in view of any real act of anointing, and here the word is a title of election and delegation as agent of God's plan; Cyrus belongs to God's providence.

The designation of the eschatological king as Messiah probably depends upon Ps. 2:2, where the historical king is designated as "Yahweh's anointed one". In the New Testament era Psalm 2 (in the *Psalms of Solomon*, in the apocalypses called *Henoch* and *Baruch*, and in *4 Esdras*, as well as in Acts 4:25f.; Heb. 1:5; Apoc. 2:27) was understood in reference to the Messiah. Accordingly the expected bringer of prosperity is called the "Messiah of God" (*Psalms of Solomon* 17:36; 18:6, 8; *Ethiopic Henoch* 48:10; 52:4). The absolute use of the name Messiah, without qualification, is not found until the first century after Christ (*4 Esdras* 7:28f.; 12:32; *Syriac Apocalypse of Baruch* 29:13; 30:1; as well as John 1:41; 4:25).

The Qumran community, even as Zech. 4:11-14, expected two Messiahs, the priestly Messiah called the "Messiah of Aaron", and the royal Messiah, the Son of David, the "Messiah of Israel." The priestly Messiah has the pre-eminence and the precedence. The royal Messiah will hold the eschatological dominion (1 QS 9:11; 1 QSa 2:12-24; 4 Q Testimonia 14; *Damascus Document* 19:10f.; 20:1).

At the time of Jesus, messianic hope had reached its zenith. Apart from the Bible, it was always politically determined by Jewish nationalism, even if partially purified. The Messiah was supposed to liberate his people from sin and purify them (*Psalms of Solomon* 17). The New Testament makes mention of some of the then current messianic movements (Acts 5:36f.; 8:9; 21:38; Matthew 24:24); others can be found in Josephus and other historical writings. The Roman occupational garrison suppressed the movements with brutal force. The title of Messiah was unclear and ambiguous. Different groups and parties, Pharisees, Sadducees, Essenes, Apocalyptics, Priests, Politicians, Zealots — all expected a Messiah, but they differed greatly in what they expected that Messiah to be.

The New Testament standing open before us affirms the fulfillment of the expectation, inasmuch as it accords the title of Messiah or Christ to Jesus with perfect certainty (Matthew 1:1; Mark 1:1; John 20:31; likewise the Epistles). Nevertheless, the state of the text is such that it is questionable whether Jesus ever bore the title Messiah. In Source Q, which can be extracted from the Synoptics, the title Christ is not attested. It is found only seven times in Mark, and increases in Matthew and Luke.

The demons recognize and acknowledge Jesus as Christ (Mark 3:11; Luke 4:41). Jesus, however, forbids them to make this public. To the question of John the Baptist, whether or not he is the Messiah, Jesus gives a veiled reply (Matthew 11:2-6). Among the disciples, certainly, Jesus himself evokes a confession (Mark 8:27-30). Peter declares: "You are the Messiah!" Jesus does not contradict him. According to Matthew 16:17, in fact, Peter, who so spoke, has been the recipient of special graces. It is not flesh and blood, but the Father in heaven who has revealed this to him. That Jesus is the Messiah is hidden from the purely human understanding, and it is supposed to remain hidden. Jesus prohibits their proclaiming their confession (Mark 8:30). Making known the Messiahship of Jesus is not the business of the disciples. All titles of majesty are possible only under the proviso of rejection and suffering (Mark 8:31).

Synoptic texts in which Jesus refers to himself as Messiah are questionable as to their historical tradition. Indeed, Mark 9:41 reports a saying of the Lord as: "Whoever gives you a cup of water to drink because of the fact that you are Christ's, truly, he shall not lose his reward." Yet the parallel in Matthew 10:42 would seem to be closer to the original: "Whoever gives to one of these little ones only a cup of cold water to drink because of the fact that the one so receiving is a disciple . . . ." Mark concretizes discipleship into the community of Christ. The saying, "Do not let yourselves be called teacher, for one only is your Teacher, the Christ" (Matthew 23:10), belongs to a group of sayings (Matthew 23:8-10) in which one can perceive the relationship of a developed community; if so, they pertain to a later time. The phrase "your Teacher, the Christ", is the community's acknowledging of the exalted Lord as the Teacher of the Church.

The Gospel of Mark knows Jesus from the very beginning as the Messiah (Mark 1:1). Even so, in the Gospel, the Messiahship of Jesus is hidden. The demoniacs recognize Jesus as Messiah (Mark 1:23f.; 1:34; 3:11f.). But Jesus commands them, just like the recipients of wonders (Mark 1:34, 44; 3:12; 5:43; 7:36) and revelations (Mark 8:26, 30; 9:9), to remain silent. Jesus conceals his message in secretive parables (Mark 4:10-12). Even the disciples do not understand Jesus (Mark 6:52; 8:17,

21). Most especially, they do not grasp the necessity of the Passion (Mark 8:32f.; 9:10).

W. Wrede, in his book *Das Messiasgeheimnis in den Evangelien* (Göttingen 1901; third edition 1963), wanted to explain the evidence in this fashion: Jesus did not know that he was the Messiah, and he did not lay claim to this dignity. Neither did the original tradition know anything of his Messiahship. When the community, after Jesus' resurrection and on the basis of his resurrection, proclaimed him as Messiah, it bridged the contradiction between the pre-paschal tradition and the post-paschal proclamation with the fiction that Jesus had indeed regarded himself as the Messiah, but had forbidden the proclamation of the fact.

The explanation offered by Wrede took a long time to get a hearing, but today professional critics are sympathetic. The secret of Messiahship is termed a Markan creation. It is his way of expressing the nature of the Messiahship of Jesus and the character of the faith of the Gospel. To faith, the secret of Jesus is unveiled; to disbelief, it is hidden. To those outside, everything is closed (Mark 4:11).

The Messiahship of Jesus must pass through the Passion. After it has begun, it can be declared (Mark 14:61f.). Not until after the completion of the Passion and after the resurrection can the secret of Jesus be recognized. Not until then and only in that way can the proclamation of Jesus take place (Mark 9:9).

In the Gospels, therefore, the Messiahship of Jesus is hidden until the last days. Jesus makes a solemn entry into Jerusalem (Mark 11:7-10). The interpretation of Scripture recognizes therein the fulfillment of the messianic prophecy. Jesus is the one "who is to come", as the expectations term the Messiah (Zcch. 14:5f; Mal. 3:1). Jesus himself probably intended to bring about the fulfillment of prophecy when he made his entry into the city as King of Peace, in accord with Zech. 9:9, one of the passages understood by the rabbis as being of messianic import. The messianic kingship was hardly any longer veiled, and at the same time its utterly unpolitical nature was made clear.

In the judicial process the Messiahhood of Jesus is confirmed. To the question of whether he is the Messiah, Jesus answers: "I am"; and he completes his profession of Messiahship with a claim to majesty as the Son of Man (Mark 14:62). Before Pilate Jesus answers with a veiled statement (Mark 15:2). As messianic King, Jesus is crucified; and thus he dies (Mark 15:26).[148] The faith and profession of the community of disciples accepted the proclamation of the Messiah and corroborated it. While the catastrophic fall of a pretender would elsewhere have contradicted and branded as false the messianic claim (Acts 5:36; Luke 24:21), the disciples grasped the gateway of Jesus through suffering and death as a divine necessity (Luke 24:46).

Jesus' works and his very manner did not correspond to the common expectation of a messianic King. A title of Messiah understood in that fashion would not have corresponded to Jesus' own consciousness of his calling. It would seem, therefore, that he did not use the title, or at any rate, that he did not demand it. It first became apparent in the resurrection and in the exaltation of Jesus that the divine majesty was hidden in the form of a servant. Such, in fact, is the declaration of the oldest messianic confession: "God made him to be Lord and Messiah" (Acts 2:36). Not until he is the Exalted One is he the Messiah.

The preaching of the apostles exhibits Jesus as the Christ and thereby gives rise to the separation between Israel and Church (Acts 17:3; 18:5). The title Christ was understood primarily as a designation of his calling — which accounts for the usage which puts the term Christ before his name, Christ Jesus — and only afterwards as a second name of Jesus, Jesus Christ. This has already come about by the time of 1 Cor. 15:3, where Paul quotes the confession of the Jerusalem community in regard to Christ (further in 1 Cor. 15:12-23). It is a remarkable fact that even though Jesus did not claim the title of Messiah, it became his own proper name as well as that of his disciples (Acts 11:26; 26:28; 1 Peter 4:16). The history of the Church but continues what was already begun in the New Testament, where the title Christ is already used perhaps five hundred times, and is the title of majesty accorded Jesus most often.

After recounting the baptism of Jesus as the revelation of his messianic Sonship, the Synoptic Gospels join to it the story of the temptation in the desert (Matthew 4:1-11 and parallels). Prior to the beginning of Jesus' messianic works, the story of the temptation is a reflection on his fullness of power. The story is a problematic composition of ingenious depth. By whom it was composed, whether by Jesus or by tradition, in any case, the gospel uses it (no matter the slight differences in the three accounts) to declare the beginning of the messianic work of Jesus, in the way that it understands the Messiah and his fullness of power.

Jesus overcomes every temptation to defect from a spiritual ministry. He refuses to misuse his calling and powers, even to satisfy such earthly needs as hunger for bread. He refuses to misuse the promise given by God; he will not turn that promise into a challenge to God. He remains obedient to the Father. Jesus finally refuses a Messiahship consisting of world dominion, politically understood. Demanding worship as a counter-god, Satan is ready to bestow in exchange all riches and glory. But the obedience of the Son, with its basis in the love of God, is stronger than every satanic temptation and power. Jesus finds God's will declared in God's word (Matthew 4:4, 7). The Spirit with which he is invested (Matthew 4:1) assists his decision and keeps him safe. After Satan has been defeated, angels minister to the Messiah, thus making manifest God's solicitude. Jesus verifies his messianic Sonship in obedience, confidence and love towards the Father.[149]

The Gospel of John repeats the Church's confident acknowledgement of the Messiah (1:17) and has for its purpose the imparting of a correct understanding of the messianic kingship. From the very beginning the disciples gather about Jesus as the Messiah and acknowledge him as such (John 1:41), and as "Son of God and King of Israel" (John 1:49).

The Samaritan woman attests that Jesus is the Messiah, who has now come (John 4:25f.). The multiplication of the loaves and the address about the bread of heaven make Jesus known as the messianic king, who does not, however, dispense earthly advantages, but everlasting life (John 6:15, 26f.). Martha believes that Jesus is "the Christ, the Son of God" (John 11:27). On the occasion of his entry into Jerusalem, he is the messianic Prince of Peace (John 12:13-15). In his high-priestly prayer Jesus speaks of himself as "Jesus Christ" (John 17:3). The conversation with Pilate presents Jesus not as King of this world, but as King of truth (John 18:33-37). The controversy with the high priests corroborates that Jesus is in reality King (John 19:21f.). This is the point over which faith and disbelief separate: whether the Messiahship of Jesus is to be acknowledged. Many of the Jews might be swayed by the marvelous deeds of Jesus (John 7:3f.; 7:26f.; 7:31, 40). Nevertheless, Jesus does not correspond to the contemporary dogmatic on the Messiah, because his origins are known (John 7:27, 42). Anyone who acknowledges Jesus as the Messiah is expelled from the synagogue (John 9:22).

The ultimate goal of the whole of John's Gospel is to lead to faith in

Jesus as the Christ and as the Son of God (John 20:31). The two titles of dignity are not the same in their content, but they are deeply bound up with each other. Jesus is the Messiah because he is the Son of God. His messianic office and his ministry both have their basis in his divine Sonship.

With an idealized conception of kingship and especially in recollection of King David (2 Sam. 7; Micah 5), the Messiah too is expected as eschatological "King" and is designated as such. The title undoubtedly derives directly from the messianic significance of Ps. 2:6 and Zech. 9:9, already so interpreted by the rabbis. And Jesus is accorded the name of king, but so seldom that one must recognize that it is not perceived as essential.

Fulfilling prophetic expectation, Jesus enters Jerusalem as king (Matthew 21:5; Luke 19:38; John 12:13, 15). The kingship theme appears already in the infancy narrative (Matthew 2:2) and afterwards clearly in the story of the Passion of Jesus (Mark 15: 2, 9, 12, 18, 32). The title occurs incidentally in John (1:49; 6:15; 12:13), and also in his Passion narrative (18:37; 19:14f.; 19:21). Yet the fourth Gospel emphasizes the title King more easily than can be done elsewhere. The tradition is mentioned in Acts 17:7, according to which the Jews in Thessalonica accused the Christians before the civil authorities of acknowledging Jesus as King. Apparently the title would have been politically ambiguous and not without its own dangers. Perhaps this prevented its use and its spread.

According to the expectation of the times, the messianic kingdom of Jesus is understood by many as an earthly one, already present or at least near at hand. This approaching eschatological kingdom is associated with Christ, the hidden King (Matthew 13:41; 16:28). His kingdom is the eschatological dominion (Luke 22:30; 23:42).

With the decline of the expectation of nearness, these foregoing notions also changed. The reign is now the kingship of the exalted Lord, which begins with his resurrection and will be perfected in his parousia. Now Christ is the Lord and King of the beyond. As such he is given the title "King of Kings and Lord of Lords" (1 Tim. 6:15). The Lamb will conquer as "Lord of Lords and King of Kings" (Apoc. 17:14; 19:16). His reign will be made manifest at the distant end of time (2 Tim. 4:1). This reign of Christ extends from the beginning to all times (Luke

1:33). The eternal kingdom beyond, originally designated the kingdom of God, can now be termed the kingdom of Christ (Eph. 5:5; 2 Peter 1:11).

Another way of conceiving it so unites the dominion of Christ with the dominion of God that finally a communication of the kingship of Christ, exercised in time, through that of the eternal God is expected (1 Cor. 15:24; Col. 1:13). The concept of the kingdom of God, so significant in the Gospels, has its own roots, other roots than those of Jesus' messianic title of King. In some passages of the New Testament the union is effected in a secondary manner.

2. SON OF MAN

Son of Man is a title of majesty which, in the Gospels, Jesus frequently uses in his own regard.[150] History of religion professors and biblical exegetes have conducted a great many investigations into the prehistory of the concept and the analysis of the New Testament evidence. The New Testament use of the term has its immediate origin and basis in the Old Testament.[151]

The New Testament Greek expression "Son of Man" ($vi\grave{o}s$ $\tauο\hat{v}$ $\dot{a}v\theta\rho\dot{\omega}\pi ου$) is, through the agency of the Septuagint, the literal translation of the Old Testament Hebrew term *ben 'adam* (or the Aramaic *bar 'enash* or *bar nasha'*). The expressions originally signified "humankind" or "man". In the New Testament, however, the term never has this simple meaning,[152] but is regularly a self-declaration of Jesus, emphasizing his position in salvation history.

It is uniformly in this sense that the expression is found in its very frequent occurrence in the four Gospels. And through its occurrences there are four streams of tradition that can be distinguished in the Synoptics: Mark (2:10; 8:31; 9:31; 10:33; 13:26; 14:62); Source Q (Matthew 8:20 = Luke 9:58; Matthew 11:19 = Luke 7:34; Matthew 12:32 = Luke 12:10; Matthew 24:27 = Luke 17:24; Matthew 24:37 = Luke 17:26; Matthew 24:44 = Luke 12:40); material proper only to Matthew (10:23); material proper only to Luke (6:22; 18:8; 19:10; 22:22, 48).

The expression Son of Man is found only in the mouth of Jesus as a designation of himself, and not in the accounts about Jesus (with the sole exception of Acts 7:56). Nevertheless, Jesus never says: I, the Son of Man. Rather, he speaks of the Son of Man in the third person, as of another. Our Gospels may be regarded as having been committed to writing between the years 70 and 100 A.D. In this period the title Son of Man had long been obsolete in proclamation and teaching, as is proved for this period and earlier by the collection of Pauline Epistles, which does not know the word. If the expression is so important to the Gospels, that can only be explained in the light of the tradition of the primitive community.

Contemporaneous Judaism did not use the term Son of Man as a title for the Messiah, even if the statement about the Son of Man in Dan. 7:13f. was interpreted by some of the rabbis as a messianic statement.

In the Old Testament the term Son of Man is used in various contexts. Son of Man can mean simply a man, designating him as a member of humankind, especially in his relationship to God. Ezechiel in his book is called "son of man" about ninety times, and is mostly so addressed by God. It was as this son of man that the prophet falls on his face before God (1:28). As son of man he is filled with the Spirit of God (2:2). Dwelling in the midst of a people who will not hear and will not see (12:2f.), he must deliver God's word to them (2:3f.). His word, therefore, becomes riddle and parable (17:2). He must prophesy against Israel (4:7) and threaten her with disaster (11:9-11). He bears suffering as a sign of the misery to come upon Israel (12:6, 17-20).

But he must also announce the future good shepherd (34:23), the cleansing by the Spirit (36:26f.), the resurrection of the dead (37:1-14), and the future glory of the new temple and of a holy land (chs. 40–48). And all these things he prophesies and announces as son of man. Such features put one in mind of the image and works of Jesus. Did Jesus take up this language and its concepts in order to explain and clarify his ministry for himself and for the people?

Elsewhere an elevated style with the term son of man describes the situation of mankind universally. "God is not a man, that he should lie, nor a son of man, that he should change his mind about anything" (Num. 23:19). "What is man, that you are mindful of him? Or the son of man, that you are concerned about him?" (Ps. 8:5). "What then with man, who is but a maggot, and the son of man, a worm?" (Job 25:6).

"Son of man" can also designate one especially chosen, as in the case of the king: "May your hand be upon the man at your right, upon the son of man, whom you have strengthened for yourself" (Ps. 80:18).

The son of man appears in another signification in apocalyptic writings. The most important text is Daniel 7:13f. Four great monsters, symbolizing four world empires, have risen from the sea as from a chaos hostile to God. They are disposed of in judgment. "Then one like a son of man came with the clouds of heaven. He came to the Ancient of Days and was presented before him. And to him was given power and glory and a kingdom. All nations and peoples and tongues must serve him, and his kingdom will never be destroyed." In the vision of Daniel the son of man is not a person, but probably, after the fashion of the four beasts which represent four worldly empires, the eschatological kingdom of God or the people Israel, the people of "the saints" (Dan. 7:21-25). As opposed to the deformity of the beasts, the son of man is the symbol of humanity.

Daniel 7 has made its way into the extra-biblical Apocalyptics. In the picturesque language of the *Ethiopic Book of Henoch* (37–71) the son of man is produced at the beginning of time before all creatures, but remains hidden in heaven until he comes at the end of the ages in order to pass judgment on the world. After the rejection of the godless he will rule over the righteous. The son of man is a pre-existing heavenly being, not yet a messianic earthly king. This picturesque imagery arose (presumably) in the first century before Christ. The texts about the son of man are lacking in the scrolls of the *Henoch* found at Qumran. The figure of the son of man, therefore, probably commanded little attention there. In a similar fashion the son of man finds entry into *4 Esdras 13*. "The Most High will redeem creation through him" (13:26). The text is certainly to be dated in the Christian era. What is significant is that in these apocalyptic writings the son of man is an individual person, just as he is in the New Testament.

In the Gospels three different circles of reference in regard to the Son of Man are recognizable.[153]

a) In some passages the statements about the Son of Man have an entirely messianic sense. Jesus operates now as Son of Man. As such he has full authority on earth to forgive sins (Mark 2:10). Jesus defends his disciples who were pulling ears of grain on the Sabbath. "For the Son of Man is Lord even over the Sabbath" (Mark 2:28). Two eschatological witnesses of God are now coming forward, John the Baptist and the Son of Man; both are rejected (Matthew 11:18f.). Jesus himself is the homeless Son of Man (Matthew 8:20). The question about the identity of the Son of Man is simply a straightforward question about the identity of Jesus, who is speaking (Matthew 16:13). A saying about the Son of Man can be a thinly veiled personal declaration of Jesus.

Of Jesus, the historical Son of Man, it is stated: "Anyone who says a word against the Son of Man, it will be forgiven him. But if anyone blasphemes against the Holy Spirit, it will not be forgiven him" (Luke 12:10). If it be supposed that in an older form a comparison was drawn between the calumniation of a man, which is to be forgiven, and the calumniation or blaspheming of the Spirit, which is unforgivable, it must, nevertheless, have its own meaning in its Synoptic form. Probably in the Gospels it states that a denial of the earthly Son of Man is not so seriously decisive and conclusive as obduracy against the Exalted One and against the Spirit operative in the community.

b) In other passages of the Gospels the title Son of Man appears in statements about the Passion of Jesus. This is the case first of all in the prophecies about the Passion that are common to the Synoptics. "The Son of Man must suffer much and be rejected by the elders, the high priests, and the Scribes, and be put to death, and after three days rise again" (Mark 8:31; similar in 9:31 and 10:33f.; and in the Synoptic parallels; also Mark 9:9, 12; 14:21; Luke 17:25; see above § 7d). His destiny to suffering is established as a divine decree. The divine will, traced out in the Scriptures beforehand, must be fulfilled. The Son of Man must be rejected, like the building stone by the builders (Ps. 118:22). The destiny of the righteous man of the Old Testament, in particular that of the "Servant of Yahweh", befalls the Son of Man. The figure of the Son of Man is united with the suffering Servant of Yahweh of Deutero-Isaiah.

Mark 9:12 certainly sounds like an echo of Is. 53:3; and Mark 10:45 re-echoes Is. 53:10-12. Man and Son of Man are placed in opposition one to another (Mark 9:31; 14:21). The byplay in the terms presents the deep humiliation of the Son of Man, since he is to be delivered up to men and made subject to them. The joining of the image of the Son of Man to that of the Servant of Yahweh takes place only in the Gospels.

Who brought this joining about? The Gospels say that it was Jesus himself.

c) In still other passages, constituting a separate group in themselves, the Son of Man is an apocalyptic figure; such is the case in the great eschatological discourse of the Synoptics. "Then will the sign of the Son of Man [154] appear in the heavens and all the tribes of the earth will lament; and they will behold the Son of Man coming on the clouds of heaven with power and great glory" (Matthew 24:30). The great judgment is depicted as revelation of the Son of Man. "When the Son of Man will come in his glory and all the angels with him, then will he seat himself on the throne of his glory, and all peoples will be assembled before him" (Matthew 25:31f.). The arrival of the Son of Man is so near that the preaching of the Gospel will not be completed even once in Israel before he comes (Matthew 10:23). Present time and eschatological future are joined. "Whoever is ashamed of me and of my words in this adulterous and sinful generation, of him too will the Son of Man be ashamed when he comes with his angels in the glory of his Father" (Mark 8:38). Is this a saying of the historical Jesus? Does it not already presuppose the situation of the persecuted community of disciples? Is Jesus speaking of the Son of Man as another apocalyptic judge, or is he speaking of himself?

Luke 12:8 is a similar passage: "Everyone who acknowledges me before men, him too will the Son of Man acknowledge before the angels of God." The angels of God are probably not thought of as abiding in heaven, but in the apocalyptic situation of the coming of the Son of Man. The saying appears in Matthew 10:32 as a first person statement of Jesus: "Everyone who acknowledges me before men, him too will I acknowledge before my Father in heaven." The saying stems from Source Q. What form had it there? Was it a first person statement or a Son of Man statement? The question can hardly be answered.

The statement of Jesus before the Sanhedrin pertains to the apocalyptic expectation of the Son of Man: "Henceforth the Son of Man will be seated at the right hand of the power of God" (Luke 22:69). This formulation seems to be more primitive than that drawn out of Dan. 7:13f. in Mark 14:62, "You shall see the Son of Man sitting at the right hand of God and coming with the clouds of heaven." In the Lukan saying Jesus, as Son of Man, has a seat at the heavenly court of judgment; the

Markan statement announces the future coming of Jesus as Son of Man. In further texts (Luke 17:24, 26; 18:8; 21:36) the Son of Man is the coming Judge. The last two verses noted are peculiar to Luke. Does Luke know a special tradition of the Son of Man sayings?

In the total picture, about half of the synoptic Son of Man sayings is of the apocalyptic sort. The connection with Dan. 7:13f. is clear. In both instances the scenes are alike. The Son of Man is at home at the throne of God; he comes on the clouds of heaven, and the dominion is transferred to him.

The phrase "the power is given to him", in the vision about the son of man in Dan. 7:14, re-echoes in the revelatory statement of the resurrected Christ in Matthew 28:18, "All power is given to me." This is probably not an accidental correspondence, but a calculated reference. In the Gospel of Matthew, Daniel 7:13f. is quoted twice in an emphatic way. In Matthew 24:30 in the apocalyptic discourse the return of the Son of Man is announced; and Matthew 26:64 speaks of the seating of the Son of Man at the right hand of God. Matthew 28:18 can scarcely mean that the eschatological return of the Son of Man is now anticipated and realized; it means rather that the prediction of Matthew 26:64 is now fulfilled, since the exalted Christ is at the right hand of God.[155]

If in this way in the Synoptics three groups of sayings about the Son of Man are distinguished according to their point of reference, then the very difficult question is raised, a question answered in very different ways, of how these groups of sayings are related one to another. Are they all original, or is the concept of the Son of Man properly original only to one group, making its entry only later into the other groups?

For a long time it was fashionable to accept as probable that the apocalyptic use of the concept was the earliest, the others being later and secondary. With his sayings about the Son of Man, so said the professional critics, Jesus may originally have been speaking about another expected apocalyptic figure, who would shortly appear and would be endorsed by Jesus and his community. If Jesus always speaks of the Son of Man in the third person — of someone else, as it were — this is in fact an indication of such origins of the concept. After Easter the community would have identified the exalted Lord with the Son of Man, and accordingly would have expected the return of Jesus as Son of Man.[156]

Today exegetes in increasing numbers are re-examining this conception and accepting the conclusion about the declaration on the earthly works and the sufferings of the Son of Man. These declarations go back to Jesus himself in their essentials.[157]

The sayings about the Son of Man are in any case quite otherwise than an everyday discourse on man and what can always happen to him. Neither are they, as ecclesiastical exegesis from St. Ignatius to St. Augustine supposed, declarations on the human nature of the Son of God; rather, they are declarations of majesty. In the totality of the New Testament sayings the claim is made that the Son of Man is the throne-companion of God, that he pre-exists and will be the eschatological Judge of the world. The peculiar character of the title is the disproportion between the straightforward meaning of the word "man" and the claim of dignity most high. As a self-designation it proclaims the Messiahship and at the same time conceals it. Only to faith can it be made manifest.

If in accord with the apocalyptic expectation of the Book of Daniel the Son of Man is predicated as the future Judge of the world, the idea of judgment experiences a strange and basic turn. The Judge is at one and the same time the human brother and the atoning Servant of God. The Judge is at the same time the God of Mercy and the Redeemer.

The Gospel of John [158] attests also in the matter of the Son of Man, as so often elsewhere, the end and the perfection of the New Testament history of belief. This Gospel uses the title Son of Man with unquestionable certainty as a messianic testimony to Jesus. It is Jesus himself who reveals himself as Son of Man. "No one has ascended into heaven except him who has descended from heaven, the Son of Man" (John 3:13; *cf.* 6:62). The earthly Jesus knows himself as Son of Man, upon whom the angels are ascending and descending (John 1:51). The Son of Man is the heavenly pre-existing one, who enters into lost humanity and ascends again to heaven in glory. Themes from Daniel, then, and from the Synoptics are employed.

The ascent begins in his being raised up on the Cross, which is in turn a sign of his being exalted in glory. "Just as Moses lifted up the serpent in the desert, so too must the Son of Man be lifted up" (John 3:14; *cf.* 8:28). The Son of Man must endure the Cross; but his Passion is his passageway to glory. So says Jesus himself at the beginning of his mortal agony: "The hour has come for the Son of Man to be glorified" (John 12:23; *cf.* 13:31). The Passion of the Messiah and the being exalted of the Son of Man are not mutually exclusive (John 12:34). For the Exalted One is the Lord of the Church who, through word and sacrament, dispenses life and spirit (John 6:27, 53-62). If there is no talk in John of the return of the Son of Man, his office as Judge is mentioned nevertheless: "He has given him power to render judgment, because he is the Son of Man" (John 5:27).

In the New Testament literature a statement about the Son of Man appears even in Acts 7:56, in the confession of Stephen: "I see the heavens opened and the Son of Man standing at the right hand of God." Stephen is probably referring to the statement of Jesus before the Sanhedrin (Luke 22:69). As Son of Man, Jesus is Judge of the world and Ruler of the world. Otherwise, there are found in the New Testament only indications that the figure of the Son of Man is known. The recipient of the vision beholds Christ "in the midst of seven lampstands, as one like to a son of man" (Apoc. 1:13). The influence of Dan. 7:13f. is clear. Likewise in Apoc. 14:14, "Behold, on the cloud there sat one who was like unto a son of man."

In other passages there is a none too certain reference to the Christological figure of the Son of Man (1 Cor. 15:20-22; Heb. 2:6). Paul does not use the title at all. The reason, no doubt, is that in the Greek world it would not be understandable as a declaration of majesty, and would have to be understood only as a declaration of the human origins of Jesus. This takes place already in St. Ignatius, in his *Letter to the Ephesians* 20:2 (Jurgens, no. 43): "Jesus Christ, who was of the family of David according to the flesh, the Son of Man and the Son of God."

The Synoptic tradition uses the term Son of Man in an otherwise unknown intensity. Exegesis accordingly agrees overwhelmingly that it was Jesus who introduced the figure of the Son of Man. In speaking of the Son of Man, was he speaking of himself, or of another who would appear in the endtime? Did Jesus know himself as the Son of Man, and declare himself such, at least in a veiled way? The evidence permits the conclusion that only hesitatingly did Jesus allow even this title of majesty to be applied to himself, because it too did not correspond sufficiently to his consciousness of his mission. If one can consider the testimony of the Gospels about the Son of Man collectively, then it indicates the presence of man — indeed, of the servant Jesus — in the expectation of divine corroboration and glorification.

3. SON (SON OF GOD)

In the New Testament Jesus is given the titles of dignity "Son" and "Son of God".[159] Here too what the precise import of the name is will have to be explained primarily from the Old Testament and from inter-testamental Judaism. In the Old Testament the connection between Yahweh and Israel is designated as a father-son relationship. "Thus says Yahweh, 'Israel is my son, my firstborn'" (Exod. 4:22). Given the status of a son, Israel can then call God its Father (Jer. 3:19f.; *cf.* Deut. 32:6).

In a special way the pious can be called sons of God (Ps. 73:15), and so too with the saints (Wis. 5:5). As representing Israel, the king can be designated as son of God. Yahweh says of him: "You are my son, this day have I begotten you" (Ps. 2:7; *cf.* Ps. 89:27f.). To the dynasty of David the promise is given that it shall endure forever. The king is promised: "I will be his Father, and he shall be my son" (2 Sam. 7:14). In distinction to the idea of a physical divine sonship of the king through begetting, such as is known in ancient presentations, the Old Testament declarations confirm the legitimacy of the king, which is established through a formula of adoption. By the manifest will of Yahweh the king is acknowledged as son, and the protection and fidelity of God is promised him. Nowhere in Hebrew texts, however, is the Messiah called Son of God.

Jesus uses the terms denoting divine Sonship in their broadest sense. If God is Father (Matthew 6:9; Luke 15:20), then all men are God's children. In a special way they are called sons of God, who are peacemakers (Matthew 5:9) and who are deemed worthy of resurrection (Luke 20:36).

In the New Testament Christology distinction must be made between the titles Son and Son of God. In the texts of the Synoptic Gospels Jesus speaks of himself as the Son, but never calls himself Son of God. The latter title is unequivocally the Church's confession of faith. Jesus speaks repeatedly of his special Sonship. In the conversation over the temple tax Jesus distinguishes himself as Son from all other Jews; and he claims a unique relationship with God (Matthew 17:25f.). The debate over Davidic sonship serves to bring out the contrast between Son of David and Son of God (Matthew 22:42-45; § 10, 1c and 3b). In the parable of the wicked vine-dressers, an allegory of salvation history, after having sent the prophets, God then sends "the one beloved Son" (Mark 12:6). As the one Son, Jesus is distinct and set apart from the prophets.[160]

As the Son, Jesus in fact occupies a position over the angels, but under the Father: "That day and that hour no one knows, not even the angels in heaven, not even the Son, but the Father only" (Mark 13:32). The statement seems to be an old one, since it unequivocally subordinates the Son to the Father, to whom the apocalyptic secrets are reserved. The saying was soon provoking scandal. Probably that is why it is lacking in Luke.[161]

An exclusive recognition joins the Father and the one Son. "Everything was delivered over to me by my Father, and no one knows the Son except the Father only, and no one knows the Father except the Son only, and him to whom the Son wants to give a revelation" (Matthew 11:27). The Old Testament speaks in many formulas and formulations about the knowledge which joins one with God. Moses was known by God, and he knew God (Exod. 33:12f.). The pious man who belongs to God knows him (Ps. 36:11; 91:14). The Messiah has the spirit of the knowledge of God (Is. 11:2). The Servant of Yahweh effects righteousness for many, by virtue of his knowledge (Is. 53:11). The highest hopes of the Old Testament are taken up and fulfilled in the word of Jesus. God knows him to be his Son, and he knows the Father as no one else does (on Matthew 11:27, see above, § 4).

In the Gospel of Luke the designation of Jesus as Son of God appears twice in the annunciation of the birth of Jesus. "He will be called Son of the Most High, and the Lord God will give him the throne of David, his father" (Luke 1:32). His Sonship is described in accord with the promise in 2 Sam. 7:14 (and Micah 4:7). Accordingly one will understand it as messianic adoption and establishment, in the same way that Israel's kings were confirmed as sons of God (Ps. 2:7). According to the word of the angel, the Child will not only be full of the Spirit, like the prophets and like John (Luke 1:5), but he will be produced by the Spirit (Luke 1:35, § 12, 2a). But how is the word of the angel to be understood? Is it to be translated:*"For this reason* the Holy One be-gotten shall be called Son of God"?

The study of the history of religion ponders the explanation that Luke wanted to say that Jesus, since he, begotten of God, has no human father, is God's Son. For the New Testament, this would be a totally unique understanding of divine Sonship. It would neutralize the other New Testament concept of the incarnation of the eternal Son of God. In the opinion of some authors Luke himself so understands the Sonship of Jesus, in accord with the saying of Jesus in Luke 10:21-23; in this in-stance was he following another tradition and conceptualization, with-out noticing the inconsistency? If one is unwilling to accept this, he will translate Luke 1:35, "The one to be born (of you) will be called holy — Son of God."

Just as penetratingly as Jesus says that God is the one heavenly Fa-ther — for which reason he teaches his disciples to pray: "Our Father" (Matthew 6:9) — do the Gospels say unequivocally that Jesus abides in an incomparably solitary relationship to the Father, a relationship which he shares with no one. The Son of Man will come "in the glory of his Father" (Mark 8:38). In prayer he calls to him: "Father!" (Mark 14:36). The Father is the Father of this Son in a completely special way (Mark 13:32). The cry of jubilation makes this relationship between Father and Son manifest (Matthew 11:27). In reference to the disciples Jesus says: "Your Father" (Mark 11:25; Luke 12:32).

Matthew augments in the sayings of the Lord the explicit mentioning of the Father of Jesus: compare Matthew 12:50 with Mark 3:35; Mat-thew 20:23 with Mark 10:40; Matthew 26:29 with Mark 14:25; Matthew 10:32f. with Luke 12:8f.; also Matthew 16:17; 25:34; 26:39. The interest of the prospering Christological confession is obvious.

What happens so often in the process of the passage of the historical tradition has happened also in this case: according to the late infancy narrative (Luke 2:49), the boy Jesus already knew about this unique Fatherhood. The sonship of the disciples is imparted through the Son-ship of Jesus (Matthew 18:10, 19; Rom. 8:15; Gal. 4:5f.). In the setting forth of the special Sonship there is the beginning of what Paul later formulates when he calls God the "Father of our Lord Jesus Christ" (Rom. 15:6 *et passim*; likewise in 1 Peter 1:3; Apoc. 14:1).

The Gospel of John never speaks of the universal Fatherhood of God.

The Father is exclusively the Father of Jesus Christ. Jesus is the one, eternal Son (John 1:18). Jesus and the Father are one (John 10:30). It is at the acknowledgement of this Fatherhood that belief and disbelief part company (John 5:18; 8:54f.). All teaching and revelation is a making known of the Father (John 10:18; 14:20; 15:15; 16:25). It is the resurrected Christ who first speaks, and then only once, of the Father of the disciples; and even here with a sharp distinction: "Your Father and my Father, your God and my God." It is the fruit of the work of salvation that the disciples are now, as "brothers" of Jesus, sons of the Father (John 20:17).

The Gospels recount that on two occasions the Father in a special way acknowledged the Messiah, Jesus, as his Son. At the baptism of Jesus (Mark 1:11) and at his transfiguration (Mark 9:7) the divine voice attested to this Sonship.[162] In the Gospel of Mark Jesus for the first time is called "Son of God". Thus the narrative could be understood, especially since it declares the Sonship with the adoption formula of Ps. 2:7, as installation into the messianic eschatological Sonship. In the Gospel of Matthew (2:15) and even more clearly in the Gospel of Luke (1:32-35), Jesus bears the title Son of God from the very beginning. The baptism narrative, then, is a making known of the Sonship which Jesus already possesses.

The baptism and transfiguration of Christ are epiphany stories, which make known the hidden glory of the earthly Jesus. The event presupposed in the life of Jesus is signified in the present narration and must first be sought for behind the narrative. The Gospel of Mark, which created the order of the stories and is therefore still of greatest utility in allowing us to recognize the original significance, assigns both narratives deliberately to their place in the general continuity of Gospel material.

The revelation about Jesus is significant at his baptism. With the acceptance of baptism he subordinates himself to John the Baptist, and he places himself in the ranks of the sinners. The scandal which one could take because of this is obvious, and is visible as the motivation and excuse for a passage peculiar to Matthew alone, Matthew 3:14f. It is necessary, therefore, to give a special assurance at the baptism of Jesus that he is the Son of God. The revelation is all the more appropriate at this time, since it is now that Jesus enters upon his public life and begins to teach openly. From the very beginning the Gospel wanted to make known who he was. To this end it employs traditional themes.

The opening of the heavens signifies apocalyptic revelation (Ezech. 1:1 *et passim*; Acts 7:56; Apoc. 4:1). Subject now to severe foreign rule, the people of God regards itself as abandoned by God and is oppressed by guilt. It is but natural to expect that, to hail the messianic eschatological time, the heavens themselves will open in a sign of favor. According to the conviction of the Church, this has now taken place through Christ (John 1:51).

Even the heavenly voice belongs in the apocalyptic scene (Dan. 4:28; *4 Esdras* 6:13; Apoc. 10:4). The rabbis were saying that prophecy, once the voice of God to his people, has been silenced; now only the *bath qôl* (the echo of that voice) still resounds. Now it issues forth as a voice from heaven at the baptism and at the transfiguration of Jesus (as also in John 12:28).

In Mark 1:11 the divine statement about Jesus combines Ps. 2:7 and Is. 42:1. In the contemporaneous expectation, Ps. 2:7 is also understood as obviously referring to the messianic Sonship. Is. 42:1 designates Jesus as the Servant of Yahweh. The coming down of the Spirit designates Jesus as the expected Messiah (Is. 11:2; § 10, 1c). The dove is the symbol of the divine Spirit (§ 12, 2a).

The consecration of the new high priest in the *Testaments of the Twelve Patriarchs: Levi* 18:6f., comes close to the story of the baptism of Jesus: "The heavens open, and from the sanctuary of glory holiness comes upon him with a paternal voice like that of Abraham to Isaac. The glory of the Most High is granted him, and the spirit of understanding and of holiness will rest upon him (in the water)." Certainly it is questionable whether this depiction is not perhaps a Christian interpolation or whether it is dependent at all upon the New Testament baptism account. Such a dependence must in any case be accepted for the assertion "in the water".

On the revelation of the Trinity at the baptism of Jesus, see § 21, 6.

The transfiguration of Jesus follows the announcement of his Passion and death, over which the disciples are scandalized (Mark 8:31-33). The transfiguration allows something of the glory of the resurrection to shine through. The voice which attests to the Sonship of Christ was, in the story of his baptism, addressed only to Christ (Mark 1:11, "You are my beloved Son"); but at the transfiguration it is a revelation for the disciples and for the world (Mark 9:7, "This is my beloved Son"). The added admonition, "Listen to him", demands consequent acceptance of the Son's message. By referring to the admonition of the departing Moses, "Him shall you hear" (Deut. 18:15), the words characterize Jesus as the prophet promised by Moses (§ 5).

Other themes of the story of the transfiguration again pertain to epiphanies and apocalpytics. The transfiguration takes place on a mountain, in all religions a place of revelation. The cloud both reveals God and conceals him (Exod. 13:21f.; 19:9; Ezech. 30:3; Dan. 7:13; Mark 14:62; Luke 21:27; Acts 1:9).

At the end of time the righteous will be transfigured in super-terrestrial brightness and shining beauty (Mark 12:25; 1 Cor. 15:51f.; *Syriac Apocalypse of Baruch* 51:3-12). White signifies the heavenly glory of the Son of Man (Apoc. 1:14), as also that of the angels (Mark 16:5 and of the transfigured blessed (Apoc. 3:4; 7:90). Elijah and Moses who appeared with Jesus are eschatological figures (Mal. 4:4f.; Apoc. 11:3-5). In the transfiguration Jesus is already surrounded by eschatological glory. The expected endtime lies hidden within him, even if for the present nothing is evident except the Son of Man who must suffer. His word is to be obeyed (Mark 9:7). But he will bring an end to the world (Mark 8:38). Probably it is possible to some extent to interpret the revelational content of the narration; but the problem is compounded by the difficulty of determining the starting point and motivation of the tradition.

The interpretation occasionally encountered, that the transfiguration is a resurrection story pre-dated into the life of Jesus, is nevertheless quite improbable. The appearance of the two witnesses, Elijah and Moses, would be quite odd in a story of the resurrection, and furthermore in any other story of a resurrection the voice of the resurrected one is always heard. The story does not present the exalted Christ, but the significance of the earthly historical Jesus. The narrative depends on the testimony of the three pillars among the apostles, Peter, James, and John (Gal. 2:9). Is there, as a basis for the transfiguration, a visionary revelation granted to them (or perhaps to Peter alone), which was afterwards decked out with additional themes?

The Gospels depict in their accounts the attestation of Jesus' divine Sonship. The sick and the demoniacs acknowledge Jesus as "Son of

God" (Mark 3:11; 5:7). Since Jewish monotheism excluded the idea of a physical divine Sonship, the title "Son of God" can only mean the chosen one of God. In the New Testament the title is one of messianic dignity, like "Holy One of God" (Mark 1:24) or "Son of David" (Mark 10:47). In this signification the confession of Peter, "You are the Messiah" (Mark 8:29), is expanded in a later formulation, "You are the Messiah, the Son of the living God" (Matthew 16:16).

In the narration about the quieting of the storm the bare account in Mark 6:51 is filled out with the attestation of the disciples, "In truth, you are the Son of God" (Matthew 14:33).

The question of the high priest, whether Jesus is the Son of the Most Blessed One, can, in his mouth, mean divine Sonship only as messianic dignity. Yet, Jesus' answer elevates the Son to the very throne of God (Mark 14:61f.).

The hearing and teaching community understood such statements handed down by tradition more and more in the later and more profound sense of an essential divine Sonship of Jesus.

In the report about the trial of Jesus the titles Messiah, Son of God, and Son of Man appear in close connection with each other in a crucial passage, when the high priest asks Jesus whether he is the Messiah and the Son of the Most Blessed One, and Jesus affirms this and adds: "You shall see the Son of Man sitting at the right hand of the Power and coming on the clouds of heaven."

The statement is taken by the court as blasphemy against God (Mark 14:61-64). The Judaism of the time of Jesus did not prosecute judicially a claim to Messiahship, but simply let it run its course to success or failure. The Messiah was not expected in Israel as Son of God. How could the high priest combine the two titles? Even the title Son of God (thus in Matthew 26:63) elsewhere in the New Testament is first of all an attestation to faith. In Jesus' answer his exaltation and his parousia are combined, which results in a remarkably singular expression on the lips of Jesus. In his statement probably Ps. 110:1 and Dan. 7:13, and perhaps even Zech. 12:10 are used. The fact that Dan. 7:13 is lacking in the parallel in Luke 22:69 may perhaps afford us a glimpse of the growth of a tradition. All three Old Testament texts are important in the theology of Scripture.

Historically it would seem likely that the Jewish court denounced

Jesus to the Romans as a messianic pretender, and demanded the death penalty. The titles of majesty, Messiah, Son of God, and Son of Man, are the Church's profession of faith in the condemned.

In the first post-Paschal testimonies it is stated that by his resurrection and exaltation Jesus was installed in his divine Sonship (Acts 2:30f.; 13:33). Even the pre-Pauline formula of faith contained in Rom. 1:3f. is so to be understood (§ 9e).

The New Testament Christology of the Sonship is presented by means of the messianic promises of 2 Sam. 7:12-14 (Acts 2:30f.; Rom. 1:3; Heb. 1:5) and of the messianically understood Ps. 2:7 (Acts 4:25f.; 13:33; Heb. 1:5). In both Old Testament texts the Messiah is represented as the Son of God. Ps. 2:7 was understood as messianic even by rabbinic exegesis. In the eschatological midrash *4 Q florilegium* from Qumran, the two texts are closely associated with each other.

For Paul the divine Sonship of Jesus is a certain declaration of the faith. To the formula of a two-stage Christology (Rom. 1:3f.) handed down by tradition, he prefixes the predication which recasts the whole: "concerning his Son" (Rom. 1:3). As God's Son the Christ was pre-existent. God sent him into the world (Rom. 8:3f.; Gal. 4:4f.). God revealed him to the apostles (Gal. 1:16). That God sent his own Son makes the grandeur of the salvational deed manifest (Rom. 5:10; 8:32; Gal. 2:20). The community of salvation is the fellowship with the Son of God, who is now the Lord (1 Cor. 1:9). The Son of God will re-appear as eschatological Judge (1 Thess. 1:10). Paul mentions (as also the Synoptics, in Mark 13:32) the subordination of the Son: "When all things will have been subjected to him, then also will the Son himself subject himself to him, who subjected all things to him, so that God may be all in all" (1 Cor. 15:28). The declaration of the divine Sonship of Jesus does not balk at a metaphysical divine equality. The goal is the glory and power of the one God. The true Sonship of Jesus is so very much the decisive basis of salvation that preaching can be described in summary fashion as the gospel of the Son of God (Rom. 1:3, 9; 2 Cor. 1:19; Gal. 1:16; similar in Eph. 4:13).

For the Epistle to the Hebrews the divine Sonship of Jesus is doctrine of the faith. It is established (Heb. 1:2; 5:5f.; 7:28) from Old Testament texts (Ps. 2:7f.; 110:4), from which in point of fact the New Testament declaration derives. The Sonship must hold good even in the Passion

(Heb. 5:8). As the Son of God Jesus is the heavenly Lord of the Church (Heb. 3:6; 4:14). It is in respect to him that the sinner is guilty (Heb. 6:6; 10:29). The divine Sonship of Jesus surpasses every other possible dignity, that of Moses (Heb. 10:29), that of the Old Testament priesthood (Heb. 7:3, 28), indeed, that of the angels themselves (Heb. 1:7f.).

In the Johannine writings too the divine Sonship of Jesus is presented in a way that reflects the more polished and perfected faith of the Church. From the very beginning John the Baptist (John 1:34) and the disciples (John 1:49) proclaim that Jesus is the Son of God. Jesus himself testifies to his own divine Sonship (John 10:36). Faith, which imparts salvation, must acknowledge that Jesus is the one Son of God (John 3:18; 5:36; 11:27; 1 John 3:23; 5:10, 12). The divine Sonship is pre-existing being of the Son with the Father (John 17:5, 24). The Father has sent the Son, and has given him up (John 3:16f.; 1 John 4:9f.). The Son will be the Judge (John 5:22). He abides forever (John 8:35).

Nevertheless, John does not intend to be stating metaphysical propositions on the unity of the Father and the Son. The nature or characteristic of the divine Sonship is intimate personal relationship and love of Father and Son (John 3:35; 5:20; 14:20). The Father is made manifest in the Son. Whoever sees the Son sees the Father (John 14:9). The operation of Father and Son is one (John 5:19). One glory belongs to both (John 5:23; 11:4; 17:9). Thus Father and Son are one (John 10:30). The love which joins Father and Son must also unite the disciples of the Church (1 John 1:3).

In the ancient world there were many different kinds of sons of gods. In the ancient East kings were regarded as divinely begotten. In Greek mythology the gods beget children with human women. Following the example of Alexander the Great, Hellenistic kings and princes bore the title "Son of God" (υἱὸς θεοῦ). In Rome emperors were divinized after their death. The (adoptive) son and successor was accordingly "Son of the Divine" (*Divi filius*). In the eastern part of the empire they were given the surname "Son of (a) God".

Men possessed of genius surpassing human measure (statesmen, philosophers) were worshipped as divine or as sons of gods (§ 10, 3c). This need not all be understood as servile flattery. The step from the human to the divine was much more easily accomplished by the men of pagan antiquity than it could be for anyone whose outlook was determined by a rigid biblical monotheism. Ancient sensitivity came to know the revelation of the divine in the most extravagantly extraordinary.

In another sense, moreover, the Stoa taught the divine sonship of all men. "We have all come into existence directly from God, and God is the Father of gods and men" (Epictetus, *Diss.* 1, 3, 1).

Investigation into the history of religion thinks it fitting that these ancient pagan notions should have contributed to the fact that Jesus came to be worshipped as Son of God. Biblical exegesis, however, emphasizes the biblical postulates for Jesus' title of Son.

According to the Synoptics Jesus designated his relationship to God as a unique filial relationship (Mark 12:6; 13:32; Matthew 11:25-27). He distinguishes this Sonship from the filial relationship of the disciples to the heavenly Father. It is hardly possible to eliminate this whole systematized report as a creation of community theology, even if the faith and theology of the community from the very beginning deepen and develop the word of Jesus, already at hand. This came about through the application of the Old Testament declaration of the messianic Sonship (Ps. 2:7; 2 Sam. 7:14 in Mark 1:11; Luke 1:32; Acts 13:33; Heb. 1:5). Accordingly, the Sonship was understood essentially as election and installation into the messianic office.

Along with this there is generally an assertion about obedience directed toward the Father (Phil. 2:8; Heb. 5:8; John 5:10; 14:28). Late Jewish expectations may also be operative here, like that in Dan. 7:14 about the Son of Man hidden from eternity with God; or the Wisdom which is God's image and which dwelt with him from eternity and has now been made manifest in Christ (Luke 7:35; 11:49; 1 Cor. 1:24); or finally, that about the Logos who, for Philo, is God's Son (§ 11, 6). Thus the Sonship is conceived as prehistorical and pertaining to the beyond. This is clear to Paul (Gal. 4:4; Rom. 8:3), who nevertheless accepts at the same time an older Christology (Phil. 2:6-11); and it is just as clear to John (1:14), and in the Epistle to the Hebrews (1:5f.). From his eternal pre-existence with the Father, the Son is sent into the world (§ 10, 6). The dogmatic theology of the Church interpreted the biblical testimony further by means of philosophical conceptualization, and it is thus that it explains the metaphysical divine Sonship.

If we call Jesus Son and Son of God, our language is making use of an image or an analogy. The term Son declares the personal communion of Jesus with the God whom he knew and taught as Father. His life was the discharge of a perfect and incomparable Sonship in obedience and love, even to a death which made the message of the Father seem to be disproven radically and to have been frustrated. The Father acknowledged the Son in the latter's exaltation. Faith and doctrine conceived the Sonship beyond experience as the basis for the existence of the unity with the Father in the diversity from him, and as a relationship internal to the Godhead within the pre-existence thereof. The universal sonship before the heavenly Father, enjoyed by all men, is essentially different from that of the one Son. Nevertheless, Jesus is the prototype of true sonship for all other sons.

4. SAVIOR

In common linguistic usage one can speak in various ways of the rescuing and saving which men experience at the hands of other men, through fortuitous circumstances, or even through the Godhead.[163] We are not concerned here with purely profane linguistic usages. Of the God of the Testaments, Old and New, it is said that he rescues, helps, and brings about salvation. (The Old Testament expresses this with the word *yasha'* while the Greek Bible uses the term σῴζειν. [*Translator's additional note*: The Hebrew term covers a rather broad variety of concepts, to deliver, to save, to help, to aid, to heal, and is associated also with notions of richness, opulence, welfare, prosperity, safety. The Greek σῴζειν is sufficiently broad to cover much the same notions; and more to our present point, the German *heilen* with its noun *Heil* covers almost precisely the same broad variety of concepts as the Hebrew, and runs the gamut from prosperity and welfare of a purely secular kind to eternal salvation. In some respects it is unfortunate that we have no single term in English sufficiently broad so as to cover this same ground, and to serve as a universal translation for *heilen* and *Heil*. The consequence of this is that it can somewhat complicate the translator's task; and he has to decide in a particular context whether *heilen* means to grant eternal salvation, to restore one to physical health, or to make one's affairs prosper, etc. Let it also be noted, however, that if this difficulty exists, it is because English has a larger vocabulary and is *more* precise than these other languages, and has perhaps two or three dozens of ways of expressing what they must express with a choice of only two or three terms. To say that a certain term in Hebrew or Greek or German can be translated by a long list of English terms means simply that, as compared to English, these other languages are less precise and are somewhat vague or fuzzy in their ability to conceptualize in a particular area]).

Man is able to rescue, and God even makes use of men to grant assistance. Nevertheless, it is much more God himself who rescues and aids, as the One who has all power at his disposal, and who therefore is best able to grant his protection and help. Israel experienced and remembered the powerful help of God in her deliverance from Egypt (Exod. 15:2; 106:21), and afterwards in her victories over her enemies (Deut. 33:29; 1 Sam. 14:23; Jer. 14:8; Hab. 3:13). The individual can anticipate God's help by reason of his membership in the people of Israel (Ps. 106:4). God helps the oppressed (Ps. 25:5; 42:6; 109:31; 145:19). This God will also give prosperity in the endtime (Is. 43:5-7; Jer. 46:27; Zech. 8:7). The endtime community will draw from the streams of salvation going out from Jerusalem (Is. 12:3). In this the whole world will have a share (Is. 45:22; 49:6).

Like later Judaism, the Qumran scrolls too make a forceful declaration of this conviction. God was Israel's aid in her history up till then (1 QM 10:4; 14:4f.; 18:7). Now he saves the poor and the pious (1 QH 2:32, 35; 5:18; 1 QM 14:10; 1 QS 10:17), which is to say, the whole community. The community is the "people of God's deliverance" (1 QM 1:12; 14:5). God grants eternal salvation (1 QM 1:12; 18:11).

In the Old Testament Greek Bible, God is called and acknowledged before all others as Deliverer and Savior (σωτήρ — in Deut. 32:15; Is. 12:2; 17:10; Ps. 27:1, 9; 62:3; 79:9; Hab. 3:18). From the Septuagint and even from those Old Testament writings originally written in Greek (Wis. 16:7; Sir. 51:1; Esther 15:5; Baruch 4:22; 1 Macc. 4:30; likewise *3 Macc.* 6:29 and *Psalms of Solomon* 3:6), it must be concluded that "Savior" (σωτήρ) was a designation of God in Hellenistic Judaism.

The biblical and the Hellenistic are joined in Philo, who can speak familiarly and easily of God as Savior (σωτήρ) and of God's saving deeds (σῴζειν). God is the "Father and Savior" (*De praemiis et poenis* 39). "God is good and the Creator and Producer of all things; and he cares for all his creatures as Savior and Benefactor" (*De specialibus legibus* 209).

Nevertheless, it is not known and is quite unlikely that in the pre-Christian era the Messiah was called Savior (σωτήρ). Moreover, this title is lacking even in the oldest New Testament writings, first appearing in books relating to Hellenistic Christianity.

The word group "to save" (σῴζειν) is of religious significance even in the Greek world. In time of danger man expects and anticipates deliverance and salvation from the gods. The mysteries grant deliverance, inasmuch as the mystēs participates in the fortune of the god who attained salvation. The Church Father Firmicus Maternus (*On the Error of Pagan Religions* 22:1) hands down as the acclamation of salvation in the mystery religions: "Be comforted, you mystēs! Since the god was saved, there is deliverance for us too from our suffering."

In Gnostic religious sentiment, it is the Gnosis which imparts salvation. The Gnosis "imparts the doctrine of how and in what way they can be redeemed" (*Corpus hermeticum* 1:29). The deliverer and savior (σωτήρ) is an important figure in the Greek religions. Greek antiquity designates gods as protectors and deliverers of peoples, communities, and of individual men; thus with Zeus; also Asclepius, the savior of the sick; the Egyptian gods Serapis and Isis, gods too of the mystery religions. These divinities are saviors as dispensers of divine life and salvation. Even creative philosphers were worshipped as saviors; and statemen and lawgivers; and in the cult of the ruler, Hellenistic princes and afterwards Roman emperors.

The New Testament attests and praises God's help, deliverance, and salvation in many ways. On the level of the Old Testament, God's help is lauded in the canticles of the infancy narrative (Luke 1:68, 77). As a matter of course in the Synoptics the words to *save* and *salvation* (σῴζειν and σωτηρία) occasionally refer to eschatological salvation (Mark 13:13, 20; Luke 13:23). God's salvation now takes place in its fullness through the work of the Messiah. Even before the birth of Jesus, that name was explained thus: "He will save his people from their sins" (Matthew 1:21). The cures worked by Jesus were frequently designated as deliverance (σῴζειν). It is faith that cures and delivers (Mark 5:34; 10:52; Luke 7:50; 17:19). The message to be proclaimed in the Acts of the Apostles is that the salvation of God has now taken place, is yet taking place, and will be perfected in Christ (4:9, 12; 11:14; 13:26; 15:11; 16:17, 30f.). All well-being has its basis, proximate or remote, in the work of Christ.

Paul uses the words *to save* and *salvation* very often in reference to God's work on behalf of man. The missionary endeavor of Paul has for its goal the effecting of deliverance and salvation (Rom. 10:1; 1 Cor. 10:33). The redeemed must work out their own salvation "in fear and trembling" (Phil. 2:12). Yet, salvation is ultimately God's eschatological operation. We are already "saved by virtue of hope" (Rom. 8:24). The gospel is "God's power unto salvation" (Rom. 1:16). This is salvation from the coming judgment in wrath (Rom. 5:9; 1 Cor. 3:15; 5:5; 1 Thess. 5:9). "The spirit shall be saved on the day of the Lord" (1 Cor. 5:5). Salvation is effected through Christ. "We are saved in his life" (Rom. 5:10). "Now is the day of salvation" (2 Cor. 6:2).

The later New Testament writings use the terms to save and salvation in a richer depth. This is true of the Pastoral Epistles. "God wills that all men be saved" (1 Tim. 2:4). "He has saved us and called us with a holy calling" (2 Tim. 1:9). "Christ Jesus has come . . . to save sinners" (1 Tim. 1:15). The redeemed can "obtain the salvation in Christ Jesus, in eternal glory" (1 Tim. 2:10). All the prophets have sought after salvation (1 Peter 1:10). Now it is real. "You are redeemed by the precious blood of the Lamb" (1 Peter 1:18f.). Salvation is represented as the "goal of faith" (1 Peter 1:9). This salvation is to be made manifest at the end (1 Peter 1:5). Christ is the author of salvation (Heb. 2:10). It is to be perfected as "eternal salvation" (Heb. 5:9). The Apocalypse of John (7:10; 12:10; 19:1) speaks of God's salvation as the eschatological victory which he gives to the Church.

In accord with the language of the Old Testament Greek Bible, the New Testament designates God as Savior (σωτήρ). Such is the case in Mary's canticle of praise, the Magnificat (Luke 1:47). In the doxology of the Epistle of Jude (25) God is called Savior. Six times do the Pastoral Epistles designate God as Savior. There seems in these instances to be a steady emphasis on the fact that God is the Savior of all. "God, our Savior, desires that all men be saved" (1 Tim. 2:3f.). "We hope in the living God, who is the Savior of all men, and especially of the faithful" (1 Tim. 4:10; similar in 1 Tim. 1:1; Titus 1:3; 2:10f.; 3:4).

The formalized designation of God as Savior can be traced to the constant linguistic usage of Hellenistic Judaism. In the Acts of the Apostles Jesus receives the title Savior. The oldest preaching, however, does not indicate that he was, already as the earthly Jesus, the Savior; rather, only now as the exalted One is he the Savior. "God has exalted him to be Author and Savior" (Acts 5:31). "From David's offspring God has had Jesus come forth as Savior for Israel" (Acts 13:23).

Just as Paul uses the verb *to save* ($\sigma\acute{\omega}\zeta\epsilon\iota\nu$) to stress the future salvation, so too he gives the predicate Savior to the Christ of the parousia. "Our home is in heaven, whence also we await the Lord Jesus Christ as Savior" (Phil. 3:20). This is the only place in the New Testament where Christ is designated Savior in reference to the eschatological consummation; elsewhere it is always in view of his already perfected or presently ongoing work of salvation. The action of the heavenly Savior is the transformation of the earthly corporeal existence of man into the life of heavenly glory by virtue of the all-embracing power of Christ (Phil. 3:20f.). In a second place, though the term Savior is not actually used, the statement is clarified; ". . . to await from heaven his Son, who will protect us against the wrath to come" (1 Thess. 1:10). Here too Christ perfects the redemption at his return.

With a somewhat different emphasis, because it speaks of a salvation that is already accomplished and is currently ongoing, Christ is called "the Head of the Church, being himself the Head of the body" (Eph. 5:23). Likewise, "By grace have you been saved" (Eph. 2:5, 8). The Epistle to the Ephesians emphasizes this salvation that has already taken place.

The Pastoral Epistles give Jesus the title Savior in broader contexts. The work of the historical Jesus is so described: "Grace was granted us in Christ Jesus before the eternal ages. Now it has been manifested through the appearance of our Savior Christ Jesus, who forced death from its throne and by the gospel brought immortal life into the light" (2 Tim. 1:9-10). As Savior Christ is the originator and basis of the life now bestowed. The frequently employed formula of greeting is broadened: "Grace and peace from God the Father and from Jesus Christ our Savior" (Titus 1:4).

After God is called Savior in Titus 1:3, in Titus 1:4 the title is appropriated also to Jesus. He has collaborated in the redemption. With God

he is called Savior. "We expect the revelation of the glory of the great
God and of our Savior Jesus Christ, who delivered himself up for us,
to redeem us from all unrighteousness and to cleanse for himself a people to be his own" (Titus 2:13-14). Christ has showed himself as Savior
by his work of redemption. "He has poured out the Holy Spirit abundantly upon us through Jesus Christ our Savior, so that we might be
justified by his grace" (Titus 3:6f.). Christ is called Savior as the agent
of salvation, just as God is called Savior as the originator of that same
salvation (Titus 3:4).

In the infancy narrative the angel announces the birth of Jesus: "Today
in the city of David there is born to you a Savior, who is Christ the Lord"
(Luke 2:11). From the very beginning and before the whole world Jesus
is proclaimed as Son of David, Savior, Messiah, and Lord. The Gospels
and the whole New Testament make it evident that these titles of Jesus
were formulated and attested to in the community of disciples after
Easter and Pentecost in a long history of reflection and kerygma. If the
message of the angel brought all of this together at the very beginning,
it is the Church's perfected confession of faith speaking here already.
[*Tr. note*: If this is so "evident", how is it that no one — friend or
enemy — had the least inkling of this for all these nineteen hundred
years, none of the ancient Fathers, none of the Doctors of the Church,
none of the great scholars of the Reformation era or even the Enlightenment down until the last few decades of our twentieth century?]

In John's Gospel the Samaritan woman acknowledges: "This is truly
the Savior of the world" (John 4:42). John's first Epistle repeats that
message: "The Father has sent his Son as Savior of the world" (1 John
4:14). Titles like Savior of the whole earth, Savior of the world (σωτὴρ
τῆς οἰκουμένης or σωτὴρ τοῦ κόσμου) were given to the Roman emperors
(Julius Caesar, Augustus, Claudius, Nero, Vespasian, Titus, Trajan,
and especially often to Hadrian) by the Eastern parts of the empire. The
Johannine writings recognize in Christ the fulfillment of the world's
longing for redemption. Therefore they attest to him with these religious
titles.

That a confrontation with the cult of the emperor might be involved
is a possibility, but an uncertain one. If the gospel puts this acknowledgement in the mouth of a Samaritan, and enemy of the Jews, perhaps

it is to make it plain that the Messiah, rejected by Israel, is Savior of the world. But the Epistle is possibly emphasizing, in opposition to the Gnosis which did not regard the world as being in need of redemption through the blood of Christ, the necessity of this redemption (1 John 1:7; 2:2; 4:2; 5:6).

The title Savior is given Jesus five times in the Second Epistle of Peter (1:1, 11; 2:20; 3:2, 18). And thereby the Epistle lets it be seen how very much, as a late book of the New Testament, it is aware of the Greek world. The Epistle is addressed to those "who have received the precious faith in the justice of our God and Savior Jesus Christ" (1:1). Here faith is already doctrine summarized in a rule of faith. Justice is surely not the justification of men through faith, but the distributive justice of God, who gives the grace of faith to all the redeemed in the same way. The phrase "our God and Savior" is comprised under a single article. A later time is indicated, when Christ is so unequivocally called God.

The kingdom, which in the Synoptics is called the kingdom of God or the kingdom of heaven, is now called "the eternal kingdom of our Lord and Savior Jesus Christ" (2 Peter 1:11). As a divine kingdom, the kingdom is eternal. Since the Gospels already speak of the eternal kingdom of Christ (Luke 1:33; 22:30; John 18:36), and the Epistles likewise (Eph. 5:5; 2 Tim. 4:1), what is said is not entirely new; however, it may be that the emphasis is newly placed. Christians are withdrawn from the world "in the knowledge of the Lord and Savior Jesus Christ" (2 Peter 2:20). The knowledge spoken of is not merely an intellectual act which grasps a teaching; rather, it comprehends Jesus Christ as personal Lord and Savior. The one recognizing him is subject to him as the Lord; the repentant sinner receives the salvation which, as Savior, he imparts to him. Furthermore Christ is repeatedly called "Lord and Savior" in a purely formalized way (2 Peter 3:2, 18). The titles in use even to our own time have their origin here.

The later New Testament writings apply the title Savior in increasing measure to God and to Christ. In so doing the New Testament is accepting and continuing Jewish Old Testament linguistic usage; but this title was afterwards used also in emphatic antithesis to the Greco-Roman world and its religious sentiment, where many saviors were worshipped.

5. THE LORD

A title of dignity which is still used for Jesus even to our own day is the appellation "Lord".[164] In oriental religious sentiment (in Egypt, Asia Minor, and especially in Syria), when the divinity is believed in as creator, he is called Lord and is worshipped as Lord. He is called upon in acclamation and prayer. In worship the community experiences his epiphany. In respect to him, man is a servant. It was otherwise with Greek antiquity, in which the gods were originally natural forces and images of being. Only later in Hellenism were the gods more customarily designated as Lord (Kyrios).

Egyptian and Greek gods of the mystery religions were celebrated as Lords, as with Lord Serapis and Lady Isis.[165] At approximately the same time in the East the rulers were addressed in worship as "Lord and God". In an inscription of the year 62 B.C., the Egyptian king is called "Lord, King, God." Even Roman emperors had themselves so addressed, at first only in the eastern parts of the empire. In an inscription from that area, Augustus is called "God and Lord." The Emperor (Nero) is called "Lord" in Acts 25:26. Domitian had the title "our Lord and God" given to himself. When during the same epoch Jesus too is called "Lord and God" (John 20:28), and "God and Savior" (2 Peter 1:1), there arose that opposition which, beginning already in the New Testament, led to the centuries-long conflicts in the persecution of the Church.

In the Old Testament Bible men can be addressed as "lord." With an emphatic exclusiveness, *'adonai* (kyrios) is a designation of the majesty of the king (Ps. 110). Even Yahweh is called "Lord" (Baal, Mara, Adon). From a reverential fear of pronouncing the sacred name of Yahweh, it came to be replaced in the recitation of the Scriptures by *'adonai*, meaning "my Lord".

The Lordship of Yahweh is unbounded. As Creator he is Lord of the world and of men, Lord over life and death. In our Septuagint the name Yahweh is rendered by Lord (Kyrios). Nevertheless the latest manuscript finds (as at Qumran) make it apparent that Judaism itself in written Greek translation designated the name of Yahweh with the Hebrew letters, in the recitation of which one would of course have said Kyrios. Accordingly Kyrios designates the God of Israel in the Book of Wisdom; and afterwards, at the time of the New Testament, fre-

quently this is the case in Philo and Josephus. Kyrios will first have been
written throughout for Yahweh in a Christian manuscript of the Septuagint.

In papyrus finds the title Mara (Lord) appears as an apostrophe or
title of address to the gods and to human authorities. The title entered
into Jewish linguistic usage both theological and profane, from the profane realm of extra-biblical usage. Examples of this are Daniel 2:47 and
5:23, as also some texts of Qumran. This linguistic usage is to be noted
in reference to 1 Cor. 16:23 (μαραναθά).

In the New Testament Kyrios can designate the master of slaves (Matthew 10:24f.; Luke 12:36f.; Eph. 6:5 *et passim*), as well as the superior
in any relationship (the owner [Mark 12:9]; the employer [Luke 16:3];
the husband in relation to his wife [1 Peter 3:6]). Or the word may signify nothing more than a mark of politeness (Matthew 18:21f., *et passim*). Just as in the linguistic usage of the Hellenistic Synagogue, so too
in the New Testament God is called Lord (Matthew 6:24; 9:38; 11:25);
and of course, this is true also in the numerous citations from the Old
Testament (Mark 12:29f.; Rom. 4:8 *et passim*).

In its application to Jesus, therefore, the title Lord will have varying
reasons and import. In the Gospels the earthly Jesus, just like other men,
is addressed with the designation Lord. In the older strata of the Synoptic
tradition some individual examples are certainly provided by Mark 7:28
and Matthew 8:8 (Source Q). In particular it is the teacher Jesus who
is to be honored with this title of address (Luke 11:1). Here Kyrios is
perhaps a translation of Rabbi or even of Mari. Even the Acts of the
Apostles (11:6) and Paul (1 Cor. 7:10) are able to use the title Kyrios
for Jesus in his capacity as earthly teacher. The title, however, is given
a decided intensification, through a stress being placed on the fact that
this teacher is the Lord, whereas his student is but a servant. "The student is not above his teacher nor is the servant above his lord" (Matthew
10:24).

"You call me Teacher and Lord, and you speak rightly; for that I am"
(John 13:13). The word of this Lord demands obedience. "Why do you
call me 'Lord, Lord', and then do not do what I tell you?" (Luke 6:46).
As Son of Man Jesus is "Lord over the Sabbath", and therefore over
God's Law (Mark 2:28). This is a Lord who can be called upon in direst
necessity. "Lord, save us, we are perishing" (Matthew 8:25).

In the title Lord one can finally begin to hear an overtone of worship. "Not everyone who says to me, 'Lord, Lord', will enter into the kingdom of heaven, but him who does the will of my Father in heaven" (Matthew 7:21). In his statements Jesus announces the will of God, whom he calls his Father. He is the Lord not only as a teacher, but as the one Son of the Father. And at the same time he is Lord because he is Judge (Matthew 7:22). The state of one's relations with this Lord decides his relationship to God.

In the marvelous story of the discovery of a riding animal for the entry of Jesus into Jerusalem, Jesus is reckoned simply as "the Lord", the omniscient and sovereign One (Mark 11:3). The evangelist and the listening congregation perceived in the title Lord increasingly a predication of the exalted Christ. Matthew (8:25; 17:4; 20:33) regularly replaces the Markan address Rabbi with Lord.

Predominant linguistic usage designates the exalted Christ as the Lord. The title is used in the Palestinian community, from whence Paul takes it. "Maranatha. The grace of our Lord Jesus Christ be with you" (1 Cor. 16:23f.). Grammatically the word Maranatha can mean "Our Lord has come" or "May our Lord come!" The former were a confession of faith, the latter a prayerful petition. In accord with 1 Cor. 11:26, Apoc. 22:20f., and *Didache* 10:6 (Jurgens, no. 7, with note 26), one will understand it as an eschatological and enthusiastic exclamatory petition, which was probably called out by the assembled congregation at the liturgy of the Lord's Supper. The cry is to be understood within the compass of the already mentioned Jewish-apocalyptic Mara styling. The exalted Christ is acknowledged and appealed to as Lord, the same who is urgently expected as Judge. In this styling, the Lord is the same as the returning Son of Man, who, as Judge, is also Lord (Matthew 25:31, 37). Since, however, in the Synagogue the coming Messiah was never called upon as Lord, the Christian community is separated from Israel by this title of its Messiah.

In the Greek speaking Gentile Christian Church another conceptual content in Jesus' title Kyrios prevailed.[166] If it acknowledges Jesus as Kyrios, then the title signifies, as in the language of Hellenistic Judaism, where Kyrios corresponds to the name of God, *'adon*, the divine Lord. Thus the profession "Jesus is Lord" (Rom. 10:9; 1 Cor. 12:3) is the shortest of all confessions of faith. The exalted Christ has likewise as Lord the highest of names, that is, the divine glory (Phil. 2:9-11).

This Kyrios is Lord over world and mankind (Rom. 14:9), as also over superterrestrial and subterranean powers and forces (Phil. 2:10; Eph. 1:20f.). He is the Lord of Lords and King of Kings (Apoc. 17:14). He stands in opposition to the gods and lords of the pagan world and deposes them (1 Cor. 8:5f.). This Kyrios is Lord of the Church (1 Cor. 4:19; 14:37; 16:7). He is manifested as the Lord in the Church's divine service. The sacramental Meal is the table of the Lord and the cup of the Lord (1 Cor. 10:21). The Church is devoted to the Lord in love (1 Cor. 16:22). The Lord gives the Apostle his office (2 Cor. 10:8; 13:10), and to the community he gives charisms and ministries (1 Cor. 3:5; 7:17; 12:5).

The whole life of the Church is determined by her belonging to this Lord (Rom. 14:8). Grace and peace are the gift of God and of Christ the Lord (Rom. 1:7; and similarly formalized in the addresses of other Epistles). The thanksgiving of the Church streams back through Christ to God (Rom. 7:25; 1 Cor. 15:57). The Lord is the Mediator between God and the Church, between God and man (1 Tim. 2:5). The Church lives before this Lord as before its present and future Judge (1 Cor. 11:27, 32). The Christian yearns to appear before this Lord as his Judge (1 Cor. 11:27, 32). This Lord will return as Judge of Church and world (1 Cor. 1:7; 1 Thess. 4:16f.) and as Savior and Perfécter (Phil. 3:20).

The exalted Christ's title of Lord is carried back to the earthly Christ. Paul mentions once that the "brothers of the Lord" are married (1 Cor. 9:5). The historical Jesus, in the backward glance of remembrance, is already called Lord. He now bears this title simply and straightforwardly in the community of the disciples. When Paul says of the Eucharist: "I received from the Lord what in turn I have handed on to you" (1 Cor. 11:23), it is the earthly Jesus who is meant, to whom the tradition goes back, who is now the exalted Christ Jesus, and who as Lord guarantees for the Church her tradition and practice.

Paul often uses, like the formula "in Christ", the formula "in the Lord". Paul is confident in the Lord (Rom. 14:14), and he bears witness in the Lord (1 Thess. 4:1). The community is to abide in the Lord (Phil. 4:1) and labor in the Lord (Rom. 16:12). Eternal life is proffered in him (Rom. 6:23). The Lord has divine dignity. He can be given synon-

ymously the title God (John 20:28; 2 Peter 1:2). In the Trinitarian structure the Lord Christ appears in the divine unity and trinity (§ 21).

It was a matter of great consequence that, to signify the person and
works of this Lord Christ, the Septuagint (or in any case, the Christian
Septuagint) translated the divine name Yahweh with Kyrios. Since the
exalted Christ also bore the name Kyrios, in the Christian reading of
the Old Testament declarations about God could be read and understood directly as declarations about Christ. An important instance is the
citation of Ps. 110:1, where the Messiah is called Lord, in Mark 12:36;
14:62; Acts 2:34f.; 1 Cor. 15:25; Eph. 1:20; Col. 1:20; Heb. 1:13.

6. PREDICATION OF DIVINITY

As Son of Man and as Son of God, Christ is on the divine side, as
opposed to man. The divine dignity and power of Jesus is expressed with
increasing clarity in the ongoing reflection on the faith. Of primary
importance are certain texts of the Epistles of Paul. "All things are yours;
you however are Christ's, and Christ is God's" (1 Cor. 3:22-23). In
mounting sequence it states: Christian existence is bound up in Christ,
and as such is free of compulsion. Christ himself is Lord, in that he belongs to God and rules for him. This can be supplemented from a Pauline
context, to the effect that Christ is the revelation of God, in that, as the
Crucified, he makes known the power and wisdom of God (1 Cor.
1:30). He brings God's work to completion, in that, as the Son, he brings
all things into subjection to God (1 Cor. 15:28).

"You ought to know, however, that the head of every man is Christ,
the head of woman is man, and the head of Christ is God" (1 Cor. 3:22f.).
In this ordering, Paul uses the concept of head, as it was used in religious
conceptualization in late antiquity.[167] In an Orphic hymn [168] Zeus is
called "the first and the last, Zeus the head and the center, the king, the
source of everything." Philo (*De specialibus legibus* 3,184) understands
the Logos as the head which directs the body of creation and gives it
life. Here there would seem to be some influence of the Gnostic speculation about the redeemer, who, as the primordial man, embraces all
things in his cosmic body. Christ is head of creation as its Lord; but he

is again its head as its source, since all is created in Christ; and as its goal, to which all creation is ordered.

The eternal God, however, is the head of Christ as his source and point of return. "For us there is one God the Father, from whom are all things and we unto him, and one Lord Jesus Christ, through whom are all things and we through him" (1 Cor. 8:6; see also *Theology of the New Testament*, Vol. 1, pp. 24–27). Christ is elevated in his nature above the world. He is the Mediator between the world and God, toward whom he turns all things. His divine dignity, then, is thought of as functional and not metaphysical.

Paul is again using the language and conceptualization of his own time when he calls Christ the image of God.[169] Disbelief does not acknowledge "the glory of Christ, who is the image of God" (2 Cor. 4:4). The Son is the image of God (Rom. 8:29). Christ is called "the image of the invisible God, the firstborn before all creation" (Col. 1:15). Here image is not to be understood as a weak copy, far removed from the prototype and intended only to recall the original to mind; rather, the image is the exact likeness, the *re*-presentation of the prototype, its revelation and epiphany. The *Corpus hermeticum* (8:2-5) describes the following progression: God is the unoriginate Creator of all; his first image is the world; his second image, man.

As representative of divinity, the ruler could be adored in worship. In the Apocalypse (13:14f.) such adoration for the "image of the beast", that is, adoration of the emperor, is challenged.

Hellenistic Judaism transferred this notion to that of divine wisdom. Wisdom is "the image of the good God" (Wis. 7:26), for she makes manifest the goodness of God. According to Philo (*De allegoriis legum* 1, 43), wisdom is the "beginning, image, and look of God". Even the Logos is, although shapeless, "the exact image of God" (*De allegoriis legum* 3, 96; *De confusione linguarum* 147).

There may also be contained in the words of Paul a recollection of Gen. 1:27, according to which Adam was created in the image of God. The glory of God was shining forth from the face of Christ (2 Cor. 4:6). The texts declare that Christ is the epiphany of God in the world.[170]

It seems to be even clearer that Gnostic conceptualizations are used in the Epistles to the Ephesians and Colossians. The Church therein is the present and earthly body of the present and heavenly Head, which is the exalted Christ (Eph. 4:15f.; 5:23; Col. 1:18). Christ is also the head of creation, since everything is created in him (Col. 1:15-17; 2:10). The resurrected Christ attains his comprehensive power, in that he draws world and Church into himself.

"God was in Christ, reconciling the world to himself" (2 Cor. 5:19). Through the Cross of Christ God was made manifest in the world as the holy and just One who demanded for sins the atonement which was made on the Cross by the Son. But God was also made manifest as the gracious and loving One who forgave sins on account of this atonement (Rom. 3:25). Atonement belongs now to the ministry of reconciliation which is practiced in the Church. God acted in Christ when, through him, he provided salvation. Its consummation is entrusted to Christ.

The revelation of God in Christ is described also in Col. 2:9, "In Christ dwells the whole fullness [171] of the Godhead [172] corporeally." The letter warns against the worship of cosmic powers. They do not bring redemption but only servitude. The fullness of redemptive power and of divine Being abides in Christ. Whoever belongs to this Lord receives his portion in him in baptism and in faith, and is filled with the forces of life (Col. 2:13). Divine Being abides in Christ "corporeally." [173] The term emphasizes the full reality of the divine indwelling. [174]

The interpretation of Titus 2:13 is not entirely certain. Are we to read "We await the epiphany of the glory of the great God and of our Savior Jesus Christ"; or "We await the epiphany of the glory of our great God and Savior, Jesus Christ"? Either is possible, the latter more probable. And in that case, Christ is here given the title of great God. The article τοῦ is used only once, and seems to direct both substantives, God and Savior, to the one person, Jesus Christ. The formula God and Savior pointedly designates the God-Savior (§ 11, 5). The glorious revelation of Christ is expected in his return (2 Thess. 2:8; 1 Tim. 6:14; 2 Tim. 1:10), whereas nothing is said elsewhere of an epiphany of God.

In the Gospel of John (1:1-14) Christ is present before the world as "Word (Logos) of God". Of the Logos it is stated that he is the revelation of God like "the light in the darkness" (John 1:5), and is the agent of creation, through whom all things were made (John 1:3). He effects salvation, inasmuch as he makes those who accept him into children of God (John 1:12). The Logos is God himself (John 1:1, 8).

The Gospel of John does not explain what the term Logos signifies. It presupposes that the reader already knows. The Old Testament describes creation through God's word (Gen. 1:3-26). The prophets announce the word of God, which brings about what it states (Is. 55:10f.; Ps. 33:9). The wisdom literature represents the wisdom of God as personified (Prov. 8:22-31; Wis. 9:9). Other ideas (probably Gnostic in origin) seem to be bound up also in the traditions then current. In the *Corpus hermeticum* (1, 6) the Logos is called Son of God. For Philo the Logos is Mediator between God and the world. He is designated as a second God (*De allegoriis legum* 2, 86); and this in view of his being the firstborn Son of God (*De agricultura Noë* 51). He is the image of God, revelation of God, and tool of creation (*De allegoriis legum* 3, 96; *De cherubim* 127). In the *Odes of Solomon* (Ode 12 especially) the Logos is the Creator and Redeemer in accord with God's plan. If the Gospel of John agrees to such mythologoumena of its milieu, then what it wants to say by so doing is that Christ is "God's Yes" (2 Cor. 1:20) even to the hopes of the Gentiles.

In John's Gospel the divinity of Jesus is repeatedly defended against "the Jews", that is, against disbelief. The Jews reason it out that Jesus, when he calls God "his own Father", is making himself "equal to God" (John 5:18). Because of this blasphemy they seek to kill him. In the mentality of the Gospel, being equal to God expresses neither extravagant arrogance nor a mythological doctrine of two Gods; rather, it states that in the unity of the Son with the Father, the Father is manifest in the Son (John 5:19).

The Jews accuse Jesus again: "You that are a man, you make yourself God"; and they want to stone him for blasphemy against God (John 10:33-38). In the argument that follows, the possibility of divine Sonship for men is established with the reference to Ps. 82:6, "I said, 'You are gods'." Finally the Jews demand that Pilate pronounce the death sentence: "According to the Law he must die, because he has made himself to be the Son of God" (John 19:7). It would appear that altercations between Synagogue and Church, from the time of the actual writing of the Gospel, have made their way into these passages. The inferences drawn in the conversations are the points of dispute in Jewish-Christian controversies. That God is Jesus' "own Father" and that Jesus is "equal to God" are already propositions of Christian dogma.

The quotation from Ps. 82:6 is probably a dispute over the proper interpretation of Scripture. The accusation of the capital crime of blasphemy against God is the constant complaint in the Jewish court against the Christian belief. At the end of John's Gospel (20:28) Thomas acknowledges (and the evangelist with him) of Jesus: "My Lord and my God!" [175] In his farewell address Jesus had stated, "Whoever has seen me has seen the Father" (John 14:9). Now the Father is gazed upon in the Son. Now the Son is acknowledged as the Logos and as God, which he was from the very beginning (John 1:1).

The Gospel of John proclaims Christ with further characteristic sayings, as Jesus says of himself: I am the bread of life (6:35), the light of the world (8:12), the door (10:7), the good shepherd (10:11); the way, the truth, and the life (14:6); the true vine (15:1). Exegesis makes it clear that these declarations tell of values which were sought after and asserted as already found, not only in the Old Testament, but also in the immediate surroundings of the Gospel (especially, no doubt, in the Gnosis). The Gospel acknowledges the quest and longing for these values as legitimate, but says that their pretended fulfillment elsewhere or in other times is insufficient or untrue. Christ is their true fulfillment. The response of the Gospel, moreover, goes beyond all limitations of place and time. For these quests and longings are pertinent not merely to the world of its own time, but to all mankind, always and everywhere. Bread is nourishment in general; water and wine are drink and refreshment; light gives brightness to life in the midst of its anxieties; way and truth give security against every kind of error or straying; the shepherd is guidance and protection in danger. Life is hope, plainly and simply. All quests find their ultimate response in Christ, all longings are fulfilled in him.

The First Epistle of John (5:20) closes with an unequivocal confession of faith: "We are in the true God, insofar as we are in his Son, Jesus Christ. He is the true God and eternal life." The Son, as the Mediator between God and men, constitutes the possibility and the basis of true existence in God. "Out of his fullness we have all received" (John 1:16). The declaration of the divine truth and reality, which is valid of the Father, is likewise valid of the Son. With this confession the Epistle concludes its depositions on the victory of faith over the world (1 John 5:4f.).

The Epistle to the Hebrews (1:1-9) begins with the high titles of dignity that belong to Christ. God has spoken his definitive Word in him (Heb. 1:1). This declaration is essentially the same as that of John 1:1f., according to which Christ is the Word of God. Through Christ the world was created, and he is its goal (Heb. 1:2). He is "the brightness of God's glory and the image of his substance" (Heb. 1:3). The letter accepts Jewish teaching about wisdom. Wisdom "is a brightness of the eternal light, a flawless mirror of divine operation, and an image of his goodness" (Wis. 7:26).

Again, therefore, in the Epistle to the Hebrews, do we encounter the theme of Christ as the image of God (2 Cor. 4:4; Col. 1:15), and that of the glory of God on the face of Christ (2 Cor. 4:6). Christ is God's first-born and only Son (Heb. 1:5f.; *cf*. Rom. 8:29; Col. 1:15). He is the "Anointed One", the Messiah, as God himself (Heb. 1:8-9). The Old Testament is prophecy referring to Christ (Heb. 1:8-10). It is of Christ that it is said: "Your throne, O God, perdures from eternity to eternity" (Ps. 45:7f.); and "In the beginning, O Lord, it was you that founded the earth" (Ps. 102:26). Old Testament declarations on the dignity of God and on his work are transferred to Christ. A rich tradition of faith, of reflection, and of teaching has been prerequisite to the Epistle to the Hebrews. The Church believes and teaches that Christ is of one nature with the eternal God.

The profession in the Second Epistle of Peter (1:1, 11; 2:20; 3:2, 18) is already firmly formalized: Jesus Christ is God as Lord and Savior. This may be an indication that the writing of the New Testament has already been protracted into the beginning of the second century. St. Ignatius of Antioch is now publicly proclaiming Christ as God with unequivocal assurance: "I give glory to Jesus Christ, the God who has made you wise" (*Letter to the Smyrnaeans* 1, 1 [Jurgens, no. 62]); "Our God, Jesus Christ, was conceived by Mary in accord with God's plan" (*Letter to the Ephesians* 18, 2 [Jurgens, no. 42]). It is just at this same time that Pliny the Younger writes, in his celebrated letter to Trajan, that in their divine service the Christians "sing a hymn to Christ as God" (*Epistulae* 10, 96, 7).

Within the ordering of the Trinity, according to biblical and ecclesiastical doctrine, Christ appears in the inscrutable divine Trinity and Unity.

In its Christology, the Gospel of Mark joins the various titles of dignity, Messiah, Savior, Son of David, Son of Man, Son, Son of God, which may have varied sources, to the unity of the gospel. This holds good also for the other primitive draft of our tradition, Source Q. Here too Jesus is the Savior of the sick and of sinners (Matthew 8:5; 11:5), the Son of Man (Luke 7:34; 9:22; 12:8-10), the Son and the Son of God (Matthew 4:3-6; 11:25-27). In the collective tradition Jesus practices the ministry of healing and of redemption through his words and works. This whole work, however, is the proclamation and the beginning of the kingdom of God (Luke 10:9; 11:20), which leads to the final salvation of creation.

The proclaiming Jesus is at the same time the event itself that he proclaims. Marcion already found a formulation for this: "In the gospel the kingdom of God is Jesus Christ himself" (Tertullian, *Against Marcion* 4, 33). Origen says that Christ is the kingdom itself (the αὐτοβασιλεία, in his *Commentaries on Matthew* [to Matthew 18:23], GCS Vol. 10 of Origen, Leipzig 1935, p. 289). The faith, the confession, and the teaching of the community of disciples express the truth and reality of Christ from the very beginning with Jesus' titles of majesty, which make an explicit Christology of that which was implicit. Beyond the historical questions in regard to the extent to which this took place in the time of the earthly Jesus, this testimony remains a valid foundation of the faith.

III
SPIRIT OF GOD

§ 12. THE SPIRIT
AS REVELATION AND AS REVEALER

Universal human experience finds that in nature the energy laden air is, although invisible, a truly mighty power. Man's breathing of air seems even to signify the presence of life. Such experiences are probably in a broad way the reason for understanding the operation of the invisible God as the presence of the divine Spirit.[176]

The pagans keep in special memory the mysterious, yes, the awesome prowess of great men and women. This is explained as emotion through contact with a divine (or demoniacal) spirit, or indeed, even as a frenzy through possession by the same. Biblical religion and its concept of the Spirit, operating in a very human milieu, reflects its awareness of such phenomena.

1. Old Testament

The many declarations of the Old Testament about the spirit of God can be separated into two groups: declarations about the work of the spirit in creation, and about his work in history. As an emphatic declaration on the spirit of creation, we read on the first page of the (Greek) Bible: "The spirit of God hovered over the waters" (Gen. 1:2).[177] To this there are added other declarations about the spirit of God as the creative force in the universe. "The heavens were made by the word of the Lord, and all their hosts by the breath of his mouth" (Ps. 33:6). God is, through his spirit, the sovereign Creator (Is. 40:13). The prophet is obliged to foretell the eventual devastation of the land, which will continue "until the spirit be poured out from on high, and then the desert will become a fruitful orchard" (Is. 32:15).

221

God's spirit is like the breath of life, the principle of human life. God blew it into the nostrils of the first man, who then became a living being (Gen. 2:7). God, who made heaven and earth, lets the human race breathe and gives the breath of life to those who walk on the earth (Is. 42:5). If God were to take back his breath of life, all flesh would perish (Job 34:14f.; Ps. 104:29). Everything that has breath, therefore, ought to praise the Lord (Ps. 150:6; Job 33:3f.).

In the Old Testament the spirit is not merely the agent of God's creation, but his continuing agent who reveals himself in the history of the operation of salvation — an operation that breaks through natural laws and while choosing, directing, and guiding, creates a people which is God's nation through appropriating it as his own. The operation of the spirit is posited primarily for individuals, and then of the whole nation. This operation of the spirit is recounted in regard to Joseph (Gen. 41:38), Moses (Num. 11:17; Is. 63:11), Josue (Num. 27:18), the Judges (Judges 3:10; 6:34; 11:29; 14:6), King Saul (1 Sam. 10:6), King David (1 Sam. 16:13), and the Prophets (4 Kings 2:9; Hos. 9:7; Ezech. 3:12; Micah 3:8; Neh. 9:30; Zech. 7:12). The spirit breaks in upon men. At first there is scarcely any notion of a continuing association. This is taken up later. And then the gift of the spirit is quieter and less obtrusive.

In particular the Messiah [178] appears as the bearer of the spirit of God. "There rests on him the spirit of God, the spirit of truth and of understanding, the spirit of counsel and of fortitude, the spirit of knowledge and of the fear of God" (Is. 11:2). God lays his spirit on his servant (Is. 42:1). In the strength of God's spirit he will bring the message of salvation to the nations (Is. 61:1-3). Even the intertestamental writings speak (in correspondence to Is. 11:2) of the Messiah's being gifted with the spirit; [179] thus in the *Psalms of Solomon* 17:42; *Ethiopic Henoch* 49:3; 62:2; *Testaments of the Twelve Patriarchs: Levi* 18:7; *Judah* 24:2. The strength and operation of this spirit are not, however, the external wonders and mighty deeds of the Messiah, but his religious and moral stature and force (*Psalms of Solomon* 17:36; 18:3-9).

Yet it is not to the Messiah only, but to the whole nation that, for the messianic era, the spirit of Yahweh is promised, who will cleanse the people of all their sins and lead them to a new way of life. The spirit will be poured out from on high; and just as the rain brings fruitfulness, he will bring justice, peace, and security (Is. 32:15-17). All Israel will be participating in this spirit (Is. 44:3). The spirit creates a new People of God: "I will impart to you a new heart and put a new spirit inside you, and will take the stony heart out of your body and give you a heart of flesh. And I will put inside you my spirit, and I will cause you to walk according to my statutes and to heed my ordinances and act accordingly" (Ezech. 36:25-27). In the great vision of the Prophet the spirit comes from the four winds and makes Israel's field of dead bones come alive (Ezech. 37:1-14).

The postexilic prophets renew this hope. The spirit of God will be poured out on all flesh (Joel 3:1-5). The spirit is guardian of the people (Haggai 2:5). It is not an army and power but the spirit of God that works salvation (Zech. 4:6).

Since God operates through his spirit, he also is represented in him. The spirit of God signifies God's omnipresence: "Whither should I go before your spirit? Whither should I flee before your face?" (Ps. 139:7); and his creative power and his wisdom: "Who has guided the spirit of the Lord?" (Is. 40:13). "The Egyptians are man, not God; their horses are flesh not spirit" (Is. 31:3). Man and flesh are earthly and human nothingness; God and spirit are divine reality and permanence.

In later prophecy and in individual Psalms, the operation of the spirit is no longer so much the individual deed of wonder, but the ongoing pious and righteous existence of man. The spirit is also granted the individual, and its being granted him is prayed for by him: "Take not the spirit of holiness from me" (Ps. 51:13). "Your spirit guides me on a straight course" (Ps. 143:10). A penitential prayer from the time of the return from exile praises God's graciousness, which gave Israel the "spirit of holiness", and supplicates its renewal (Is. 63:7-19).

In Wisdom, the spirit achieves independent and personal status. God sends "Wisdom and holy Spirit from above" (Wis. 9:17). "The Spirit of the Lord fills the whole earth" (Wis. 1:7). God's "unchanging Spirit is in all things" (Wis. 12:1). The teacher prays to receive "the holy Spirit" (Wis. 1:5; 9:17). The Spirit fills the prophets (Sir. 48:13). God and his holy Spirit produce and inspire the writing down of the Law and the Apocalyptics (*4 Esdras* 14:22-26). There is a strengthening of the conviction of the rabbis that the canonical books are prompted by the holy Spirit, and that he speaks through them (§ 1, 3).[180]

The Qumran scrolls state that man has his measure of spirit as a portion of the spirit of God. The writing designated 1 QS is dominated by the notion of two spirits who circle about men and between whom man has to choose. These are the spirit of light, of truth, of knowledge, and the spirit of darkness (1 QS 3:18f.; 4:23f.). The counsels of the good spirit invite one to virtue. Man lives not by his own strength, but by the spirit of God. "Man's path is not firm, except in the spirit whom God produced" (1 QH 4:31). While the petitioner praises God's demonstrations of grace, he also thanks him again and again for his having bestowed his "spirit of holiness" (1 QH 7:6f.; 9:32; 12:11f.; 16:12). An expression of blessing reads: "May the Lord be gracious to you with the holy spirit and mercy" (1 QSb 2:24).

The Old Testament texts speak for the most part of the "spirit of Yahweh"; but Ps. 51:13 and Is. 63:10-14 tell of the "spirit of holiness", a phrase which in the Septuagint is translated "holy spirit" ($\pi\nu\epsilon\tilde{\upsilon}\mu\alpha$ $\check{\alpha}\gamma\iota o\nu$). The formulation appears also in the Greek of Daniel 5:12 and 6:4, as also in the original Greek of the Book of Wisdom 1:5; 7:22; 9:17. The phrase is familiar to Qumran. This manner of expression is used also by the rabbis, probably because intertestamental Judaism avoided the name of God as much as possible. The spirit is called holy, because he is the spirit of God, who is by nature holy; holy spirit properly signifies divine spirit (see *Theology of the New Testament*, Vol. 3, pp. 171-175).

According to the broadened notion of the Gnosis, God is of pneumatic substance. In the creation, pneumatic parts are bound into matter. The gathering and leading back of these parts into their heavenly homeland is redemption. The Gnostic notion and language may perhaps be operative here and there even in the New Testament.

2. New Testament

The New Testament announces that the expectation of the old covenant has been fulfilled. The Spirit-endowed Messiah has come, and his community has been filled by the Holy Spirit.

When the New Testament speaks simply of the spirit, it is seldom the human spirit ("the soul"), as opposed to the body, that is meant, but almost always the Spirit of God, who is now bestowed upon men.

a) The Spirit-endowed Messiah

On the threshold of the New Testament John the Baptist is preaching that the Messiah to come after him will baptize the people with the Holy Spirit and fire (Matthew 3:11).

According to the accounts of his baptism, the Messiah begins his messianic office in the fullness of the Spirit. "As soon as he came up out of the water, he saw the heavens open, and the Spirit soaring down upon him like a dove" (Mark 1:10). Even if they differ in some details, the gospel accounts agree unanimously that the Spirit appeared in the form of a dove. Exegesis looks for an explanation of this tradition. It recalls Old Testament concepts.

The pious man "takes refuge under the wings of Yahweh" (Ruth 2:12). "In the shadow of God's wings do the children of men take refuge" (Ps. 36:8; 57:2). A rabbinic saying compares the hovering of the spirit of God over the waters (Gen. 1:2) to that of the dove over her brood. The "voice of the turtledove" (Cant. 2:12) is explained in the targum as referring allegorically to "the voice of the holy Spirit." In other literature the dove symbolizes Israel, inasmuch as it signifies the captive people led away into exile, lamenting and imploring God's help; so too in the interpretation of the Canticle of Canticles (2:12). The image of the dove can be seen as especially appropriate for the Holy Spirit, since the dove is without guile (Matthew 10:16). "The image is so charged with the force of symbolism from proverb and legend, from the usages and customs of worship, from the holy lore of the patriarchs and prophets of the Old Covenant, that in this moment when God is pledging himself to his Son, the dove is the almost uniquely appropriate form for the appearance of the Holy Spirit of God, and could be immediately and rightly understood." [182]

The infancy narratives of the Gospels, in a longer perspective than that of the baptism, testify that from the very beginning of his existence Jesus was the product of the Spirit (Matthew 1:18, 20; Luke 1:35; § 10, 3c).

Some few texts of the Gospels depict Jesus as a bearer of pneumatic strength. After being filled with the Spirit in baptism, Jesus remains under the superior strength of the Spirit: "Immediately the Spirit drove him forth into the desert" (Mark 1:12). The later Gospels temper this singular declaration somewhat.

Jesus refers to his being gifted with the Spirit: "If by the Spirit of God I cast out demons, then indeed has the kingdom of God come to you" (Matthew 12:28). To judge by the wording, however, Luke 11:20 must needs be the more primitive form: "If by the finger of God I cast out demons . . ." . This is archaic language (Ps. 8:4; Exod. 31:18), which has been shaped by Matthew in accord with Is. 42:1, and from the community's later experience of the Spirit. The old Gospels are very reserved in such portrayals. Jesus is not the bearer of the Spirit like one of the prophets. He is something else, He is more. He effects God's eschatological salvation.

Luke [183] is able to present Jesus somewhat otherwise. He does this through his special interest in the phenomenon of the Spirit, the outpouring of the Spirit that he has to describe in the Acts of the Apostles. Luke inserts reflections on Jesus' being endowed with the Spirit. The deeds and works of Jesus take place in the power of the Holy Spirit (Luke 4:1, 14). Jesus refers the statement about the Servant of Yahweh to himself: "The spirit of the Lord rests on me" (Is. 61:1). Thus does Jesus proclaim his Gospel, and thus does he effect his mighty deeds (Luke 4:18). Jesus rejoices in the Holy Spirit (Luke 10:21). The Spirit is manifested in Jesus' preaching (Luke 12:10). To those who ask it of God, the Holy Spirit will be given (Luke 11:13). After his resurrection Jesus dispenses the Spirit to the community (Luke 24:29; Acts 3:33).

b) The Filling of the Community with the Spirit

Only a few texts of the early Gospels speak of the Spirit's filling the community. Blasphemy against the Holy Spirit will not be forgiven (Mark 3:29). Probably the saying was already somewhat enigmatic when the Gospels were being written; at any rate, they have interpreted the saying further. In Source Q (Matthew 12:31; Luke 12:10) it must have stated that blasphemy against the Son of Man can be forigven; not, however, that against the (Holy) Spirit. Did the saying originally state that sinning against a man ("son of man" in Aramaic, as also in Syriac, means simply a human being) can be forgiven, but not sins against the Spirit of God?

In its present form the saying warns against holding in contempt through disbelief the Spirit revealed in the word and work of the community, in which the exalted Lord is manifested. The saying already presupposes the possession of the Spirit by the post-paschal community. Mark 3:30 (and following him, Matthew 12:32) interprets the saying probably secondarily in reference to the pneumatic strength of Jesus: "For they had said, 'He has an unclean spirit'".

There is another saying which may also point to the time of the Church: "If they lead you away to deliver you up, be not anxious beforehand about what you should say. . . . For it is not you who are speaking, but the Holy Spirit" (Mark 13:11). This saying seemingly presupposes a lengthy period of missionary endeavor and experience, a circumstance which is even more clearly verified in the parallels in Matthew 10:18-20 and Luke 12:11f. This scarcity of texts which speak of the Spirit in the communities is an indication of the fidelity of tradition. The Church's experience of the Spirit should not go back to the time of Jesus.

At the accepted time the New Testament represents the Church as the messianic congregation, filled, according to expectation, with the Spirit. The Acts of the Apostles describes the pouring out of the Spirit upon the Church. The Pentecost narrative (Acts 2:1-13) [184] contains the recollection of the first charismatic appearance before Israel of the community of disciples, an event which took place on the Jewish Feast of Weeks. An outbreak of ecstatic speech, the glossolalia, is depicted by the Acts of the Apostles as miraculous speech, in such a way that each of the foreigners was able to hear it as his own language. The event is interpreted in the schema of promise and fulfillment, as fulfillment of the prophecy in Joel 3:1-5 (Acts 2:16f.). The Spirit, when he comes from God upon men, is received as something unexpectedly and inconceivably new. He appears "suddenly" (Acts 2:2), without any preparatory formalities. "He settles down on each" (Acts 2:3). To the Spirit belongs dynamic and awesome noumenal power. This is intimated with signs like fire and storm (Acts 2:2f.), and shaking (Acts 4:31).

The signs or symbols referred to will have to be explained from the Old Testament. The Old Testament experienced the revelation of God in storm (2 Sam. 5:24; 3 Kings 19:11; Ps. 104:4) and in fire (Exod. 3:2; 13:21f.; Ps. 104:4). The tongues signify the charismatic speech of the proclamation. They settle down on each one present. It is one Spirit, yet he is specially imparted to each (1 Cor. 12:4, 11). The power of the Spirit is made evident in ecstatic speech (Acts 2:4; 10:44, 46; 19:6) and preaching (Acts 4:8; 5:32), in the fearless candor of the apostles (Acts 4:31), in martyrdom (Acts 7:55) and in the conquest of illnesses (Acts 3:6) and of demoniacal spirits (Acts 5:3; 8:7; 13:9f.). The Spirit re-awakens prophecy, thought to have died out long since (Acts 11:28; 21:9-11; Rom. 12:6f.; 1 Cor. 12:10).

Yet the Spirit does not produce only the extraordinary and miraculous. To the believer the gift of the Spirit is imparted in baptism (Acts 2:38; 9:17; 19:5f.). Imposition of hands by the apostles imparts the Spirit (Acts 8:12). God bestows the Spirit of faith even upon the Gentiles (Acts 15:8). The Spirit, along with wisdom, is given to the seven dea-cons (Acts 6:3, 10). The Spirit guides the mission. He singles out Paul and Barnabas for the evangelization of the Gentiles (Acts 13:2) and leads them (Acts 13:4; 16:6f.). For men like Stephen (Acts 6:5) and Barnabas (Acts 11:24), the Spirit is their strength of faith. The Spirit is meaningful understanding and perseverance and submission. He is active in the ministerial office (Acts 6:3; 13:2, 9; 18:25; 1 Tim. 4:14; 2 Tim. 1:6f.). Anyone who cheats the community cheats the Spirit (Acts 5:3). Whatever the community proclaims is the proclamation of the Spirit (Acts 13:2; 15:28). The Spirit is not free and unbridled; rather, he is already the Spirit of communion, inasmuch as he is operative in the united community, and in the organized Church as a visible institution.

c) Paul's Witness to the Spirit

Paul bears witness to the fullness of the Spirit in the primitive com-munity.[185] The Spirit is creative, in that he produces life. It was through the Spirit that Jesus was raised up from the dead (Rom. 1:4; *cf.* 1 Peter 3:18). The Spirit will likewise effect the general resurrection (Rom. 8:11). He is now the pledge of our hope of resurrection (2 Cor. 1:22). The Spirit creates the Church. Just as by the Spirit Christ was made the Son (Rom. 1:4), so now that Spirit makes Christians to be sons of God (Rom. 8:23; Gal. 4:6).

Paul treasures the Spirit as the vigor of the extraordinary and miracu-lous. He enumerates the gifts of the Spirit as utterance of wisdom, utter-ance of knowledge, faith, charismatic gift of healing, working of mira-cles, utterance of that to which one was inspired, distinguishing of spirits, speaking in tongues (probably an enraptured speech delivered in enthusiasm and not understandable to others), and the ability to interpret the same (1 Cor. 12:4-11; 14:13-16). Paul otherwise adduces as gifts of the Spirit: inspired utterance, ministerial work, teaching, admonishing, presiding, mercy, and love (Rom. 12:6-9). The capacity for extraordinary ministry in the community is listed by Paul along with the capacity for ordinary ministry. Listing them all together as if in some way proportionate, Paul enumerates as the Spirit-endowed officials of the community and their ministries: "Apostles, prophets, teachers, miraculous powers, charismatic gifts of healing, services of help, powers of administration, speaking in various tongues" (1 Cor. 12:28).

The community receives the Spirit "not from works of the Law, but from the preaching of the faith" (Gal. 3:2). God "gives the Spirit and performs marvels by virtue of faith" (Gal. 3:5). Paul describes his own ministry as "word and work, power of signs and wonders, power of the Spirit" (Rom. 15:18f.); not as "persuasive words of [human] wisdom" but as "demonstration of the Spirit and of the power" (1 Cor. 2:4); as "proclaiming of the gospel not merely in speech, but also in power and in the Holy Spirit and in great confidence" (1 Thess. 1:5).

The overflowing richness of the gifts of the Spirit is not to be repressed. Paul warns, "Do not extinguish the Spirit" (1 Thess. 5:19). Certainly Paul says that those endowed with the Spirit no longer have control over themselves; they are "impelled" by the Spirit (Rom. 8:14; Gal. 5:18). And yet Paul investigates and classifies the movement of the Spirit. He thanks God that he has the gift of tongues more than others do (1 Cor. 14:18).

But in exemplary fashion, he rates even this gift of the Spirit according to the good it can do in service to the community. Ecstasies, in the midst of which Christ is contemned, do not come from the Spirit of God (1 Cor. 12:3). Speech in tongues that are not understood serves to edify the community and is meaningful, only when the one who is in ecstasy or someone else can, as a prophet, offer an interpretation of what was said (1 Cor. 14:1-33). More valuable than such ecstatic speech is the intelligible word, spoken rationally. "In the assembly I would rather speak five words with my understanding, so that I might also instruct others, than ten thousand words in tongues" (1 Cor. 14:19).

Attitudes and deeds in which daily life is supported are also for Paul the operations and gifts of the Spirit. Thus in his lists he mentions faith, mercy, presiding in the community, and again and again, preaching and speaking words of consolation (1 Cor. 12:4-11; 14; Rom. 12:6-9). It is by the Holy Spirit that "the love of God is poured out in our hearts" (Rom. 5:5). The Spirit is accepted by the heart, *i.e.*, by the emotion and by the will of a man. In prayer, love is turned back toward God. Praying correctly, therefore, is a gift of the Spirit (Rom. 8:26f.; Gal. 4:6).

The working of love in the community is operation of the Spirit (1 Cor. 13; Rom. 15:30). The true Spirit is the Spirit of gentleness (1 Cor. 4:21). Celibacy is a gift of the Spirit (1 Cor. 7:7). Experiencing the Spirit is subordinate to the love of neighbor and the edification of the community. True endowment with the Spirit is that which makes itself subordinate to the simplicity of the faith and to everyday necessity, and serves the whole. "The revelation of the Spirit is given to each for the profit of the community" (1 Cor. 12:7).

The Spirit is never any kind of fanaticism or selfishness, but communion and order. He is the Spirit of Christ (Rom. 8:9). Paul says straight out: "The Lord is the Spirit" (2 Cor. 3:17). The heavenly Christ in his glory is the Spirit operating in the Church. Through his being raised up from the dead he became "a life-giving Spirit" (1 Cor. 15:45f.; Rom. 1:4). "The law of the Spirit of the life in Christ has set you free from the law of sin and of death" (Rom. 8:2). The expressions "in Christ" and "in the Spirit" are interchangeable. Justification takes place in Christ and in the Spirit (1 Cor. 6:11; Gal. 2:16f.). So too with mortification (1 Cor. 1:2; 1 Cor. 6:11) and with being sealed (Eph. 1:3; 4:30). Christ and the Spirit grant love (Rom. 5:5; 8:39) and life (Rom. 6:23; 2 Cor. 3:6).

Christ receives the Spirit from the Father, and pours him out on the Church (Acts 2:33). The Spirit is proper to the collective Church. He is imparted to each believer at baptism. This is the common viewpoint of Christianity, which Paul shares: "In one Spirit we were all baptized into one body . . . and we were all given to drink of one Spirit" (1 Cor. 12:13). The apostolic office transmits the Spirit. The Corinthians are a "letter of Christ, prepared by the Apostle not with ink, but with the Spirit of the living God, written not on stone tablets but on the tablets of human hearts" (2 Cor. 3:3). The Church is "the fellowship of the Spirit" (2 Cor. 13:13). She is the temple of the Spirit (1 Cor. 3:16; 6:19). Since the Spirit is a gift to the whole Church, all her members are "spiritual people." "You, all of you, are not in the flesh but in the Spirit; for indeed, the Spirit of God dwells in you" (Rom. 8:9).[186]

Since holiness designates the divine world, while the human world is characterized by Paul as flesh, then (Holy) Spirit and flesh are antithetical. Flesh can even signify simply human existence (2 Cor. 7:5; Gal. 4:13). Mostly, however, the term flesh is so accentuated that it designates man in his futility and ultimately in his sinfulness (Rom. 7:14; 8:5; *Theology of the New Testament*, Vol. 1, pp. 133–136). The Galatians have now begun in the spirit, and they must take care not to end in the flesh (Gal. 3:2-5). Their existence in faith is established by God's gift of salvation. They must not now attempt, by doing the works of the law, to live as if salvation were their own achievement. In the same sense it is said that "we serve God in the spirit and not trusting in the flesh" (Phil. 3:3).

The opposition between law and grace is designated as just such an opposition as exists between the letter which kills and the spirit which gives life (2 Cor. 3:6), and between "a newness of spirit and the absoluteness of the letter" (Rom. 7:6). Even the opposition between the son of the enslaved Hagar and the son of the freewoman Sarah, and thereby between the old covenant and the new, is conceived as an opposition between spirit and flesh (Gal. 4:29). Accordingly, to live in the spirit means, freed from the law, to risk living by grace.

Sin is foreign to the spirit, just as it is to the Holy Spirit. Paul says again and again that the spirit is the strength of conducting oneself in a holy manner. "The flesh lusts against the spirit, and the spirit against the flesh" (Gal. 5:17). To live according to the flesh brings death. "Those who, in the spirit, kill the deeds of the flesh, will live" (Rom. 8:13). The spirit must be the norm and mode of living. "Who sows in his flesh will, from the flesh, reap corruption; who sows in the spirit will, from the spirit, reap eternal life" (Gal. 6:8; cf. Rom. 8:4, 6). "We must walk not according to the flesh but according to the spirit" (Rom. 8:4; Gal. 5:25). This means serving others in love and in that way fulfilling the law (Gal. 5:13f.). Paul exhorts: "Walk in the spirit and do not fulfill the lusts of the flesh" (Gal. 5:16). Since it is only he in whom the spirit is operative that is truly in the spirit, Paul is able — in seeming contradiction to his assertion that the Spirit is given to each of the baptized —

to distinguish among Christians those who are spiritual and those who are carnal (1 Cor. 3:1-3).

The Spirit is joy in all tribulation (1 Thess. 1:6). He is the Spirit of adoption into sonship with God (Rom. 8:15). Spirit is collective Christian existence in general. "The fruit of the Spirit is love, joy, peace, patience, affability, goodness, fidelity, gentleness, and self-control" (Gal. 5:22). The Spirit is the beginning and the anticipation of perfection. He is "earnest-money" (Rom. 8:23) and the "pledge" (2 Cor. 1:22; 5:5) of future glory. The Spirit as indestructible life-force is the conquest of death, the assurance of the resurrection and of eternal life (Rom. 8:10f.). The resurrection-body will be a "spiritual body" (1 Cor. 15:44).

d) The Gospel of John and his First Epistle

In the Gospel of John, in its doctrine of the Spirit, there is lacking any reference to the ecstatic aspects of being endowed with the Spirit.[187] At most, one might find a hint about prophecy in the statement: "The Spirit will not speak on his own authority, but he will speak whatever he has heard; and he will proclaim to you the things that are to come" (John 16:13). The remark of Jesus to the effect that streams of living waters will flow from the body of one who believes in him is explained by the evangelist: "He said this of the Spirit, whom those who believed in him were to receive. But the Spirit was not yet given because Jesus had not yet been glorified" (John 7:39). The Spirit is the gift of the exalted Christ. Not until after Jesus' consummation is the Church equipped with the Spirit. (This concurs with the hesitancy that the older Gospels have in letting the earthly Jesus speak of the Spirit).

The world of the Spirit is the divine world. The Spirit is imparted to men as heavenly gift. God gives us of his Spirit (1 John 4:13). Indeed, "God is Spirit". That is why the true worshipper must worship in spirit and in truth (John 4:24; § 19, 1). Christian existence is always being in the Spirit. The Spirit is a gift to the whole Church. The resurrected Christ imparts the Spirit to the Church (John 20:22). He is the full authority of the forgiveness of sins in the Church. The Spirit is imparted to all in baptism (John 3:5). He is given out beyond all measure (John 3:34). The Spirit effects new birth from above. The opposition between old covenant and new, between world and God, is designated just as in

Paul (Rom. 8:5; Phil. 3:3), as opposition of flesh and spirit (John 3:6; 6:63). The spirit is new creation by the power of God.

In John's Gospel in the sayings about the Paraclete [188] the Spirit is promised to the Church as her support (John 14:16-28; 15:26; 16:7-15). Above all else, with this concept John explains anew and in a deeper way the general Christian doctrine of the Holy Spirit. As their mediator of truth, Jesus was until now his disciples' Paraclete (John 14:16). They must not remain unprotected in an inimical world (John 15:18f.). "Another Paraclete" (John 14:16) will now be their helper and advocate. Christ is no longer visible in the world and at their disposal. He is to be experienced only in faith. As Spirit of truth the Paraclete is to make the presence of the Father and of the Son able to be experienced in faith (John 14:16-23).

As witness and plaintiff in the legal battle between God and the world, the Paraclete places on exhibit the disbelief of the world and the justice of Jesus (John 3:18-20; 16:8-11). He operates in the testimony of the disciples as presence of God, which is operative in the apostolic proclamation to the community. The disciples bear witness by recalling what they saw and heard when in the company of Jesus (John 15:27), and through them the Spirit bears witness (John 15:26). Through the operation of the Paraclete the words of the historical Jesus get their permanent force and real effectiveness. The words of the Spirit are the testimonials spoken in the fully authoritative proclamation to the community (John 20:22f.). The Spirit bears Christ's testimony (1 John 5:6-8). He gives life to the word and thereby to the Church (John 6:63).

There is also a false "inspiration" or "enrapturement in the spirit", leading to error. The Church dares not trust every spirit. She must test spirits and distinguish among them. The Spirit of God is recognized by the fact that he "confesses that Jesus Christ has come in the flesh" (1 John 4:1-3). The genuinity of the spirit is distinguished by its position in regard to Christ (see 1 Cor. 12:1-3).

As a strength for the fulfilling of the commandments, the Spirit is the principle of the moral life. "Whoever keeps his commandments abides in God and God in him." That God abides in us, "we recognize by the Spirit, whom he has given us" (1 John 3:24). Only where there is love, is there life (1 John 3:14). Therefore the teachers of error, who rend the unity and love of the Church, do not have the Spirit of God (1 John 4:13).

The Paraclete is equal beside Father and Son. The "other Paraclete" is given and sent by the Father and the Son, just as the Son was sent by the Father (John 14:24, 26). Like the Son, he proceeds from the Father (John 15:26; 16:27). The testimony of the Spirit derives from the reality of the Son just as the testimony of the Son derives from the reality of the Father (John 14:10; 16:13).

e) Substance of the Spirit

In looking at the Church's teaching on the Trinity, one can notice, historically speaking, intimations of a granting of autonomy to what the "spirit" is. The first hints in this direction can be found in the Old Testament and in intertestamental Judaism.

The Old Testament is rigidly monotheistic. Nevertheless, just as in the wisdom literature Wisdom experiences a certain hypostatization, a comparable process occurs with the *Spirit*: "The *spirit* of the Lord fills the earth" (Wis. 1:7).

In the Qumran scrolls along with the "Holy Spirit" other spirits too are named: spirits of truth and of falsehood; spirits of light and of darkness (1 QS 3:18f., 24f.; 4:23).

In the New Testament the declarations are clearer. The spirit appears as an impersonal force; but it is also personified. Then the Spirit is separated from God as the One given by God and the One sent from God (Gal. 4:6). God pours out the Spirit (Acts 2:17). "He has saved us by the bath of rebirth and renewal, which is effected by the Holy Spirit whom he has poured out upon us abundantly through Jesus Christ" (Tit. 3:6f.).

The Spirit is gift. But his being given is no more a contradiction of his personal independence than it is in the case of the Son, who is given up. The Spirit is sent. The Son too is sent into the world (John 3:17; Rom. 8:3). Nevertheless, the Spirit can also be the subject, not just something but someone; not just operated upon, but the One who is operating; not just the Gift, but the Giver. The Spirit himself testifies along with our spirit (Rom. 8:16). He entreats for us with God (Rom. 8:26). He bestows his gifts where he will (1 Cor. 12:11). The Spirit speaks in the writings of the Old Covenant (Heb. 3:7; 1 Peter 1:11f.; 2 Peter 1:21), as also in the Church (1 Tim. 4:1). He teaches the community (Apoc. 2:7). It is possible to oppose the Spirit (Acts 7:51). It is possible to grieve him (Eph. 4:30).

The Gospel of John speaks of the Father, who is manifest in the Son, and of the Spirit who works in closest union with him and is yet independent. As Paraclete, the Spirit is the helper and support of the Church (John 15:26). The Father sends the Spirit at the request of Jesus (John 14:16) and in the name of Jesus (John 14:26). Jesus himself also sends him forth from the Father (John 15:26; 16:18). The Spirit proceeds from the Father and the Son and is therefore separate from the Father and the Son (John 15:26). After the exaltation of Christ the Spirit is the other support (John 14:16). "The Paraclete, the Holy Spirit, whom the Father will send in my name — He (ἐκεῖνος) will teach you all things, and will recall to your minds everything that I have said to you" (John 14:26). In this passage the Spirit, as agent of Christ in the community, is represented so personally that, although πνεῦμα is neuter, the masculine of the personal pronoun ἐκεῖνος is used.

In the "triad texts" witnessing to the initial stages of the developing doctrine of the Trinity, the Holy Spirit will appear even more clearly in his substantial independence, a matter which we will pursue in chapter 21, below.

IV

BELIEF IN GOD
AND DOCTRINE ABOUT GOD

§ 13. THE QUESTION OF GOD TODAY

In modern theology the question of God is propounded with new and greater intensity.[189] Properly, of course, this is the essential question of *theo*-logy. In general, can one speak accurately of God; and if so, how? This is a question with which men have always occupied themselves. It is the question weighed by both Testaments of the Bible, Old and New. It was and is the question which philosophy and natural theology have always seen as confronting them. It is a basic question of Christian theology and philosophy from Origen and Augustine through the scholastics and mystics to the reformation and to era of idealism.

Just as in every age, so too today, radical atheism, at an opposite pole from theology, strives actively to substitute for theology. We even hear of formulations in theology which make us prick up our ears, formulations which must be carefully examined as to their tendency. We hear catch phrases about an "a-theistic theology" and a "God-is-dead theology."

This a-theistic theology wants to be a theology without and against philosophical theism. It explains that the God of philosophy, who is the ultimate cause in a series of compelling conclusions, is not the biblical God, the sovereign Lord. Christianity is not an instance of a theistic religion, but, as revelation of God, something quite otherwise. Indeed, the celebrated *Mémorial* of Blaise Paschal already speaks of just such an antithesis: "Fire. God of Abraham, God of Isaac, God of Jacob. Not of the philosophers and of the learned. Certitude, feeling. Joy, peace, God of Jesus Christ."

Today a-theism too expresses itself with the saying "God is dead."

236

According to this school the God who is dead is the God who is self-evident to us. God is a coin we have spent all too freely, even frivolously. Now it is worn out by constant handling and its value is debased. "God is dead" means that, because of the darkness of the times, which are full of awesome happenings, he is absent. "God is dead" means that he is not available to us. Have we ever understood this sufficiently? Have we not consigned God to the innumerable theses of our dogmatic handbooks? Was it not a temptation of Canon Law in the past and ecclesiastical bureaucracies in the present to manage God?

The term "God" is a word found in all religions. Biblical faith recognizes in a thoroughly critical way that, with the term *God*, it makes use of a word which, employed outside the faith, designates something which does not properly exist. "Not knowing God you have served gods who in reality do not exist at all" (Gal. 4:8). The term "God", used by the pagans, designates nothing that is true and real. Pagan culture, therefore, though it worships many gods, can be characterized by the saying: "You were in this world without God" (Eph. 2:12). The biblical term "God" is always turned against the idolatrous misuse of the term God. It has always the task of "de-idolizing" this word.

On the other hand it must never be forgotten that even biblical and Christian assertions about God are always analogous assertions. The statement of the Fourth Lateran Council must be kept in mind: "No similarity can be affirmed between Creator and creature without there being affirmed at the same time an even greater dissimilarity between them" (Schönmetzer's Denziger, *Enchiridion symbolorum*, 33rd edition, Freiburg 1965, no. 806).

God is never a matter from which the speaker can stand apart at some distance, in order to make some assertion about him. The speaker is himself always supported and embraced by God in the eternal act of creation. God, therefore, is never the object, but always conjointly the subject of every theological assertion. Talking about God is possible only when this relationship is acknowledged and accepted. God is not an object occupying space, but the determination of every existence.

The talk about an absent and hidden God can certainly, it seems, appeal to the Bible. Moses asks the God who was speaking to him from the thornbush for his name. The answer he receives is: "I am the I here present" (Exod. 3:13f.). God has no name, such as the gods of the

Egyptians and the gods of the pagans have, according to which these religions believe that one must know the name of God, the name by which he himself wants to be called, in order to call upon him, indeed, in order to be able to control him. Yahweh is always present as the one nearby and the helper. Nevertheless, he will be present in the way that he determines, and not in the way that man thinks and desires. God is ever the Unavailable and Hidden One.

Authors in the fields of exegesis and the history of dogma tell us that it was not only highly significant but really quite unfortunate that Christian theology from the second century onwards — and then to an ever increasing degree — in its association with Greek philosophy took up the latter's concept of God, and relocated the biblical Christian God in the "highest being" (*summum ens*) of philosophy, and fused both concepts of God into one. This was made easier for the Fathers of the Church by the fact that the Septuagint translated the name of Yahweh in Exod. 3:14 as "I am who exists." The Fathers intended thereby to designate God simply as being. This seemed to them to be a confirmation of Greek philosophy, insofar as the latter designated the Godhead as the highest being. The Church's theology equated the biblical Creator-God with the metaphysical world-principle.

The first two prohibitions of the decalogue forbid the worship of strange gods and the misuse of the revealed name of God (Exod. 20:1-5; Deut. 5:6-11). Forbidden too is the setting up of images, which took place as a matter of course in the pagan religions. The God of Israel is not comprehensible nor at one's disposal by means of images.

No man can see God; he would have to die (Gen. 32:31; Judges 6:22; 13:22). When Moses, the prince of Israel and friend of God, requested to be allowed to behold the glory of God, it was granted him only to see God's back and to hear the name of the Lord (Exod. 33:18-23). When Yahweh appears, he is still hidden in a cloud. He goes past Moses, who only hears the message of God's mercy (Exod. 34:5f.). Darkness is God's veil (Ps. 18:12; 97:2). These narrations are mythological in form, like many other stories which tell of the transactions of the gods with men. But the biblical stories destroy every mythology insofar as they say that man cannot treat with God as his equal, but that he must perish if he so much as sees God.

The Old Testament often says that God hides himself from his people and from those who seek him and pray to him. He remains silent, he turns away, he hides His face (Ps. 13:2; 69:18; Is. 1:15; 8:17; Job 13:24). This hiddenness of God is his reaction to sin and guilt. His hiddenness, however, is temporally bounded, since God again wills to bestow his favor upon the petitioner and again makes his countenance shine upon him (Ps. 80:4).

In some passages of the Old Testament there is talk even of God's being hidden in his mystery and in his incomprehensibility. "In truth you are a hidden God, God of Israel, the Savior" (Is. 45:15). God's dealings are hidden; for he chooses the Gentile Cyrus for his anointed one (Is. 44:28; 45:1). Filled with mystery is the significance of the Servant of Yahweh. The prophet says of the latter, "Who has believed our report?" (Is. 53:1).

The stricken Servant of Yahweh (probably Israel in her grief) is now the sign of the incomprehensible dealings of God. These texts pertain to the historical associations of the last years of the exile. They bear witness to a new insight. God's dealings had until now shown themselves in triumph and power. Now, however, it is a hidden control which men cannot understand.

In the New Covenant the highest and final revelation of God takes place in Christ. But in him the Word of God has become flesh. There is always the possibility of being scandalized in the man Jesus. Now "the blind see, the lame walk, the lepers are made clean, the deaf hear, the dead are raised to life, and the poor have the gospel preached to them." Nevertheless, these wonders do not compel belief. "Blessed is he who is not scandalized in me" (Matthew 11:4-6). Jesus himself says that the work of God "is hidden from the wise and prudent and revealed to the little ones" (Matthew 11:25).

The ultimate revelation and at the same time the most profound concealment of God takes place in the Cross of Christ. It is incomprehensible to human judgment, "a scandal to the Jews, and foolishness to the Gentiles" (1 Cor. 1:23). God's dealings look like weakness (2 Cor. 13:3f.). No proclamation and interpretation can take that away. What is more, even the preaching of the Cross looks like foolishness (1 Cor. 1:18, 21). Incapacity and weakness too is the appearance of the Church, which bears the mortal sufferings of Christ in her body so that the life also of Jesus may be manifest in her body (2 Cor. 4:10). Even in weakness the strength of God must be consummated in a hidden way (2 Cor. 12:9). The revelation remains "God's mystery" (1 Cor. 2:1). God's wisdom is to be proclaimed in the mystery (1 Cor. 2:7). Christ is not only the revelation of God, but his mystery also (Col. 2:2).

God is hidden even in the ages. In a backward glance at the history of Israel and of the Gentiles, Paul cries out: "How inscrutable are his decisions and unsearchable his ways! For who has known the mind of the Lord, and who has been his counsellor?" (Rom. 11:33-34).

God can be known only to the extent that he allows. "If anyone thinks he has known anything, he has not yet known as he ought to know. But if anyone loves God, he is known by him" (1 Cor. 8:2f.; *cf.* Gal. 4:9). Paul does not say that a man who loves God knows God; but, in a tumultuous reversal of his thought, he says that true knowledge can never be had except by God. God knows the man in choosing him. The decision and action of God always precede the decision and action of man. God is the Hidden One, unless he himself suspends his hiddenness.

§ 14. OLD TESTAMENT BELIEF IN GOD
AND THE GREEK CONCEPT OF GOD

The nature and practice of a religion is determined by its idea of God.[190] The biblical belief in God and the Greek concept of God are to be considered in greater detail in surveying the New Testament. The terms "biblical belief in God" and "Greek concept of God" are used of set purpose, it being intended to show by their difference an awareness of the fact that biblical belief in God knows very well that it cannot form an adequate concept of God, while philosophy continues to expend its efforts to form just such a concept of God.

1. OLD TESTAMENT BELIEF IN GOD

The history of religion highly esteems Israel's belief in God as pure, imageless monotheism. As such it really had a virtually inestimable significance and importance in the history of religion and religions. Monotheism is at the same time one of our primary classificational points in the modern scientific study of religions. Israel's belief in God certainly does not bespeak the notion of monotheism unequivocally and from the very beginning. Israel's belief in God has its history.

In the beginning of this history of belief Israel acknowledged God as her peculiar God, whom the nation had experienced in the course of her history as her helper. From the earliest ages onward God is the God of the covenant on the basis of covenanted agreements with Noah, Abraham, and Moses.

The union between this God and his people is not bound up with nature, in the way that the relationship between god and people was broadly understood in the ancient orient; rather, the covenant relationship is established by God's free choice. God chose Israel purely by grace, gave her the promises and fulfilled them. He practices fidelity (Exod. 20:6). Israel too is obligated to fidelity. This fidelity demands of Israel exclusive devotion to her God, and prohibits the worship of other gods. Thus speaks the Lord of the covenant: "I am the Lord, thy God, who led thee out of the land of Egypt, out of the house of bondage. Thou shalt have no other gods besides me" (Exod. 20:2-3). Israel's God is a "jealous God" (Exod. 20:5). The whole Old Testament warns menacingly of this zeal of Yahweh (Deut. 4:24; Is. 8:1-15; Ezech. 5:13; Zech. 1:14).

Other nations can worship other gods, who have their own validity and reality. In the beginning, at any rate, their existence is not expressly denied by Israel; and, indeed, it is actually acknowledged at times in the belief of the people (Judges (11:23f.; 1 Sam. 26:19; 4 Kings 3:27). Ancient formulas do not say that the God of Israel is the only God, but that he is the highest God, and is superior to all other gods. Songs and psalms praise the God of Israel as highest King among all gods (Ex. 15:11; Ps. 86:8; 95:3; 96:4). God himself holds judgment over the gods of the nations and overthrows them (Ps. 82; Deut. 32:37-39). The conclusion is drawn and declared as a conviction that the highest God is alone God and Lord of all nations and kingdoms (3 Kings 8:60; 4 Kings 19:15; Deut. 4:35).

The absolute exclusiveness of Yahweh certainly pertains to the religion of Moses. This exclusiveness is afterwards made statutory in legal texts, which can be elucidated and clarified only on the supposition of monotheism. The formulations of the Law, nevertheless, even if they are shifted to the time of Moses, are probably later and belong to the deuteronomic period. The Law reads: "Thou shalt have no other gods besides me." And Israel, with her imageless worship, is separated thereby from all worship of idols (Exod. 20:3f.; Deut. 5:7f.).

The solitary God of Israel is one in his nature. As one and only he can and must demand total and exclusive submission. In response to this demand it is stated in the commandment that is of absolute authority for Israel: "Hear, Israel! Yahweh is our God, Yahweh alone. You shall love Yahweh, your God, with your whole heart, with your whole soul, and with your whole strength" (Deut. 6:4f.). From this follows the further commandment that the one God is to be ministered to in the one place of worship which he himself has chosen, Jerusalem (Deut. 12).

The rigid Hebrew monotheism is established in these laws. In the New Testament era the Jewish mission in the diaspora proclaimed its One-God-Belief among the Gentiles. The true God is preached as εἷς θεὸς and as μόνος θεὸς. "There is one God, the Sole-Sovereign, the Inexpressible, who is enthroned in the heavens" (*Sibylline Oracles* 3, 11). "He is sole God; besides him there is no other" (*Sibylline Oracles* 3, 629). Even the Gentile will finally come to know that this One alone is God (2 Macc. 7:37). Exclusiveness characterizes God. Thus Philo says, in his *De allegoriis legum* 2, 1: "Only the One is alone. The One, however, who shapes a unity for himself, is God, and there is nothing similar to God. It is good that the truly Existing is alone." For men, however, it is said: "It is not good that he be alone" (Gen. 2:18). The one God is the Father of all. "The Jews believe that God is one, the Father and Creator of the world" (Philo, *De legatione ad Caium* 115; similar in his *De decalogo* 64). The Christian mission took over this preaching and continued it among the nations (§ 15, 1; § 16, 1).

On this point of monotheism, however, an orthdoxy took shape which Israel had to defend with most extraordinary vigor throughout the course of her history, even with many martyrs. Finally the monotheism of Judaism refused even to accept the revelation of God in his Son Jesus Christ and retreated into an irreconcilable opposition to the Christian belief in the Triune Godhead.

In Israel's history the revelation of the name of Yahweh was of incomparable significance for her understanding of the nature of God (Exod. 3:14 in the Elohist; Exod. 6:3 in the Priestly text). Old Testament investigation comes to the well-nigh unanimous conclusion that the name is probably to be translated: "I will be present as the I will be present" (Martin Buber).[191] The name must not be understood in the mentality of Greek metaphysics, as the Jewish philosophy of religion understood it from the time of the Septuagint onwards, and as patristic theology also thought to understand it, as a declaration of the uncreated divine being. Much more it is a promise of the permanent nearness of God. Thus Yahweh now assures Israel of his help in the midst of her mortal danger in an inimical Egypt (and this promise is always valid for Israel). Yahweh does not first have to be called down, as others believe of their gods; rather, he is always present. He is surely present where and how he determines. He acts always in perfect and sovereign freedom.

The little nation of Israel had to preserve and authenticate her faith in the midst of nations and powers often politically and culturally far superior to herself. In this confrontation there was a growing awareness of the peculiarity of her spiritual belief in God and of her imageless worship of God. The confrontation is carried on by the prophets. Elijah led the battles against the nature religion of Baal (3 Kings 17f.). Israel challenged Babylon, world power though she was.

The shocking indictments levelled by the prophets, like that of Jeremiah 44:15-23 and Ezechiel 8, provide a picture of how broadly and deeply the false gods of the Gentiles could infiltrate Israel. The prophets had to deliver the message that the misfortunes and disasters which befell the nation were a punishment for her apostasy from the true God (Is. 10:11; Jer. 9:12-15; Ezech. 8:17f.). The prophets deepened and clarified the faith, when they proclaimed forcefully and unequivocally that the pagan gods are not gods at all. "Has ever a nation changed its gods? — and indeed, they are not gods! And my nation has exchanged her God for that which avails nothing" (Jer. 2:11; *cf*. 10:7; 16:20).

Deutero-Isaiah experiences the overpowering knowledge of the uniqueness of God. "Before me there was no god, and after me none will be. I am the Lord, and besides me there is no helper" (Is. 43:10f.). He alone can lay claim to the names El and Elohim (i.e., God). All other gods are nothings (Is. 41:24, 29). Idols are but creations of human hands; they do not see, they do not hear, and they accomplish nothing (Hos. 8:4-6; 13:2; Ps. 135:15-18). Yahweh will annihiliate the false gods (Is. 10:10f.; Ezech. 6:4-6). On the day of judgment men will cast aside their idols (Is. 2:18-21). The polemic of the Deutero-Isaiah is especially vehement in the situation of the exile, when Israel was obliged to live in the land of a grandiose and imposing religion of effigies. The manufacture of images is ridiculed (Is. 40:19f.; 41:6; 44:9-20). The idols are not able to protect the city of Babylon; they themselves are obliged to go along into captivity (Is. 46:1-7).

Progressive reflection understood Yahweh as Creator of heaven and earth. In relation to the world, he is the One who is superior, the transcendent One (see Schelkle, *Theology of the New Testament*, Vol. 1, pp. 3–13). He is not the Creator just once and in the beginning, but in perduring operation. He is the "breath of life in all flesh" (Num. 27:16). It is the God who is separated from the world who answers to this description. The Transcendent One is the Immanent One.

Amos (9:2-6) proclaims the Avenger-God, who is everywhere, whom man cannot escape. Even Psalm 139:7-12, probably ancient, praises God as superterrestrial and filling up the world, one before whom man cannot flee. Nothing created, whatever and wherever it may be, is comparable to God. God is nowhere confined in place, much less in an image. "You are not to make for yourself any image of God, nor any kind of image at all, neither of those things in heaven above, nor of those things on the earth below, nor of those things which are in the waters and beneath the earth" (Exod. 20:4).

Not even the temple can contain Yahweh, and certainly no other place. At the consecration of the temple Solomon prays: "If heaven and all the heavens of heaven are not able to contain you, how much less, then, this house" (3 Kings 8:27). Isaiah (6:1-3) beholds the temple and the whole world filled up with the glory of Yahweh. Yet the temple contains only the hems of his cloak.

God is superior even to all times, and is present in all times. He is "the First and the Last" (Is. 44:6; 48:12). "Before the mountains were born, before the earth and the world were created — O God, you are, from eternity to eternity!" (Ps. 90:2). God, therefore, is the Lord of all history. He is the King of nations and of times (Is. 24:23; 52:7; Jer. 10:7, 10; Ps. 24:7-10; 33:8-11). God's substance is his holiness (Amos 4:2; Is.

6:3). He is "the Holy One of Israel" (Is. 1:4; *Theology of the New Testament*, Vol. 3, pp. 171–174). God is the Righteous One, who leads justice to victory (*ibid.*, p. 179f.). He manifests himself at all times as the One who is acting in all history. He is the personal God. His personality is already declared in the name Yahweh (Exod. 3:14), since this name signifies: "I am present as the I am present."

Since man is created in the image of God, man has a certain relationship to God, and God to him (Gen. 1:27). God is the "Thou" of conversation and response. God is gracious and merciful (Exod. 33:19; Ps. 103:8). He forgives guilt (Exod. 34:6f.). In the covenant of his love God embraces the whole nation. "When Israel was young, I prized him dearly; and out of Egypt I did call my son" (Hos. 11:1). He is the Father of the people Israel (Exod. 4:22f.; Is. 63:16; Jer. 31:9). Although Yahweh is depicted as a person through the harmless employment of numerous anthropomorphisms, the faith knows well enough that this God can never be compared to a man (Hos. 11:9). He is "without compare" (Is. 40:18). Consequently it is not possible for there to be any image of him, nor permissible to attempt such (Deut. 4:15-18).

From the beginning of the third century before Christ, Judaism found itself face to face with the paramount culture of Greece. The altercation became violent in the time of the Maccabees; otherwise it was carried on broadly as a spiritual struggle. The Wisdom literature continues the polemic against the worship of images (Wis. 13:10-16; 14:12-21; 15:4-8; Baruch 6; Dan. 14:1-22).[192] Paganism is always, however, a dangerous reality. Demoniacal powers, or so it is believed, are at work in it and keep it alive. The cult of idols pollutes; and it stirs up God's wrath (Exod. 32:33-35). The Septuagint introduces the term and concept of demons into the Greek Bible (Septuagint: Psalm 95:5; 105:37; Is. 65:11; Deut. 32:16f.). Whatever is sacrificed to idols is received by the impure demons (*Ethiopic Henoch* 19, 1; 99, 7; *Book of Jubilees* 11, 4f.).

In the New Testament era finally the opponent of Judaism was the Roman government. The New Testament is well aware of the enmity between Jewish zeal and the Roman Empire. Messianic movements, which wanted to shake off foreign rule, broke out again and again, and were suppressed with blood. The Apocalypse of John (13:1-10) depicts the battle between the community and the government, which, according to the biblical view, was idolatrous in its cult of the emperor (*Theology of the New Testament*, Vol. 3, pp. 333-350).

In the era of intertestamental Judaism, reverential fear in the presence of God's majesty was heightened more and more, and even exaggerated. The name of God was no longer pronounced, in order to preclude any irreverence. Substitute terms were used in place of the name of God, such as "heaven", "name", and "power". Judaism separated God from the world. He could operate in the world and deal with men only through a system of intermediary powers and angelic beings.

In the writings from the Qumran community the name Yahweh never appears, but the word El, meaning God, is not infrequent. He is called "the Prince of the Gods and King of the Highly Worshipped and Lord of every Spirit and Ruler of every Creature" (1 QH 10:8). He is "King of Kings" and "God of Gods" (1 QM 14:16). God is the Creator of the world and of men (1 QH 10:12). He made also the spirits of light and of darkness, through whom he accomplishes his works (1 QS 3:25). God is the Just (1 QH 14:15), the Wise (1 QH 9:17), the Truthful (1 QH 15:25), the Holy One (1 QM 19:1), and in a special way the "God of Israel" (1 QM 1:9f.), and the "Father of the Sons of Truth" (1 QH 9:35). He is worshipped as the God of mysteries and the Dispenser of salvation: "Out of the wellspring of his righteousness comes my Law, the light of his wonderful mysteries shines in my heart" (1 QS 11:5). To the "Sons of His Good Pleasure" he shows favor, kindness, goodness and mercy (1 QH 4:32f.; 7:30; 11:29). He forgives guilt and re-establishes righteousness (1 QH 4:37; 1 QM 11:13f.). This is the experience of the pious who, chosen from eternity, belong to his community (1 QH 7:34; 9:30). "The godless, however, are made for the time of wrath and from their mother's womb are destined for the day of slaughter (1 QH 15:17).

2. THE GREEK CONCEPT OF GOD

The "pagan" religion in the milieu of the New Testament was in part still mythology (Greek especially), and in part religious philosophy and mysticism. This religion was by its very nature polytheistic. It did have, however, a henotheistic aspect, in that even in its polymorphous character it conceived and frequently spoke of the unity of the religious world. The divinities and religious notions of various religions were equated and combined in a broadly syncretistic fashion.

Apart from the archeological monuments, we first encounter the world of the Greek gods in the epics of Homer. The multiplicity of the gods already appears as an ordered whole. Ultimately they are represented in Zeus, the "father of men and gods" (*Iliad* 15, 47), the "highest and best of the gods" (*Odyssey* 19, 303).

Philosophy endeavors from its very beginnings to shed some light upon religious viewpoints, and especially upon mythology. The pre-Socratics were already subjecting the myths to severe criticism. Xenophanes (*fl. ca.* 538 B.C.) states: "Homer and Hesiod have attributed to the gods everything that is regarded by men as shame and disgrace: theft and adultery and deception of each other" (Fragment 11 in H. Diels and W. Kranz, *Die Fragmente der Vorsokratiker*, Vol. 1, 7th edition, Berlin 1954). "If oxen and horses and lions had hands or could paint with their hands and make images such as men do, horses would paint the shapes of their gods and fashion their bodies to look like horses, oxen would make theirs like oxen. . . . The Ethiopians are of a mind that their gods are broad-nosed and black; the Thracians, blue-eyed and with red hair" (*Ibid.*, Fragm. 15 and 16). The philosopher himself has the following concept of God: "God is one only, the greatest among gods and men, similar to mortals neither in form nor in idea" (*Ibid.*, Fragm. 23).

Heraclitus (*fl. ca.* 513 B.C.) reproaches the very idea and practice of religion: "They seek to be cleansed of blood guilt, while they but contaminate themselves with more blood . . . And they pray even to the images of gods, as if one were to carry on a conversation with a house; which can only show that he does not recognize the gods and heroes for what they are" (Diels and Kranz, *op. cit.*, Heraclitus, Frag. 5).

The first Greek philosophers tried to discover the principle (the ἀρχή) of things. By the originating principle they understood the "source, primitive cause, and the boundless as the predominantly governing element in everything." They called this ultimate basis or originating principle "the divine"; thus according to the report of Aristotle (see Anaximander, *Life* A 15, in Diels and Kranz, *op. cit.*).

In the multiplicity of the gods philosophy sought to recognize a divine unity. According to Heraclitus the divine Logos is realized in the All; according to Anaxagoras (*fl. ca.* 450 B.C.), it is the divine Nous that is so realized. Plato (*Republic* 517 B.C.) represents God as the idea of the good. Aristotle conceives reason (the Nous) as the absolute and the divine.

In later antiquity, especially among the Stoics, the godhead was pantheistically conceived as idea, world-reason, the good, being, the alone, fate. The all-embracing order in the world can be called Zeus. Marcus Aurelius (7, 9) is able to offer a formulation of the recognition of God as provided by Stoic philosophy: "The world is one from all, and God is one through all, and being is one with the law." Divine law and natural law are one (Marcus Aurelius 4, 23): "Everything which your passing seasons bring, O Nature, is profit unto me. From you are all things, in you are all things, unto you are all things." [*Translator's note*: This same passage was quoted on page 22 of Vol. 1 of the present *Theology of the New Testament*, in which place we inadvertently omitted the important clause "*in you are all things*": the reader may correct the quotation in the margin of Vol. 1 from the passage as quoted immediately above].

The New Testament comes close to such statements of Hellenistic mysticism as the above; thus in Rom. 11:36, "From him and through him and unto him are all things" (see Schelkle, *Theology of the New Testament*, Vol. 1, pp. 22–23). The Acts of the Apostles (17:16-34) recognizes a relationship between Greek religion and Christianity, which is indicated with a quotation from Aratus: "We too are surely offspring of God" (Acts 17:28; see below, § 16, 1; and in Vol. 1 of the present work, pp. 42–43).

The religious sentiment of philosophy nevertheless holds fast to polytheism as an expression of the power of the divine, which is visible and operative in many appearances and under many names. The Greek gods are the archetypes and basic powers of the world. What Thales says at the very beginning of philosophy, then, is verified: "Everything is full of the gods" (according to Plato and Aristotle; in Diels and Kranz, op. cit., Thales, *Life* A 22). The cosmos as a whole is a revelation of God and itself divine.

According to Heraclitus (Diels and Kranz, *op. cit.*, Fragm. 30) this world is eternal: "It was not one of the gods nor yet a man who created this ordering of the world, which is the same for all; on the contrary, it was always in existence. It is and will be eternally living fire, flaring up in dimensions and dying down in dimensions." In this mysterious primordial principle gods and men alike have their origins. Pindar (*Nemean Odes* 6, 1) says as much: "One is the race of men, one is the race of gods. By one mother we are both given breath; yet we are separated by powers utterly disparate." Plato (*Timaeus* 92 C) explains: "Equipped and brought to completion with mortal and immortal living creatures, this cosmos itself has become a visible living creature embracing the visible creatures, the image of the intelligible, a perceivable God, the greatest and the best, the most beautiful and most perfect, this sole and only-begotten All" (see Schelkle, *Theology of the New Testament*, Vol. 1, p. 56). Nevertheless, Plato (*Timaeus* 28 C) can also designate God as the Maker or as the Orderer of the All: "Certainly it is difficult to find the Maker and Father of this All; and even when one has found him, it is impossible to talk about him in such a way that everyone will understand."

The God of philosophy is the manifestation of the glory of being, but not in the way that this may be said of the God of biblical faith. The God of the philosophers does not stand in relation to the world as its Creator. He is not the "totally other", such as the Holy One of Israel is. The divine is the shape, order, form, and mentality of reality.

§ 15. NEW TESTAMENT BELIEF IN GOD

If we now consider the community of disciples and the Church of the New Testament, their belief in God is a fact of unquestionable certainty.[193] It requires no demonstration. Paul is convinced that God's existence can be deduced from the world (Rom. 1:19f.) and from moral consciousness or conscience (Rom. 2:14; § 2, 2 above). God can also be recognized from his wisdom, manifested in the world (1 Cor. 1:21). Paul's argumentative preaching in the midst of the Areopagus may very well be a calling to mind of the philosophical recognition of God (Acts 17:26-28). But the belief in God is never referred to such deliberations nor does it rest on such. Faith has its certitude on other grounds, which essentially are two.

There is the revelation of God vouchsafed to the nation of Israel in the Old Covenant; and there is the present and definitive revelation of God in Christ. "Many times and in many different ways God has spoken to the fathers through the prophets; but now, at the end of these days, he has spoken to us through his Son" (Heb. 1:1f.). New Testament belief in God was obliged to analyze itself when confronted by its contemporary world.

1. New Testament Belief in God, and Pagan Religion

The first Christians lived in a pagan milieu and experienced the impact of opposing religious beliefs.[194] This was true of Jesus as well as of the primitive community. The Synoptic Gospels mention several sojournings of Jesus in the pagan frontier districts (Mark 6:14-8:26). Nevertheless, the Gospels say nothing of any preaching that Jesus may have done there, and are silent about such in their history. But even in the land of Israel one could not but come into contact with paganism. In the midst of the land of the patriarchs stood the grand temple of Roma and Augustus in Samaria, then called Sebaste (*i.e.*, City of Augustus). Jesus too saw the city and its temple often enough from the Plain of Sichem. The extensive ruins can still give us some idea of the beauty of the structure and grounds. In the temple itself a magnificent priesthood ministered. According to a saying of Jesus the pagan divine services were wordy, empty displays (Matthew 6:7). This may have reflected Jewish criticism of Gentile worship in contrast to their own imageless synagogue services.

Everywhere, in the marketplaces, on the streets, the Jew came into contact with pagan strangers, Roman soldiers, officials and merchants, even Greek philosophers. Their commercial life would have seemed to the pious Jew to be a restless and agitated existence, filled with apprehensions unstilled by faith (Matthew 6:31f.; *Theology of the New Testament*, Vol. 3, pp. 86 and 210). But the Jews must live together with the Roman army of occupation. Challenged with the question about the tax coin, Jesus answers, "Render to the emperor what belongs to the emperor, to God what belongs to God" (Mark 12:17). The statement should not be taken to mean that the political and religious spheres are separate and independent; rather, it means that the state and civil affairs are bounded and circumscribed by God (*Theology of the New Testament*, Vol. 3, § 26).

The altercation with paganism became more urgent and more severe when the gospel had made its passage from the Jewish to the Gentile world. Witnesses to this fact are the Acts of the Apostles, the Epistles of Paul, and the Apocalypse of John. In comparison to the tiny and forlorn Christian community, paganism was an overpowering and menacing religious, cultural and sociological reality. Christianity was obliged to engage in a life and death struggle for its very existence.

In the face of the surrounding paganism and its worship of idols the first reaction of Judaism was pride in its pure monotheism. And Paul shares in this pride. We hear it coming through in his description of the abominations of the worship of idols in Rom. 1:18-32. In respect to the Judaizers who boast of their fidelity to the Law, Paul says: "We ourselves are Jews by birth and not sinners from among the Gentiles" (Gal. 2:15).

In opposition to pagan polytheism, biblical monotheism is proclaimed with the gospel (§ 14, 1 above). The Acts of the Apostles provides examples of this, when it tells of the conflict with pagan mythology. Faith in one God and the teaching thereof is unquestionably superior to polytheism. The mission preaching of this was pursued in Lystra (Acts 14:11-18), in Athens (Acts 17:22-31), in Ephesus (Acts 19:23-40), and in Malta (Acts 28:3-10). The Epistles of Paul occasionally make it evident that his preaching began with the doctrine of the One God. Paul reminds the Thessalonians of "the welcome acceptance which we received among you, and how you returned from idols to God" (1 Thess. 1:9). Paul reminds the Corinthians too about their conversion from mute idols (1 Cor. 12:2); and the Galatians, of their turning away from the servitude of the gods of the elements, who really do not exist, to the freedom of God (Gal. 4:8f.). The Apostle repeats: "One only is God" (1 Cor. 8:4; Gal. 3:20). If it is but seldom that the Epistles mention those first mission sermons of Paul, it is understandable. The Epistles discuss and settle questions which arose later in long established and firmly grounded communities.

The Epistle of James likewise brings biblical monotheism to the fore (2:19; 4:12).

It is self-evident that Christian converts could have nothing more to do with the pagan worship of idols. The catalogs of sins put idolatry among the pagan vices which Christians have renounced. It is mentioned among the "works of the flesh" (Gal. 5:20). No idolater has his lot in the kingdom of Christ and of God (Eph. 5:5; *Theology of the New Testament*, Vol. 3, p. 209f.).

In the struggle of the Church against paganism, Old Testament themes continue to be operative. In Israel prophets and teachers of wisdom had defended pure monotheism against idolatry (§ 14, 1 above). Like the Old Testament, the New also speaks of the nothingness of idols. Criticism and derision of the images of gods re-echoes when Paul says: "They have exchanged the sublimity of the incorruptible God for the image and shape of corruptible men and birds and four-legged beasts and things that crawl" (Rom. 1:23). The idols are mute (1 Cor. 12:2). In the style of ancient polemics, Acts 17:29 says: "We ought not suppose that the Godhead is like gold or silver or stone, like an image graven of human art and imagination." The Ephesians accuse Paul of having impugned the worship of the great Artemis (Diana), when he said, "things made by hands cannot be gods" (Acts 19:26).

The problem about the reality of the gods and about paganism arises in Corinth with the question of whether or not one may eat meat if it was ritually slaughtered, however perfunctory the religious rite. Paul replies: "Now as to the eating of meat sacrificed to idols, we know that there is no such thing as an idol in the world, and that there is no God except the One" (1 Cor. 8:4). Paul repeats: "What then do I mean? That flesh sacrificed to idols is anything or that an idol is anything? No. . . ." (1 Cor. 10:19-20). So too in Gal. 4:8; "Formerly, when you did not know God, you served idols, which in reality are not gods."

Accordingly, and with the philosophy of the Greek Enlightenment, the Corinthians argued that if there is no reality to idols one can, without anxiety, eat meat that was sacrificed to idols. Paul says — at first, at least — that their argument is correct. It follows that when the Corinthians are buying meat at the market they need not question how it comes there, nor inquire whether it is perhaps from meat sacrificed to idols, which, after the sacrifice, was sold in the market (1 Cor. 10:25; see Vol. 1 of the present work, pp. 27–28). All anxiety and all the legalism which gives rise to anxiety is to be put aside.

Yet Paul continues the discussion, to point out that metaphysically the gods are nothing (1 Cor. 8:4). He adds: "Even if there be so-called gods, whether in heaven or on earth, and if there be in fact many gods and lords, yet there is for us but one God and Father" (1 Cor. 8:5). The assertion that the gods do not exist is not sufficient. It skirts the existential significance of idolatry. The gods exist in virtue of the power by which they captivate the minds of men. It does not suffice to confess One God verbally and to disavow the gods; rather, the gods must be overthrown.

Later Judaism is convinced that the idolatry and service of the pagan gods is a highly dangerous reality, through which the demons are active (§ 14, 1). Paul is now of this mind also, that demons cooperate in the pagan ritual of worship. It is they who accept the sacrificial gifts. "What the Gentiles sacrifice they sacrifice to demons, not to God. I would not have you become the companions of demons" (1 Cor. 10:20).[195] The demons lead men astray to the worship of the gods. "You know that when you were pagans you let yourselves be attracted irresistably to mute idols, even as you were led" (1 Cor. 12:2). The gods are mute, dead idols. No operation of any kind, therefore, can proceed from them.

Nevertheless, there is a mighty force that does proceed from idolatry. It comes from the demoniacal powers behind it. If one participates in the worship of idols, he makes them into something real. Idolatry, therefore, is not a matter of indifference, but a genuine outrage. Paul warns against frivolously allowing oneself to be so endangered. Anyone who participates in such cult "becomes a companion of demons." Who would want to provoke God's judgment? "Are we perhaps stronger than he?" (1 Cor. 10:21f.).

For Paul, writing under the inspiration of the Holy Spirit, there is no question but that there are good and evil spirits, and that the latter lead men astray and do them harm. He will use the idea that the demons, dwelling in the space between heaven and earth as "rulers of the universe", disrupt the peace between God and men (Eph. 6:12). Paul does not intend to teach a superstitious demonology; on the contrary, he wants to free the faith from such. That is the import of his teaching and admonition: "We know that there is no such thing as an idol in the world, and that there is no God except the One. And if there really are so-called gods in heaven or on earth . . . nevertheless, for us there is only the one God, the Father, from whom are all things and we unto him, and the one Lord Jesus Christ through whom are all things, and we through him" (1 Cor. 8:5-6). The redeemed are in the protection of the mightiest and greatest Powers, the Creator and Father of the world, and Christ the Lord. Christians proceed from this God and return again to him. Through him they are withdrawn from the demoniacal world. No inimical power can do any harm.

The traditional polemic against the worship of idols finds expression once more in the Apocalypse, 9:20, "They did not repent and turn away from the works of their hands, they did not cease worshipping demons and idols of gold and silver and brass and stone and wood, which can neither see nor hear nor walk."

Paul appropriates still other notions and suppositions of his own time. The pagan religion signifies subjection to the "elements of the world" and therefore the forfeiture of Christian freedom (Gal. 4:3, 9; Col. 2:8, 20). The elements of the world (fire, earth, water, air, as well as sun, moon, and stars) were raised to the power of divine beings. In worshipping the gods, therefore, man serves the elements of nature. And our modern study of the history of religion certainly agrees that in the world of the gods, forces of nature were represented (see Schelkle, *Theology of the New Testament*, Vol. 1, p. 30f.).

2. NEW TESTAMENT AND JEWISH BELIEF IN GOD

That the God of the Old Covenant is the God also of the New Covenant is forever expressed in the name of Jesus. In its Hebrew form Y*e*hoshua*ᶜ*, the name signifies "Yahweh saves" or "Yahweh is (my) Savior." The name Jesus declares that the God of Israel is likewise the God of the Church.

Jesus expressly acknowledged Israel's belief about God as his own. When one of the scribes asked him about the most important commandment, he quoted the synagogue's confession of faith, structured in accord with Deut. 6:4f.: "Hear, Israel, the Lord our God is *one* Lord; and you shall love the Lord your God with your whole heart" (Mark 12:29-30). Jesus and the community of disciples with him accepted this confession. Another saying of the Lord designates the God of Abraham, of Isaac and of Jacob as the living God, operative now and always (Matthew 22:32, quoting Exod. 3:6). Those whom Jesus healed gave praise to the God of Israel (Matthew 15:31). Thus it is an essential declaration also of the New Testament doctrine about God, that God is *one*, that he is the Lord and that man lives in a relationship of love for him. New Testament belief in God and New Testament doctrine about God have at the same time received the old confession anew, from the mouth of the Son. For "no one knows the Son except the Father only, and no one knows the Father except the Son only, and him to whom the Son wishes to give a revelation" (Matthew 11:27).

The preaching of the apostles further states that the God whom the Christians worship is the God and Father of Israel. "The God of Abraham, of Isaac, and of Jacob, the God of our fathers, has glorified his Son" (Acts 3:13; *cf.* 5:30). In many declarations Paul acknowledges the unity of the Old and New Testament belief in God. As an especially penetrating passage we may quote: "The God who said, 'Out of darkness let the light shine forth', has shone forth in our hearts, to give enlightenment to the recognition of the glory of God, shining on the face of Christ" (2 Cor. 4:6). In a grand panorama Paul brings together and unifies every revelation of God, from the beginning through the present, and even to the last day. It is one and the same God who reveals himself in the creation and therefore in the book of creation, the Old Testament; who reveals himself in the face of Christ, and therefore in the New Testament Scriptures as testimonial to Christ; and who reveals himself in the hearts of the faithful, to the recognition of his Son.

In spite of the total agreement between Old and New Testament on the doctrine about God, there are remarkable differences in their designations of God. In the New Testament the most frequent term for God is θεὸς (the usual Septuagint translation for Elohim). Judaism at the time of the New Testament did not use the term God, but only circumlocutions like Power, Name, Heaven, the Holy One, the Only One, and others. Unlike Judaism, the New Testament has no timidity about using the name of God, even if there remains the requirement that it be used reverentially. The use of his name in an oath, which puts God at man's disposal, is therefore prohibited (Matthew 5:34).

In any case, the earlier hesitancy still produces its after-effect; for Matthew speaks very seldom of the kingdom of God, in place of which he quite regularly refers to the kingdom of heaven. And if the New Testa-

ment can unhesitatingly vocalize the term God, it must also be taken
into consideration that Hellenistic Judaism was much freer with its use
of the term God than was the rabbinate. The New Testament will also
have been influenced in its linguistic usage by the ubiquitous use of the
term God in a Greek milieu.

However that may be, it is also possible that the linguistic usage of the
New Testament is significant as an expression of the new relationship
between man and God, here defined by a certain frankness of speech or
parrhesia.

In speaking of God, the New Testament seldom uses the term κύριος,
the Septuagint translational term for Yahweh; and when it does use it,
it is mostly in quotations from the Old Testament. The term is, however, a very frequent title of dignity for Jesus Christ (§ 11, 5 above).

The great point of divergence between the Old Testament and the
New is the New Testament confession of Jesus Christ. Israelitic monotheism is continued in the Christian confession of Christ as Son of God.
But Israel sees it as a lapse from the One God, even while Christianity
is nevertheless convinced that it is preserving the doctrine of the One
God. This opposition between Church and Synagogue remains even to
the present day.

Yet the whole of the New Testament is a testimony to the confession
of One God, while confessing Christ. The opposition is penetratingly
declared in a statement of belief like that of 1 Cor. 8:6, "For us there is
only *one* God, the Father, from whom are all things and we unto him;
and *one* Lord, Jesus Christ, through whom are all things and we through
him." Here Paul will be making use of a formula handed down to him,
a structured confessional formula already in use in the Church. We can
recognize in it the beginnings of the later Apostles' Creed. This creed
which Paul quotes firmly maintains that there is only one God, the
Father. Here God is the Father, not so much as the Father of Jesus Christ,
but as the Creator. He is "the Father, from whom are all things".

Israel too knows how to speak of the Creator as Father (see Vol. 1 of
the present work, pp. 103–106). To this extent the confession of the
Church and that of the Synagogue agree. But then the old credal formula, "There is *one* God", develops further and becomes the confession:
"One God, the Father — One Lord, Jesus Christ." Christ is the one Lord;

and the title signifies divine dignity (§ 11, 5 above). He is the agent of creation, and therefore in the Unity of God from all eternity (*Theology of the New Testament*, Vol. 1, pp. 24–27).

§ 16. ONE GOD AND ONE CHURCH

1. ONENESS OF GOD

The New Testament expresses its confession of the one God very frequently with the formula "one God" (εἷς θεὸς) and less frequently in the formula "one only God" (μόνος θεός).[196] Either term can express the idea that God is the sole One, besides whom there is no other. The term εἷς θεὸς can also signify that God is one, in whom there subsists no kind of difference or multiplicity. This signification is brought to the fore with the word εἷς when the unity of the Church is inferred from the unity of God.

Just as rigid monotheism is Israel's bequest to the Gentiles, so it is her legacy to the New Testament and the Church (§ 14, 2; § 15, 2).

Nevertheless, it is not the Bible only that speaks of the *one* God. Even ancient philosophy and mysticism had a presentiment of it. Oneness and unity in general are absolutely universal ideals and yearnings, far beyond their biblical concepts; and there is even a religious motivation to their expression. Along with the Old Testament heritage, these thoughts too will have found entry into the New Testament. And here too there is a validity to what Paul says, that Christ is the great "Yes" of God (2 Cor. 1:18f.). He is the fulfillment even of mythology and philosophy. In mythologies there is a oneness which stands at the beginning, out of which the genealogies of the gods are derived; or as a divine primordial matrix, out of which the world comes forth as emanation or as creation. According to Gnostic mythology the redeemer gathers together the flashes of light that have been disseminated throughout the world and restores them to their original heavenly unity.

In the sixth century before Christ, Xenophanes was able to give expression to the discernment of the unity of God as a conclusion of radical criticism of religion, and of passionate reflection: "One only God, the greatest among gods and men, similar to mortals neither in form nor in idea" (§ 14, 2 above).

In Orphic theology Zeus is conceived as "all-embracing Godhead." "The God holds the beginning and end and center of everything." "Zeus is the first, Zeus the last, the flinger of thunderbolts, Zeus the head, Zeus the center, from Zeus has everything come into existence. He is the one strength, the one divine power (δαίμων), the great beginning of all, a royal shape in which everything is enclosed."

The Stoa teaches the oneness of mankind, which has its basis in the one divine world-reason. In the *Hymn to the Most High* of Cleanthes (331–232 B.C.) we read: "Zeus, immortal, most high, the many-named ruler of the universe, do thou dispose all things in one, the good and the wicked, that from all the one and eternal (ordering of) reason may come to be." Marcus Aurelius, the imperial Stoic, ponders the idea: "The world is one from all, and God is one through all and one being and one law, the reason common to all living beings; and one truth, one perfection as it were, of all living beings which have conjointly come to be and to share in the same reason." [197]

Old Testament belief and Greek philosophy are joined one with the other in the speculations of later Judaism. Here the ideal oneness has its basis in the oneness of the personal God and of true religion, rather than in the one world, understood as divine. The *Syriac Apocalypse of Baruch* (48), for example, says: "We are all one people, who bear a highly celebrated name, since we receive one Law from the One." Josephus, in his *Against Apion* (2, 193) explains: "There is one only temple for the only God, for like is disposed to prefer like, a universal sanctuary for the universal Godhead." In a similar fashion Philo says: "It is proper that there be only one sanctuary, just as there is but one God" (*De specialibus legibus* 1, 67).

Such a union of biblical and Hellenistic ideas is found also in the praises of God in the New Testament, coming there from Hellenistic Judaism. Thus in 1 Tim. 1:17, "To the King of the ages, to the immortal, invisible, and only God, to him be honor and glory in the ages of ages." A ceremonial liturgical text, it uses the cultic language of Hellenistic Judaism. Above all, its negative assertions of immortality and invisibility show that it is the language of Greek philosophy (see below, § 20). 1 Tim. 6:15f. can also be cited: "The epiphany of our Lord Jesus Christ will be made known, and that in his own good time, by the blessed and only Ruler, the King of Kings and Lord of Lords, who alone has immortality and dwells in light unapproachable, whom man has never seen nor is able to see." Again the praises of God are sung in Hellenistic Jewish language. Epicurus, Plutarch, Philo, and Josephus also speak of the blessedness of God (see below, § 20, 4). The intensified "King of Kings . . ." is shaped after the elevated titles of oriental monarchs (Ezech. 26:7; Dan. 2:37; 2 Macc. 13:4). Even today the ruler of Iran (Persia) is not simply the Shah, but the *Shah-in-Shah.*

The New Testament says that the verbal confession of the *one* God is in itself of no significance. Orthodoxy and protestation of belief is not necessarily true faith. With the *Shema* of Deut. 6:4f. the Jews twice daily declare their confession of the one God. And Jesus still calls them "an unbelieving generation" (Mark 9:19). St. James says: "You believe that God is one? You do well! But the demons believe it too, even while they tremble" (2:19).

The *one* God of the Christian faith must be acknowledged, with all its inferences and consequences. Faith is not only belief in God, but personal trust in him. "Abraham believed God, and this was accounted to him as righteousness" (Rom. 4:3). He alone has faith, who hopes in God. "Hoping against hope, he believed" (Rom. 4:18). At very least, God is not to be thwarted. Peter says, "Who am I, then, that I should be able to interfere with God?" (Acts 11:17). And God is not to be tempted. "Thou shalt not tempt the Lord thy God" (Matthew 4:7).

To know God is not enough; faith is a passionate zeal for God. "There is none who is just, none who has understanding, none who is zealous for God" (Rom. 3:10f.). One who confesses the soleness of God can have no other gods besides him — and no idols goes without saying. "Flee from the worship of idols . . . you cannot drink the cup of the Lord and the cup of demons. You cannot partake at the table of the Lord and at the table of demons" (1 Cor. 10:14-21). "What concord can there be between the temple of God and idols?" (2 Cor. 6:16).

But there are other things which this God does not suffer to be near him, and which are much more difficult to abolish. Mammon must not become one's god. "You cannot serve God and mammon" (Matthew

6:24). Neither is a man to make a god of his "belly" (Phil. 3:19). Nor shall self-glory be made an idol, which one might prefer to God. This would be having confidence in the flesh in place of confidence in God. "We glory in Christ Jesus and place not our confidence in the flesh" (Phil. 3:3; *cf.* 1 Cor. 4:7).

There must be no respecting of persons, not even of governmental authorities, of such a kind as would detract from the reverence due the one God. "Render to Caesar what is Caesar's, and to God what is God's" (Matthew 12:17). "One must obey God rather than men" (Acts 5:29). Paul enumerates all the powers and forces of present and future, of height and depth, which could come between God and man, and must not be allowed to do so: "Neither death nor life, neither angels nor principalities, neither present nor future, nor powers, neither height nor depth, nor any other creature" (Rom. 8:38f.).

Paul names death and life first. The destructive force of death will not separate a man from God. Nor is it empty rhetoric when Paul completes his statement about death with its polar opposite, life. Life is the worship of life, which lets God be forgotten. The various forms of Baal, for whom Israel had many times betrayed God, were in fact false gods of the life that is in nature and man, who were worshipped in an orgiastic cult of an unrestrainedly sensual character. Other demoniacal powers are mentioned by Paul as adversaries of men in a comparable statement in 1 Cor. 8:4-6.

Disbelief is rebuked in John 5:44, "How can you believe, when you receive glory from one another, and do not seek the glory that is from the only God?" Here the one God is contrasted to the multiplicity of men's dealings with each other.

In contrast to Mosaic monotheism the New Testament acknowledges the oneness of God in the unity between the Father and his Son Jesus Christ. Thus in the proposition of the faith: "For us there is only one God, the Father, from whom are all things and we unto him; and one Lord, Jesus Christ, through whom are all things and we through him" (1 Cor. 8:6).[198] Israel's confession of one God, the Father, is broadened around the other confession, one Lord, Jesus Christ (see above, § 15, 2). A further instance, God and Christ are united in the New Testament doxologies. Praise is accorded God through Christ. "To the only wise God through Jesus Christ, to him be glory in the ages of ages" (Rom.

16:27). "To the only God our Savior, through Jesus Christ the Lord, belong glory and majesty, power and dominion" (Jude 25). Praise is accorded the Father and Christ: "One Lord, one faith, one baptism, one God and Father of all" (Eph. 4:5f.).

The one Mediator Jesus Christ corresponds to the one God. "There is one God, and there is one Mediator between God and men, the Man Jesus Christ" (1 Tim. 2:5). This seems to be emphasized in order to counteract the Gnostic theory which accepted two gods, the most high god and the creator-god placed after him, as well as numerous intermediary beings as mediator between god and men.

The Gospel of John also speaks of the oneness between Father and Son. This oneness signifies that the Father is manifested in the Son. "Whoever sees me, sees him who sent me" (John 12:45; *cf.* John 14:9). The Father operates in the Son, and the Son executes the orders of the Father. "The Son can do nothing of himself, but only what he sees the Father doing" (John 5:19). Eternal life is "knowing the one true God and him whom he sent, Jesus Christ" (John 17:3). This knowledge always embraces Father and Son conjointly and in one. The Father is revealed in the Son, and he operates in him; and the Son is to be acknowledged even as Son of the Father. In this knowledge, man arrives at God; since God is the Creator, with him man finds life. The oneness of operation, however, is in an even more profound way a oneness of being and nature. "I and the Father are one" (John 10:30; 17:11).[199]

2. Oneness in Church and World

The oneness and soleness of God are the basis and objective of a oneness so far-reaching as to be of boundless dimensions.[200]

The oneness of mankind and of nations has its basis in the creation of the *one* man by the *one* God. This oneness remains in spite of all differences, and was not destroyed even by the sin of Adam (Acts 17:24-28). Indeed, at the very beginning of the history of mankind, Adam, by his disobedience, became the cause of the death sentence hanging over all men. The one Christ, however, by his obedience, brought all to life (Rom. 5:12-21).

The oneness of God is the basis and origin of the oneness of the Church; for this reason its unity must not be encroached upon or destroyed. The same is stated in many texts of the New Testament. These texts, however, probably presume an already present danger to the unity of the Church. Division in the Church does not arise for the first time with the schisms and heresies recorded in the history of the Church. Divisions have always threatened the Church by reason of the failure and guilt of men.

Already in the Synoptics the word of Christ contains an admonition to unity (Matthew 23:8-11). "*One* is your Father, who is in heaven." The unity of the disciples, therefore, must not be dissolved, as it would be if they were to call any on earth their fathers. "*One* is your teacher, the Christ. You, however, are all brothers." None, therefore, is to let himself be called rabbi or teacher. A respected rabbi claimed the title father, and accordingly groups and schools were formed around him. While Jesus lived, and in close connection with him, a disciple could hardly have had himself called father or rabbi. The admonition presumes that there is already a striving after honors and positions of honor in the community. The saying as such, then, is probably not a statement of the historical Jesus, but a testimonial to the ecclesial community's solicitude for its unity stemming from the spirit and content of Jesus' teaching.

The apostles developed the doctrine of the unity of the Church. The work of salvation is one. "One has died for all; therefore all have died" (2 Cor. 5:14). The once-only event is the once-for-all event (Heb. 9:26-28; 1 Peter 3:18). The Church is one primarily through unity with and in her Lord. "Whoever receives the Lord is one spirit with him" (1 Cor. 6:17). Through the one God one and the same justification is now allotted to all, Jews and Gentiles alike. On that account the Church, though made up of Jews and Gentiles, must be one (Rom. 3:29f.; 10:12). In baptism all have put on Christ. In faith and in reception of the gift of salvation all are "one in Christ Jesus", without distinction of nation or stock. In the new existence all comprise together the one body of Christ (Gal. 3:28).

Paul has experience of quarrels and factions in the community of Corinth. People there are saying: "I belong to Paul, I to Apollos, I to

Cephas, I to Christ" (1 Cor. 1:12). Stirred to action by this, Paul urgently affirms the oneness of the Church; and in preaching he establishes its theological basis. He admonishes and rebukes: "Has Christ been divided up?" (1 Cor. 1:13). Jealousy and quarrelsomeness are human and of the flesh. The Church is God's planting; a building erected on the one foundation of Christ; the temple of God, in which the Spirit of God dwells. "If anyone (through quarrelling) drags down the temple of God, him will God drag down" (1 Cor. 3:17).

Paul describes the unity of the Church with the verbal figure of the one body of Christ. All are in the one body of the Lord, and do themselves comprise this body. "In one Spirit we have all been baptized into one body, whether Jews or Greeks, whether slaves or free; and we were all given to drink of the one Spirit" (1 Cor. 12:13; *cf.* Col. 3:15). Paul continues to exhort to unity, while he explains the concept of the body of Christ (1 Cor. 10).[201] Here he takes cognizance of a plurality and a unity of names and references, which is not very easy for us to understand.

First of all, the body of Christ is the body which was surrendered to the Cross. "With the body of Christ, you have died to the Law" (Rom. 7:4). "He has reconciled you by virtue of his fleshly body, through the death thereof" (Col. 1:22). And in the Eucharistic liturgy, "This is my Body, which is for you" (1 Cor. 11:24), the body is the one surrendered in death, since the same thing is then said of the blood of Christ (1 Cor. 11:25). Body and blood are signs and reminders of his historical sacrifice on the Cross, which is now made present and effective in the ritual meal, the sacrifice of the Mass. If body and blood of Christ in this text are catch-phrases for the reality of Christ's surrendering of himself to the Cross, Paul's concern is not with the material substance of the bread (the Body) or of the wine (the Blood). The sacramental Meal is a sharing in that reality.

Paul alludes further to the unity of the Meal, represented by the palpable unity of the one Bread and the one Cup. By means of the tangible elements all participate in the one sacramentally present Body and Blood of Christ, that is, in the blessing of Christ's salvific death (1 Cor. 10:16f.). In this way, as Paul explains in another anacoluthic leap of his mental processes, the many become the one body of the Church. Paul does not say only that the Church is comparable to the well-membered organism of a human body (as in 1 Cor. 12:12-28), but that the Church is in fact one body. "We, the many, are one body" (1 Cor. 10:17). "We, the many, are one body in Christ" (Rom. 12:5). Paul can also say that Christ himself is that body which is the Church (1 Cor. 12:12). The many become this one body of the Church through the one body which is present in the Sacrament and which is ultimately the one body of the crucified Christ.

The one body of the Church is prefigured in the body of Christ on the Cross and in the sacramental Body of the Eucharist. The unity of the Church does not arise from the fact of its being a human communion, though the Church is that also. In its origins, this oneness transcends all human efforts. Certainly men are able to destroy it, as the Corinthians are doing or are on the point of doing. So much the more, then, must the Church, in her daily life, accomplish and realize the unity asserted in the Sacrament.

The Epistle to the Ephesians deepens the perspective of oneness. It exhorts its readers "to preserve the unity of the Spirit through the bond of peace: One body and one Spirit, just as also you were called to the one hope imparted in your calling; one Lord, one faith, one baptism; one God and Father of all, who is over all and through all and in all" (Eph. 4:3-6). The above text has the form of an acclamation and a hymn. The unity of the Church is not established and created by Christians; rather, it has its foundation in the unity of God, through the salvific power of the one Christ, and through the one Spirit of God who is given to the Church. This unity is indicated by the unity of the Sacrament. One also is the calling, and one the hope to which that calling gives a firm basis. Christians must have a regard for this unity and maintain it in the common peace. The destruction of unity would obscure even the unity of God. God, who is over all, is able to bring into being, over and above the unity of the Church, the unity of the world.

Another apostolic admonition in 1 Tim. 2:1-6 emphasizes that the one God and the one Mediator Christ, who surrendered himself for all, reveal God's universal will to save. Therefore the Church must be concerned for all and in her prayer she must intercede with God for all men. The result of this will be peace.

The oneness or unity of the Church is a special concern of John's Gospel. Against the background of prophecy (Ezech. 34:23; 37:24), which promises a Davidic king in the endtime as the one shepherd of the one flock, the parable of the good shepherd depicts the unity of the flock. The Church, made up of Jews and Gentiles — that is what is meant — will be "one flock with one shepherd" (John 10:16). The mission of the Church gathers disciples from among all nations.

Christ himself is operative in the mission of the Church. He must "gather them all to himself, and they will heed his voice" (John 10:16). But the Father too is operative in the work of unification. The faith is always immediacy to God. The Father has given everything to the Son, and no one can snatch anything out of the hand of the Father; for the Son and the Father are one (John 10:30).

The unity of the Church is the deep concern of Jesus' high-priestly prayer. Concern and petition for the unity of the ecclesial community reach out beyond all place and time. Unity is effected through the word of preaching and through faith (John 17:20). Behind it all there is the obligation of love (John 13:34f.; 15:12). In its own way the unity of the disciples is comparable to the unity between Father and Son; just as the latter are to each other, so too should the disciples be in respect to one another: "*Just as* you, Father, are in me, and I in you" (John 17:21).

This unity of the Church has its basis in the revealed divine truth and in the very event of the revelation of God himself (John 17:6). Unity is the task and goal of the Church, in order that she may represent the divine unity: "*So that* they may be one even as we are One" (John 17:22). Unity is the gift of Christ to his Church. "I have given them the glory that you gave to me, so that they may be one" (John 17:22). The unity of the Church resides in the divine glory. In the revelation of Christ, however, this has become recognizable in the light of faith, while to the world it remains invisible. For the most part the world rejects the Messiah. It will be the same too with the glory of the one Church. It is hidden from the world.

Unity is the work of God. "Protect them in your Name, which name you gave to me, so that they may be one even as we are" (John 17:11). The name of Christ, as Son of God, accomplishes and maintains unity. This is not a human work. It is not accomplished through human institutions, not even through officially defined dogmas, which in fact are more likely to result in a dividing of the Church rather than in the achievement of unity. Unity is a future perfection; but it is also a perfection belonging to the present ("that they may be perfected in unity" — John 17:23).

We might be inclined to say that unity is the prerequisite of the Church's realization of her potential in the world; unity, then, would be the means to an end. But in John it says that unity itself is the goal and end in view. It is even as the one Church and only as the one Church that the Church represents in the world the unity of the Father and of the Son, and thereby the divine glory. Her unity, therefore, is the perfection of the Church, while her division is her destruction.

The unity of Church is ultimately to be the unity of mankind. Without understanding or willing it, the high priest speaks as a prophet: Jesus will die for the people; "and not only for the nation, but also that he might gather into one the children of God scattered abroad" (John 11:51f.). Israel expects that in the messianic time the scattered members of the twelve tribes will be gathered together. John's Church, however, is a Church made up of Jews and Gentiles. The children of God in the whole world are redeemed by the death of Jesus. They are God's property, and the gift of the Father to his Son (John 17:10).

If the unity of the Church is a matter of such deep concern to the Gospel of John, perhaps it is because by the time that Gospel was written this unity was already endangered. This danger was present especially because of the Gnosis; and there are many passages in John's Gospel as well as in his Epistles which probably represent argumentation against Gnosticism.

In the final perspective the Apocalypse of John sees all peoples united in eschatological salvation by the unity of God. "You alone are holy . . . All nations will come and fall down before you, because your righteous deeds have become manifest" (Apoc. 15:4). God's righteous rule is as much his judicial sentence as his action which creates justice and salvation. Ultimately they will conquer, resulting in great peace.

The unity of the Church is not left to the good will of the Church and of the churches; rather, it is consequence and demand of faith in God and the proclamation of the Gospel.

§ 17. GOD: CREATOR, LORD AND FATHER

The biblical God is the God of history and of men. As Creator, he is at the beginning of all history. As the Creator, he is the absolute Lord (Deut. 6:4; Mark 12:29).[202]

The Old Testament heralds the theme of creation. Jesus too attests Israel's belief in creation. The world had its beginning in the creation (Mark 10:6; 13:19). The Creator sustains the world (Luke 12:22-31). God gives life to man every day (Matthew 6:27), and calls it back again (Luke 12:20).

Paul says of God as Creator, that he "calls things that are not as though they are" (Rom. 4:17) — that is, his command calls into existence what did not exist. Even justification is creation unto life (Rom. 4:24f.). Creation is "from him, through him, and unto him" (Rom. 11:36). The Creator maintains and supports creation and leads it on to its goal. Creation is a continuously ongoing event. We cannot understand the biblical representation of the creation (especially Gen. 1 and 2) as historical accounts primarily. According to our explanation the story of creation is not the telling of something that happened once and a long time ago. Much more it is a call to every man to understand himself as creature, and as a sinful creature. The New Testament declarations are open to such an interpretation when they state that creation is a continuing and ongoing event.

If God, then, is the Lord, man, in relation to him, is a servant (see *Theology of the New Testament*, Vol. 1, pp. 101–103).

God, who sustains creation, is, in his solicitude for man, like a Father; indeed, plainly and simply, he is the Father. The history of religion tells us that God could be spoken of as Father by the pagan religions of the New Testament milieu. The Greeks call Zeus "father of the gods and of men", understanding the divinity in a pantheistic-physical way as the primordial basis of the All.

Israel too can call God Father, even if it is rare that she does so. "Now however, Yahweh, you are our Father" (Is. 64:7). "Lord, you are my Father, you are my God and the Champion of my well-being" (Sir. 51:10). Nevertheless, and this holds good especially for the New Testament period, in the prayer of the Synagogue (as also in Qumran) it was not customary to address God as Father. It was a new message of the Gospel that God as Father is the one ever near, ever present, ever caring, ever forgiving, and that in prayer the disciples are always to address God as Father (Matthew 6:9; *Theology of the New Testament*, Vol. 1, pp. 103–105).

If God is the Father, then man is his child (Vol. 1, pp. 105–106).[203]

§ 18. GOD'S HOLINESS AND GLORY

1. GOD'S HOLINESS

The God of the Old and New Testaments is the Holy One.[204] The Hebrew word *qadosh*, meaning *holy*, belongs to those terms deriving from the root *qadash*, meaning *to be separated* or *to be apart*. God is apart from the world, to which his relationship is that of Creator. God's holiness signifies his transcendence. That God is the Holy One is basically the same concept as that expressed by the philosophy of religion when it designates God as the "totally other."

Old Testament exegesis separates from the Pentateuch the Law of Holiness (Leviticus, chs. 17 to 26) as a Book of Law, which demands of the people of Israel a holiness in accord with the holiness of Yahweh. Its keynote is expressed in Lev. 19:2; "Be holy, for I, your God, am holy." As God's holy people Israel must keep apart from other nations.

Prophetic theology developed the concept of God's holiness further. It recognizes and reveals that the Holy One, if he is apart from the world, is especially apart from sin. That is how Isaiah, in the vision imparted when he receives his vocation to be a prophet, comes to know God. He sees Yahweh on the heavenly throne. Seraphim soar about him, and they cry out: "Holy, holy, holy is Yahweh of the hosts." His glory fills the temple and the earth. As a sinner the prophet is lost. A seraph brings a glowing coal from the altar and purifies the lips of the prophet, while saying, "Your guilt is blotted out and your sins forgiven" (Is. 6:1-7).

God is the primordial Holy One. Whatever he takes into his domain is holy. As God's dwelling, heaven is holy (Ps. 20:7). The places of the manifestations of God, Sinai (Exod. 19), the temple (Ps. 5:8), and Jerusalem (Is. 52:1) are holy. Israel, as God's community, is holy (Exod. 19:5f.).

In the proclamation of Jesus too God is the Holy One, even if its express attestation is much rarer than in the Old Testament. Jesus makes it a concern of his disciples' prayers that God be manifest as the Holy One: "Hallowed be thy name" (Matthew 6:9). God's name is his nature. God himself is asked to make known the holiness and glory of his nature before the nations in grace and judgment. Jesus uses the address for God: "Holy Father" (John 17:11).

The preaching of the apostles unveils the depths of guilt in the face of God's holiness. Sin operates from Adam onwards, and all have fallen forfeit to it (Rom. 3:9, 23; 5:19f.). Nevertheless, the community of God is withdrawn from sin. It is the community of "the holy ones, the saints", as Paul often addresses the congregations (Rom. 1:7; 1 Cor. 1:2; 2 Cor. 1:1; Phil. 1:1). Christians are "the elect of God, the holy and beloved ones" (Col. 3:12). Holiness is first of all cultic consecration through God's calling and bestowing of grace. The gift of Christian life becomes the command to be holy. "This is God's will, your sanctification" (1 Thess. 4:3). "Hallow the Lord Christ in your hearts" (1 Peter 3:15). Final perfection will consist in holiness. "God will give the reward to his servants, the prophets and the saints" (Apoc. 11:18).

God's holiness becomes in respect to sin, God's wrath.[205] The Old Testament does not hesitate to speak in a very human way of God's wrath as the near and final judgment. "Behold, a storm goes out from the Lord, a burning wrath; and a whirlwind plunges down upon the head of the evildoer" (Jer. 30:23). The wrath of God is announced for the general judgment. "Behold, the name of the Lord comes from afar. He is like burning wrath and heavy burden, his lips are full of anger and his tongue like consuming fire" (Is. 30:27). If the prophets had the special task of proclaiming God's wrath in view of Israel's guilt, certainly they had also to announce God's grace. "In the boiling up of my wrath for a moment I hid my face from you, but with eternal kindness I have shown mercy to you" (Is. 54:8).

In the Gospels the wrath of God is disclosed when they tell of Jesus' being provoked to anger, a characteristic which pertains to his total image. "And he was moved to anger [reading ὀργισθείς rather than σπλαγχνισθείς], stretched forth his hand, touched him and said to him: 'I will, be thou made clean'. Immediately the leprosy left him; and he addressed him angrily, and drove him off while saying to him: 'Take care! Tell no one anything!" (Mark 1:40-44).[206] His anger was directed against the destructive demon of illness.

Christ is angered by the unfaithful generation surrounding him (Mark 3:5; Matthew 9:30; John 2:17). John the Baptist proclaims the impending judgment which is to take place in the midst of God's wrath (Matthew 3:7). According to a saying of Jesus the world is rushing on to the wrath of God as to eschatological peril: "Woe to expectant and nursing mothers in those days! For there will be great distress on earth and anger against this people "(Luke 21:23).

As the Holy One, God can only be the Judge in reference to sin. The Holy One is the Just One. In deepest earnest Jesus proclaims this judgment between salvation and calamity, when he announces the nearness of the kingdom of God. It has, in fact, already commenced. "If I cast out demons by the finger of God, God's kingdom is with you already" (Luke 11:20). The absolute will of God and his perfect sovereignty are so overwhelming that the world pales before them. The temporal interval between the present and the judgment and kingdom of God is lost. The world is even now in the midst of the judgment (Mark 9:1).

For Paul the world, because of its godlessness and injustice, is, beginning with nature itself, under the wrath of God, which is revealed even now (Rom. 1:18) and is expected definitively on the day of judgment (Rom. 2:5). Every man is under the obligation of the Law and no man can fulfill it. Thus "the Law works wrath." First of all the Jew, but at the same time every man, is a "vessel of wrath" (Rom. 9:22). Every man must appear before the Judge (2 Cor. 5:10). The biblical testimony to the wrath and judgment of God is no mythical notion, even if the graphic manner of its expression in the New Testament makes use of mythological images like those of the judgment seat of God or of the fire and darkness of hell. This testimony affirms that the decision between good and evil is the proper content of human history.

As Creator, God is the Father; and as Holy One, he is the Judge. This constitutes a most extraordinary antithesis. He is extolled as a God who is prepared to forgive. "Praised be you, O Lord, who forgive abundantly": so says the Jew in his daily recitation of the *Eighteen Benedictions*. But this forgiveness is accorded the pious man of Israel, to whom God extends his favor, and whose sin God overlooks. The sinner and the godless, however, can expect nothing of God except damnation. It is well-stated by a worshipper: "Your righteousness and kindness, O Lord, are made manifest even in this, that you show mercy to those who have no treasure of good works" (*4 Esdras* 8:31-36). At this the angel replies: "You, therefore, will receive of the highest glory, because you have humbled yourself, as is proper, and have not counted yourself among the just. Therefore the honor you are to receive will be so much the greater" (*4 Esdras* 8:47-49). When the pious man realizes that he cannot appeal to his own good works, he will nevertheless point to his humble confession of sin, and in that way solicit divine favor.

According to Israel's belief, it is in the pious and just that God has his true pleasure. The pledge that God has more joy in a converted sinner than in ninety-nine just (Luke 15:7), has nothing like it in the literature of Israel.[207] Jesus, however, says that God is inclined to mercy and is, in his dealings, the forgiving One. "The tax-collector stood afar off, could not once lift up his eyes to heaven, but beat his breast and said, 'O God, be gracious to me, a sinner!' I tell you, this man went back to his house justified" (Luke 18:13f.).

The tax-collector, unlike the pious man, does not know that, because he humbled himself, he is to be counted among the just. He knows that as a sinner he is nothing, and he neither supposes nor dares hope that underneath it all he is still a just man. When man is reduced to utter silence and finds nothing more in himself, that is when he experiences forgiveness. For he cannot of himself, by the performance of penance or works, compensate for his sins or expunge them; rather, they can be forgiven him only as a totally free gift. In accepting this forgiveness, he bows beneath God's judgment as a man judged and condemned, in order to receive his life again as a gift from God's hand. "Whoever lets his life go . . . saves it" (Mark 8:35). Jesus did not simply promise a future forgiveness by God, but he made that forgiveness real and operative in the present, as the friend of the poor, of tax-collectors and sinners, when he went about in their company (Matthew 11:19; Luke 7:48).

The sign of forgiveness and of peace is the Cross of Christ. Paul shows that the Cross, revelation of the justice and holiness of God (Rom. 3:21), is still more the revelation of the freely bestowed love of God; and that it produces atonement, forgiveness, and salvation. It is at the Cross that the loving work of God and Christ reaches its goal. As the Just One, it is God who makes man just (Rom. 3:26).

2. GOD'S GLORY

An essential, biblical attribute of God is his glory. In the Old Testament the divine glory is designated as *kabôdh* (heaviness, weightiness). Revelations of the glory of God are his past, present, and future epiphanies.

Creation itself is an epiphany of God, in which his glory is recognizable (Ps. 19:2; Is. 6:3). The glory of God shows itself in powerful manifestations of nature, as in storms (Ps. 29; 97). In an apparition of glory God reveals the decalogue on Mount Sinai (Exod. 24:15f.). Veiled in the clouds over the tent of the heavens, God escorts his people; he likewise fills up the holy tent (Exod. 40:34f.), as afterwards the temple (3 Kings 8:10f.). In visions the prophets behold the glory of God (Is. 6:1-4; Ezech. 10:4; 43:2-5). Finally it will be made manifest even to the nations (Ps. 57:6; Is. 66:18f.). Yahweh is "the King of Glory" (Ps. 24:7-10).

The Greek translation of the Old Testament renders the term *kabôdh* with *doxa*. The Greek term first signifies opinion, and then it comes to mean the good opinion others have of someone, and as a consequence of that meaning, honor and fame. The Septuagint fixed upon the last mentioned meaning of the Greek word in employing it as a translation of *kabôdh*.

Accordingly in the New Testament also the term *doxa* signifies the divine glory and power. God is the "God of Glory" (Rom. 1:23; Acts 7:2), the "Father of Glory" (Eph. 1:17), simply the "Great Glory" (2 Peter 1:17). He is "rich in glory" (Eph. 3:16). *Doxa* is characteristic of God in his qualities of ulteriorness and eternity. Many doxologies so attest; Luke, for example, in 2:14 ("Glory [is proper] to God on high; and on earth [there is] peace to men of his favor"); also Luke 19:38; Rom. 11:36; 16:27; Gal. 1:5; Eph. 3:21; Phil. 4:20; 1 Tim. 1:17; Apoc. 1:6.

German-speaking people are accustomed to the translation "*Ehre sei Gott*", which means "*Honor be to God*"; but this is incorrect. *Doxa* is to be translated not by *Ehre* (honor) but by *Herrlichkeit* (glory). In German and in English the lack of a verb in Luke 2:14 and similar passages is commonly supplied for by turning the passage into a wish or petition expressed in the subjunctive ("May glory be to God" or just "Glory be to God . . ."). It should be interpreted, however, as a simple statement of his praises: God has the glory for his own. This latter is stated unequivocally in 1 Peter 4:11; where the verb is expressed: "God's is the glory and the power in the ages of ages."

God's glory is celebrated in the heavenly liturgy (Apoc. 4:9; 7:12). In the salvation event this glory is now made manifest. The glory of God shines round about the angels (Luke 2:9). At the transfiguration on the mountain Moses and Elijah appear in glory. The disciples see the glory of the transfigured Christ (Luke 9:31f.; 2 Peter 1:17). Christ appears in glory to his Apostle on the road to Damascus (Acts 22:11). In company with his glory, God's strength can be named (2 Thess. 1:9), or his power (Col. 1:11), or his salvation and power (Apoc. 19:1). The well-known formalized prayer conclusion which found its way into certain manuscripts at Matthew 6:13 mentions his kingdom (dominion) and power along with his glory.

The glory of God is manifested in Jesus Christ. His being raised up from the dead, an action of divine power, took place in the glory of God (Rom. 6:4). In that raising up, God gave Jesus the glory (1 Peter 1:21). Stephen beholds the exalted Christ in the glory of God (Acts 7:55). In the whole apppearance and history of Christ "God's glory shone forth" (2 Cor. 4:6). This glory is powerful in the salvational work of justification. "All have sinned; and lacking the glory of God, they now are justified by the free gift of his grace" (Rom. 3:23).

God's glory will be manifested in its fullness in the eschatological consummation, "when the Son of Man comes in the clouds with great power and glory" (Mark 13:26; Matthew 16:27). The Church expects "the revelation of the glory of the great God" (Titus 2:13). God's eternal kingdom is his glory (1 Thess. 2:12). God's glory fills the eschatological heavenly sanctuary (Apoc. 15:8) and in the end the whole of the eternal city (Apoc. 21:11, 23).

John recognizes already in the earthly life of Jesus the revelation of the glory of the Father. Such is the case with his wondrous deeds, performed as signs of that glory (John 2:11; 11:4). The Passion of Jesus is his entry into heavenly glory (John 12:23). Nevertheless, the Pre-existing One was already in the glory of God (John 17:5, 24). The evangelist sums up his testimony: "We have seen his glory as the glory of the only-begotten Son of the Father" (John 1:14).

§ 19. GOD: SPIRIT, LIGHT, LOVE

In the Johannine writings of the New Testament, God is denominated with three titles that are similar in form, full and pregnant in content: God is Spirit (John 4:24), God is Light (1 John 1:5), God is Love (1 John 4:8).

Such passages are not declarations about a metaphysical nature of God, his very being; rather, they are assertions about the event, manner and style of his revelation. He manifests himself as Spirit, Light, Life, and Love. "The Life was the Light of men" (John 1:4). Everything is stated in reference to the way in which God deals with man.

1. "GOD IS SPIRIT, AND THE TRUE WORSHIPPER MUST WORSHIP IN SPIRIT AND IN TRUTH" (JOHN 4:24)

The statement is not to be interpreted according to what any particular philosophy or *Weltanschauung* understands by spiritual worship of God, but in accord with the meaning of the terms in the New Testament and in particular in John.[208]

Spirit does not mean the internal, spiritual worship of God as opposed to a religion which practices external rites and presents visible, material sacrifices; nor as opposed to a religion which has specific places of worship. Truth is not a philosophically refined knowledge of God or a philosophical religion in which piety is the seeking of truth and the serving of truth when found. Were this the case, the hour of which Jesus speaks would not be a new era at all (John 4:23). For philosophy already knew that God is a spiritual being and had to be worshipped in an internally spiritual religion.

At the same time it is not only a spiritual worship of God that is demanded, not merely an intellectual worship, such as the prophets had already demanded when they preferred such a divine service to ritual and cult. At the dedication of the temple this knowledge finds expression in the prayer of Solomon: "Behold, if heaven and the whole heaven of heavens cannot contain you, how much less this house which I have built" (3 Kings 8:27; similarly in Is. 66:1). The piety of the prophets says it forcefully. "Is the Lord pleased by many thousands of rams? Am I to surrender my firstborn? You have been told, O man, what is good and what the Lord requires of you: nothing else than to do justice and to love kindness and to walk humbly before your God" (Micah 6:7f.). "Bloody sacrifice you do not desire, and were I to give a burnt offering it would not please you. The offering that is pleasing to God is a humbled spirit; a battered heart, O God, you will not scorn" (Ps. 51:18-19).

In Qumran too such offerings as the latter are required: The community in Qumran was of a mind that in Jerusalem unhallowed priests performed an unhallowed ministry. Since the pious of Qumran kept themselves aloof from the temple in Jerusalem, they could present no material sacrifices, but only spiritual offerings. "When these things obtain in Israel, as defined by these provisions, the Holy Spirit will indeed rest on a sound foundation; truth will be evinced perpetually; the guilt of transgression and the perfidy of sin will be shriven; and atonement will be made for the earth more effectively than by any flesh of burnt-offerings or fat of sacrifices. The 'oblation of the lips' [*i.e.*, prayer] will be in all justice like the erstwhile 'pleasant savor' on the altar; righteousness and integrity like that free-will offering which God deigns to accept" (1 QS 9:3-5, in Theodore H. Gaster's *The Dead Sea Scriptures in English Translation*, New York 1956, p. 57).

The statement of Jesus (John 4:23) speaks of a new hour in the process of perfecting, which is greater than anything heretofore. In John's Gospel as for the most part throughout the New Testament, spirit is not human spirit, but God's Holy Spirit, which brings forth what is new. Spirit stands in opposition to the flesh. Flesh is the human, worldly sphere; spirit is the holy and divine world separated from the flesh. Those who are designated here as true worshippers are those who are begotten anew by the Spirit (John 3:3-8). Those who worship in the spirit are those who are born again of the Spirit.

In John's Gospel, truth is the reality of God which is revealed in Christ. "I am the way, the truth, and the life" (John 14:6). "Your word is truth" (John 17:17). The true worshippers are "sanctified in the truth" (John 17:19). The hour of true worship is now present with the truth revealed in Christ and with the Spirit of Christ now operative.[209]

Other texts of the New Testament are to be understood in this same sense. For example, Rom. 12:1, "I exhort you, my brothers, for the sake of God's mercy, to present your bodies (*i.e.*, your lives) as a living and holy sacrifice pleasing to God, as your spiritual worship (τὴν λογικὴν λατρείαν ὑμῶν — *lit.*, your logical worship, *i.e.*, your worship in accord with Logos [reason], your spiritual worship)." The concept of sacrifice remains, the primitive term in every worship. The Gospel does not abandon it but perfects it.

Sacrifice, however, is not a means of winning God over, for his mercy precedes it. The sacrifice, then, can only be an offering in thanksgiving. In this sacrifice man does not give away some part of his possessions, but his body, that is, himself. The offering is not slain; rather, man presents himself there in his own life. The offering is holy, because the ones offering it are the elect saints. This is now to be the manner of worship. It is suited to the Logos; it is rational, of the spirit; it is spiritual. Even Greek mysticism spoke of sacrifice suited to the Logos, as opposed to the bloody sacrifice of animals. Thus in the *Corpus hermeticum* 1, 31, "Accept the pure offering, suited to *reason* (logos), of a soul and of a heart, which is held out towards you, the Unutterable, the Ineffable, the One to be named only in silence." In Rom. 12:1 Paul takes up and makes use of terms and notions of Hellenistic mysticism which come to him by way of Hellenistic Judaism.

Only a spiritual worship can correspond to the nature of God, who is Spirit (John 4:24). This term too is not to be understood as a philosophical definition, as if one were to say that God's nature is immaterialness. Greek philosophy too describes God's nature as Spirit. The Stoa calls God "thinking Spirit"; the Gnosis calls him "invisible Spirit."[210] In that way philosophy describes God's nature in accord with a phenomenon which it knows and can deal with. But that is philosophy.

John's Gospel is something else again. His assertion is to be understood in accord with what spirit means in the Bible. Spirit in the Bible is a wonderful divine power and substance, the openness of God toward men. God is Spirit, as the One who deals with mankind. God is Spirit, and he desires to be worshipped in spirit and in truth. Man is not able of himself to be in spirit and in truth; he can be such only as a new creation of God. Only if God deals with a man beforehand, only if God has sanctified him can a man worship God in truth. All natural religion, which proceeds from man, remains simply a human undertaking and is therefore inadequate. A relationship of man to God which is not rooted in a relationship of God to man cannot be a true relationship to God.

2. "God is Light" (1 John 1:5)

Light is a prerequisite of all life.[211] Darkness is death. Man cannot himself produce light. Light, therefore, is respected as a divine gift, and indeed sometimes even worshipped as itself divine. The divine world is imagined as bathed in light.

The Old Testament, confronted by a milieu that divinized light, emphasized that light and darkness are the creation of God (Gen. 1:3-5; Is. 45:7; Jer. 31:35).

Light connaturally symbolizes God. Light is God's mantle (Ps. 104:2). His epiphany takes place with light (Exod. 24:17; Ps. 97:3f.; Ezech. 43:2). As man's salvation God himself is called light (Ps. 27:1). Of this mentality is the prayer that God may "raise up the light of his countenance" upon his people (Ps. 4:7). God's word (Ps. 119:105), God's law (Ps. 19:9; Prov. 6:23), and God's wisdom (Wis. 7:10, 26) are the brightening and redeeming light of men. The servant of God is "light for the illumination of the nations" (Is. 42:6; 49:6). God's directive is light for all nations (Is. 51:4). In the end God will be the eternal light and the glory of his people (Is. 60:19).

The Qumran community teaches a dualism of darkness and light. The children of light (1 QS 1:9; 2:16; 3:13) are engaged in a struggle with the sons of darkness (1 QS 1:10, 24; 2:5, 19). The present day and end-time struggle is depicted in the book entitled *War of the Sons of Light with the Sons of Darkness*. To the internal subjective antipathy of light and darkness there corresponds a metaphysical antipathy between the princes of light (1 QS 3:20f.; 1 QM 13:10) and the angels of darkness, as lords of the present world (1 QS 3:19-21). God is the Creator of both

(1 QS 3:25). They are engaged in a conflict with each other in the world and in man. Light and darkness are asserted as antitheses of creation, but they are also decisions which man makes and ways in which he walks (1 QS 3:18f.). The pious man receives God's light: "In your glory give light to my light; you have made a light shine upon me out of the darkness" (1 QH 9:26f.). According to the decision which a man makes now, light or darkness will be his lot in eternity (1 QS 2:7f.; 4:6-8, 12f.).

In the most ancient Greek literature, that of Homer and of the classical age, light is understood as a priceless gift. The world of the gods is in the fullness of the light. As a divine gift to men, light is "holy" and "heavenly" (in Homer, Hesiod, Sophocles and Euripides). This light enables man to enjoy a full life in the world. It is his salvation. This light is in the first place always the physical brightness of natural life. The opposite is the darkness of night and the darkness of death. The bitterness of dying is in the fact that it is a departure from the light. Euripides says: "The most precious thing that man has here is to behold the light! Below is naught."

This primordial Greek understanding of light underwent a radical change in later times. The earthly day and the earthly world and the natural light that fills the world are now understood as darkness. Darkness is this side, light is the heavenly beyond. Earthly light is designated as "dark light." The divine Father of all is described as "light and life" (*Corpus hermeticum*, 1, 21). Redemption and salvation begin when a man is ready to acknowledge that abiding here, he is in the dark. A yearning for the light beyond grips him, and he desires to be admitted to it. The consecration of the mystery religions is called "illumination." Consecration imparts immortality. This is also the terminology and conceptuality of Gnosticism. The divinity is the light. Souls originate in the world of heaven's light and are exiled here below in the darkness. They desire to return and must be returned into the world of light (examples quoted in R. Bultmann and H. Conzelmann, in the works cited in footnote 211).

The New Testament too validates the idea that God's world is light. As messengers from the heavenly world, angels appear in glorious light (Luke 2:9; Matthew 28:2f.; Acts 12:7). The epiphany of Christ himself takes place in light and splendor (Matthew 17:2; Acts 9:3). Luke 2:32 refers Isaiah 49:6 to the person of Christ: "A light for the illumination of nations"; and Matthew 4:16 refers Isaiah 8:23 to the beginning of the gospel's proclamation: "The people who sat in darkness saw a great light." As children of God, the disciples are "children of the light" (Luke 16:8). Inasmuch as the disciples disseminate the light they have received, they are "the light of the world" (Matthew 5:14-16).

In a grand panorama of all salvation history Paul recognizes God wherever there is light, and light wherever God is. "God who said, 'Out of the darkness let light shine,' has shone in our hearts as the bright light of the knowledge of the glory of God that shines on the face of Christ" (2 Cor. 4:6). God made light at the creation of the world; it shone forth on the face of Christ, and it is the clarity of the faith of every man. Christ, in his glory, is the "image of God"; preaching is "the light of the gospel of the glory of Christ" (2 Cor. 4:4). Christ is the day (Rom. 13:12). In preaching and sacrament Christ streams forth as light (Eph. 5:14). Who once were darkness are now "light in the Lord" (Eph. 5:8). The divine gift of light turns the faithful into light. "You are all sons of the light and of the day" (1 Thess. 5:5). Christians ought to shine "like starry lights of heaven in the world" (Phil. 2:15). The promise is of "participation in the inheritance of the saints in light" (Col. 1:12).

The Johannine writings develop a meaningful theology of the light. It can hardly be explained from the Old Testament alone; much more, it uses the ideas and formulas of the Gnosis. But while in the Gnosis the opposition between light and darkness is a mythological dualism in their creation, in John it is a dualism in the decision between belief and disbelief; therefore, a moral dualism.

According to the prologue of John's Gospel, Christ, the Logos, was and is light and life for men. Light and darkness are the divine world and the world hostile to God (John 1:4f.). Light is the strength of life. "The true light that enlightens every man came into the world (in Christ)" (John 1:9). The emphatic "the true light" (as in 1 John 2:8) means that there are also false assertions about the light, either simply because men deceive themselves, or perhaps it is said in a polemical way, because there are in fact false teachings (perhaps the Gnosis) about pretended light. Christ himself says: "I am the light of the world. Whoever follows me will not walk in the darkness, but will have the light of life" (John 8:12). Christ is the light, and he gives the light.

The cure of the man born blind makes manifest by way of a sign the

fact that Christ is "the light of the world" (John 9:5). In the revelation
of Christ the world is brightened. It is in this revelation that man first
comes to understand himself. "For this purpose have I come into the
world: so that no one who believes in me will remain in the darkness"
(John 12:46). Those who believe are themselves a light in the world and
for the world. "Believe in the light, so that you may become children of
light" (John 12:36).

The First Epistle of John continues the symbolism of light, but with
certain nuances, such that in spite of what the Epistle has in common
with the Gospel, we may conclude to different authors for the two works.

At the very beginning the Epistle affirms: "This is the message which
we have heard from him and which we announce to you: that God is
light, and there is no darkness in him" (1 John 1:5). According to this,
it is Christ's word and teaching that God is light. There is no saying of
Jesus which states this expressly; but the letter simply intends by its remark to state the import of the doctrine of Jesus.

The Gospel of John speaks of the revelation of the light. It is the dynamic event of revelation that the Gospel describes in such a way; but
here in the Epistle, with the statement "God is light", it is rather God's
being itself that is described. Light radiates and brightens. The statement
can be applied also to the glory, the purity, and the holiness of God, and
then no doubt also to the illuminating truth of God. The Epistle says,
"Darkness is not in him." This is in opposition to all dualism, which
perceives in God two inimical principles of good and evil, or which at
least makes God the Creator even of evil.

When the Epistle admonishes us to walk in the light (1 John 1:6-7),
it intends to summon us to a life free of darkness, that is, free of sin.
One cannot get hold of the light in some mystical way; rather, one possesses it only in a moral way. Since the light is identical with the truth
(1 John 1:6), and truth is the reality of God, a reality made accessible
in revelation, the light is to be apprehended in faith. Those who walk
in the light have fellowship with each other (1 John 1:7).

The Epistle takes up a second time the admonition to live in the light
(1 John 2:8-10). The true light makes its appearance with the entry of
Christ into the world; it shines now, and provides the opportunity of
a new life. Christians must remain in the light. "Whoever hates his

brother is in the darkness; but whoever loves his brother abides in the light" (1 John 2:9-10). The opposition of darkness and light is represented in the opposition of hatred and love.

The eschatological consummation is sharing in the world of light. As yet God dwells "in inaccessible light" (1 Tim. 6:16). Now God's word is "a light shining in a dark place, until the dawn breaks and the morning star rises in your hearts" (2 Peter 1:19). The world is enveloped in darkness. Its natural light is darkness. Just as darkness is accorded no value in the viewpoint of late antiquity and of the Gnosis, so also in the New Testament (Matthew 4:16; John 1:5; Eph. 6:12). The word of God is light (Ps. 119:105; *4 Esdras* 12:42). Expectation looks to the day which is Christ's parousia. But while in Rom. 13:12 this day is to be a revelation for the world, in 2 Peter 1:19 it is understood in a psychological way in regard to individuals: with the coming of the day, light will send its beams into hearts. The expected parousia is delayed. The point of interest turns away from the universal and comprehensive event of the endtime and settles upon a personal eschatology.

3. "GOD IS LOVE" (1 John 4:8, 16)

Aristotle teaches that it is senseless to speak of a love of the gods for men, because the gods themselves require nothing to complete their bliss.[212] Likewise it would be absurd for anyone to say that he loves Zeus (*Nicomachean Ethics* 9, 1158 B, 35; *Magna moralia* 2, 11, 1208). This is of consequence for his natural and philosophical sense of religion. In the human concept of love, as Plato so wonderfully represents it in the *Symposium*, love is the movement toward that which is recognized as full of worth and which is therefore aspired to as worthy of love. A person who loves is seeking, in giving and receiving, the enrichment of himself from the worth of the one loved. According to this concept, the God of philosophy cannot love. Being perfect, he already possesses the perfection of every good thing.

The love of the biblical God is quite otherwise. It is not covetous of worth; rather, it bestows worth and creates worth. It turns toward the worthless, indeed, to that which is of negative worth, the sinner. It makes worthy of love that which formerly was unworthy of love.

Thus the Old Testament describes God as him who chooses and loves Israel. Prophets like Hosea (1–3), Isaiah (54:4-8), and Jeremiah (2:2; 31:32f.) describe the relationship of God to Israel as a covenant of love which God has founded (see *Theology of the New Testament*, Vol. 3, pp. 113–115).

The God of the Old Testament is the perfect and absolute Good, as also the One who is good. Israel's confession of God is in accord with God's revelation to Moses: "The Lord, the Lord is a merciful and gracious God, patient and rich in kindness and fidelity, who maintains mercy even to the thousandth generation, and pardons guilt and misdeed and sin" (Exod. 34:6-7). God's goodness is proclaimed already in creation. "God saw all that he had made, and behold, it was very good" (Gen. 1:31).

Israel experienced God's goodness constantly in her history. The deliverance from Egypt (Exod. 18:9), the promise and actual bestowal of the land in which Israel is to dwell (Num: 29), are mentioned as special acts of God's kindness. The Law is a gift of God's goodness (Deut. 30:15; Ps. 34:8f.; Prov. 28:10). For the future Israel expects a good gift and restoration to be given her (Is. 52:7). God promises the eternal new covenant with good things and salvation for Israel and her children (Jer. 32:42f.). The pious man experiences and praises God as the Good and Gracious One (Ps. 25:7; 34:8f.; 86:5; 106:1; 136:1-26; Wis. 15:1; 2 Macc. 1:24). Israel keeps faith in God's goodness, even if she recognizes that in appearance and in the actual experience of life, God's goodness often remains hidden for a time (Eccl. 3:11f.; 5:17; 7:25). The worshipper in Qumran praises God on account of "the abundance of his kindness" (1 QS 11:14).

The basic term in Hebrew for the goodness or kindness of God is *ṭôbh*. In the Septuagint, God is called ἀγαθός, καλός, and above all, χρηστός. His goodness is χρηστότης. These terms are found also in the New Testament.

Platonic philosophy recognizes and teaches that God is the highest idea of the good (ἀγαθόν; *Republic* 7, 517 B.C.; *Philebus* 65 A). The good is also the beautiful, which Eros constantly seeks and aspires to (*Symposium* 204 B). The *Corpus hermeticum* gives expression to the formulas: "God is the good, and the good is God" (2, 16); and "God can do only what is good" (11, 17). Biblical faith, however, recognizes God not as the good, but as the personally good, the One who is good.

Jesus calls God the "only one who is good" (ἀγαθός; Mark 10:18). The term good, rich as it is in content, belongs to God only and ought not be applied frivolously to men. In reference to God, it asserts his moral perfection, and his kindness as well. The kindness of God the Father is all-embracing. "He is kind (χρηστὸς) to the ungrateful and to the wicked" (Luke 6:35). Christ says: "My yoke is smooth (χρηστὸς) and my burden easy" (Matthew 11:30). In the message and person of Christ the goodness of God is made manifest. In Jesus' parabolic manner of speech, he himself is the "good shepherd" (καλὸς ποιμήν), that is, the true shepherd, because he lays down his life for his own (John 10:11). Even as the good shepherd he makes God's goodness manifest. God's love is active in the ministry of Christ, who devotes himself to the poor, to the sick, and to sinners. The parable of the prodigal son declares that the Father accepts sinners, because Jesus accepts them (Luke 15:11-32). The love of God devoted itself to the world when God delivered up his Son on the world's behalf (John 3:16).

Paul too makes God known as the One who is good. "God showed his love for us by the fact that when we were still sinners Christ died for us" (Rom. 5:18; Gal. 2:20f.; Titus 3:4). Now the love of God is clear to the world and is effective in it. "The love of God is poured out in our hearts through the Holy Spirit, who has been given to us" (Rom. 5:5). As the gracious One, God does not desire the death of the sinner, but his salvation (Rom. 11:22; Eph. 2:7). God manages everything for the good of those who are his own (Rom. 8:28). God's kindness, nevertheless, must not be understood simply as his being good-natured. It is patient forbearance, which awaits conversion to him (Rom. 2:4).

God always negotiates the beginning. He acts first, not man. The love of God (Rom. 5:5) is God's love for us, not our love for God. There would be no constancy in love on the part of mankind. Love is poured out by the Holy Spirit, who is the Mediator between God and world (John 14:26). "We are victorious in everything because of God who has loved us" (Rom. 8:37). The love of God is clear to us in Christ, and nothing can separate us from this love (Rom. 8:39). It is God's plan "to perfect in the ages to come the overwhelming richness of his grace in kindness toward us" (Eph. 2:7). Grace and kindness of God express equivalently the fullness of salvation.

"The goodness and kindness-toward-mankind (χρηστότης καὶ φιλανθρωπία) of God our Savior have appeared" (Titus 3:4). The Epistle is employing a Hellenistic terminology. Kindness toward mankind (φιλανθρωπία) is literally philanthropy, and can also be translated affability or sociability; it is a vritue celebrated in literature and in inscriptions in reference to rulers; and not infrequently goodness and this kindness which loves mankind are mentioned together.

All Christians have tasted "that the Lord (Christ) is good (χρηστός)" (1 Peter 2:3). χρηστός, a predicate of God in the Psalms, is applied to Christ. The former gracious dealing of God with the fathers is one and the same as that of the present, which took place in Christ. The ultimate good things of the future world must be hoped for from the good God. He will perfect the good work of the Christian life (Phil. 1:6). Christ is the High Priest of the good things to come (Heb. 9:11).

The brief statement, "God is Love" (1 John 4:8, 16), is an impressive summarization of the basic message of the New Testament. The Epistle does not intend to describe God's metaphysical being in itself. Neither does it demonstrate the correctness of the statement with philosophical explanations; rather, it derives it and establishes it simply from history itself. That God is love is to be recognized from the fact that "He sent his Son into the world so that we might receive life through him." The Son whom he sent is to be a propitiation for our sins (1 John 4:9f.). Since God took the sinner to himself, he is shown as the One who was first to offer his love (1 John 4:10; *cf.* Rom. 5:8). God's love goes out to the whole world, embracing the whole of it (1 John 4:9, 14). All restraint is set aside. The love of God, the Father's love, makes one a child of God. "Whoever loves is begotten of God" (1 John 4:7). The love of God should bring forth, in the one upon whom it is bestowed, a love of others. Only one who loves others can abide in love (1 John 4:11).

Such statements as the above may be directed against the false Gnosis, which sought for union with God but forgot about moral obligations. The statement that God is love is an assertion about his dealings in and with men.

§ 20. PHILOSOPHICAL PREDICATES OF GOD

Biblical belief in God is elucidated in the terminology of Hellenistic conceptuality especially in the later writing of the New Testament, and those writings particularly concerned with the Greek world. This phenomenon is the result for the most part of Jewish Hellenism.[213]

1. ETERNAL GOD

The concept of eternity as a timelessness which is beyond past, present, and future presumes abstract philosophical thought. There is scarcely any precedent for this in the Bible. In its unsophisticated understanding eternity is viewed from the human standpoint as time reaching backwards and forwards without bounds. That is the way, in any case, that the oldest declarations about it are to be understood. "Abraham called upon the name of Yahweh, the God of primordial time" (Gen. 21:33). God's life is ever such that he can simply be termed the One Who Lives (Deut. 5:26; 32:40). God's time outlasts all generations (Ps. 102:25-28). He operates constantly; he is the One Who Lives. His kindness and fidelity are eternal (Ps. 89:2-5). The covenant established by him shall remain forever (Is. 55:3). He constantly gives Israel new strength and vigor (Is. 40:28-31). The idols cannot act and are dead (Is. 46:7; Hab. 2:18f.). That too is the difference between God and man: man is mortal (Gen. 3:22) and the span of his life is short (Gen. 6:3). Even the span allotted to the world has temporal limits.

The Septuagint and Hellenistic Judaism designated time, infinite time and eternity with the terms αἰών and αἰῶνες.[214] The plural αἰῶνες and its duplication αἰῶνες τῶν αἰώνων (Ps. 84:5; 1 Chron. 16:36) signify infinitely long and eternal time. Later texts, under the influence of Greek philosophy, are able to form a more abstract concept of eternity. Divine Wisdom exists before time: "From eternity on was I fashioned, from the beginning, before the origin of the world" (Prov. 8:23; similarly in Sir. 1:1-4). The problem of the concept of time is recognized. God lets time succeed itself in successive periods for the sake of men;

then it will vanish, and the eternal and immutable age of the world will come (*Slavic* [*i.e.*, Old Bulgarian] *Apocalypse of Henoch* 65).

The New Testament continues the use of Old Testament formulas, and deepens their significance. God's eternity is restated with the expression that he is Lord of the ages (i.e., eons, αἰῶνες); and the short formula "in all ages" (Rom. 11:36) is augmented through the use of the duplicated plural "from ages to ages" (twenty-one instances in the New Testament; *e.g.*, Rom. 16:27; Gal. 1:5; 2 Tim. 4:18; Apoc. 1:6. This is the "*per omnia saecula saeculorum*" of the Latin liturgical prayer conclusion, generally translated "forever" or "forever and ever" or "world without end" in English). The predication of God as Lord of the ages can be employed in signifying pre-temporal eternity (Eph. 3:9; Col. 1:26; Jude 25) as well as post-temporal eternity (John 6:51; 1 John 2:17; 2 John 2; Heb. 1:8; 5:6).

In 1 Timothy 1:17 God is designated "King of the Ages." The title is found in a similar way in Jer. 10:10; Sir. 36:19; Tob. 13:6, 10; and in the *Ethiopic Apocalypse of Henoch* 9:4 and 12:3. Apparently 1 Timothy is using a Jewish ritual formulation. It designates God as eternal King, and as the one who rules over the ages or eons, in which context the ages or eons are to be understood both as areas of time and as areas of place. (Again, this explains how, in the Latin liturgical prayer ending, *saeculum* can translate αἰών, and how *per omnia saecula saeculorum*, literally "through all ages of ages," can be rendered "world without end").

Ancient formulas are also being taken up anew when divine predication is expressed in such terms as: "I am the Alpha and the Omega, says the Lord God, who was and who is and who is coming, the almighty Sovereign" (Apoc. 1:8).[215] "I am the Alpha and the Omega, the beginning and the end" (Apoc. 21:6). Alpha and Omega are examples of a mystical use of the alphabet. The sum of the letters of an alphabet is the symbol of fullness, of totality, of consummate perfection. The first and last letters of the alphabet stand for the whole. [*Translator's note*: This obvious symbolism was utterly lost in those much-antiquated translations of Scripture into Germanic vernaculars which rendered the passage, in effect, "I am the A and the O!" We might suggest for an English translation the use of an archaic term for Z, which seems to capture something of the passage's high sense of dramatic mystery: "I am the

A and the Izzard". With the term Izzard one fairly hears the cosmic winds whistling through the hoary locks of the Godhead.]

It is true that we find no precedent for such a use of the letter Alpha and Omega; but certainly the terminal letters of other alphabets are so used, the Hebrew letters Aleph and Taw among them. (Izzard, archaic and dialectic English for Z, no longer serves any other function in the language; why not let it earn its keep here?).

The formula "who is, who was, and who is coming" is known, as an embodiment of all time, even in extra-biblical literature. It is said of Zeus: "Zeus was, Zeus is, Zeus will be." In rabbinic writings we find: "I am who I have been; and I am the self-same now and am the self-same in the future." The three period formula probably passed over from Greek into Jewish tradition and from thence into the Apocalypse.[216] In the Apocalypse the third member of the formula means "who is coming here", in accord with the urgent expectation which the Apocalypse has of the parousia.

In the conclusion of the Epistle to the Romans (16:25-27), a passage which is almost certainly a post-Pauline addition, God is predicated as the one who is eternal and beyond all ages: the mystery, silent through eternal ages, is now publicly preached and made manifest in accord with the commission given by the eternal God; to him belongs glory in the ages of ages. God is called "eternal" in his capacity as Lord of the ages from the primordial time even to the (present) endtime. The Old Testament knows the title "eternal God" (Gen. 21:23; Is. 14:28; Dan. 13:42; Baruch 4:8; 2 Macc. 1:25), and so too does late Judaism (*Ethiopic Henoch* 75:3; *Book of Jubilees* 12:29). Even Greek literature speaks of the eternal gods (Plato, *Timaeus* 37 C). In an inscription paying homage to Augustus, the "eternal and immortal nature of the All" is glorified. Like other divine attributes, that of being "eternal" is ascribed to the Emperor (H. Sasse, Article αἰώνιος, in the *Theol. Dict. N. T.*, Vol. 1, p. 208).

Whatever pertains to God shares in his divine eternity: God's eternal spirit (Heb. 9:14), his eternal gifts (2 Cor. 4:18), eternal consolation (2 Thess. 2:16), eternal covenant (Heb. 13:20), eternal salvation (Heb. 5:9), his eternal glory and the good things thereof (2 Cor. 4:17; 1 Tim. 6:16; 2 Tim. 2:10; 1 Peter 5:10). The eschatological consummation of perfection perdures eternally (Luke 16:9; 2 Cor. 5:1; Heb. 9:15; 2 Peter 1:11).

The biblical concept of eternity underwent a certain evolution. It signified, at least originally, the powerful contemporaneousness of God in reference to all history from the creation to the consummation. A biblical *Weltanschauung* was probably also in touch with the concept of the divine eternity as the transcendence of time and as the eternal and self-sufficient cause of the world. Finally, the biblical concept of God's eternity comes to understand that eternity now and then and with greater or lesser clarity, even as God's timelessness and unchangingness.

2. INVISIBLE GOD

Critical reflection must have taken place for a long time before God could be described in philosophy by means of negations. At that point positive assertions about God's nature and properties are avoided or no longer hazarded. Negations express the fact that God is otherwise than men and the experience of mankind. There are three such negations, in particular, which are to be found in the New Testament: God is invisible, imperishable, and immortal.

In many narratives of the Old Testament, Israel was told how God associated with the fathers and, at least to chosen men, was quite visible, even if his presence was full of mystery, terror, and danger.[217] After the struggle at night with the apparition of God, Jacob says: "I have seen God face to face and am still alive" (Gen. 32:30; see also Exod. 3:6; Judges 6:22f.; 3 Kings 19:13). As prince of Israel and friend of God, Moses was permitted to look upon the face of God (Exod. 24:9f.; 33:11; Num. 12:7f.). It is also stated, however, that Moses, when he asked to be permitted to look upon the glory of God, was given the answer: "You cannot look upon my face; for no man looks upon me and remains among the living" (Exod. 33:20). The prophets were given to understand that sinful man cannot survive a personal encounter with the holy God (Is. 6:5). God, however, lets his countenance shine upon the pious, when he is bestowing his favor (Num. 6:25f.; Ps. 4:7).

Greek mythology was in no way abashed at speaking of the traffic of the gods with men. But philosophical criticism arrived finally at the teaching that God is invisible to men, and, at most, he is apprehensible to reason. Philo is quite able to call God the "invisible"; thus in his *De migratione Abrahami* 75 f.: "God is invisible. He did not wish to be apprehended by the bodily eyes, perhaps because it were not right that any mortal should come into contact with the eternal, and perhaps also because of the weakness of our sense of sight"; and again in his *De specialibus legibus* 1, 46: "God is invisible. He is apprehensible only to reason."

According to the Gnosis, God is separated from the world, as the one one who is beyond; there is, however, the possibility of seeing God in an ecstatic occurrence, which God can grant. It is depicted in the *Corpus hermeticum* 1, 26: "They ascend the ranks toward the Father, surrender themselves to the powers, become powers themselves and pass into God. That is the good end of those who have received the knowledge of being divinized." Apuleius, in the *Metamorphoses* 11, 23, portrays his initiation into the mysteries: "I went to the boundary between life and death. I set foot on Proserpina's threshold, and after I had passed through all the elements, I came back again. At the time of deepest midnight I saw the sun beaming with the brightest light. I gazed upon the lower and higher gods face to face and worshipped them in their own presence."

If the New Testament speaks repeatedly of the invisibility of God, it is borrowing, in disregard of Old Testament narratives, the ideas of philosophy. The Old Testament is even subjected to a certain refinement by these ideas. Moses "persevered, as if seeing him who cannot be seen." Certainly the Old Testament passages according to which Moses spoke with God face to face are known to the Epistle. But the Epistle ignores these passages in order to represent Moses as an example of the faith which believes without having seen.

The assertion that God is invisible is formulated in the doxology: "To the King of the ages, to the imperishable, invisible, and one only God, [there is] honor and glory" (1 Tim. 1:17). Praises are offered the "blessed and only Sovereign . . . who alone has immortality, who dwells in inaccessible light, whom no man has seen nor can see" (1 Tim. 6:15f.). Both statements are undoubtedly cast in the mold of Jewish and Christian liturgy.[218]

God is invisible, but he does become manifest. This takes place in creation (Rom. 1:19f.). And it takes place too in the word of God and in

the appearance of Christ. He is "the image of the invisible God" (Col.
1:15; *cf.* 2 Cor. 4:4). Since the time of Plato (*Timaeus* 92 C), and especially in Hellenistic religion, the All is designated as "image of God."
Hellenistic Judaism calls Wisdom the image of the good God (Wis.
7:26). Assisted by this tradition, Col. 1:15 says that God is invisible but
is manifested in Christ (§ 11, 6 above). John's Gospel likewise says that
although no one has ever seen God, Christ has revealed him (1:18).
That God has never been seen is stated again in 1 John 4:12; "No one
has seen God. If we love one another, God abides in us." The statement
is directed against Gnostic teachers of error, who taught an immediate
ecstatic vision of God. The Epistle states to the contrary, that love is the
prerequisite and preparation for God's fellowship.

3. Imperishable and Immortal God

In late antiquity when God and world are separated from each other,
the world beyond is depicted as imperishable, while this world is portrayed as perishable.[219] Thus in the *Corpus hermeticum* 11, 4 and 12, 16,
we read that the world is changeable and perishable, while God is un-
changeable and imperishable. Epicurus (*To Menoeceus* 123) teaches
God's imperishability and blessedness: "Regard God as an imperishable
and blessed living being, such as is the universal idea that men have of
God, and add nothing to him which were foreign to his imperishability
or incompatible with his blessedness. Believe of him instead, everything
that is guaranteed by his blessedness and imperishability" (cf. 1 Tim.
1:11; 6:15). Plutarch (*Stoic Inconsistencies* 38, 3) quotes the statement
of the Stoic Antipater of Tarsus: "We think of God as a blessed and imperishable being."

Hellenistic Judaism says of the Spirit of God: "Your imperishable
Spirit is in all" (Wis. 12:1). According to Philo (*De vita Mosis* 2 [3],
171), Moses reprimands the idolatrous Jews: "They called perishable
created beings with the name of the Imperishable and·Increate." Again
Philo says, in his *Quod Deus sit immutabilis* 26, that God is "the imperishable and blessed One." Josephus (*Antiquities* 10, 278) is convinced

that "the universe is governed by the blessed and immortal One, so that the whole of it may perdure."

In the New Testament, God and his world possess imperishability (ἀφθαρσία). Paul depicts the worship of idols: "They exchanged the glory of the imperishable God for an image in the shape of perishable men" (Rom. 1:23).

Imperishable are the good things of divine salvation. Christ has brought life and imperishability into the world (2 Tim. 1:10). The Blood of Christ participates in divine imperishability (1 Peter 1:18f.). Christians are reborn "not of perishable but of imperishable seed, through the living and abiding Word of God" (1 Peter 1:23). The spirit imparted by God is imperishable (1 Peter 3:4). For Paul, imperishability is a strictly eschatological salvational good, which will first make its appearance with the parousia (1 Cor. 15:42, 50, 53f.). This future salvational benefit is "the imperishable, undefiled and unfading inheritance reserved in heaven" (1 Peter 1:4). If the First Epistle of Peter employs the term "imperishable" with notable frequency, this too is perhaps an index of its openness to Greek thought.

The assertion of the unchangeability of God is essentially the same as that of his immortality.[220] In opposition to the death which is the universal lot of mankind, the God of the Bible, like the gods of the Greeks, possesses ever-continuing life as his own. A Hellenistically influenced doxology says that God is "the only one who is immortal" (1 Tim. 6:16). This life can, at any rate, be bestowed upon men as a divine gift. Plato says as much in his celebrated book on immortality, *Phaedo* (106 C–D), and it is self-evident in the Bible. God, the Creator of life, is Lord and Source of all life (Ps. 36:10). He alone is, by his very nature, the one who lives (Deut. 5:23). Just as he is the one who lives, so too he is the one who makes others to live (1 Thess. 4:14; 2 Cor. 1:9). The eternal Word of God is the course and agency of all life. "In him was the life" (John 1:4).[221]

The word immortality (ἀθανασία) is a term of Greek philosophy. Possibly it was first used by Plato; that it has been in use since his time is demonstrable. Basically it is a word foreign to the Bible, because the very term and concept of immortality imparts immortality to man as a universal and natural endowment by reason of his immortal soul, whereas eternal life, biblically conceived, is a gift of God. It is first in the Greek books of the Old Testament and in the post-canonical writings that the hope of eternity is designated as immortality (Wis. 3:4; 15:3; *4 Macc.* 14:5), and the soul is specified as immortal (*4 Macc.* 14:6; 18:23). The term and concept of immortality are quite familiar to Philo (*e.g.*, his *De virtutibus* 9) and Josephus (*Jewish War*, 7, 340 and 7, 372).

In the New Testament, other than in the Hellenistic doxology of 1 Timothy 6:16; the term immortality occurs only in 1 Cor. 15:53, where Paul uses the language of Hellenistic Judaism to describe the opposition between the earthly manner of existence and that of the resurrection as perishability and imperishability, and mortality and immortality.

4. BLESSED GOD

Since the time of Homer the Greeks have recognized the gods as the blessed ones (μάκαρες, μακάριοι) [222] who, by the nature of their life, are more than a match for troubles, toils, and death. From this stance Hellenistic religious sentiment lauds the imperishable blessedness of the gods (see § 20, 3 immediately above, for texts from Epicurus, Plutarch, the *Corpus hermeticum*, and Judaism). Hellenistic Judaism too speaks in this way about God. According to Philo, God is "the only one who is happy and blessed" (*De specialibus legibus* 2, 53), "more blessed than blessedness, happier than happiness, if there can be anything more perfect than the concepts themselves" (*De legatione ad Caium* 5); the divine nature is "uncreated, imperishable, full of happiness and blessedness" (*De somniis* 1, 94). Josephus (*Against Apion* 2, 190) speaks in a similar fashion: "God has everything. He is perfect and blessed." [223]

The Pastoral Epistles likewise employ such language. "The gospel of the glory of the blessed God" is now to be announced (1 Tim. 1:11). "God is the blessed and only Sovereign" (1 Tim. 6:15). "We look forward impatiently to the blessed hope and the revelation of the glory of our great God" (Titus 2:13). This hope is called blessed because it awaits expectantly the eternal good things of heaven. Here Greek speculations on the nature of God take the place of biblical assertions about God's operation in history.

5. Most High God

Biblical and extra-biblical documents acclaim God as the "Most High" (ὕψιστος) or the "highest God." [224] Zeus is not infrequently accorded the predicate "Most High" (in Pindar, the tragic poets, Pausanias, and in inscriptions). The same title is also given to other high gods as an absolute superlative.

This predication to God of being the "Highest" is frequently found in the Septuagint as a translation for the old designation of God as the *'El 'Elyon* or *'El 'Elîm* (God of Gods), which Israel may perhaps have borrowed from the Canaanite religion. This name for God appears also in the deuterocanonical books of the Greek Bible (especially frequent in Sirach) and in the apocrypha, though it is rare in Philo. Its widespread use on a popular level is attested by inscriptions designating synagogues as "dedicated to the Most High." The Jewish diaspora probably prized the expression as an ecumenical designation of God. Be that as it may, it is ultimately a reflection of a Greek attribute of God.

In the New Testament it is stated repeatedly that God dwells "in the heights" or "on high" (ἐν ὑψίστοις — Mark 11:10; Luke 2:14). The designation of God as "the Most High" is found nine times in the New Testament. A thoughtful Jew would no doubt simply say "the Most High", whereas among non-Jews one might expect "the Most High God", an expression which can be understood polytheistically of a most high god who has other gods subject to him.

As a name of God the term is heard on the lips of Jesus in Luke 6:35, "that you may be sons of the Most High"; but the original form of his statement will be recognized as that of the parallel passage, Matthew 5:45, "so that you may become sons of your Father in heaven." In Luke's infancy narrative the precursor John is called "prophet of the Most High" (Luke 1:76); Jesus is "Son of the Most High" (Luke 1:32); and the Spirit is termed "Power of the Most High" (Luke 1:35). The basis of this will be found in the fact of the influence which the Greek of the Septuagint clearly had upon these chapters of the Gospel.

Stephen says in his address that "the Most High does not dwell in temples made by men" (Acts 7:48-50).

The name "the Most High" is deliberately chosen in order to point out God's superterrestrial quality as opposed to anything of man's domain.

The designation of God by this term in the form "the Most High God" is used repeatedly by demoniacal spirits (Mark 5:7 and its parallel in Luke 8:28; Acts 16:17). In these instances this particular form of the expression probably seemed to be a suitable designation of God, because it leaves the confession of God somewhat in doubt. Ultimately, even pagans use such an expression.

The designation of God as "the Most High" is used in the New Testament without any special emphasis, and apparently it has no import that is peculiar to the New Testament. The name occurs with its greatest frequency in the Lukan writings, which are directed especially to the Greek world. The term can perhaps be designated as a syncretistic intrusion in the New Testament.

6. ALMIGHTY SOVEREIGN GOD

The term almighty sovereign ($\pi\alpha\nu\tau o\kappa\rho\acute{\alpha}\tau\omega\rho$) is used outside the Bible, even if rather infrequently, as a predicate of divinities such as Hermes and Isis.[225]

The term is of frequent occurrence in the Septuagint, and serves as a translation for the Hebrew *Zebaôth* and *Shaddai*, attributes understood as names of God. It is an especially useful term in the writings of the prophets, and also appears frequently in deuterocanonical literature (Judith, Baruch, Second Maccabees; and *Third Maccabees* as well). Philo uses it, but rather infrequently; in his *De gigantibus* 64 he calls God "the only King and Almighty Sovereign."

The term occurs in 2 Cor. 6:18 in the concluding line in a long series of Old Testament quotations, either as a quotation from the Septuagint (perhaps after 2 Sam. 7:8) or as a free construction. Exegesis is of a mind, however, that 2 Cor. 6:14–7:1 is an interpolation not originating with Paul.[226]

The attribute God Almighty, *i.e.*, Sovereign or Omnipotent, occurs with great frequency in the Apocalypse of John (1:8; 4:8; 11:17; 15:3; 16:7, 14; 19:6, 15; 21:22). As a title it sometimes sums up the declaration, "Who is, was, and is coming" (Apoc. 1:8; 4:8; 11:17), and thus places an emphasis also on the totality of time. The frequency of the use of this attribute may be indicative of a change in the image of God. The viewpoint is elevated from the ever personal belief to a view of unlimited extension and perfection of the divine sovereignty in space and time. Ultimately this is indeed the great theme of John's Apocalypse.

§ 21. THE DIVINE TRINITY

In the confrontations of Christian faith with other religions and philosophies, the dogma of the Trinitarian God is the distinguishing feature. It is this doctrine which distinguished Christianity and set it apart from Judaism and Islam. It is also this dogma which separates Christianity from every purely rational-philosophical doctrine about God. Judaism, Islam, and philosophical Theism are unitarian; Christianity is trinitarian.[227]

1. Prior Considerations
from the History of Religion

Certainly it would be difficult to overestimate the importance of the triad throughout the world and in all times even down to the present, and the significance which it has in religion, myth, art, literature, and even in everyday life. Three constitutes the smallest group that is complete in itself, comprising a beginning, a middle, and an end. The number three, moreover, is of the greatest importance throughout the whole Bible.

Various religions are aware of divinities in sets of three. The three sons of Kronos, to wit, Zeus, Poseidon, and Hades, have mastery over the world, consisting of heaven and earth, sea, and the underworld. In Rome there was the Capitoline triad of Jupiter, Juno, and Minerva.

Immediately, then, a distinction must be made between triple and trinitarian groups. While a triple group *i.e.*, a triad, simply counts three together, a trinity makes the three into a unity. We might say that a triplex reckons three as a unit, while trinity makes them into a unity.

In the New Testament there is a purely triadic or triplex listing which is repeatedly in evidence: God, Christ, angels (Mark 13:32; Luke 9:26; 1 Tim. 5:21; Apoc. 1:4f.). It is the task of exegesis to explain whether and to what extent the triad of Father, Son, and Spirit is to be understood already in the New Testament as a Trinity.

2. OLD TESTAMENT

With the New Testament revelation as a starting point, exegesis and dogmatics ask whether any hints of a doctrine of the Trinity can be found already in the Old Testament. The Church Fathers explained numerous Old Testament passages as referring to the Trinity; thus with the We-formulas in statements made by God (Gen. 1:26; 3:22; 11:7; Is. 6:8). Reports about triads were understood by the Fathers of the Church as prior revelations of the divine Trinity; thus with the three men who visited Abraham in Gen. 18:1-16; thus with the threefold request for a blessing in Num. 6:24-26; and thus too with the "Holy, holy, holy" of the seraphim in Isaiah 6:3. Such an interpretation of the literal sense seems to us today to be quite impossible.

Nevertheless, it can be pondered in the light of the history of religion and of revelation, whether or not within rigid Old Testament monotheism there can be found ideas of a fullness of life internal to the Godhead, and the external revelation thereof, whereby the Old Testament might seem to have opened a way for the New.

The Old Testament speaks of forces and beings through which and in which God operates externally and becomes present in history. When one no longer dared speak of direct and personal appearances of Yahweh as matter of course events, then the "Angel of Yahweh" (*mal'akh Yahweh*) made an entry as the mediator between Yahweh and Israel. It is he that guides Israel in her wandering in the desert (Exod. 14:19). He aids the afflicted (Gen. 16:7; 3 Kings 19:5; 4 Kings 1:3). The angel of God makes known the strength (Zech. 12:8) and knowledge (2 Sam. 14:20) of God. He protects the pious (Ps. 34:8). Occasionally the angel appears in the identity of Yahweh himself (Gen. 31:11, 13; Exod. 3:2, 4;

Hosea 12:4f.). The "angel of the Lord" is a form in which God reveals himself.

The "word of God" is likewise a manner of God's self-disclosure in the Old Testament. Just as for the oriental in general, so too for the Old Testament, the word is more than a transitory sound; it has great power and creative strength (Gen. 1:3-24; Is. 55:10f.). This mentality is expressed in a deeper way in later texts of the Old Testament (Ps. 33:6; Wis. 9:1; 18:15; Sir. 39:17). The Word now appears as a personification. The influence of this on the New Testament is conspicuous in the prologue to John's Gospel (1:1), where Christ is designated as the Word of God.

In the postexilic wisdom literature, Wisdom comes forward as being nearly separate from God, acting independently, and finally as a hypostatized and pre-existing power (Prov. 1:20-33; 8; 9:1-6; Sir. 24; Wis. 6:12-25; 7:22-8:1). In the New Testament Christ occasionally appears as Wisdom (Matthew 11:19; 1 Cor. 1:24, 30).

Finally, of course, there is the Old Testament doctrine about the spirit, for which see § 12 above.

The Old Testament concept of God can, in such assertions as the above, be understood as preparing and opening the way for the New Testament revelation. Even here the Old Testament can be explained as a "shadow of the future" (Heb. 10:1).

3. Duplex Formulas in the New Testament

Exegesis understands and describes the confession of the Trinity within the New Testament as the end product of a process of development. This confession proceeds from the belief in the one God, whom the New Testament has in common with the Old. From this there arises the confession of the dyad of Father and Son, and finally of the triad of Father, Son, and Spirit. The development takes place both in forms and in their content. Here too it is possible to speak of a critical account of forms and traditions, as well as of faith and doctrine, in the New Testament.

The duplex formulas are found in sayings of the Lord, which speak of the narrow and exclusive communion between the Father and Jesus as Son (thus in Matthew 11:27; Mark 13:32; John 5:30; 10:30; 17:3. On the Christology of these texts see above, § 11, 3 and § 16, 1).

The Lukan writings, which attend especially to the operation of the Spirit (§ 12, 2a), advance to triplex groupings. Already at the annunciation to Mary, God, Holy Spirit, and Son of God are mentioned (Luke 1:35). While in Matthew 11:27 the cry of jubilation mentions only Father and Son, in the parallel in Luke 10:21 we read: "In that same hour Jesus rejoiced in the Holy Spirit and said, 'I praise you, Father, Lord of heaven and earth.' " The martyrdom of Stephen is depicted thus: "Filled with the Holy Spirit, he looked up to heaven and saw the Glory of God, and Jesus standing at the right hand of God; and he said: 'Behold, I see the heavens opened'" (Acts 7:55). In both passages the Father, Jesus, and the Holy Spirit are mentioned one after another and even with an internal coördination. The Holy Spirit is operative in the verbal testimony of Jesus and of Stephen, and in both testimonies he confesses God.

In the letters of the apostles the confession of the dyad is sometimes expressed in a brief formula, and sometimes in greater detail. A very simple statement is found in Gal. 4:4, "God sent his Son." We might mention also the statement in 1 Tim. 2:5, "There is one God, and one Mediator between God and men, the Man, Jesus Christ." Such a statement takes the unity of God for its point of departure. Through the one Mediator, the divine unity is present and effective in the redemption. As an early and detailed attestation of the dyad, there is the passage in 1 Cor. 8:6, "For us there is one God, the Father, from whom are all things and we unto him, and one Lord, Jesus Christ, through whom are all things and we through him" (see above § 15, 2). The Jewish confession of rigid monotheism is continued even in the duplex assertion of one God and one Lord. In this way the conformity and unity of creation and redemption is expressed.

The greetings of the Epistles are occasionally stated in duplex formulas. "Grace be to you, and the peace of God, our Father, and of the Lord Jesus Christ" (Rom. 1:7; Gal. 1:3). In accord with the universal style of confessions of faith and prayer in the New Testament, God is called "Father." Since Jesus was exalted as Lord in the resurrection, and is now the heavenly dispenser of blessings, he is mentioned in association with the Father. This is clearly the case with Gal. 1:1, "Paul, an Apostle, not of men nor through a man, but through Jesus Christ and God, the

Father, who raised him from the dead." The duplex formula can be developed into a triplex formula for a more solemn greeting (2 Cor. 13:13; see below).

As a duplex formula of another kind, however, we might mention 2 Cor. 3:17, "The Lord is the Spirit." Certainly Paul does not intend in this passage to oppose his numerous declarations about the basically trinitarian structure of Christian existence with a declaration about a binitarian structure. Just as those statements are valid, in which Paul distinguishes between Christ and the Spirit, so too is this one, in which he equates the two. Here the Spirit is to be understood as Christ's continuing revelatory existence in the Church. Christ is not present merely as a memory or through his word and example; rather, he is the powerful, spiritual presence and reality in the faith and life of each member of the Church, and ultimately in the collective Church.

4. TRIPLEX FORMULAS IN THE EPISTLES

We will consider the texts individually, taking them simply in the sequence of the New Testament writings.

a) "Paul, singled out for the gospel of God . . . (the gospel) about his Son, born of the seed of David according to the flesh, constituted as Son of God in power according to the Spirit of holiness in consequence of the resurrection of the dead" (Rom. 1:3f.). In this address of the Epistle to the Romans, Paul is probably making use of an older Christological formula (§ 9e above). The antiquated schema of a two-stage Christology seems to be used, which distinguishes the earthly and human lowliness of Jesus from his subsequent heavenly and divine glory (as also in Acts 2:36).

But what is ever so much more significant is the fact that in this formula Father, Son, and a "spirit" are mentioned in connection with each other. From his existence as Son of David, *i.e.*, the Messiah, Jesus was exalted after and by reason of his resurrection and was constituted as Son and Lord in power. This took place "according to the Spirit of holiness". Even this peculiar designation may be pre-Pauline, and in any case it is difficult to interpret. Whatever belongs to God's domain is holy (see *Theology of the New Testament*, Vol. 3, pp. 171–175).

The Spirit of holiness is probably divine spirit and divine power. But what is the relationship between Son and Spirit? To what extent are they thought of as a unity or as a dyad? Is the "spirit of holiness" the divine substance of the Son, which belongs to him even now and always, and which will be powerfully manifested in the resurrection and exaltation of Jesus (*cf*. 2 Cor. 3:17)? In that event, the spirit would not be a divine person of the Trinity. Or is the "spirit of holiness" a specific divine strength, which produces all this? Then the formula would seem more likely to have been conceived already in accord with the notion developed later of the divine triad. In Rom. 1:3f., then, there is an expression of the Trinity at least in a primitive and formational way.

b) "You are not in the flesh but in the spirit, if the Spirit of God does in fact dwell among you. If, however, anyone does not have the Spirit of Christ, he is not Christ's own . . . If the Spirit of him who raised Jesus from the dead dwells in you, then also will he that raised Jesus from the dead make your mortal bodies alive through the indwelling of his Spirit among you" (Rom. 8:9-11). Twice in this dynamic text the triad is spoken of, God, Christ, and Spirit. The Spirit is the life of the community. This Spirit is called equally Spirit of God and Spirit of Christ. Whoever does not have this Spirit does not belong to the community. Where the Spirit of Christ is, there Christ himself is present (2 Cor. 3:17). God, who raised Jesus from the dead, will, through the Spirit which dwells in Christ, also make mortal bodies have life. Through his Spirit God gives the pledge of life. In the Spirit, God's truth and power are manifest and effective, even as they are in the word and work of Christ.

c) "I admonish you by our Lord Jesus Christ and by the love of the Spirit, to join my struggle in prayers to God for me, that I may be rescued from the disobedient in Judea" (Rom. 15:30-31). Paul speaks of Christ first, as the one who is Lord over the Apostle himself and over the Church. He speaks then of the Spirit, who produces the fellowship of love; and finally he speaks of God, to whom the common prayer is to be directed. God is the goal, "God all in all" (1 Cor. 12:6).

d) "You are washed, you are sanctified, you are justified by the name of the Lord Jesus Christ and by the Spirit of our God" (1 Cor. 6:11). The gift of baptism is described in two triplex formulas. Baptism is purification, sanctification, and justification. It has its basis in the name, that is, in the work of Christ. It is in his name, therefore, that baptism is bestowed, inasmuch as it signifies a proprietary conversion to Christ (1 Cor. 1:13). Christ is present through the Spirit. Since this Spirit is designated Spirit of God, salvation is traced back to God.

e) "No one speaking in the Spirit of God can say, 'Jesus is cursed!' And no one can say, 'Jesus is Lord', except he be speaking in the Holy Spirit" (1 Cor. 12:3). There is false ecstasy and genuine ecstasy. Whoever in ecstasy reviles Jesus (perhaps, as in 1 Cor. 1:23, one who reviles Jesus as the Crucified), is unmasked. Speaking in the Spirit of God, one must confess that Jesus is Lord. Christ, Spirit, and God are a unity.

f) "There are different kinds of charismatic gifts, but the same Spirit. And there are different kinds of ministerial duties, but the same Lord. And there are different kinds of operations, but the same God who effects all in all" (1 Cor. 12:4-6). The triplicity is conspicuously stylized and objectively expressed. The matter under discussion is divided into three lots. The apportionings are objectively determined. The charismatic gifts are attributed to the Spirit, the operation of the more extraordinary charisms pertaining to that Spirit in a special way. The ministerial duties are the special province of Christ, the Lord (1 Cor. 4:1), who summons others to the service of the community (2 Cor. 4:1) and is himself its servant (Rom. 15:8). The operations are collectively an effluence of the omnipotence of God. The three different ranks again strive toward God as the goal of all activity. The formal triplicity expresses an objective unity. Paul is attempting to put in order and to explain the fullness and the richness of Christian experience. He conceives it in a trinitarian schema.

g) "The grace of the Lord Jesus Christ and the love of God and the fellowship of the Holy Spirit be with you all" (2 Cor. 13:13). Paul's practice is to close his letters by wishing the recipients the grace of Christ or by asserting his love in Christ. "The grace of our Lord Jesus Christ be with you" is his conclusion in Rom. 16:20; 1 Cor. 16:23; Gal. 6:18; Phil. 4:23; 1 Thess. 5:28; and 2 Thess. 3:18. In the conclusion just now cited from 2 Cor. 13:13, the one-member formula is expanded to a three-member formula. The triplex character of the formula may correspond to the liturgical way of achieving a greater solemnity (see the triplex benediction of Num. 6:24-26). With this final sentence of the letter, there is a conclusion also to Paul's roll-call of those engaged in the public worship. The series Christ, God, and Spirit shapes the plan of salvation. In Christ the Father's love was made manifest. That love is devoted to the Church by the Spirit. The three genitives must be understood uniformly as subjective genitives.[228] Christ gives grace, God loves men, the Spirit produces the fellowship which embraces all.

h) "Because you are sons, God sent the Spirit of his Son into our hearts, which Spirit cries out from there, 'Abba, Father' " (Gal. 4:6). In his Son, God has accepted us as sons. Now he bestows also the Spirit of his Son, which Spirit manifests in his prayerful cry the status of sonship in relation to the Father, and makes it possible to have subjective experience of that relationship. The Spirit of the Son of God is the Son himself, in the power of his and God's presence.

i) "We are the (spiritual) circumcision, we who worship God in the Spirit and who glory in Jesus Christ" (Phil. 3:3). Paul is opposing the Judaizers, who demand that Christians accept circumcision. The corporeal rite of circumcision is to be understood spiritually. The Spirit bestowed upon the Church brought the new arrangement in which the true worship of God now takes place. The newness has its basis in salvation through Christ, in whom henceforth the community prides itself.

j) "We, however, must thank God at all times on account of you, brethren beloved of the Lord, because God has chosen you as the firstlings unto salvation and unto holiness through the Spirit. Thus too has he called you . . . to obtain the glory of our Lord Jesus Christ" (2 Thess. 2:13f.). In this vocation it is God who chooses. The election is effective in the love which Christ shows to those who are called. The Spirit produces the sanctification, which is equivalent to living a Christian life and belonging to the holy Church (*Theology of the New Testament*, Vol. 3, pp. 171-178). The Spirit effects this in accord with his nature as designated in the attribute "Holy" Spirit. The eschatological goal is the glory of Christ. Christian life and the fullness of the Church are being described in a trinitarian fashion.

k) "Blest is the God and Father of our Lord Jesus Christ, who has blest us with every spiritual blessing [*i.e.*, every blessing of the Spirit] in the highest heavens in Christ" (Eph. 1:3). The great praise of God (Eph. 1:3-14) begins with a formula of blessing. Salvation was manifested and became an actualized event, inasmuch as God, as the Father of Christ, has blest us in the Spirit. The Father has determined upon salvation, and has arranged it in Christ, and he bestows it in the Spirit. There is a correspondence between the trinitarian event of salvation and the thanksgiving for it that is formulated in a trinitarian fashion.

m) "One body and one Spirit, even as you are called in one hope of your calling. One Lord, one faith, one baptism; one God and Father of all" (Eph. 4:4-6). The phrases have the conspicuous appearance of a formula. Perhaps the passage contains a liturgical acclamation which the Epistle has expanded. The basic structure is a confession of unity — and this is of special importance, frequently being aimed in a specific direction (see § 16 above). The confession of unity clashes with the confession of triplicity. The one Spirit produces and maintains the unity of the Church, since he is bestowed upon all Christians (Rom. 8:9-11; 1 Cor. 6:19). This Spirit is the Spirit of God in Christ. It is in this Spirit that the Church is erected as God's house (Eph. 2:22); the Spirit is the filling up of the body of Christ, which is the Church (Eph. 1:23). The abundance and fullness of the salvational event in Christ and in the Spirit pushes forward to its goal, to the one God and Father, who gathers all into unity.

n) Baptism is "the bath of rebirth and renewal through the Holy Spirit, whom God has poured out abundantly upon us through Jesus Christ our Savior" (Titus 3:5 *cf.* 2 Tim. 1:9). The divine triplicity is a unity in the plan of salvation.

o) "How much more, then, will the blood of Christ, who by the eternal Spirit has presented himself as an unblemished sacrifice to God, cleanse our conscience from dead works, for the worship of the living God" (Heb. 9:14). Just as the high priest on the Day of Atonement enters into the temple's holy of holies, so too does Christ enter into the heavenly sanctuary (Heb. 9:12). The Old Testament prototype, nevertheless, remains far behind its fulfillment. Now there is a true sanctuary, an eternal High Priest, and a Sacrifice of infinite value. Like the Old Testament sacrifice (Lev. 17:11; Heb. 9:22), this sacrifice too requires blood. The blood of Christ, however, is not to be regarded as the matter and substance of the sacrifice; rather, the term blood signifies the surrender and the carrying out of the totality of the sacrifice which was Christ himself. Priest and offering are identical. Christ is given his task by the Spirit of God. The Spirit is "eternal", because he belongs to the eternal world of God. Probably the Spirit is Christ's own, but he seems to be conferred on Christ, and therefore given to him and separate from him.

The Old Testament laws of worship require an unblemished sacrificial animal (Exod. 29:1; 1 Peter 1:19). The sacrifice of an irreproachable and holy Christ does not produce "purity of the flesh" (Heb. 9:13f.), for it is not a ceremonial, ritual cleansing; rather, it brings about the cleansing of conscience, *i.e.*, of the innermost and total existence of a man. What are dead works? Probably, in accord with Heb. 6:1, it is sin that is meant, *i.e.*, our former existence which was in death and not in life. The goal of all is the worship of the living God, which is performed in the community (Heb. 12:28). In Heb. 9:14 Christ, God, and Spirit are spoken of in connection with each other. They are manifest and present in the work of salvation.

p) "To those chosen in accord with the foreknowledge of God the Father, in sanctification by the Spirit, unto obedience and sprinkling with the blood of Jesus Christ" (1 Peter 1:2). The salvational event is described in a carefully formulated triplex formula rich in content. Salvation has its source in the precognitive and predeterminative decree of the Father, who at the same time, since he chooses lovingly, shows himself as Father. The election becomes effective in the sancitification which is produced by the Spirit. The designation of the Spirit as Holy Spirit is presupposed; and the phrase is to be understood with the significance of that designation even though unexpressed. The goal in the arrangement of salvation is "obedience and sprinkling with the blood of Jesus Christ", therefore, fellowship and community in Christ. If obedience calls to mind the fact that in this matter man must make a decision (a typically Pauline statement about obedience unto faith, as in Rom. 1:5), so too the "sprinkling with the blood of Christ" calls to mind God's working through Christ and the gift of the sacrament of baptism. The sequence Father — Spirit — Son is determined simply by the structure of the description of what has taken place. The triplex formula describes an undivided event. Probably it can be designated not only as triadic but as exemplarily trinitarian. The passage, as not a few places in 1 Peter, is already under the influence of Pauline theology.

q) "Build yourselves up in your most holy Faith. Pray in the Holy Spirit. Keep yourselves in God's love, awaiting impatiently the mercy of our Lord Jesus Christ unto eternal life" (Jude 20-21). The sequence ·

Spirit — God — Christ is probably arranged in this way so that it takes for its starting point the personal existence of the reader, *i.e.*, his being in the Spirit. The love of God is of continuing perdurance (and here the love of God surely means the love which God has for men, and not man's love for God). Eternal life by the grace of Christ is the eschatological goal. As the Church's dogma of Faith, this triplicity is a "most holy Faith." The dogma of the Trinity is taking shape.

The numerous triplex groupings of the New Testament Epistles still lack a rigid and formulational manner of expression, and they are not yet dogmatically composed. God is designated sometimes as Father, sometimes as God; Jesus is Son, Christ, or Lord. The sequential order is not yet determined in the fashion customary today as Father, Son, and Spirit. The passages in question are not ontological and metaphysical declarations on a statically self-sufficient nature of a triune God, but declarations on the dynamic operation of God in revelation and in history. The eternal Father was revealed in the Son. The Spirit is the presence of God in the Church. At the same time, however, the Spirit is also removed from a pure functionality, and is personified and granted autonomy (see above, § 12, 2e).

Within the texts of the letters of the apostles, from the earliest Pauline passages until those of the late Apostolic age (Titus, Hebrews, First Peter), there seems to be a gradual firming up of their formulational characteristics, until finally (Jude 20f.) the consciousness of a trinitarian belief is designated as the norm of the Church's Faith. Most of these passages express something of a basic trinitarian consciousness on the part of the Church and of her theology, which theology is just then in the process of formation.

5. Divine Triplicity in the Gospel of John

To the texts of the letters of the apostles, those from the Gospels may be added. Here they appear as sayings of Jesus or at least within the history of Jesus. In this regard scarcely anyone will deny that these texts were written down at a notably later time than, at very least, the (older) Epistles of Paul. Indeed, the texts reveal such a thematically developed trinitarian theology that even by reason of their form and content they must be regarded as later than the Pauline Epistles.

First we may mention two sayings of Christ from the Gospel of John. "The Advocate, the Holy Spirit, whom the Father will send in my name, will teach you all things and will recall to your minds all that I have said to you" (John 14:26). "But when the Advocate comes, whom I will send you from the Father, the Spirit of Truth, who proceeds from the Father, he will bear witness concerning me" (John 15:26).

Both sayings mention Father, Christ, and Spirit in closest connection with each other. The Spirit will continue the revelation of Jesus, when he preserves and renews the word of Jesus, and bears witness to Christ. Since the Son is the revelation of the Father and is one with him (John 17:22), when the word of Jesus is made present the Father is also spoken of, and the Father is revealed in that word. All revelation is revelation of the Father through the Son; and if this is true in the history of Jesus, it is equally true after his departure and in the era of the Church. Therefore the Spirit proceeds from the Father and is sent by him. The Gospel of John also bears witness to an awareness of the belief of the Church that she has received the Spirit as a gift of God after the exaltation of the Lord and through his mediation. Like other texts, John too can say that Jesus sends the Spirit (John 15:26; Mark 1:8; Luke 24:49; Acts 2:33), and that the Father sends him (John 14:26; Acts 2:17; 2 Cor. 1:22; Heb. 2:4).

6. Trinitarian Texts in the Synoptics

The report about the baptism of Jesus (Mark 1:9-11) [229] depicts a substantial revelation of the Trinity. Over the Son, the voice of God resounds from heaven, and the Spirit soars down in the form of a dove. The triad are brought together in single and unique occurrence. The baptism, however, is not simply a narrative about the life of Jesus; rather, it is an epiphany story, containing a body of themes and reflecting various influences. Even the very representation of the Trinity at the baptism reflects the developed theology of a later time (see above, § 11, 3; on the appearance of the dove, § 12, 2a).

The trinitarian formula in the commission to baptize, in Matthew

28:19, is also the result of a lengthy process of development. "Baptize in the name of the Father and of the Son and of the Holy Spirit" (Matthew 28:19). The divine Triad is brought together under one name and in one sacramental action. An unequivocal and certain trinitarian confession is found here on the lips of the resurrected Christ himself. Such a precise confession, however, is out of place here at the very beginning of the Church's history. A trinitarian confession so well-developed is much more likely to have been set down in this way only after it had taken shape and drawn its form and content from the Church with which Matthew was familiar.

The context of Matthew 28:19 seems to point to a later time. In the command to baptize, the apostles are twice directed — before and after the commission to baptize — to teach the nations. Is this a reflection of the ordering of the catechumenate, according to which the catechumens were probably instructed before baptism on the distinctive Christian teachings, but only after baptism on the totality and depth of the mysteries of the Faith and of Christian living? It may be that the account is to be understood as referring to the baptismal catechesis. The baptized is always accepted by God as his child, and is endowed with the Spirit of sonship (Rom. 8:15f.; Gal. 4:6). When the trinitarian confession of Matthew 28:19 appears in the command to baptize, it recalls to mind also that even at the reception of baptism a confession of faith was necessary and was required (Acts 8:37 [the rejected reading with the confession of the Ethiopian eunuch]; 16:31; Heb. 10:22f.).

Since baptism, as is attested in the Acts of the Apostles (2:38; 8:16; 10:48; 19:15) and in Paul (Rom. 6:3; 1 Cor. 1:13; 6:11; Gal. 3:27), was at first conferred in the name of Jesus, the trinitarian formula in Matthew 28:19 is shown to be a later formulation. In Matthew 28:19 it is probably the primitive Christian order of baptism that is depicted.[230]

Someone wanted to read in the New Testament another unequivocal trinitarian declaration, and added it as an interpolation at 1 John 5:7f. in the so-called Johannine comma. The original text of 1 John 5:7 must have read: "There are three who bear witness on earth, the Spirit, the water, and the blood; and these three are one." Christ is attested as Son of God by the revelation at his baptism; by his salvific death, which is represented in the Eucharistic Lord's Supper; and by the Spirit abiding in the Church (1 John 4:13-15). To this was added: "There are three who bear witness in heaven, the Father, the Word, and the Spirit; and these three are one." The interpolation was added, probably by the beginning of the third century and probably in North Africa. [*Translator's note*: A knowledge of the Johannine comma seems to be reflected in Tertullian († *ca.* A.D. 220) and Cyprian of Carthage († A.D. 258). See Jurgens, *The Faith of the Early Fathers*, point 235 in the Doctrinal Index].

The profusion of the trinitarian declarations of the New Testament laid a foundation for the Church's dogma of the Trinity and a terminus for dogmatic speculation. Catholic theology has always affirmed the trinitarian dogma, defended it against objections as a divine mystery, and attempted to establish it and clarify it from Scripture and history.

Broad circles of Protestant theology have either abandoned or re-interpreted the ecclesiastical teaching of the Trinity, since the time of Deism and the Enlightenment. The Trinity was explained as consequent upon the recognition of the divinity of Jesus and the presence of the divine Spirit in the Church (F. Schleiermacher). The Trinity was understood in a pantheistic philosophical way as God's eternal becoming. The generation of the Son, therefore, is God's otherwise-being in finite creation, to which he reconciles himself in the finite spirit (G. W. Fr. Hegel).

In modern Protestant theology Karl Barth has revalidated the dogma of the Trinity.[231] In a comprehensive presentation and with penetrating assimilation he exhibits the doctrine of the Trinity as an interpretation of the biblical testimony, and again interprets the doctrine in the light of this testimony. As God's self-exposition, revelation is the primary basis of the Church's doctrine of the Trinity. This in turn is again a systematic exposition of revelation, and ultimately of divine being. Representing the historicity of revelation and redemption in the plan of salvation, the doctrine of the Trinity keeps the Christian teaching about God from lapsing into mythology or metaphysics.

The fact that in the formation of the dogma of the Trinity (as is quite broadly the case in the history of dogmas) the conceptuality of Greek metaphysics and of Latin scholasticism was accepted and employed in the interpretation and advancement of biblical revelation is matter for the course on special problems in the theology of the Trinity. The terms and concepts that now are important in dogmatics — hypostasis and substance, prosopon and person — can be used in regard to the dogma of the Trinity in the passage from the human to the divine only in a markedly analogical and relative sense, differing from their philosophical and anthropological usage elsewhere. A concomitant weakness is that some of these concepts and terms are not used with precisely the same meaning in Christology that they have in the doctrine of the Trinity. Ultimately it must be noted that today some of these terms and concepts — and "person" is a noteworthy example of this — have, in philosophy and in general everyday usage, a very considerably different meaning and import than they had at the time the dogmas were taking shape and being crystallized.[232]

That is why in our foregoing exposition, for the sake of a better understanding and description of biblical theology, we have of set purpose and insofar as possible avoided the use of this later dogmatic terminology.

NOTES

[1] Among the more recent expositions of New Testament theology we might mention: (1) From the viewpoint of Catholic theology: O. Kuss, *Paulus. Die Rolle des Apostels in der theologischen Entwicklung der Urkirche*, Regensburg 1971. M. Meinertz, *Theologie des Neuen Testaments*, 2 vols. Bonn 1950. B. Rigaux, *Saint Paul et ses lettres*, Desclée de Brouwer 1962 [translated by S. Yonick, ·*The Letters of St. Paul*, Chicago 1968]. K. H. Schelke, articles "The Letters of Paul" and "Pauline Theology" in English edition of *Sacramentum mundi*, Vol. 3, New York and London 1969, pp. 198–203 and 220–227. R. Schnackenburg, *Neutestamentliche Theologie*, 2nd edition, Munich 1965 [this was first published in French under the title *La théologie du nouveau testament* in 1961, and an English translation by David Askew, under the title *New Testament Theology Today* was published at New York, Herder and Herder, in 1963].

(2) From the viewpoint of Protestant theology: R. Bultmann, *Theologie des Neuen Testaments*, 6th edition, Tübingen 1968 [translation of an earlier edition was done by Kendrick Grobel, *Theology of the New Testament*, 2 vols., New York 1951–1955]. H. Conzelmann, *Grundriss der Theologie des Neuen Testaments*, 2nd edition, Munich 1968 [translation of 2nd German edition by John Bowden, under title *An Outline of the Theology of the New Testament*, New York 1969]. G. Eichholz, *Die Theologie des Paulus im Umriss*, Neukirchen-Vluyn 1972. J. Jeremias, *Neutestamentliche Theologie, 1: Die Verkündigung Jesu*, Gütersloh 1971 [English edition translated by John Bowden under title *New Testament Theology, 1: The Proclamation of Jesus*, New York 1971]. W. G. Kümmel, *Die Theologie des Neuen Testaments nach seinen Hauptzeugen*, Göttingen 1969. H. Ridderbos, *Paulus. Ein Entwurf seiner Theologie*, translation, Wuppertal 1970.

As an addenda to the dictionaries mentioned in volumes 1 and 3 of the present *Theology of the New Testament*, we can now make reference to the excellent and only recently completed work of L. Coenen (general editor with numerous collaborators), *Theologisches Begriffslexikon zum Neuen Testament*, 3 vols. Wuppertal 1967–1971.

[2] R. Bultmann, Art. γινώσκω, in the *Theol. Dict. N. T.*, Vol. 1 (1964), pp. 689–719; also of Bultmann, Art. δηλόω, *ibid.*, Vol. 2 (1964), pp. 61–62; A Oepke, Art. καλύπτω, *ibid.*, Vol. 3 (1965), pp. 556–592; R. Bultmann and D. Lührmann, Art. ψαίνω, *ibid.*, Vol. 9 (1974), pp. 1–10. Werner Bulst, *Offenbarung. Biblischer und theologischer Begriff*, Düsseldorf 1960 [translated by Bruce Vawter under title *Revelation*, New York 1965]. Oscar Cullman, *Heil als Geschichte*, Tübingen 1965 [translated by Sidney G. Sowers *et al.*, under title *Salvation in History*, New York 1967]. Avery Dulles, *Revelation Theology*, New York 1969. J. Feiner and M. Löhrer (editors), *Mysterium salutis I*, Einsiedeln 1965 (pp. 1–496, on salvation

311

history, revelation, and Sacred Scripture). F. Konrad, *Das Offenbarungsverständnis in der evangelischen Theologie*, Ismaning/Munich 1971. W. Pannenberg, R. and T. Rendtorff, and U. Wilckens, *Offenbarung als Geschichte*, 4th edition, Göttingen 1970 [earlier edition translated by David Granskou, under title *Revelation as History*, New York 1968]. M. Seybold *et al.*, *Die Offenbarung*, in the *Handbuch der Dogmengeschichte* I/1, Freiburg 1971.

³ Werner Bulst, *Revelation*, trans. by Bruce Vawter, New York 1965, p. 17.

⁴ P. Grelot, *La bible, parole de Dieu*, Paris 1965. K. H. Schelkle, *"Wort Gottes"*, in *Wort und Schrift*, Düsseldorf 1960, pp. 11–30. H. Schlier, *Wort Gottes*, 2nd edition, Würzburg 1962; also of Schlier, *"Grundzüge einer Theologie des Wortes Gottes"* in *Das Ende der Zeit*, Freiburg 1971, pp. 16–24. L. Alonso-Schökel, *La palabra inspirada*, Barcelona 1966, of which the English translation by Francis Martin, *The Inspired Word*, was published at New York already in 1965.

⁵ Late Judaism (the Rabbinic writings; Philo, *De vita Mosis* 2,292; Josephus, *Jewish Antiquities* 10,210) called the Bible "Sacred Writings", *i.e.*, "Holy Scripture", in the same way that whatever pertained to the realm of the divine was termed holy. The New Testament follows the same practice (Rom 1:2; 2 Tim. 3:15); see G. Schrenk, Art. βίβλος, in the *Theol. Dict. N. T.*, Vol. 1 (1964), pp. 615–620; also of Schrenk, Art. ἱερός, *ibid.*, Vol. 3 (1965), pp. 221–283.

⁶ This is stated likewise by the Second Vatican Council in its Constitution on Divine Revelation, *Dei verbum* 6, 24; "The Sacred Scriptures contain the word of God and, since they are inspired, they really are the word of God."

⁷ E. Sjöberg, in Art. πνεῦμα in the *Theol. Dict. N. T.*, Vol. 6 (1968), especially p. 381f.

⁸ Karl Rahner, *Über die Schriftinspiration*, Freiburg 1958 [translated by Charles H. Henkey, *Inspiration in the Bible*, New York 1961], explains the inspiration of Scripture through Scripture's coming forth from the primitive Church, which was entirely and in every respect created by the Spirit and filled with him. Therefore New Testament Scripture too is the creation of the Spirit. And the New Testament knows and recognizes the Old Testament as the word of the Spirit.

⁹ H. Kleinknecht, in Art. πνεῦμα, in the *Theol. Dict. N.T.*, Vol. 6 (1968), p. 343f.; E. Schweizer, in same article, p. 452f. F. L. Strack and P. Billerbeck, *Kommentar zum Neuen Testament*, Vol. 4/1, 1928, pp. 435–451.

¹⁰ Norbert Lohfink, *"Die Irrtumslosigkeit"*, in *Das Siegeslied am Schilfmeer*, Frankfurt 1965, pp. 44–80 [translated into English by R. A. Wilson, *The Christian Meaning of the Old Testament*, Milwaukee 1968, chapter entitled "Inerrancy", pp. 24–51].

¹¹ Karl Barth, *Die kirchliche Dogmatik*, Vol. I/1, 5th edition, Zürich-Zollikon 1947, pp. 147–173; Vol. I/2, 4th edition, Zürich-Zollikon 1948, pp. 324–356 [translation by G. T. Thomson and others, from 2nd and later German editions, under title *Church Dogmatics*, Vol. I/1, Edinburgh 1936 (repr. 1963), pp. 162–184; Vol. I/2, Edinburgh 1956 (repr. 1963), pp. 325–336]. Under Barth's influence but going even further, Dietrich Bonhoeffer (*Widerstand und Ergebung*, edited by

Eberhard Bethge, 8th edition, Munich 1958, pp. 183, 219, 233–239; published in English translation by Reginald Fuller, revised by Frank Clarke, under the title *Letters and Papers from Prison*, New York 1953, revised ed. 1956, pp 125, 148, 158–162) demands a "non-religious interpretation of biblical concepts." According to Bonhoeffer's notion religion can be characterized as "the metaphysical and the inwardness". "Religionlessness", then, is the sustaining of the truth before God, just as if God did not exist at all. "Man's religiosity makes him look in his distress to the power of God in the world. . . . The Bible directs man to God's powerlessness and suffering" (*Ibid.*, German ed., p. 272; English ed., p. 188). This is faith in genuine worldliness. It is, moreover, a call to responsible action. See Gerhard Ebeling, *"Die 'nichtreligiöse Interpretation biblischer Begriffe'"* in *Wort und Glaube*, Tübingen 1960, pp. 90–160 [translation by James W. Leitch, under title *Word and Faith*, Philadelphia 1963, chapter "The 'Non-religious Interpretation of Biblical Concepts'"*, pp. 98–161]. E. Feil, *Die Theologie Dietrich Bonhoeffers*, Munich and Mainz 1971, pp. 380–396.

[12] H. Koester, Art. φύσις, in the *Theol. Dict. N. T.*, Vol. 9 (1974), pp. 251–277, R. Bultmann, *"Die Frage der natürlichen Offenbarung"*, in *Glauben und Verstehen*, Vol. 2, Tübingen 1952, pp. 79–104. W. Eltester, *"Schöpfungsoffenbarung und natürliche Theologie im frühen Christentum"*, in *New Testament Studies*, Vol. 3 (1956/1957), pp. 93–114. J. Heiselbetz, *Theologische Gründe der nichtchristlichen Religionen*, Freiburg 1967. K. Rahner, *"Das Christentum und die nichtchristlichen Religionen"*, in *Schriften zur Theologie*, Vol. 5, Einsiedeln 1962, pp. 136–158 [translated by K. H. Kruger, "Christianity and the Non-Christian Religions", chapter in *Theological Investigations*, Vol. 5, London and Baltimore 1966 (repr. 1969), pp. 115–134]. H. R. Schlette, *Die Religionen als Thema der Theologie*, Freiburg 1963 [translated by W. J. O'Hara, *Towards a Theology of Religions*, New York 1966].

[13] Rudolf Bultmann, *"Die Unsichtbarkeit Gottes"*, in *Exegetica*, Tübingen 1967, pp. 174–197. E. Fascher, *"Deus invisibilis"*, in *Marburger theologische Studien*, Vol. 1, Gotha 1931, pp. 41–77. D. Lührmann, *Das Offenbarungsverständnis bei Paulus und in paulinischen Gemeinden*, Neukirchen-Vluyn 1965, pp. 21–26. E. Norden, *Agnostos Theos*, 4th edition, Darmstadt 1956, pp. 24–29. M. Pohlenz, *Paulus und die Stoa*, Darmstadt 1964, pp. 6–19.

[14] The teaching of the wisdom books and of late Jewish Theology is clearly recognizable in Paul. What is questionable is whether Paul draws directly upon the wisdom literature or whether he but stands in a tradition the influence of which is seen both in the wisdom literature and in Paul. Besides the usual commentaries, see G. Bornkamm, *"Gesetz und Natur (Röm. 2, 14–18)"*, in *Gesammelte Aufsätze*, Vol. 2, Munich 1959, pp. 93–118. Stanislaus Lyonnet, *Quaestiones in epistolam ad Romanos 1*, Rome 1955, pp. 68–108.

[15] Ch. Maurer, Art. σύνοιδα, in the *Theol. Dict. N. T.*, Vol. 7 (1971), pp. 898–919. See also our present *Theology of the New Testament*, Vol. 1, p. 137.

[16] Paul's Areopagus speech is likely to have been constructed by Luke as a model of a missionary sermon to pagans, in accord with a form that had already become

customary. See M. Dibelius, *Aufsätze zur Apostelgeschichte*, 2nd ed., Göttingen 1953, pp. 29–70. B. Gärtner, *The Areopagus Speech and Natural Revelation*, Upsala 1955. F. Mussner, *"Anknüpfung und Kerygma in der Areopagrede (Apg. 17, 22b–31)"* in *Praesentia salutis*, Düsseldorf 1967, pp. 235–243. W. Nauck, *"Die Tradition und Komposition der Areopagrede"*, in *Zeitschrift für Theologie und Kirche*, Vol. 53 (1956), pp. 11–56. H. P. Oven, "The Scope of Natural Revelation in Romans I and Acts XVII", in *New Testament Studies*, Vol. 5 (1958/1959), pp. 133–143.

[17] On this point see M. Lackmann, *Vom Geheimnis der Schopfung. Die Geschichte der Exegese von Röm I, 18–23; II, 14–16 und Acta XV, 17–19, XVII, 22–29 vom 2. Jahrhundert bis zum Beginn der Orthodoxie*, Stuttgart 1952, pp. 36f., 98–101, 180–190, 198, 204, 213–215. This violent exegesis is found also in Karl Barth, *Die kirchliche Dogmatik*, Vol. I/2, 4th edition, Zürich-Zollikon 1948, p. 332; and Vol. II/1, 2nd edition, Zürich-Zollikon 1947, pp. 131–133 and 145 [translation by G. T. Bromley *et al.*, under title *Church Dogmatics*, Vol. I/2, Edinburgh 1956 (repr. 1963), p. 304f; Vol. II/1, Edinburgh 1957 (repr. 1964), pp. 119–121 and 133]. This interpretation was defended by Augustine (among others) against Pelagius. Since Pelagius extolled man's natural ability very highly, Augustine minimized it in order to emphasize the necessity of grace; see K. H. Schelkle, *Paulus, Lehrer der Väter*, 2nd edition, Düsseldorf 1959, pp. 81–83. F. Flückiger, *"Die Werke des Gesetzes bei den Heiden"*, in *Theol. Zeitschrift*, Vol. 8 (1952), pp. 17–42.

[18] F. Büchsel, Art. ἀλληγορέω, in the *Theol. Dict. N.T.*, Vol. 1 (1964), pp. 260–263. G. Delling, Art. πληρόω, *ibid.*, Vol. 6 (1968), pp. 286–298. H. Krämer, R. Rendtorff, R. Meyer, and G. Friedrich, Art. προφήτης, *ibid.*, pp. 828–861. A. C. Joosen and J. H Waszink, Art. *Allegorese in Reallexikon für Antike und Christentum*, Vol. 1 (1950), pp. 283–293. H. L. Strack and P. Billerback, *Kommentar zum Neuen Testament*, Vol. 3 (1926), pp. 384–399. S. Amsler, *L'ancien testament dans l'église*, Neuchâtel 1960. James Barr, *Old and New in Interpretation*, New York 1966. M. Black, "The Christological Use of the Old Testament in the New Testament", in *New Testament Studies*, Vol. 18 (1971/1972), pp. 1–14. K. Berger, *Die Gesetzesauslegung Jesu*, Neukirchen-Vluyn 1972. J. Bonsirven, *Exégèse rabbinique et exégèse paulinienne au temps de Jésus Christ*, 2 vols., Paris, 1934f. C. H. Dodd, *According to the Scriptures*, Dingswell-Place 1961. E. E. Ellis, *Paul's Use of the Old Testament*, Edinburgh 1957. L. Goppelt, *Typos. Die typologische Deutung des Alten Testaments im Neuen*, Gütersloh, 2nd edition, 1969. P. Grelot, *Sens chrétien de l'Ancien Testament*, Tournai 1962. F. Hesse, *Das Alte Testament als Buch der Kirche*, Gütersloh 1966. M. Karnetzki, *Die alttestamentlichen Zitate in der synoptischen Tradition*, typed dissertation, Tübingen 1955. C. Larcher, *L'actualité chrétienne de l'Ancien Testament*, Paris 1962. B. Lindars, *New Testament Apologetic. The Doctrinal Significance of the Old Testament Quotations*, London 1961. U. Luz, *Das Geschichtsverständnis des Paulus*, Munich 1968. S. Lyonnet, *Il Nuovo Testamento alla luce dell'Antico*, Brescia 1972. K. H. Schelkle, *"Auslegung als Symbolverständnis"*, in *Theol. Quartelschrift*, Vol. 132 (1952), pp. 129–151. Also

of Schelkle, *"Von alter und neuer Auslegung"*, in *Wort und Schrift*, Düsseldorf 1966, pp. 201–215.

[19] Otto Betz, *Offenbarung und Schriftforschung in der Qumransekte*, Tübingen 1960. H. Braun, *Qumran und das Neue Testament*, 2 vols., 2nd edition, Tübingen 1969. Frederick Fyvie Bruce, *Biblical Exegesis in the Qumran Texts*, The Hague 1960. M. Limbeck, *Die Ordnung des Heils*, Düsseldorf 1971 (especially pp. 119-189, *"Das Gesetzesverständnis der Gemeinschaft von Qumran"*).

[20] G. Schrenk, Art. τὸ ἱερόν, in *Theol. Dict. N. T.*, Vol. 3 (1965), pp. 230–247. O. Michel, Art. ναός, *ibid.*, Vol. 4 (1967), pp. 880–890. Y. M. J. Congar, *The Mystery of the Temple*, translated by R. F. Trevett, Westminster, Maryland 1962. B. Gärtner, *The Temple and the Community in Qumran and the New Testament*, Cambridge 1965. R. Pesch, *Naherwartungen. Tradition und Redaktion in Mk 13*, Düsseldorf 1968. N. Walter, *"Tempelzerstörung und synoptische Apokalypse"*, in *Zeitschrift für die neutestamentliche Wissenschaft*, Vol. 57 (1966), pp. 38–49.

[21] Exegesis ponders the question of whether or not this passage gives expression to the problem of Palestinian Christians of Jewish origin, who paid the temple tax upon coercion, although they no longer regarded themselves as obliged to pay it. In view of the appearance in the course of the narrative of the fabled theme of a treasure in the mouth of a fish (§6, 3e), the historicity of the account, at least in that episode, is questionable.

[22] According to the saying of the Lord in Matthew 5:17–19, even the least commandment of the Law must remain. The passages are probably the substance of a debate over the Law in the primitive congregation; and in the present instance it is a rigid Judaism that speaks. In Matthew 5:20 the counterposition is taken, to the effect that the righteousness of the Law is worthless. The Jewish Christian position is certainly taken again, when in Matthew 23:3 an adherence to all that Pharisaism teaches is demanded. As criticism it is stated that the Pharisees do not act in accord with their own teaching.

[23] G. Delling, Art. στοιχεῖον, in *Theol. Dict. N. T.*, Vol. 7 (1971), pp. 670–687.

[24] S. Schulz, Art. σκιά, in *Theol. Dict. N. T.*, Vol. 7 (1971), pp. 394–400.

[25] It may be indicative of a curious and not infrequently encountered misunderstanding. The rabbis calculated that there were 613 commands and prohibitions to which men were obligated. This is not to be regarded simply as the expression of a legalism with which no man could comply. In fact, 613 is a symbolic number, as the sum of the 350 days of the lunar year and of the 263 members of which the opinion of the times would have it the human body was composed. The number 613 signifies, therefore, that the whole man at every moment is under God's command, *i.e.*, at God's disposal.

[26] J. Bihler, *Die Stephanusgeschichte im Zusammenhang der Apostelgeschichte*, Munich 1963.

[27] If Paul employs the first person singular in this exposition, it is not on that account to be understood as autobiographical, as if he, as a Jew and a Pharisee, which he was (Phil. 3:5), had experienced the Law as an unbearable burden and

as unfulfillable in its demands. Paul speaks with the insight born of faith, a knowledge which discloses and continues to disclose the uselessness of works. The "I" of Rom. 7 describes the situation prior to the coming of the faith, therefore of the Jews and pagans, not of Christians. But the Christian is in danger of falling back into the situation of Rom. 7. Christian existence in the Spirit is expounded upon in Rom. 8.

[28] R. Bultmann, *"Der Begriff der Offenbarung im Neuen Testament"*, in *Glauben und Verstehen*, Vol. 3, Tübingen 1960, pp. 1–34. D. Lührmann, *Das Offenbarungsverständnis bei Paulus und in paulinischen Gemeinden*, Neukirchen-Vluyn 1965. H. Schulte, *Der Begriff der Offenbarung im Neuen Testament*, Munich 1949. For further bibliography see footnote no. 2 above.

[29] G. Bertram, Art. νήπιος, in the *Theol. Dict. N. T.*, Vol. 4 (1967), pp. 912–923. O. Michel, Art. ὁμολογέω, *ibid.*, Vol. 5 (1967), pp. 199–220. P. Hoffmann, *Studien zur Theologie der Logienquelle*, Münster 1962. D. Lührmann, *Die Redaktion der Logienquelle*, Neukirchen-Vluyn 1969. A. P. Polag, *Die Christologie der Logienquelle*, typed dissertation, Trier 1968.

[30] Besides the usual commentaries see also Rudolf Bultmann, Art. γινώσκω in *Theol. Dict. N. T.*, Vol. 1 (1964), pp. 689–719. E. Schweizer, Art. υἱός, *ibid.*, Vol. 8 (1972), p. 372f. The derivation of Matthew 11:27 from Hellenism took place decisively and produced long after-effects according to E. Norden, *Agnostos Theos*, 4th edition, Darmstadt 1956, pp. 277–308. J. Jeremias points out idiosyncracies of Semitic language in Matthew 11:27, in *Abba*, Gottingen 1966, pp. 47–54 [in John Bowden's English translation in *The Prayers of Jesus*, Naperville, Illinois 1967, see pp. 45–52]. Also of Jeremias, *Neutestamentliche Theologie*, Vol. 1, Gütersloh 1971, pp. 62–67 [translated by John Bowden, under title *New Testament Theology: The Proclamation of Jesus*, New York 1971].Jeremias explains Matthew 11:27 as an image in accord with the transfer of knowledge from a father to his son in the Jewish family. In regard to the Qumran texts see O. Betz, *"Die Geburt der Gemeinde durch die Lehrer"*, in *New Testament Studies,* Vol. 3 (1956/1957), pp. 314–326; also of Betz, *"Das Volk seiner Kraft"*, in Vol. 5 (1958/1959) of the same, pp. 67–75.

[31] In most of the pertinent passages of the New Testament, and especially in St. Paul, the status of the child is derogated. See our present *Theology of the New Testament*, Vol. 3, pp. 331–332.

[32] R. Baumann, *Mitte und Norm des Christlichen*, Münster 1968, pp. 171–279.

[33] Such texts are cited also in the rabbinic literature. It bespeaks the hope that God will himself instruct his people in the Torah. See Strack and Billerbeck, *Kommentar zum Neuen Testament*, Vol. 2 (1924), pp. 484f. (on John 6:45); Vol. 3 (1926), p. 634 (on 1 Thess. 4:9); Vol. 3, p. 704 (on Heb. 8:8–12), Vol. 4/1 (1928), p. 153f.

[34] K. H. Rengstorf, Art. διδάσκω, in the *Theol. Dict. N. T.*, Vol. 2 (1964), pp. 135–165; also of Rengstorf, Art. μαθητής, *ibid.*, Vol. 4 (1967), pp. 390–461. H. Krämer, R. Rendtorff, R. Meyer, G. Friedrich, Art. προφήτης, *ibid.*, Vol. 6 (1968), pp. 781–

861. E. Lohse, Art. ῥαββί, *ibid.*, Vol. 6 (1968), pp. 961–965. H. W. Bartsch, *Jesus, Prophet und Messias aus Galiläa*, Frankfurt 1970. M. Hengel, *Nachfolge und Charisma*, Berlin 1968. E. Jüngel, *"Jesu Wort und Jesus als Wort Gottes"*, in *Unterwegs zur Sache*, Munich 1972, pp. 126–144. R. Meyer, *Der Prophet aus Galiläa*, Leipzig 1940 (repr. Darmstadt 1970). F. Norman, *Christos Didaskalos*, Munster 1966. H. Schürmann, *Traditionsgeschichtliche Untersuchungen zu den synoptischen Evangelien*, Düsseldorf 1968.

[35] The following will serve as a general bibliography to the whole of part 2, §§ 5–11: W. G. Kümmel, *"Jesusforschung seit 1950"*, in *Theologische Rundschau*, new series Vol. 31 (1965/1966), pp. 15–46 and 289–315. H. R. Balz, *Methodische Probleme der neutestamentlichen Christologie*, Neukirchen-Vluyn 1967. Otto Betz, *Was wissen wir von Jesus?*, 2nd edition, Stuttgart 1967 [translated by Margaret Kohl under title *What Do We Know about Jesus?*, Philadelphia 1968]. J. Blank, *Paulus und Jesus*, Munich 1968. Günther Bornkamm, *Jesus von Nazareth*, Stuttgart 1965 [translated by Irene and Fraser McLuskey with James M. Robinson, *Jesus of Nazareth*, New York 1960]. H. Braun, *Jesus. Der Mann aus Nazareth und seine Zeit*, 2nd edition, Stuttgart 1970. R. Bultmann, *"Das Verhältnis der urchristlichen Christusbotschaft zum historischen Jesus"*, in *Exegetica*, Tübingen 1967, pp. 445–469. Lucien Cerfaux, *Christ in the Theology of St. Paul*, English translation by Geoffrey Webb and Adrian Walker, New York 1959. Oscar Cullmann, *Die Christologie des Neuen Testaments*, 4th edition, Tübingen 1966 [translated from 1957 edition by Shirley C. Guthrie and Charles A. M. Hall, under title *The Christology of the New Testament*, Philadelphia 1959]. C. H. Dodd, *The Founder of Christianity*, London 1971. C. Dautzenberg, *Christusdogma ohne Basis?*, Essen 1971. J. Ernst, *Anfänge der Christologie*, Stuttgart 1972. J. Feiner and M. Löhrer (editors), *"Das Christereignis"*, in *Mysterium salutis*, Vol. III, 1/2, Einsiedeln 1969f. E. Fuchs, *Jesus, Wort und Tat*, Tübingen 1971. R. H. Fuller, *The Foundations of New Testament Christology*, New York 1965. J. Gnilka, *Jesus Christus nach frühen Zeugnissen des Glaubens*, Munich 1970 and Leipzig 1972. E. Gütgemanns, *Der leidende Apostel und sein Herr, Studien zur paulinischen Christologie*, Göttingen 1966. Ferdinand Hahn, *Christologische Hoheitstitel. Ihre Geschichte im fruhen Christentum*, 3rd edition, Göttingen 1966 [translated by Harold Knight and George Ogg as *The Titles of Jesus in Christology: Their History in Early Christianity*, New York 1969]; also of Hahn, *"Methodenprobleme einer Christologie des Neuen Testaments"*, in *Verkündigung und Forschung*, Vol. 15 (1970), pp. 3–41. I. Hermann, *Kyrios und Pneuma. Studien zur Christologie der paulinischen Hauptbriefe*, Munich 1961. M. Horstmann, *Studien zur markinischen Christologie*, Münster 1969. E. Jüngel, *Paulus und Jesus*, 3rd edition, Tübingen 1967. H. W. Kuhn, *"Der irdische Jesus bei Paulus als traditionsgeschichtliches und theologisches Problem"*, in *Zeitschrift für Theologie und Kirche*, Vol. 67 (1970), pp. 295–320. E. Larsson, *Christus als Vorbild*, Uppsala 1962. X. Léon-Dufour, *Les Évangiles et l'histoire de Jésus*, Paris 1963 [translated and edited by John McHugh, under title *The Gospels and the Jesus of History*, New York 1967]. Willi Marxsen, *Anfangs-*

probleme der Christologie, Gütersloh 1967 [translated by Paul J. Achtemeier under title *The Beginnings of Christology: A Study of the Problems*, Philadelphia 1969]. J. P. Miranda, *Der Vater, der mich gesandt hat*, Bern and Frankfurt 1972. G. Muschalek, *"Gott in Jesus"*, in *Zeitschrift für katholische Theologie*, Vol. 94 (1972), pp. 145–157. K. Niederwimmer, *Jesus*, Göttingen 1968. Wolfhart Pannenberg, *Grundzüge der Christologie*, 2nd edition, Gütersloh 1966 [translated by Lewis L. Wilkins and Duane A. Priebe, *Jesus, God and Man*, Philadelphia 1968]. W. Pesch (editor), *Jesus in den Evangelien*, Stuttgart 1970. K. Rahner and W. Thüsing, *Christologie — systematisch und exegetisch*, Freiburg 1972. A. J. E. Rawlinson, *The New Testament Doctrine of the Christ*, 3rd edition, London 1949. H. Ridderbos, *Paul and Jesus*, Philadelphia 1958. H. Ristow and K. Matthiae (editors), *Der historische Jesus und der kerygmatische Christus*, 2nd edition, Berlin 1964. J. Roloff, *Das Kerygma und der irdische Jesus*, Göttingen 1970. L. Sabourin, *Les noms et titres de Jésus*, Paris 1963 [translated by Maurice Carroll, *The Names and Titles of Jesus*, New York 1967]. G. Schneider, *Die Frage nach Jesus*, Essen 1971. Piet Schoonenberg, *Hij is een God van mensen*, translated into English by Della Couling under title *The Christ: A Study of the God-man Relationship in the Whole of Creation and in Jesus Christ*, New York 1971. K. Schubert (editor), *Der historische Jesus und der Christus unseres Glaubens*, Vienna 1962; also edited by Schubert, *Vom Messias zum Christus*, Vienna 1964. H. Schürmann, *Das Geheimnis Jesu*, Leipzig 1972. E. Schweizer, *Jesus Christus im vielfältigen Zeugnis des Neuen Testaments*, 2nd edition, Hamburg 1970 [translated by David E. Green, under title *Jesus*, Richmond 1971]. E. Stauffer, *Jesus war ganz anders*, Hamburg 1967. V. Taylor, *The Names of Jesus*, London 1953; also of Taylor, *The Person of Christ in New Testament Teaching*, London 1958. H. Thüsing, *Per Christum in Deum*, 2nd edition, Münster 1969. W. Trilling, *Fragen zur Geschichtlichkeit Jesu*, 3rd edition, Düsseldorf 1969; also of Trilling, *Christusverkündigung in den synoptischen Evangelien*, Munich 1969. E. Trocmé, *Jésus de Nazareth vu par les témoins de sa vie*, Neuchâtel 1971. A. Vögtle, *"Exegetische Erwägungen über das Wissen und Selbstbewusstsein Jesu"*, in *Das Evangelium und die Evangelien*, Düsseldorf 1971, pp. 298–344. G. Voss, *Die Christologie der lukanischen Schriften in Grundzügen*, Paris 1965. B. Welte (editor), *Zur Frühgeschichte der Christologie*, Freiburg 1970. H. Weinacht, *Die Menschwerdung des Sohnes Gottes im Markusevangelium*, Tübingen 1972.

[36] A. Oepke, Art. ἐπιστάτης, in *Theol. Dict. N. T.*, Vol. 2 (1964), pp. 622–623. O. Glombitza, *"Die Titel Didaskalos und Epistates für Jesus bei Lukas"*, in *Zeitschrift für die neutestamentliche Wissenschaft*, Vol. 49 (1958), pp. 275–278.

[37] In the parallel passage in Luke 6:40 only the first half of the saying of Matthew 10:24 is reported. If the second half is an expansion, it bespeaks at the same time the further development of Christology from within the community.

[38] H. J. Schoeps, *"Die jüdischen Prophetenmorde"*, in *Aus frühchristlicher Zeit*, Tübingen 1950, pp. 126–143. O. H. Steck, *Israel und das gewaltsame Geschick der Propheten*, Neukirchen-Vluyn 1967.

[39] The expectation of a prophet, reaching its highest point of tension precisely in the New Testament era, was responsible for the appearance of numerous false prophets and messianic pretenders, of whom the New Testament has something to say (Acts 5:36f.; 21:38), and Flavius Josephus even more. See O. Michel, "*Spätjüdisches Prophetentum*", in the *Zeitschrift für die neutestamentliche Wissenschaft*, special number 21 (*Festschrift R. Bultmann*), 1954, pp. 60–66.

[40] R. Schnackenburg, "*Die Erwartung des Propheten nach dem Neuen Testament und den Qumrantexten*", in *Texte und Untersuchungen*, Vol. 73 (1959), pp. 622–639. H. M. Teeple, The *Mosaic Eschatological Prophet*, Philadelphia 1957.

[41] J. Jeremias, Art. Μωυσῆς, in *Theol. Dict. N. T.*, Vol. 4 (1967), pp. 848–873. Aage Bentzen, *Messias — Moses redivivus — Menschensohn*, Zürich 1948 [Bentzen himself translated his own work into English, under the title *King and Messiah*, London 1955; 2nd edition, ed. by G. W. Anderson, Oxford 1970].

[42] F. Normann, *Christos Didaskalos*, Münster 1966, pp. 137–177.

[43] Wolfhart Pannenberg, *Grundzüge der Christologie*, pp. 218–232 [pp. 212–225 in the English edition referred to in note 35 above].

[44] W. Foerster, Art. δαίμων, in *Theol. Dict. N. T.*, Vol. 2 (1964), pp. 1–20; also of Foerster, Art. διαβάλλω, *ibid.*, pp. 71–81. W. Grundmann, Art. δύναμαι, *ibid.*, pp. 284–317. G. Bertram, Art. θαυμάζω, in *Theol. Dict. N. T.*, Vol. 3 (1965), pp. 27–42. W. Beyer, Art. θεραπεία, *ibid.*, pp. 128–132. A. Oepke, Art. ἰάομαι, *ibid.*, pp. 194–215. W. Foerster and K. Schäferdieck, Art. σατανᾶς, in *Theol. Dict. N. T.*, Vol. 7 (1971), pp. 151–165. K. H. Rengstorf, Art. σημεῖον, *ibid.*, pp. 200–269; also of Rengstorf, Art. τέρας, in *Theol. Dict. N. T.*, Vol. 8 (1972), pp. 113–126. K. Thraede, Art. *Exorzismus*, in the *Reallexikon für Antike und Christentum*, Vol. 8 (1970), pp. 44–117. O. Böcher, *Christus Exorcista*, Stuttgart 1972. K. Bornkamm, *Wunder und Zeugnis*, Tübingen 1968. G. Delling, "*Das Verständnis des Wunders im Neuen Testament*," in *Studien zum Neuen Testament und zum hellenistischen Judentum*, Göttingen 1970, pp. 146–159. P. Fiebig, *Jüdische Wundergeschichten des neutestamentlichen Zeitalters*, Tübingen 1911. Reginald Horace Fuller, *Interpreting the Miracles*, Philadelphia 1963. R. M. Grant, *Miracle and Natural Law in Graeco-Roman and Early Christian Thought*, Amsterdam 1952. R. and M. Hengel, "*Die Heilungen Jesu und das medizinische Denken*", in *Medicus Viator (Festschrift R. Siebeck)*, Tübingen and Stuttgart 1959, pp. 331–361. R. Herzog, *Die Wunderheilungen von Epidauros*, (*Philologus*, Suppl. 22,3), Leipzig 1931. K. Kertelge, *Die Wunder Jesu nach dem Markusevangelium*, Munich 1970. H. van der Loos, *The Miracles of Jesus*, Leiden 1965. Louis Monden, *Signs and Wonders*, New York 1966 [this is an English translation of Monden's own French version, *Le miracle: signe de salut*, of his original Flemish *Het Wonder*]. F. Mussner, *Die Wunder Jesu*, Munich 1970 (and with it, the *Theolog. Revue*, Vol. 68 [1972], pp. 177–185). R. Pesch, *Jesu ureigene Taten?*, Freiburg 1970. G. Schille, *Die urchristliche Wundertradition*, Berlin 1966. O. Weinreich, *Antike Heilungswunder*, Giessen 1909 (repr. Berlin 1969).

[45] This is the viewpoint also of the Hellenistic Judaism that was contemporaneous

with the New Testament, as it is seen in the writings of Philo and Josephus. See G. Delling, *"Wunder — Allegorie — Mythus bei Philon von Alexandrien"*, in *Studien zum Neuen Testament und zum hellenistischen Judentum*, Göttingen 1970, pp. 72–129; and in the same work, *"Josephus und das Wunderbare"*, pp. 130–145.

[46] Besides the usual commentaries see also E. Helzle, *Der Schluss des Markusevangeliums Mk 16,9–20 und das Freerlogion Mk 16,14 W, ihre Tendenzen und ihr gegenseitiges Verhältnis*, typed dissertation, Tübingen 1959.

[47] Besides the articles in the *Theol. Dict. N. T.* and in the *Reallexikon für Antike und Christentum* (see above, note 44), see also O. Böcher, *Dämonenfurcht und Dämonenabwehr*, Stuttgart 1970. Strack and Billerbeck, *Kommentar zum Neuen Testament*, Vol. 4 (1928), pp. 501–535, on ancient Jewish demonology.

[48] Synopses of the stylized themes of exorcisms of demons and miraculous cures can be found in Rudolf Bultmann, *Die Geschichte der synoptischen Tradition*, 7th edition, Göttingen 1967, pp. 223–260 [in English, *The History of the Synoptic Tradition*, translated by John Marsh from the 2nd German edition (1931), New York 1968, pp. 209–244]; in M. Dibelius, *Die Formgeschichte des Evangeliums*, 6th edition, Tübingen 1971, pp. 78–88; 169–172 [in English, *From Tradition to Gospel*, translated by Bertram Lee Woolf in collaboration with Dibelius himself, from the 2nd German edition; New York 1965, pp. 70–103; 164–177]; in L. J. McGinley, *Form-Criticism of the Synoptic Healing Narratives*, Woodstock 1944; also in H. van der Loos, *The Miracles of Jesus*, Leiden 1965, pp. 117–138; and O. Weinreich, *Antike Heilungswunder*, Giessen 1909 (repr. Berlin 1969), pp. 195–201.

[49] Strack and Billerbeck, *op. cit.*, Vol. 4 (1928), pp. 745–763.

[50] The remarks concerning Jesus' cures of the blind, the lame, *etc.*, (not only in Matthew 8:17, but also such passages as Matthew 15:30-31; 21:14; Luke 14:13), are to be understood in relation to the Old Testament instructions like that of Lev. 21:16–23, whereby those in any way blemished or crippled were excluded from priestly service; and perhaps also against the background of 1 QSa 2:3–9, specifying that the sick, the crippled, the lame, the blind, the deaf, the mute, or those marked in the flesh by any blemish, or an old man who trembles, none of these may enter into the communion (of divine service). "For the angels of holiness are in the community." Rabbinic determinations of exclusion have a similar ring to them. But according to the gospel, even all of these outcasts are called.

[51] R. Pesch, in *Jesu ureigene Taten?*, Freiburg 1970, p. 135, comes to the conclusion: "The question of whether Jesus cured lepers was not able to be answered positively on the basis of the extant traditions. The historian does not find himself in a position to offer even such a qualified answer as 'probably'." This does no violence to the sense of the accounts.

[52] J. Becker, *"Wunder und Christologie"*, in New Testament Studies, Vol. 16 (1969/1970), pp. 130–148. S. Hofbeck, Σημεῖον, Münsterschwarzach 1966. A. Smitmans, *Das Weinwunder von Kana*, Tübingen 1966.

[53] R. Pesch, *Der Besessene von Gerasa*, Stuttgart 1972. Pesch suggests that the

story of the swine and their downfall was added only later to the narrative of the healing of the possessed man, but at a time still prior to the writing of Mark's Gospel. See also H. Schürmann, *Das Lukasevangelium*, Vol. 1, Freiburg 1969, pp. 479–487.

[54] Josephus, *Jewish Antiquities* 8,46–49. Philostratus, *Apollonius* 4,20.

[55] Old Testament stories in 3 Kings 17:17–24 and 4 Kings 4:8–37. For rabbinic narratives, see P. Fiebig, *Jüdische Wundergeschichten*, p. 36f.; Strack and Billerbeck, *op. cit.*, Vol. 1 (1922), p. 580. For Graeco-Roman accounts: Empedocles (in H. Diels and W. Kranz, *Fragmente der Vorsokratiker*, 7th edition, Berlin 1954, p. 353f.; and Diogenes Laertius 8,67); Philostratus, *Apollonius* 4,45; Lucian, *Philopseudes* 26; Apuleius, *Florida* 19.

[56] Especially noteworthy among the commentaries is H. Schürmann, *Das Lukasevangelium*, Vol. 1, Freiburg 1969, pp. 308–405; and A. Harbarth, *Die Erweckung des Jünglings von Nain Lk 7,11–17*, typed dissertation, Freiburg 1969.

[57] Coming upon a sick man lying on a stretcher, Asclepius heals him (inscription at Epidaurus; see R. Herzog, *Die Wunderheilungen von Epidauros*, Leipzig 1931 [Philologus, Suppl. 22,3], p. 18f.). Apollonius meets the funeral procession of a dead bride at the gates of Rome (Philostratus, *Apollonius* 4,45). The physician Asclepiades meets a funeral procession, stays the bier, and calls the dead person back to life (Apuleius, *Florida* 19). Lucian (*Philopseudes* 11) ridicules not only belief in wonders but makes a joke of the fact that so often they take place at a chance encounter on the road.

[58] Günther Bornkamm, *"Die Sturmstillung in Matthäusevangelium"*, in *Überlieferung und Auslegung im Matthäusevangelium*, 4th edition, Neukirchen 1965, pp. 48–53. G. Schille, *"Die Seesturmerzählung Mk 4,35–41 als Beispiel neutestamentlicher Aktualisierung"*, in *Zeitschrift für die neutestamentliche Wissenschaft*, Vol. 56 (1965), pp. 30–40.

[59] Rabbis calm storms at sea (P. Fiebig, *Jüdische Wundergeschichten*, Tübingen 1911, pp. 33 and 61; Strack and Billerbeck, *op. cit.*, Vol. 1 [1922], pp. 452, 489f.). The Dioscuri, Castor and Pollux, assist sailors in distress (*Homeric Hymns* 33,6–17; Theocritus, *The Fishermen* 1,17–22; H. Jaisle, *Die Dioskuren als Retter zur See*, dissertation, Tübingen 1907). Asclepius and Serapis rescue seafarers (Publius Aelius Aristides 2,337 and 2,362; see also O. Weinreich, *op. cit.*, p. 14). The sailor Apion writes a letter home, in which he gives thanks to Serapis for his being rescued from peril at sea (P. Deissmann, *Licht vom Osten*, 4th edition, Tübingen 1923, pp.145–150). At sea, Aeneas prays for the rescuing hand of the divinity (Vergil, *Aeneid* 6,370). The divine emperor turns back storms (Calpurnius Siculus, *Bucolica* 4,97f.).

[60] R. Pesch, *Der reiche Fischfang (Lk 5,1–11 / Jo 21,1–14)*, Düsseldorf 1969. H. Schürmann, *Das Lukasevangelium*, Vol. 1, Freiburg 1969, pp. 264–274.

[61] A. Heising, *Die Botschaft der Brotvermehrung*, Stuttgart 1966.

[62] Strack and Billerbeck, *Kommentar zum Neuen Testament*, Vol. 1 (1922), pp. 614–675. R. Meyer, *"Der Ring des Polykrates, Mt 17,27 und die rabbinishe*

Überlieferung", in *Orientalische Literaturzeitung*, Vol. 40 (1937), pp. 665–670. H. Schwarzbaum, *Studies in Jewish and World Folklore*, Berlin 1928, pp. 262, 270, 273, 477.

[63] Rudolf Bultmann, "*Zur Frage des Wunders*", in *Glauben und Verstehen*, Vol 1, Tübingen 1933, pp. 214–228 [in translation by Louise Pettibone Smith, "*The Question of Wonder*", in *Faith and Understanding*, New York 1969, pp. 247–261].

[64] W. Michaelis, Art. πάσχω, in *Theol. Dict. N. T.*, Vol. 5 (1967), pp. 904–939. J. Schneider, Art. σταυρός, *ibid.*, Vol. 7 (1971), pp. 572–584. H. Riesenfeld, Art. ὑπέρ, *ibid.*, Vol. 8 (1972), pp. 507–516. A. Dauer, *Die Passionsgeschichte im Johannesevangelium*, Munich 1972. G. Delling, *Der Kreuzestod Jesu in der urchristlichen Verkündigung*, Göttingen 1972. H. Kessler, *Die theologische Bedeutung des Todes Jesu*, Düsseldorf 1970. B. Klappert (editor), *Diskussion um Kreuz und Auferstehung*, Wuppertal 1967. E. Linnemann, *Studien zur Passionsgeschichte*, Göttingen 1970. E. Lohse, *Die Geschichte des Leidens und Sterbens Jesu Christi*, Gütersloh 1964 [translated by M. O. Dietrich under title *History of the Suffering and Death of Jesus Christ*, Philadelphia 1967]. F. J. Ortkemper, *Das Kreuz in der Verkündigung des Apostels Paulus*, Stuttgart 1967. W. Popkes, *Christus traditus*, Zürich 1967. K. H. Schelkle, *Die Passion Jesu in der Verkündigung des Neuen Testaments*, Heidelberg 1949. L. Schenke, *Studien zur Passionsgeschichte des Markus (Mk 14,1–42)*, Würzburg and Stuttgart 1971. G. Schneider, *Verleugnung, Verspottung und Verhör Jesu nach Lk 22,54–71*, Munich 1969. J. Schreiber, *Die Markuspassion*, Hamburg 1969. F. Schütz, *Der leidende Christus*, Stuttgart 1969. M. Seils, "*Zur Frage nach der Heilsbedeutung des Kreuzestodes Jesu*", in *Theol. Literaturzeitg.*, Vol. 90 (1965), pp. 881–894. A. Vanhoye, *De narrationibus passionis Christi in evangeliis synopticis*, Rome 1970. P. Viering (editor), *Das Kreuz Christi als Grund des Heils*, Gütersloh 1967; also edited by Viering, *Zur Bedeutung des Todes Jesu, Exegetische Beiträge*, Gütersloh 1967.

[65] E. Benz, *Der gekreuzigte Gerechte bei Plato, im Neuen Testament und in der alten Kirche*, Wiesbaden 1950; also of Benz, "*Christus und Sokrates in der alten Kirche*", in the *Zeitschrift für die neutestamentliche Wissenschaft*, Vol. 43 (1950/1951), pp. 195–224.

[66] W. Thüsing, *Die Erhöhung und Verherrlichung Jesu im Johannesevangelium*, 2nd edition, Münster 1970.

[67] W. Zimmerli and J. Jeremias, Art. παῖς θεοῦ, in the *Theol. Dict. N. T.*, Vol. 5 (1967), pp. 654–717. E. Fascher, *Jesaia 53 in christlicher und jüdischer Sicht*, Berlin 1958. J. Jeremias, "παῖς (θεοῦ) *im Neuen Testament*", in *Abba*, Göttingen 1966, pp. 191–216. Otto Kaiser, *Der königliche Knecht*, 2nd edition, Göttingen 1962. E. Lohmeyer, *Gottesknecht und Davidssohn*, 2nd edition, Göttingen 1953. E. Lohse, *Märtyrer und Gottesknecht*, 2nd edition, Göttingen 1963.

[68] H. Schürmann, *Jesu Abschiedsrede Lk 22,21–38*, Münster 1957, pp. 126–128.

[69] The more Pilate is exonerated, so much more are the Jews blamed. Does antisemitism have its beginnings in the New Testament? In the prophecies of the Passion it is the Jews who bear the principal culpability (Mark 8:31). It is "the

Jews" who crucified Jesus; the active role of the Romans is scarcely mentioned (Acts 2:23; 3:14f.; 5:30; 1 Thess. 2:15). It is "the Jews" who call down the blood of Jesus upon themselves (Matthew 27:54). According to P. Winter, *On the Trial of Jesus*, Berlin 1961, on the contrary, the Romans arrested, condemned, and executed Jesus as a political agitator. The high priest may have yielded to Roman demands. Jesus appears as the primordial figure of the Jew, persecuted in the world and condemned to unspeakable suffering.

[70] The prayer for his enemies (*i.e.*, the Jews) in Luke 23:34a is lacking in the more ancient manuscripts, even in P 75, the oldest presently known. The majority of the Greek manuscripts, of the ancient translations, and of the Church Fathers read the verse. Was the verse added in order to demonstrate Jesus' love of enemies, or was it omitted? The only conceivable reason for omitting it would seem to be that hatred for the Jews would not want Jesus' prayer for the Jews to remain. [*Translator's note*: Deliberate omission of a verse seems of its very nature much more difficult to admit than the addition of a verse. But besides the reason which Schelkle suggests as a possible motive for addition, *i.e.*, to demonstrate Jesus' love of enemies, it could also have been added in an antisemitic spirit, to impress again upon the reader that it was "the Jews" who were the enemy rather than the Romans. On the other hand, if the addition were intended to point specifically at either Jew or Roman, one would expect it to name the group; and the passage does not. I frankly doubt that antisemitism enters into the question at all in this particular passage, whether the passage be regarded as addition or as omission.]

[71] Luke 22:43f. is found only in a portion of the manuscripts. Were the verses added later as a note of comfort, or were they deleted lest Christ, in being strengthened by the angel, might seem to be ranked beneath the angels? According to Col. 1:16 and Heb. 1:4-7, Christ, as Creator, is exalted even above the angels.

[72] Besides the usual commentaries, which will offer further examples, see also: C. Schneider, Art. καταπέτασμα, in the *Theol. Dict. N. T.*, Vol. 3 (1965), pp. 628–630. Günther Bornkamm, Art. σείω, *ibid.*, Vol. 7 (1971), pp. 196–200. H. Conzelmann, Art. σκότος, *ibid.*, pp. 423–445. Ch. Maurer, Art. σχίζω, *ibid.*, pp. 959–964.

[73] Rudolf Bultmann, *"Bekenntnis- und Liedfragmente im 1. Petrusbriefe"*, in *Exegetica*, Tübingen 1967, pp. 285–297. R. Deichgräber, *Gotteshymnus und Christushymnus in der frühen Christenheit*, Göttingen 1967, pp. 140–143 and 169–173. C. H. Hunzinger, *"Zur Struktur des Christushymnen in Philipper 2 und 1 Petrus 3"*, in the Festschrift for Joachim Jeremias edited by Ch. Burchard *et al.*, *Der Ruf Jesu und die Antwort der Gemeinde*, Göttingen 1970, pp. 142–156. K. H. Schelkle, *Die Petrusbriefe. Der Judasbrief*, 3rd edition, Freiburg 1970, pp. 110–112.

[74] Explanations offered by the study of the history of religion, explanations which suggest that Paul may be describing the death of Christ and baptism as sacrament of that death by analogy to a mystery cult, in which the mystes participates in the death and resurrection of the divinity, or which place Paul's descriptions in the category of the Gnostic myth according to which redeemer and redeemed are paired in one body, upon critical examination are shown to be precarious. See

C. Colpe, *Die religionsgeschichtliche Schule. Darstellung und Kritik ihres Bildes vom gnostischen Erlösermythus*, Göttingen 1961. G. Wagner, *Das religionsgeschichtliche Problem von Römer 6,1–11*, Zürich 1962.

[76] M. Hengel, "Christologie und neutestamentliche Chronologie", in the Festschrift for Oscar Cullmann edited by H. Baltensweiler and B. Reicke, *Neues Testament und Geschichte*, Zürich and Tübingen 1972, pp. 43–67.

[76] F. Büchsel, Art. καταλλάσσω, in *Theol. Dict. N. T.*, Vol. 1 (1964), pp. 254–259. O. Procksch and F. Büchsel, Art. λύω, *ibid.*, Vol. 4 (1967), pp. 328–356. C. Andresen, Art. *Erlösung*, in the *Reallexikon für Antike und Christentum*, Vol. 7 (1969), pp. 54–219. C. Colpe, "Traditionsüberschreitende Argumentationen zu Aussagen Jesu über sich selbst", in the Festschrift for K. G. Kuhn edited by G. Jeremias *et al.*, *Tradition und Glaube*, Göttingen 1971, pp. 230–245. A. Holl, *Jesus in schlechter Gesellschaft*, Stuttgart 1971. J. Jeremias, *Der Opfertod Jesu Christi*, 2nd edition, Stuttgart 1966. H. Leroy, *Vergebung und Gemeinde nach dem Zeugnis der Evangelien*, typed inaugural dissertation, Tübingen 1972. E. Lohse, *Märtyrer und Gottesknecht*, 2nd edition, Göttingen 1963. J. Moltmann, *Der gekreuzigte Gott*, Munich 1972. H. Patsch, *Abendmahl und historischer Jesus*, Stuttgart 1972. J. Roloff, "Anfänge der soteriologischen Deutung des Todes Jesu", in *New Testament Studies*, Vol. 19 (1972/1973), pp. 38–64. H. Thyen, *Studien zur Sündenvergebung im Neuen Testament und seinen alttestamentlichen und jüdischen Voraussetzungen*, Göttingen 1970.

[77] The theme of the forgiveness of sin is regarded by some exegetes as a later addition to the story of the cure. This is the judgment, for example, of I. Maisch, *Die Heilung des Gelähmten*, Stuttgart 1971: The forgiving of sins in Mark 2:5b-12 is a secondary addition to an original story of a cure. The community, practicing forgiveness, bases its action on the life of Jesus. It does this in remembrance of the love of Jesus for sinners.

[78] The pericope is parallel with Mark 14:3-9, where only the anointing is recounted, and not the forgiving of sins. Accordingly, some exegetes hold that the latter theme is of secondary origin in Luke 7:36-50.

[79] Mark 10:45 is accepted as an original saying of Jesus by F. Büchsel, Art. λύτρον, in *Theol. Dict. N. T.*, Vol. 4 (1967), pp. 340–349; by C. Colpe, Art. ὁ υἱὸς τοῦ ἀνθρώπου, *ibid.*, Vol. 8 (1972), p. 455; by O. Cullmann, *Die Christologie des Neuen Testaments*, 4th edition, Tübingen 1969, p. 64; by J. Jeremias, "Das Lösegeld für viele (Mk 10,45)", in *Abba*, Göttingen 1966, pp. 216–229; and by E. Lohse, *Märtyrer und Gottesknecht*, Göttingen 1955, pp. 116–122. W. Popkes, *Christus traditus*, Zürich 1967, attributes the saying to the semitic speaking Jewish Christianity, holding that in view of its explicit soteriology and its use of Is. 53 it can hardly be attributed to Jesus himself. K. Wengst, *Christologische Formeln und Lieder des Urchristentums*, Gütersloh 1972, pp. 35–77, refers to the fact that even Hellenism knows and glories in the laying down of one's life for persons and ideals. He is of a mind that the formula in Mark 10:45 received its whole shape in the Hellenistic-Jewish Christian Community.

[80] Luke 22:27 employs terminology of the Hellenistic community and milieu. ἡγούμενος (Acts 15:22), νεώτερος (Acts 5:6,10), διάκονος (Acts 6:1), εὐεργέτης is Hellenistic nomenclature. To this extent, in any case, Luke 22:27 is secondary in comparison to Mark 10:45.

[81] J. Betz, *Die Eucharistie in der Zeit der griechischen Väter,* Vol. 2/1, Freiburg 1961, pp. 1–129. J. Jeremias, *Die Abendmahlsworte Jesu,* 4th edition, Göttingen 1967 [the 3rd edition was translated by Norman Perrin under the title *The Eucharistic Words of Jesus,* New York 1966].

[82] It is said of the martyrs in *4 Macc.* 17:22, "They have become, as it were, a substitute (ἀντίψυχον) for the sins of the people. By the blood of those pious people and the atoning sacrifice of their death, God's providence has saved Israel, until now sorely oppressed." See also the *Testaments of the Twelve Patriarchs: Benjamin* 3:8 (Christian interpolation?). In *4 Macc.* 6:29 the priest Eliezer prays: "Make my blood a purificatory sacrifice (καθάρσιον) for them, and take my life as substitute for their life (ἀντίψυχον αὐτῶν λαβὲ τὴν ἐμὴν ψυχήν)." These texts belong to the New Testament era. The conceptual and verbal correspondence with Mark 10:45 is evident.

[83] On the prepositions see the articles in the *Theol. Dict. N. T.*: F. Büchsel on ἀντί, Vol. 1 (1964), pp. 372–373; A. Oepke on διά, Vol. 2 (1964), pp. 65–70; H. Riesenfeld on περί, Vol. 6 (1968), pp. 53–56; and Riesenfeld again on ὑπέρ, Vol. 8 (1972), pp. 507–516.

[84] F. Büchsel and J. Herrman, Art. ἵλεως, in the *Theol. Dict. N. T.*, Vol. 3 (1965), pp. 300–323. E. Käsemann, "*Zum Verständnis von Röm 3,24–26*", in *Exegetische Versuche und Besinnungen*, Vol. 1. Göttingen 1960, pp. 96–100. W. G. Kümmel, "*πάρεσις und ἔνδειξις. Ein Beitrag zum Verständnis der paulinischen Rechtfertigungslehre*", in *Heilsgeschehen und Geschichte*, Marburg 1965, pp. 260–270. A. Pluta, *Gottes Bundestreue. Ein Schlüsselbegriff zu Röm 3,25a,* Stuttgart 1969.

[85] Johannes Behm, Art. θύω, in *Theol. Dict. N. T.*, Vol. 3 (1965), pp. 180–190. J. Jeremias, *Der Opfertod Jesu Christi,* 5th edition, Stuttgart 1965. O. Michel, *Der Brief an die Hebräer,* 13th edition, Göttingen 1968, see index therein under θυσία.

[86] Johannes Behm, Art. αἷμα, in the *Theol. Dict. N. T.*, Vol. 1 (1964), pp. 172–177. C. Hunzinger, Art. ῥαντίσω, *ibid.,* Vol. 6 (1968), pp. 976–984. J. H. Waszink, Art. *Blut,* in the *Reallexikon für Antike und Christentum*, Vol. 2, (1954), pp. 459–473. Ceslaus Spicq, *L'Épître aux Hébreux*, Vol. 2, 3rd edition, Paris 1953, pp. 271–285. See also the other standard commentaries on the Epistle to the Hebrews.

[87] A. Oepke, Art. ἀνίστημι, in the *Theol. Dict. N. T.*, Vol. 1 (1964), pp. 368–372; also of Oepke, Art. ἐγείρω, *ibid.,* Vol. 2 (1964), pp. 333–339. F. X. Durwell, *Die Auferstehung Jesu als Heilsmysterium,* Salzburg 1958. G. Friedrich, "*Die Auferstehung Jesu, eine Tat Gottes oder ein Interpretament der Junger?*" in *Kerygma und Dogma,* Vol. 17 (1971), pp. 154–177. R. H. Fuller, *The Foundation of the Resurrection Narratives,* New York 1971. A. Geense, *Auferstehung und Offenbarung.* Göttingen 1971. H. Grass, *Ostergeschehen und Osterberichte,* 4th edition, Göt-

tingen 1970, G. Kegel, *Auferstehung Jesu — Auferstehung der Toten*, Gütersloh 1970. G. Koch, *Die Auferstehung Jesu Christi*, 2nd edition, Tübingen 1965. J. Kremer, *Das älteste Zeugnis von der Auferstehung Jesu Christi (1 Kor 15,1–11)*, 2nd edition, Stuttgart 1967; also of Kremer, *Die Osterbotschaft der vier Evangelien*, Stuttgart 1967. K. Lehmann, *Auferweckt am dritten Tag nach der Schrift*, Freiburg 1968. Willi Marxsen, *Die Auferstehung Jesu von Nazareth*, Gütersloh 1968 [translated by Margaret Kohl under the title *The Resurrection of Jesus of Nazareth*, Philadelphia 1970]. Also of Marxsen, in collaboration with U. Wilckens, G. Delling, and H. G. Geyer, *Die Bedeutung der Auferstehungsbotschaft für den Glauben an Jesus Christus*, Gütersloh 1966 [English edition under editorship of C. D. Moule, translated by Dorothea M. Barton and R. A. Wilson, under title *The Significance of the Message of the Resurrection for Faith in Jesus Christ*, London 1968]. Franz Mussner, *Die Auferstehung Jesu*, Munich 1969. K. H. Rengstorf, *Die Auferstehung Jesu*, 5th edition, Witten 1967. E. Ruckstuhl and J. Pfammatter, *Die Auferstehung Jesu Christi*, Lucerne 1968. H. Schlier, *Über die Auferstehung Jesu Christi*, Einsiedeln 1968, J. Schmitt, *Jésu ressuscité dans la prédication apostolique*, Paris 1949. Ph. Seidensticker, *Die Auferstehung Jesu in der Botschaft der Evangelisten*, Stuttgart 1967; also of Seidensticker, *Zeitgenössische Texte zur Osterbotschaft der Evangelien*, Stuttgart 1967. Eduard Schweizer, *Erniedrigung und Erhöhung bei Jesus und seinen Nachfolgern*, 2nd edition, Zürich 1962 [first edition translated into English by A. R. Allenson, under title *Lordship and Discipleship*, Naperville 1960]. P. de Surgy et al., *La Résurrection du Christ et l'exégèse moderne*, Paris 1969.

[88] Among the copious literary productions special reference may be made to H. Conzelmann, *Der erste Brief an die Korinther*, Göttingen 1969, pp. 291–311; E. Güttgemanns, *Der leidende Apostel und sein Herr*, Göttingen 1966, pp. 53–94; J. Kremer, *Das älteste Zeugnis von der Auferstehung Christi*, Stuttgart 1966, pp. 14–24; K. Lehmann, *Auferweckt am dritten Tag nach der Schrift*, Freiburg 1968, pp. 17–157.

[89] Lexicography shows that the terms and concepts ἁμαρτία, ὤφθη, ἐγήγερται, κατὰ τὰς γραφάς, οἱ δώδεκα are un-Pauline. The Greek style can be recognized as that of the Septuagint, and it points, therefore, to a Greek-speaking community, *i.e.*, probably to a Hellenistic-Jewish community.

[90] Willi Marxsen attributes the message to "the experiencing of the vision". The witnesses saw (again) the crucified (1 Cor. 9:1). "The living presence of the crucified Jesus" means the resurrection. "Awakened by the experiencing of the vision, the cause of Jesus continues on" (Marxsen, *"Die Auferstehung Jesu als historisches und als theologisches Problem"*, in Marxsen et al., *Die Bedeutung der Auferstehungsbotschaft für den Glauben an Jesus Christus*, pp. 29, 37f.). The post-paschal faith has no other content than that of the pre-paschal. This content is: "The encounter with God in this life, liberation unto love, self-abnegation for the sake of neighbor" (W. Marxsen, *Die Auferstehung Jesu von Nazareth*, pp. 128–150). The question remains: What happened in the experiencing of the vision? Was some-

thing seen, or was it a hallucination? Paul "saw Jesus our Lord" (1 Cor. 9:1); therefore, the Crucified as the Exalted. To that extent, at least, the post-paschal faith has a content other than that of the pre-paschal. The broad and profound New Testament interpretation, therefore the understanding of the vision interpreted here, is without meaning for Marxsen. The New Testament attestation to the resurrection proclaims Jesus as the Resurrected, and because he is the Resurrected, his preaching and his cause is proclaimed all the more (Rom. 1:3f.; 10:9; 1 Cor. 15:3f.).

[91] K. Schubert, *"Das Problem der Auferstehungshoffnung in den Qumrantexten und in der frührabbinischen Literatur"*, in *Wiener Zeitschrift für die Kunde des Morgenlandes*, Vol. 56 (1960), pp. 154–157; also of Schubert, *"Der Entwicklung der Auferstehungslehre von der nachexilischen Zeit bis zur frührabbinischen Zeit"*, in *Biblische Zeitschrift*, new series, Vol. 6 (1962), pp. 177–214.

[92] The passage can hardly say only that God caused Jesus to "come forth" or "come forward", so that only his mission in general were meant.

[93] W. Grundmann, Art. δέξιος, in the *Theol. Dict. N. T.*, Vol. 2 (1964), pp. 37–40. G. Bertram, Art. ὕψος, *ibid.*, Vol. 8 (1972), pp. 602–620. Eduard Schweizer, *Erniedrigung und Erhöhung bei Jesus und seinen Nachfolgern*, 2nd edition Zürich 1962 [English translation from first edition under title *Lordship and Discipleship*, Naperville 1960]. W. Thüsing, *Erhöhungsvorstellung und Parusieerwartung in der ältesten nachösterlichen Christologie*, Stuttgart 1969.

[94] Here the realm of the flesh is not understood as sinful and estranged from God, as it is so often elsewhere in Paul, but only as finite and ephemeral. Here the flesh is the earthly sphere of the entwining kinships of generations (as in Rom. 9:3 and in the Old Testament, starting at Gen. 2:23). See E. Schweizer, *"Röm 1,3f und der Gegensatz von Fleisch und Geist"*, in *Neotestamentica*, Zürich 1963, pp. 180–189. Also: M. E. Boismard, *"Constitué fils de Dieu (Rom 1,4)"*, in *Revue Biblique*, Vol. 60 (1953), pp. 5–17; A. Sand, *Der Begriff "Fleisch" in den paulinischen Hauptbriefen*, Regensburg 1967, pp. 160–163, 291–305; H. Schlier, *"Zu Röm 1,3f"*, in H. Baltensweiler and B. Reicke (editors), *Neues Testament und Geschichte (Festschrift Oskar Cullmun)*, Zürich and Tübingen 1972, pp. 207–218.

[95] The Christian exegesis of Psalm 110 continues the Jewish, which already interpreted the royal psalm as messianic (Strack and Billerbeck, *Kommentar zum Neuen Testament*, Vol. 4 [1928], pp. 452–465).

[96] W. Thüsing, *Die Erhöhung und Verherrlichung Jesu im Johannesevangelium*, 2nd edition, Münster 1970.

[97] Besides the usual commentaries, see G. W. Tromph, "The First Resurrection Appearance and the Ending of Mark's Gospel", in *New Testament Studies*, Vol. 18 (1971/1972), pp. 308–330.

[98] B. Steinseifer, *"Der Ort der Erscheinungen des Auferstandenen"*, in *Zeitschrift für die neutestamentliche Wissenschaft*, Vol. 62 (1971), pp. 232–265.

[99] E. L. Bode, *The First Easter Morning: The Gospel Accounts of the Women's Visit to the Tomb of Jesus*, Rome 1970. H. von Campenhausen, *"Der Ablauf der*

Osterereignisse und das leere Grab", in *Tradition und Leben*, Tübingen 1960, pp. 48–113 [there is an English translation done by A. V. Littledale, under title *Tradition and Life in the Church*, Philadelphia 1968]. W. Nauck, "*Die Bedeutung des leeren Grabes für den Glauben an den Auferstandenen"*, in *Zeitschrift für die neutestamentliche Wissenschaft*, Vol. 47 (1956), pp. 243–267. Wolfhart Pannenberg, *Grundzüge der Christologie*, 2nd edition, Gütersloh 1966, pp. 97–99 [p. 100f. in the English edition, *Jesus: God and Man*, Philadelphia 1968, translated by Lewis L. Wilkins and Duane A. Priebe]. L. Schenke, *Auferstehungsverkündigung und leeres Grab*, Stuttgart 1968.

[100] J. Broer, *Die Urgemeinde und das Grab Jesu*, Munich 1972, p. 78, comes to the conclusion: "Matthew himself invented the story of the watchmen at the tomb, apparently in order to refute the explanation of the empty tomb then current among the Jews as impossible and as a base calumny. The story of the watchers at the grave, therefore, is comparatively recent."

[101] H. Traub, Art. οὐρανός, in the *Theol. Dict. N. T.*, Vol. 5 (1967), pp. 497–543. R. Balz, Art. τεσσαράκοντα, *ibid.*, Vol. 8 (1972), pp. 135–139. G. Lohfink, *Die Himmelfahrt Jesu*, Munich 1971.

[102] G. Delling, Art. τρεῖς, in *Theol. Dict. N. T.*, Vol. 8 (1972), pp. 216–225. With a detailed demonstration, K. Lehmann (*Auferweckt am dritten Tag nach der Schrift*, Freiburg 1968, pp. 159–290) shows that it was a conviction of faith, according to the contemporary Targumic and Midrashic literature, that God would not leave the righteous man in distress for more than three days. This was established from the Old Testament, referring to such examples as Gen. 22:4; Exod. 19:16; Hosea 6:2; Jonah 2:1. It is from such a background as this that the "according to the Scriptures" of 1 Cor. 15:4 results. The third day, accordingly, is not a calendar computation at all, but signifies the day of salvation.

[103] Joachim Jeremias, Art. ᾅδης, in the *Theol. Dict. N. T.*, Vol. 1 (1964), pp. 146–149; and Art. παράδεισος, *ibid.*, Vol. 5 (1967), pp. 765–773. Also of J. Jeremias, "*Zwischen Karfreitag und Ostern"*, in *Abba*, Göttingen 1966, pp. 323–331. W. Bieder, *Die Vorstellung von der Höllenfahrt Jesu Christi*, Zürich 1949.

[104] In regard to this passage, some exegetes are of a mind that the Epistle to the Ephesians may not be speaking of the descent of Christ into the underworld or Hades, but that the descending may mean his coming down to the earth in the incarnation, while the ascending refers to his ascension into heaven, in which ascent Christ made captives of the spirits ruling in the air.

[105] See the usual commentaries in the pertinent place (among others, K. H. Schelkle, *Die Petrusbriefe. Der Judasbrief*, 3rd edition, Freiburg 1970); also B. Reicke, *The Disobedient Spirits and the Christian Baptism*, Copenhagen 1946; and W. J. Dalton, *Christ's Proclamation to the Spirits*, Rome 1965.

[106] The literature mentioned in note 35 above will serve well for the present chapter §10. Additional bibliographical material will be noted at pertinent places throughout the chapter, in notes 106 to 143. On the texts from the Pauline Epistles, besides the usual commentaries, see also A. van Dülmen, *Die Theologie des Gesetzes*

bei Paulus, Stuttgart 1968; and A. Sand, *Der Begriff "Fleisch" in den paulinischen Hauptbriefen*, Regensburg 1967.

[107] The history of the interpretation of the passage is presented by E. de Roover, "*La maternité virginale de Marie dans l'interprétation de Gal 4,4*", in *Analecta Biblica*, Vol. 18 (Rome 1963), pp. 17–37.

[108] In biblical linguistic usage "born of woman" is a way of saying "a human being." Thus, in *4 Esdras* 7:46, we read: "Who of those born of woman has never broken your covenant?"; or in 1 QH 13:14, "He that is born of woman, what is he among your works?" *Cf.* 1 QH 18:12-16,23; Job 11:2,12; 14:1 in Sept.: "For mortal man, born of woman, ..." Matthew 11:11 speaks likewise of men as those "born of woman".

[109] G. Schneider, in his "*Die Davidssohnfrage (Mk 12,35-37)*", in *Biblica*, Vol. 53. (1972), pp. 65–90, distinguishes between the pre-Markan tradition of the pericope and the Markan redaction, and comes to the conclusion that the debate can hardly go back to Jesus, who surely did not lay claim to the current messianic title. It represents a debate in the community over the question of Jesus' Davidic sonship. In Mark's Gospel it is not denied, but is nevertheless put into a relative perspective. An uncompromisingly genealogical understanding of the title "Son of David" is rejected. Mark acknowledges the Davidic sonship of Jesus. This, however, is surpassed by his enthronement as Son of God after the resurrection.

[110] ὁμοίωμα signifies not the likeness of similarity, but the likeness of the isomorphic image. Paul knows how to use the term even otherwise than in describing the incarnation; for example, in Rom. 1:23 and Phil. 2:7. It is, therefore, a part of Paul's considered terminology. See J. Schneider, Art. ὁμοίωμα, in the *Theol. Dict. N. T.*, Vol. 5 (1967), pp. 191–198.

[111] Worthy of special note among the rich literature on the New Testament hymns are: M. Reese, "*Formeln und Lieder im Neuen Testament*", in *Verkündigung und Forschung*, Vol. 15 (1970), pp. 75–95; of the commentaries on Phil. 2:5-11, above all, J. Gnilka, *Der Philipperbrief*, Freiburg 1968, pp. 108–147. Also M. Black, *The New Testament Christological Hymns*, Cambridge 1971. R. Deichgräber, *Gotteshymnus und Christushymnus in der frühen Christenheit*, Göttingen 1967. E. Lohmeyer, *Kyrios Jesus. Eine Untersuchung zu Phil 2,5-11*, 2nd edition, Darmstadt 1961. R. P. Martin, *Carmen Christi Phil 2,5-11 in Recent Interpretation and in the Setting of Early Christian Worship*, Cambridge 1967. J. T. Sanders, *The New Testament Christological Hymns*, Cambridge 1971. G. Schille, *Frühchristliche Hymnen*, Berlin 1967. K. Wengst, *Christologische Formeln und Lieder des Urchristentums*, Berlin 1971; also of Wengst, "*Der Apostel und die Tradition. Zur theologisches Bedeutung urchristlicher Formeln bei Paulus*", in *Zeitschrift für Theologie und Kirche*, Vol. 69 (1972), pp. 145–162.

[112] Words that can be pointed out as un-Pauline are μορφή in verses 6 and 7; ἁρπαγμὸς in verse 6; σχήματι in verse 7; and ὑπερύψωσεν in verse 9.

[113] It is generally surmised that among the Pauline additions are the phrases θανάτου δὲ σταυροῦ in verse 8, and εἰς δόξαν θεοῦ πατρὸς in verse 11.

[114] In profane Greek literature μορφὴ means first of all "form of appearance, shape, image"; in the Hellenistic period its meaning changes to "divine substance and power"; see J. Behm, Art. μορφή, in the *Theol. Dict. N. T.*, Vol. 4 (1967), pp. 742–759; and E. Käsemann, *"Kritische Analyse von Phil 2,5-11"*, in *Exegetische Versuche und Besinnungen*, Vol. 1, Göttingen 1960, pp. 51–95.

[115] In the Septuagint the term ὑπερυψοῦν always designates the action of Yahweh; thus in Ps. 96(97):9. See G. Bertram, Art. ὕψος, in the *Theol. Dict. N. T.*, Vol. 8 (1972), pp. 602–620.

[116] On the hymn in 1 Tim. 3:16 see W. Stenger, *"Der Christushymnus in 1 Tim 3,16"*, in *Trierer theol. Zeitschr.*, Vol. 78 (1969), pp. 33–48, with the literature on the New Testament hymns mentioned therein in note 5. Among the commentaries see especially M. Dibelius and H. Conzelmann, *Die Pastoralbriefe*, 3rd edition, Tübingen 1965, pp. 48–51; G. Holtz, *Die Pastoralbriefe*, Berlin 1965, pp. 89–96; Ceslaus Spicq, *Les Épîtres Pastorales*, Vol. 1, 4th edition, Paris 1969, pp. 468–475 and 482–492.

[117] Günther Bornkamm, Art. μυστήριον, in the *Theol. Dict. N.T.*, Vol. 4 (1967), pp. 802–828. On the concept of "piety" see our present *Theology of the New Testament*, Vol. 3, §18, pp. 224–226.

[118] Following E. Norden, *Die Geburt des Kindes*, 3rd edition, Darmstadt 1958, pp. 116–128, J. Jeremias too, in his *Die Briefe an Timotheus und Titus*, 3rd edition, Göttingen 1963, pp. 21–24, wanted to rediscover in 1 Tim. 3:16 the ritual of an oriental accession to the throne. The action takes place in three scenes: exaltation of the new ruler, his presentation before the people, and his coronation or actual accession to the throne. At most a comparison can be drawn between such a ritual and the lines of the hymn; but the ritual can hardly have been the model for the hymn.

[119] See R. Bultmann and D. Lührmann, Art. φαίνω, in the *Theol. Dict. N. T.*, Vol. 9 (1974), pp. 1–10. F. Pfister, Art. *Epiphanie*, in the Pauly-Wissowa *Realencyklopädie der klassischen Altertumswissenschaft*, Suppl. Vol. 4, 1924, pp. 277–323. H. Frank, *"Zur Geschichte von Weihnachten und Epiphanie"*, in the *Jahrbuch für Liturgiewissenschaft*, Vol. 12 (1932), pp. 145–155; Vol. 13 (1933), pp. 1–38. D. Lührmann, *"Epiphaneia"*, in the Festschrift for K. G. Kuhn, *Tradition und Glaube*, edited by G. Jeremias *et al.*, Göttingen 1971, pp. 185–199. E. Pax, *Epiphaneia*, Munich 1955; and also of Pax, the article *Epiphaneia*, in the *Reallexikon für Antike und Christentum*, Vol. 5 (1962), pp. 832–909.

[120] F. Hiller von Gaertringen, *Inscriften von Priene*, No. 105, Göttingen 1906. W. Dittenberger, *Orientis Graeci inscriptiones selectae*, Vol. 2, No. 458, Leipzig 1905 (reprinted at Hildesheim 1960). E. Bloch, *Das Prinzip Hoffnung*, Vol. 2, Frankfort a. M. 1959, p. 1483f. A. Deissmann, *Licht vom Osten*, 4th edition, Tübingen 1923, pp. 313–317. W. Foerster, *Neutestamentliche Zeitgeschichte*, Vol. 2, Hamburg 1956, p. 31f. F. C. Grant, *Ancient Roman Religion*, New York 1957, pp. 173–174. M. P. Nilson, *Geschichte der griechischen Religion*, Vol. 2, Munich 1961, p. 388f.

[121] On the Synoptic infancy narratives, among the commentaries see especially H. Schürmann, *Das Lukasevangelium*, Vol. 1, Freiburg 1969, pp. 18–145. Also J. Kosnetter, *"Der Geschichtswert der Kindheitsgeschichte Jesu", in Festschrift F. Loidl*, Vol. 3, Vienna 1971, pp. 73–93. E. Nellessen, *Das Kind und sine Mutter*, Stuttgart 1969. H. Raisänen, *Die Mutter Jesu im Neuen Testament*, Helsinki 1969. K. H. Schelkle, *"Die Kindheitsgeschichte Jesu"*, in *Wort und Schrift*, Düsseldorf 1966, pp. 59–75. A Vögtle, *Messias und Gottessohn. Herkunft und Sinn der matthäischen Geburts- und Kindheitsgeschichte*, Düsseldorf 1971; *"Offene Fragen zur lukanischen Geburts- und Kindheitsgeschichte"*, in *Das Evangelium und die Evangelien*, Düsseldorf 1971, pp. 43–56; and also of Vögtle, in the same work, *"Die Genealogie Mt 1,2-16 und die Matthäische Kindheitsgeschichte"*, pp. 57–102.

[122] According to Vergil, *Aeneid* 2,694–698, Aeneas was guided on the journey from Troy to Latium by a star. The commentary of Servius remarks in respect to this, or so Varro says, that the star was constantly visible and only ceased to shine when Aeneas had reached Latium, by which fact Aeneas understood that he had at last arrived at his goal. According to St. Clement of Alexandria, *Stromateis* 1,24,163 Thrasybulus, with those whom he was leading, was guided by a fire which went before them to their goal, near Munychia, where the altar of Phosphorus (*i.e.*, the light-bringer) now stands ("now" referring, of course, to Clement's own time). See also note 124 below.

[123] J. Jeremias, Art. Μωυσῆς, in the *Theol. Dict. N. T.*, Vol. 4 (1967), pp. 848–873. R. Bloch, *"Die Gestalt des Moses in der rabbinischen Tradition"*, in *Moses in Schrift und Überlieferung*, (trans.) Düsseldorf 1963, pp. 164–171.

[124] The Haggadoth tell of miraculous apparitions of light at the birth of Abraham, of Isaac, and of Moses; see Strack and Billerbeck, *op. cit.*, Vol. 1 (1922), pp. 76–78. According to the commentary of Servius on the *Aeneid* 10,127, a comet appeared when Augustus acquired dominion. There it portended that great joy would be the lot of every people. F. Ferrari d'Occhieppo, *Der Stern der Weisen — Geschichte oder Legende?*, Vienna 1969.

[125] E. Lohse, Art. υἱὸς Δαυίδ, in the *Theol. Dict. N. T.*, Vol. 8 (1972), pp. 478–488. Ch. Burger, *Jesus als Davidssohn*, Göttingen 1970. J. Fitzmyer, "The Son of David Tradition and Matthew 22,41–46 and Parallels", in *Concilium*, Vol. 20, New York and Glen Rock 1966, pp. 75–87. A Suhl, *"Der Davidssohn im Matthäus-Evangelium"*, in *Zeitschrift für die neutestamentliche Wissenschaft*, Vol. 59 (1968), pp. 57–81.

[126] H. L. Strack and P. Billerbeck, *Kommentar zum Neuen Testament*, Vol. 1 (1922), p. 35.

[127] On the theology of the virgin birth, see G. Delling, Art. παρθένος, in the *Theol. Dict. N. T.*, Vol. 5 (1967), pp. 826–837. Th. Booslooper, *The Virgin Birth*, London 1962. H. J. Brosch and J. Hasenfuss (editors), *Jungfrauengeburt gestern und heute*, Essen 1969. H. von Campenhausen, *Die Jungfrauengeburt in der Theologie der alten Kirche*, Heidelberg 1962. M. Dibelius, *"Jungfrauensohn und Krippenkind"*, in *Botschaft und Geschichte*, Vol. 1, Tübingen 1953, pp. 1–18. K. S. Frank

et al., Zum Thema Jungfrauengeburt, Stuttgart 1970. H. Gese, *"Natus ex virgine"*, in H. Wolf (editor), *Probleme biblischer Theologie (Festschrift G. von Rad)*, Munich 1971, pp. 73–89. J. Graystone, *Virgin of all Virgins*, Rome 1968.

[128] E. Brunner-Traut, *"Die Geburtsgeschichte der Evangelien im Lichte ägyptologischer Forschungen"*, in *Zeitschrift für Religions- und Geistesgeschichte*, Vol. 12 (1960), pp. 97–111; also of Brunner-Traut, *"Pharao und Jesus als Söhne Gottes"*, in *Antaios*, Vol. 2 (1960), pp. 266–284. H. Brunner, *Die Geburt des Gottkönigs*, Wiesbaden 1964. And with the last, see also J. Hasenfuss, *"Die Jungfrauengeburt in der Religionsgeschichte"*, pp. 11–23 in the work edited by Brosch and Hasenfuss, noted above in footnote no. 127.

[129] The points of similarity and the differences, as discovered from the study of the history of religions, are discussed, for example, by G. Delling, Art. παρθένος, in *Theol. Dict. N. T.*, Vol. 5 (1967), pp. 826–837; by E. Sjöberg and E. Schweizer, Art. πνεῦμα, *ibid.*, Vol. 6 (1968), pp. 375–455; E. Schweizer, Art. υἱός, *ibid.*, Vol. 8 (1972), p. 376f.

[130] Today Is. 7:14 is universally translated: "Behold, the young woman will conceive and bear a son, and she will call his name Emmanuel." In regard to its meaning see P. F. Ellis, *The Men and the Message of the Old Testament*, 3rd edition 1976, pp. 306ff.; M. McNamara, M.S.C., *Isaiah 1–39* in the *Old Testament Reading Guide* series, no. 16, pp. 44–47.

[131] On the other hand, it is questionable whether the Qumran community expected a divine begetting of the Messiah (furthermore, be it noted, a divine begetting and a virgin birth are not in themselves synonymous notions). O. Michel and O. Betz, in the chapter *"Von Gott gezeugt"*, in *Judentum — Christentum — Kirche (Festschrift J. Jeremias)*, edited by W. Eltester, Berlin 1960, pp. 3–23, find this expressly declared in 1 QSa 2:11f., where they read and translate: "God will beget the Messiah." This doctrine might be discovered in the declarations on the divine sonship of the Messiah in Ps. 2:7 and 2 Sam. 7:14, as quoted in Qumran. The text of 1 QSa 2:11f., however, is uncertain. E. Lohse, in *Die Texte aus Qumran, hebräisch und deutsch*, Darmstadt 1964, reads and translates: "When (God) causes the Messiah to be born among them."

[132] Even in the articles *"Ein alttestamentliche Ausführungsformel im Matthäusevangelium"*, in the *Bibl. Zeitschr.*, new series, Vol. 10 (1966), pp. 220–245; Vol. 11 (1967), pp. 79–97; and *"Der Gottessohn im matthäischen Evangelienprolog"*, in *Biblica*, Vol. 48 (1967), pp. 395–420. R. Pesch states that the virgin birth is a theologoumenon; Matthew 1 and 2 make use of the Moses Haggadah; the pericope of Matthew 1:18-25 is a free creation of the evangelist.

[133] In my work entitled *Die Mutter des Erlösers*, 3rd edition, Düsseldorf 1967, I have attempted to explain the biblical and ecclesiastical tradition of the Virgin birth not only as a meaningful symbolism and legend, but as a meaningful event.

[134] H. Gollinger, *Das "Grosse Zeichen" von Apokalypse 12*, Würzburg and Stuttgart 1971. A Kassing, *Die Kirche und Maria. Ihr Verhältnis im 12. Kapitel der Apokalypse*, Düsseldorf 1958. P. Prigent, *Apokalypse 12. Histoire de l'exégèse*,

Tübingen 1959. A. Vögtle, "*Mythos und Botschaft in Apokalypse 12*", in G. Jeremias, *et al.*, editors, *Tradition und Glaube (Festschrift K. G. Kuhn)*, Göttingen 1971, pp. 395–415.

[135] H. Braun, *Qumran und das Neue Testament*, Vol. 1, Tübingen 1966, pp. 313–318. A. Dupont-Sommer, "*La Mère du Messie et la mère de l'Aspic dans un hymne de Qumrân*", in *Revue de l'histoire des religions*, Vol. 47 (1955), pp. 174–188.

[136] A. Debrunner, H. Kleinknecht, O. Proksch, G. Kittel, G. Quell, and G. Schrenk, Art. λέγω, in *Theol. Dict. N. T.*, Vol. 4 (1967), pp. 69–192. Among the commentaries, see especially Rudolf Bultmann, *Das Evangelium des Johannes*, 19th edition, Göttingen 1968, pp. 1–57. R. Schnackenburg, *Das Johannesevangelium*, Vol. 1, 2nd edition, Freiburg 1967, pp. 197–269. A. Feuillet, *Le prologue du quatrième évangile*, Brussels 1968.

[137] Such speculations are attested in the *Corpus hermeticum*, in the *Odes of Solomon*, in the Mandaean writings, in the Coptic Gnostic writings from Nag Hammadi, as well as in the anti-Gnostic writings of the Church Fathers. The written sources are nearly all of later date than the New Testament; consequently, one must reckon with the possibility of New Testament influences. Nevertheless, the traditions are older. See R. Bergmeier, "*Quellen vorchristlicher Gnosis*", in G. Jeremias *et al.*, (editors), *Tradition und Glaube (Festschrift K. G. Kuhn)*, Göttingen 1971, pp. 200–220. W. Foerster has a collection and interpretation of the sources in 2 volumes, *Die Gnosis*, Zürich 1969.

[138] U. Wilckens and G. Fohrer, Art. σοφία, in *Theol. Dict. N. T.*, Vol. 7 (1971), pp. 465–528. P. Benoit, "*Preexistence et Incarnation*", in *Revue Biblique*, Vol. 77 (1970), pp. 5–29. F. Christ, *Jesus Sophia*, Zürich 1970. A. Feuillet, "*Jésus et la sagesse divine d'après les évangiles synoptiques*", in the *Revue Biblique*, Vol. 62 (1955), pp. 161–196; also of Feuillet, *Le Christ Sagesse de Dieu dans les Épîtres pauliniennes*, Paris 1966. K. H. Schelkle, "*Die Schöpfung in Christus*", in G. Bornkamm and K. Rahner (editors), *Die Zeit Jesu (Festschrift H. Schlier)*, Freiburg 1970, pp. 208–217. R. Schnackenburg, *Das Johannesevangelium*, Vol. 1, 2nd edition, Freiburg 1967, pp. 290–302. E. Schweizer, "*Die Herkunft der Präexistenzvorstellung bei Paulus*", in *Neotestamentica*, Zürich 1963, pp. 105–109.

[139] H. L. Strack and P. Billerbeck, *Kommentar zum Neuen Testament*, Vol. 1 (1922), p. 974; Vol. 2 (1924), pp. 334–335 and 353–357.

[140] Robert McL. Wilson, *The Gospel of Philip*, New York 1962, pp. 116–117. J. E. Ménard, *L'Évangile selon Philippe*, Paris 1964, pp. 33–34 and 84.

[141] D. Wiederkehr, "*Entwurf einer systematischen Christologie*", in J. Feiner and M. Löhrer (editors), *Mysterium salutis*, Vol. 3/1, Einsiedeln 1970, pp. 477–648, especially 534–540.

[142] More of Schoonenberg in *Die Antwort der Theologen*, edited by Karl Rahner *et al.*, Düsseldorf 1968, pp. 48–55. K. Reinhardt, "*Die menschliche Transzendence Jesu Christi*", in *Trierer theol. Zeitschr.*, Vol. 80 (1971), pp. 273–289. A decree of the Sacred Congregation for the Teaching of the Faith, dated February 21, 1972,

"in relation to some errors of most recent times", seems to have been called forth by the above-mentioned attempts at an explanation of Christological dogma.

¹⁴³ See Wolfhart Pannenberg, *Grundzüge der Christologie*, 2nd edition, Gütersloh 1966, pp. 150–158.

¹⁴⁴ The literature mentioned in note 35 will serve also for chapter § 11. Additional bibliographical material will be noted at pertinent places throughout the chapter, in notes 145–175.

¹⁴⁵ Other titles of majesty have already been discussed. For Prophet, see § 5; Son of David, § 10,3bb.

¹⁴⁶ For presentations treating directly of the numerous titles of majesty and dignity which are accorded Jesus, see O. Cullmann, *Die Christologie des Neuen Testaments*, 4th ed., Tübingen 1966 [translated into English by Shirley C. Guthrie and Charles A. M. Hall under title *The Christology of the New Testament*, Philadelphia 1959]. F. Hahn, *Christologische Hoheitstitel*, 3rd edition, Göttingen 1966 [translated by Harold Knight and George Ogg under title *The Titles of Jesus in Christology*, New York 1969]. L. Sabourin, *Les noms et titres de Jésus*, Bruges [Brugge] 1963 [translated by Maurice Carroll, *The Names and Titles of Jesus*, New York 1967]. V. Taylor, *The Names of Jesus*, 2nd edition, London 1962. See also Ph. Vielhauer, "*Zur Frage der christologischen Hoheitstitel*", in *Theol. Literaturzeitg.*, Vol. 90 (1965), pp. 570–587. K. Berger, "*Zum traditionsgeschichtlichen Hintergrund christologischer Hoheitstitel*", in *New Testament Studies*, Vol. 17 (1970/1971), pp. 391–425.

¹⁴⁷ H. Kleinknecht, G. von Rad, G. Kuhn, and K. L. Schmidt, Art. βασιλεύς, in the *Theol. Dict. N. T.*, Vol. 1 (1964), pp. 564–593. W. Grundmann, F. Hesse, M. de Jonge, A. S. van der Woude, Art. χρίω, in the *Theol. Dict. N. T.*, Vol. 9 (1974), pp. 493–580. O. Eissfeldt and J. Kollwitz, Art. *Christus*, in the *Reallexikon für Antike und Christentum*, Vol. 2 (1954), pp. 1250–1262. J. Coppens, *Le messianisme royal*, Paris 1968. E. Dinkler, "*Petrusbekenntnis und Satanswort. Das Problem der Messianität Jesu*", in *Signum crucis*, Tübingen 1967, pp. 283–312. Werner R. Kramer, *Christos Kyrios Gottessohn*, Zürich 1963 [English translation by Brian Hardy, under title *Christ, Lord, Son of God*, London 1966]. G. Minette de Tillesse, *Le secret messianique dans l'Évangile du Marc*, Paris 1968. A. Vögtle, "*Messiasbekenntnis und Petrusverheissung*", in *Das Evangelium und die Evangelien*, Düsseldorf 1971, pp. 137–170.

¹⁴⁸ Jews might have called the Messiah "King of Israel" (as in fact the priests do, in Mark 15:32), but hardly "King of the Jews." The title is undoubtedly a Roman formulation, and therefore a political interpretation of the messianic claim.

¹⁴⁹ H. Seesemann, Art. πεῖρα, in *Theol. Dict. N. T.*, Vol. 6 (1968), pp. 23–36. Jacques Dupont, *Les tentations de Jésus au désert*, Paris 1968. E. Fascher, *Jesus und der Satan*, Halle 1949. K. P. Köppen, *Die Auslegung der Versuchungsgeschichte unter besonderer Berücksichtigung der alten Kirche*, Tübingen 1961.

¹⁵⁰ C. Colpe, Art. ὁ υἱὸς τοῦ ἀνθρώπου, in *Theol. Dict. N. T.*, Vol. 8 (1972), pp. 400–477. F. H. Borsch, *The Christian and Gnostic Son of Man*, London 1970. P. Hoff-

mann, *Studien zur Theologie der Logienquelle*, Münster 1972, pp. 81–233. R. Leivestad, *"Der apokalyptische Menschensohn — ein theologisches Phantom"*, in the *Annual of the Swedish Theological Institute*, Vol. 6 (1967/1968), pp. 49–105; also of Leivestad, "Exit of the Apocalyptic Son of Man", in *New Testament Studies*, Vol. 18 (1971/1972), pp. 243–287. G. Lindeskog, *"Das Rätsel des Menschensohnes"*. in *Studia theologica*, Vol. 22 (1968), pp. 149–175. R. Maddox, *"Methodenfragen zu der Menschensohnforschung"*, in *Evang. Theologie*, Vol. 32 (1972), pp. 143–160. U. B. Müller, *Messias und Menschensohn in jüdischen Apokalypsen und in der Offenbarung des Johannes*, Gütersloh 1972. F. Neugebauer, *Jesus der Menschensohn*, Stuttgart 1972. E. Schweizer, *"Der Menschensohn"*, in *Neotestamentica*, Zürich 1963, pp. 58–84; also of Schweizer and in the same work, "The Son of Man Again", pp. 85–92. E. Sjöberg, *Der verborgene Menschensohn in den Evangelien*, Lund 1955. Heinz Eduard Tödt, *Der Menschensohn in der synoptischen Überlieferung*, 2nd edition, Gütersloh 1963 [translated into English by Dorothea M. Barton, *The Son of Man in the Synoptic Tradition*, Philadelphia 1965].

[151] In the present context we are obliged to ignore the difficult question of the possible extra-biblical background of the idea and title Son of Man.

[152] At most, the term is used in its simpler sense when in the plural. Thus, in Mark 3:18, "Everything will be forgiven the sons of men."

[153] Comparison of passages leads some critics to the conclusion that the term Son of Man has been inserted into sayings of Jesus handed down by tradition. The evangelists tend to convert first person declarations of Jesus into third person Son-of-Man declarations. Compare Matthew 13:37; 16:13,28; 19:28; Luke 6:22; 12:8; and 22:48 with their parallels. John uses the title thirteen times.

[154] The "sign of the Son of Man", mentioned only in Matthew 24:30, is not explained. Is the sign the Son of Man himself, or is it a sign that refers to him? See K. H. Rengstorf, Art. σημεῖον, in *Theol. Dict. N. T.*, Vol. 7 (1971), pp. 236–238.

[155] A. Vörtle, *"Das christologische und eschatologische Anliegen Mt 28,18-20"*, in *Das Evangelium und die Evangelien*, Düsseldorf 1971, pp. 253–272.

[156] This is the explanation defended by a number of authors, among them Rudolf Bultmann, *Theologie des Neuen Testaments*, 6th edition, Tübingen 1968, pp. 35–39; also F. Hahn and E. Tödt in their works mentioned above in notes 35 and 150. Others oppose this view and deny that Jesus spoke at all of the Son of Man; thus E. Käsemann, *"Das Problem des historischen Jesus"*, in *Exegetische Versuche und Besinnungen*, Vol. 1, 4th edition, Göttingen 1965, pp. 187–214; similarly in Ph. Vielhauer, *"Gottesreich und Menschensohn in der Verkündigung Jesu"*, in *Aufsätze zum Neuen Testament*, Munich 1965, pp. 55–91; and the same author in the same work, *"Jesus und der Menschensohn"*, pp. 92–140.

[157] Thus with E. Schweizer (note 150 above), who supposes that Jesus follows the linguistic usage of Ezechiel and applies it to his own ministry; similarly in R. Leivestad (his work mentioned above in footnote 150). J. Jeremias explains in *Neutestamentiche Theologie*, Vol. 1, pp. 245–263, that in speaking of the Son of

Man in the third person Jesus is distinguishing between the present and the future. He is not yet the Son of Man, but he will be exalted and become the Son of Man. [158] J. Blank, *Krisis*, Freiburg 1964, pp. 161–164. R. Schnackenburg *"Der Menschensohn im Johannesevangelium"*, in *New Testament Studies*, Vol. 11 (1964/1965), pp. 123–137. S. Schulz, *Untersuchungen zur Menschensohnchristologie im Johannesevangelium*, Göttingen 1957.

[159] P. Wülfing von Martitz, G. Fohrer, E. Schweizer, E. Lohse, W. Schneemelcher, Art. υἱός, in *Theol. Dict. N. T.*, Vol. 8 (1972), pp. 334–397. J. Bieneck, *"Sohn Gottes"*, in *Zeitschrift für die neutestamentliche Wissenschaft*, Vol. 47 (1956), pp. 113–133. B. M. F. van Iersel, *Der "Sohn" in den synoptischen Jesusworten*, Leiden 1961. Th. de Kruijf, *Der Sohn des lebendigen Gottes*, Rome 1962. E. Lövestam, *Son and Saviour*, Lund 1961. C. Maurer, *"Knecht Gottes und Sohn Gottes im Passionsbericht des Markus"*, in *Zeitschrift für Theologie und Kirche*, Vol. 50 (1953), pp. 1–53. P. Pokorny, *Der Gottessohn*, Zürich 1972. E. Schweizer, *"Sohn Gottes"*, in *Beiträge zur Theologie des Neuen Testaments*, Zürich 1970, pp. 83–111.

[160] The parable itself presupposes the then current relationships in Galilee, in the management of a large agricultural property (M. Hengel, *"Das Gleichnis von den Weingärtnern Mk 12,1–12 im Lichte der Zenonpapyri und der rabbinischen Gleichnisse"*, in *Zeitschrift für die neutestamentliche Wissenschaft*, Vol. 59 [1968], pp. 1–39). On the other hand, the parable clearly refers to the Passion (Mark 12:7f.) and exaltation (Mark 12:10f.) of Jesus (in the parallel accounts in Matthew 21:38f. and Luke 20:14f. there is an even closer correspondence to the events themselves). The mission to the Gentiles is already in progress (Mark 12:9). Thus there are themes in the parable which seem to be introduced or interpreted allegorically after the events had already taken place. Some exegetes are of a mind that the whole parable is the creation of the community (see W. Kümmel, *"Das Gleichnis von den bösen Weingärtnern"*, in *Heilsgeschehen und Geschichte*, Marburg 1965, pp. 207–217). The parable is found in a simpler form in the *Gospel of Thomas* (65), which says: "Then the lord sent his son." Now and then it is conjectured that this comes closer to the original composition. Did the community take the statement about a son and give it a Christological intensification? (Thus J. Jeremias, *Die Gleichnisse Jesu*, 7th edition, Göttingen 1965, pp. 67–75). This would be a most unusual circumstance, however, since elsewhere the *Gospel of Thomas* presupposes the existence of the Synoptics, and not infrequently gives them a Gnostic interpretation (W. Schrage, *Das Verhältnis des Thomasevangeliums zur synoptischen Tradition und zu den koptischen Evangelienübersetzungen*, Berlin 1964, pp. 137–145).

[161] If the reasons given above seem sufficient to conclude to the antiquity of the saying, nevertheless, R. Pesch (*Naherwartungen*, Düsseldorf 1968, pp. 190–195), is of a mind that a more ancient saying, which might possibly go back to Jesus, would have read, "No one knows that day, not even the angels in heaven, but God only." Mark would be responsible for the addition, "not even the Son". Lack of knowledge about the time of the day of judgment, and the postponement of it,

might well have been the cause of considerable unrest in the community; and Mark might have been seeking to quiet that unrest by indicating that Jesus himself did not know when that day would come.

[162] Among the commentaries see especially H. Schürmann, *Das Lukasevangelium*, Vol. 1, Freiburg 1969, pp. 188–197 and 552–567. See also A. Oepke, Art. βάπτω, in *Theol. Dict. N. T.*, Vol. 1 (1964), pp. 529–546. J. Behm, Art. μεταμορφόω, in *Theol. Dict. N. T.*, Vol. 4 (1967), pp. 755–759. H. Baltensweiler, *Die Verklärung Christi*, Zürich 1959. A. Feuillet, *"Le baptême de Jésus"*, in *Revue Biblique*, Vol. 71 (1964), pp. 321–352. F. Lentzen-Deis, *Die Taufe Jesu nach den Synoptikern*, Frankfurt 1970. H. Riesenfeld, *Jésus transfiguré*, Lund 1947. E. Schlink, *Die Lehre von der Taufe*, Kassel 1969.

[163] W. Foerster and G. Fohrer, Art. σῴζω, in *Theol. Dict. N. T.*, Vol. 7 (1971), pp. 965–1024. F. Dornseif, Art. σωτήρ, in A. Pauly and G. Wissowa, *Realencyklopädie der klassischen Altertumswissenschaft*, II/5 (1927), pp. 1211–1221. L. Cerfaux and J. Tondriau, *Le culte des souverains*, Tournai 1957. H. Linssen, θεὸς σωτήρ, dissertation, Bonn 1929. S. Lyonnet, *De vocabulario redemptionis*, Rome 1960.

[164] G. Quell and W. Foerster, Art. κύριος, in *Theol. Dict. N. T.*, Vol. 3 (1965), pp. 1039–1098. K. G. Kuhn, Art. μαραναθά, in *Theol. Dict. N. T.*, Vol. 4 (1967), pp. 466–472. W. Bousset, *Kyrios Christos*, Göttingen 1913 (5th edition, 1965). L. Cerfaux, *"Le titre Kyrios et la dignité royale de Jésus"*, in *Recucil Lucien Cerfaux*, Vol. 1, Gembloux 1934, pp. 3–63. I. Hermann, *Kyrios und Pneuma*, Munich 1961. W. Kramer, *Christos Kyrios Gottessohn*, Zürich 1963. E. Lohmeyer, *Kyrios Jesus. Eine Untersuchung zu Phil 2,5-11*, 2nd edition, Darmstadt 1961. E. Schweizer, *"Der Glaube an Jesus den 'Herrn' in seiner Entwicklung von den ersten Nachfolgern bis zur hellenistischen Gemeinde"*, in *Evang. Theologie*, Vol. 17 (1957), pp. 7–21. S. Schulz, *"Maranatha und Kyrios Jesus"*, in *Zeitschrift für die neutestamentliche Wissenschaft*, Vol. 53 (1962), pp. 125–144.

[165] W. Bousset maintained in his book *Kyrios Christos* (see preceding note), a work which had a significant influence on later authors, that it was on this level in Hellenistic Christianity that the Christ cult arose, and that it was in that same Hellenistic Christianity that Christ was first worshipped as Lord. Modern exegesis, however, accords a validity also to its Old Testament roots.

[166] Of the passages in which the term *Kyrios* is employed in the New Testament, the majority are found in the Lukan (210 times) and Pauline (275 times) writings, which is to say, in the writings which are related in a special way to the Greek world. It is clear that in the Greek world the term was received with a special understanding and interest.

[167] H. Schlier, Art. κεφαλή, in *Theol. Dict. N. T.*, Vol. 3 (1965), pp. 673–682. P. Benoit, *"Leib, Haupt und Pleroma in den Gefangenschaftsbriefen"*, in *Exegese und Theologie*, (translation) Düsseldorf 1965, pp. 246–279. H. J. Gabathuler, *Jesus Christus — Haupt der Kirche, Haupt der Welt*, Zürich 1965.

[168] Otto Kern, *Orphicorum fragmenta*, Berlin 1922, frag. no. 168, pp. 201–207.

[169] G. Kittel, G. von Rad, and H. Kleinknecht, Art. εἰκών, in *Theol. Dict. N. T.*, Vol. 2 (1964), pp. 381–397. W. Eltester, *Eikon im Neuen Testament*, Berlin 1958. H. Wildberger, *"Das Abbild Gottes"*, in *Theol. Zeitschr.*, Vol. 21 (1965), pp. 245–259, 481–501.

[170] There is a problem in exegesis, as to how Rom. 9:5 is to be understood. Is the doxology, "Who is present over all, God, blessed unto ages", to be referred to Christ, or does it stand alone? This latter seems to be the more probable. However, see H. Thüsing, *Per Christum in Deum*, 2nd edition, Münster 1969, pp. 147–150.

[171] The concept of the "fullness" (πλήρωμα), stemming from the philosophical religious (probably Gnostic) milieu of the Epistle, has a rich intellectual content in its use in the letters to the Colossians and to the Ephesians. "The whole fullness (of God) was pleased to make its dwelling in him (Christ)" (Col. 1:19). The expression describes the total oneness of God and of his Son, which is made known in revelation and in operation. See G. Delling, Art. πλήρωμα, in *Theol. Dict. N. T.*, Vol. 6 (1968), pp. 298–305. Of the commentaries, E. Lohse's *Die Briefe an die Kolosser und an Philemon*, Göttingen 1968, is especially valuable. See also J. Ernst, *Pleroma und Pleroma Christi*, Regensburg 1970. N. Kehl, *Der Christushymnus im Kolosserbrief (Kol 1,12–20)*, Stuttgart 1967.

[172] θεότης no doubt designates the being of God as power and life. To be distinguished from θεότης is θειότης (Rom. 1:20), whereby Godhead is designated according to its nature, divinity. Col. 2:9 brings the revelation of God in Christ into relief.

[173] In Col. 2:17, σῶμα can mean the "reality". Is the word σωματικῶς in Col. 2:9 to be understood in this same way? Or does the term here refer also to the σῶμα of the Church, as it does in Col. 1:18? Does it mean that the divine indwelling fills up the body of the Church? Or does σωματικῶς designates the corporeality, *i.e.*, the incarnation and perfect humanity of God in Christ? See F. Baumgärtel and E. Schweizer, Art. σῶμα, in *Theol. Dict. N. T.*, Vol. 7 (1971), pp. 1024–1094.

[174] Basing itself on biblical Christology, in which Christ is termed "Word of God" and "Image of God" (see above, present section, § 11,6), whereby the Revealer and the Revealed are identical, modern Protestant theology interprets the divinity of Jesus as God's self-revelation and God's disclosure of his nature in Christ. Thus the Christ event pertains to the nature of God himself. God is the one "who makes the dead to be alive" (Rom. 4:17), because he is the one "who has raised Jesus up from the dead" (Rom. 8:11). The proposition "Christ is God" is likewise valid when it is turned about, "God is Christ." See Karl Barth, *Die Kirchliche Dogmatik*, Vol. 1/1, pp. 435–470; and Vol. 1/2, pp. 145–187. W. Pannenberg, *Grundzüge der Christologie*, 2nd edition, Göttingen 1966, pp. 124–131.

[175] The use of the formula "Lord and God" has prior examples in the Old Testament (Ps. 35;23; Jer. 38:17; Zech. 13:9) and also in Hellenism (Epictetus, *Diss.* 2,16,13, [the Lord God]; and dedicatory inscriptions [to the God·and Lord]). See Rudolf Bultmann, *Das Evangelium des Johannes*, 19th edition, Göttingen 1968, p. 538f.

[176] H. Kleinknecht, F. Baumgärtel, W. Bieder, E. Sjöberg, and E. Schweizer, Art.

πνεῦμα, *Theol. Dict. N. T.*, Vol. 6 (1968), pp. 332–455. C. Barrett, *The Holy Spirit and the Gospel Tradition*, 2nd edition, London 1966. F. Büchsel, *Der Geist Gottes im Neuen Testament*, Gütersloh 1926. G. Hasenhüttl, *Charisma, Ordnungsprinzip der Kirche*, Freiburg 1969. L. Hermann, *Kyrios und Pneuma*, Munich 1961. F. Lieb, "*Der Heilige Geist als Geist Jesu Christi*", in *Evang. Theologie*, Vol. 23 (1963), pp. 281–298. K. L. Schmidt, "*Das Pneuma Hagion als Person und als Charisma*", in *Eranos-Jahrbuch*, Vol. 13 (1945), pp. 187–235. E. Schweizer, "*Gegenwart des Geistes und eschatologische Hoffnung bei Zarathustra, spätjüdischen Gruppen, Gnostikern und den Zeugen des Neuen Testaments*", in *Neotestamentica*, Zürich 1963, pp. 153–179.

[177] Modern translations and commentaries (M. Buber, K. Galling, G. von Rad, C. Westermann) determine their rendering of Gen. 1:2 on the basis of linguistic, religious-historical, and exegetical considerations: "A storm of God (*i.e.*, a frightful storm) moved over the waters." The statement, therefore, is by way of describing the chaos. F. Baumgärtel rejects this view (*Theol. Dict. N.T.*, Vol. 6 [1968], pp. 363 and 366) and still understands Gen. 1:2 in respect to the creative Spirit of God. The Septuagint translation in any case was able to be understood, along with other similar passages (Ps. 33:6; Is. 32:15), as referring to the Creator Spirit. That, in fact, is how it was understood; and it worked its influence accordingly.

[178] M. A. Chevalier, *L'Esprit et le Messie dans bas-judasime et le Nouveau Testament*, Paris 1958. R. Koch, *Geist und Messias*, Vienna 1950.

[179] W. Foerster, "*Der heilige Geist im Spätjudentum*", in *New Testament Studies*, Vol. 8 (1961/1962), pp. 117–134.

[180] Strack and Billerbeck, *op. cit.*, Vol. 2 (1924), p. 134f.; Vol. 4 (1928), pp. 435–451.

[181] F. Nötscher, "*Geist und Geister in den Texten von Qumran*", in *Vom Alten zum Neuen Testament*, Bonn 1962, pp. 175–187; J. Schreiner, "*Geistbegabung in der Gemeinde von Qumran*", in *Bibl. Zeitchr.*, new series, Vol. 9 (1965), pp. 161–180.

[182] H. Greeven, Art. περιστερά, in *Theol. Dict. N. T.*, Vol. 6 (1968), pp. 63–72. A. Feuillet, "*Le symbolisme de la colombe dan les récits évangéliques du baptême*", in *Recherches de science religieuse*, Vol. 16 (1958), pp. 524–544. F. Lentzen-Deis, *Die Taufe Jesu nach den Synoptikern*, Frankfurt 1970, pp. 170–183; 265–270. On other themes of the baptism account, see § 11,3 and § 21,6 in the present work.

[183] H. von Baer, *Der Heilige Geist in den Lukasschriften*, Stuttgart 1926. G. W. H. Lampe, "The Holy Spirit in the Writings of St. Luke", in D. E. Nineham, *Studies in the Gospel*, Oxford 1955, pp. 159–200.

[184] E. Lohse, Art. πεντηκοστή, in *Theol. Dict. N. T.*, Vol. 6 (1968), pp. 44–53. W. Grundmann, "*Der Pfingstbericht der Acta in seinem historischen Sinn*", in *Texte und Untersuchungen*, no. 102, 1961, pp. 584–594.

[185] E. B. Allo, "*Sagesse et Pneuma dans 1 Cor.*", in *Revue Biblique*, Vol. 43 (1934), pp. 321–346. E. Fuchs, *Christus und der Geist bei Paulus*, Leipzig 1932. P. Gaechter, "*Zum Pneumabegriff des heiligen Paulus*", in *Zeitschrift für katholische Theologie*,

Vol. 53 (1929), pp. 345–408. U. Luck, *"Historische Fragen zum Verhältnis von Kyrios und Pneuma bei Paulus"*, in *Theol. Literaturzeitg.*, Vol. 85 (1960), pp. 845–848. K. Stalder, *Das Werk des Geistes in der Heiligung bei Paulus*, Zürich 1962.

[186] K. H. Schelkle, *Ihr alle seid Geistliche*, Einsiedeln 1964.

[187] G. Johnston, *The Spirit-Paraclete in the Gospel of John*, Cambridge 1970. H. Schlier, *"Zum Begriff des Geistes nach dem Johannesevangelium"*, in *Besinnung auf das Neue Testament*, Freiburg 1964, pp. 264–271.

[188] In profane Greek the term "paraclete" is associated with juridical process. It signifies one called upon for assistance, one who speaks for or in behalf of another, an advocate (in the legal sense). In Judaism, the paraclete, employed as a loanword, is one who speaks for God, a mediator. The study of the history of religions shows that the New Testament idea of the Paraclete goes back to late Jewish apocalyptic traditions of mediational speakers for God; but Gnostic (Mandaean) notions of revealers and helpers have also been accepted, since just such functions as these are proper to the Johannine Paraclete. The multiplicity of helpers acknowledged elsewhere, however, is concentrated in John on Christ and the Spirit. See J. Behm, Art. παράκλητος, in *Theol. Dict. N. T.*, Vol. 5 (1967), pp. 800–814. O. Betz, *Der Paraklet*, Leiden 1963.

[189] Gerhard Ebeling, *"Gott und Wort"*, in *Wort und Glaube*, Vol. 2, Tübingen 1969, pp. 396–432. H. Gollwitzer, *Die Existenz Gottes im Bekenntnis des Glaubens*, 5th edition, Munich 1968. H. Grass, *"Die Gottesfrage in der gegenwärtigen Theologie"*, in *Theol. Rundschau*, new series, Vol. 35 (1970), pp. 231–269; Vol. 37 (1972), pp. 1–42. R. Spaemann, *"Die Frage nach der Bedeutung des Wortes Gott"*, in *Internationale katholische Zeitschrift*, Vol. 1 (1972), pp. 54–72. J. Sudbrack, *Abwesenheit Gottes*, Zürich 1971. H. Thielicke, *"Was meint das Wort 'Gott'?"*, in *Studium generale*, Vol. 23 (1970), pp. 23–46. H. Zahrnt, *Die Sache mit Gott*, Munich 1966.

[190] F. Büchsel, Art. εἴδωλον, in *Theol. Dict. N. T.*, Vol. 2 (1964), pp. 375–380. G. Quell, E. Stauffer, K. G. Kuhn, Art. θεός, *ibid.*, Vol. 3 (1965), pp. 65–123. M. Buber, *"Die Götter der Völker und Gott"*, in O. Betz *et al.*, editor, *Abraham unser Vater (Festschrift O. Michel)*, Leiden 1963, pp. 44–57. W. Eichrodt, *Theologie des Alten Testaments*, Vol. 1, 8th edition, Stuttgart 1968, pp. 110–189. V. Hamp, *"Monotheismus im Alten Testament"*, in *Bibliotheca Ephemeridum Theologicarum Lovaniensum XII–XIII*, 1 (1959), pp. 516–521. M. Rehm, *Das Bild Gottes im Alten Testament*, Würzburg 1951. H. D. Preuss, *Verspottung fremder Religionen im Alten Testament*, Stuttgart 1971. J. Schildenberger, *"Die Religion des Alten Testaments"*, in F. König, *Christus und die Religionen der Erde*, Vol. 3, 2nd edition, Freiburg 1961, pp. 439–521. W. H. Schmidt, *Alttestamentlicher Glaube und seine Umwelt*, Neukirchen-Vluyn 1968. Th. C. Vriezen, *Theologie des Alten Testaments in Grundzügen*, Wageningen 1957, pp. 123–168. W. Jaeger, *Die Theologie der frühen griechischen Denker*, Stuttgart 1953 (repr. Darmstadt 1964). W. Weischedel, *Der Gott der Philosophen*, 2 vols., Darmstadt 1971/1972.

[191] R. Mayer, *"Der Gottesname Jahwe im Licht der Forschung"*, in *Bibl. Zeitschr.*,

new series, Vol. 2 (1958), pp. 26–53. R. Rendtorff, *"El, Baal und Jahwe"*, in *Zeitscrift für die alttestamentliche Wissenschaft*, Vol. 78 (1966), pp. 277–292.

[192] H. Eising, *"Der Weisheitslehrer und die Götterbilder"*, in *Biblica*, Vol 40 (1959), pp. 393–408. M. Hengel, *Judentum und Hellenismus*, Tübingen 1969, pp. 199–670. G. von Rad, *Weisheit in Israel*, Neukirchen-Vluyn 1970, pp. 229–239. The Jewish polemicism corresponds to the ancient criticism of cultic images and their worship. The explanation of the cult of images in Wis. 14:15–21 matches the theory of Euhemerus. See I. Geffcken, *"Der Bilderstreit des heidnischen Altertums"*, in *Archiv für Religionswissenschaft*, Vol. 19 (1916/1919), pp. 286–315. V. Müller, Art. *Kultbild*, in A. Pauly and G. Wissowa, *Realencyklopädie der klassischen Altertumswissenschaft*, Suppl. Vol. 5, Stuttgart 1931, pp. 472–511.

[193] H. Kleinknecht, G. Quell, E. Stauffer, K. G. Kuhn, Art. θεός, in *Theol. Dict. N.T.*, Vol. 3 (1965), pp. 65–123. C. Bussmann, *Themen der paulinischen Missionspredigt auf dem Hintergrung der spätjüdisch-hellenistischen Missionsliteratur*, Bern and Frankfurt 1971. G. Delling, *"Partizipale Gottesprädikationen in den Briefen des Neuen Testaments"*, in *Studia theologica*, Vol. 17 (1963), pp. 1–59. H. M. Féret, *La connaissance biblique de Dieu*, Paris 1955. R. Rahner, *"Theos im Neuen Testament"*, in *Schriften zur Theologie*, Vol. 1, Einsiedeln 1954, pp. 91–167; also of Rahner, *"Bemerkungen zur Gotteslehre in der katholischen Dogmatik"*, in *Schriften zur Theologie*, Vol. 8, Einsiedeln 1967, pp. 165–185. R. Schäfer, *Jesus und der Gottesglaube*, Tübingen 1970. G. Schneider, *"Urchristliche Gottesverkündigung in hellenistischer Umwelt"*, in *Biblische Zeitschrift*, new series, Vol. 13 (1969), pp. 59–75.

[194] P. Dalbert, *Die Theologie der hellenistich-jüdischen Missionsliteratur unter Ausschluss von Philo und Josephus*, Hamburg-Volksdorf 1954. Ferdinand Hahn, *Das Verständnis der Mission im Neuen Testament*, Neukirchen 1963 [translated by Frank Clarke under title *Mission in the New Testament*, Naperville 1965]. J. Jeremias, *Jesu Verheissung für die Völker*, Stuttgart 1956 [translated by S. H. Hooke under title *Jesus' Promise to the Nations*, Naperville 1958]. Ulrich Wilckens, *Die Missionsreden der Apostelgeschichte*, Neukirchen 1961.

[195] Paul bases his teaching in 1 Cor. 10:20 on Deut. 32:1f., in which latter passage the Septuagint says of Israel's unfaithfulness, "They sacrificed to demons, which are not God". The Hebrew text reads, "They sacrificed to new gods, which Israel had not known until now."

[196] E. Stauffer, Art. εἰς, in *Theol. Dict. N. T.*, Vol. 2 (1964), pp. 434–442. G. Delling, "Μόνος θεός", in *Studien zum Neuen Testament und zum hellenistischen Judentum*, Göttingen 1970, pp. 391–400. E. Peterson Εἰς θεός, Göttingen 1926; also of Peterson, *"Der Monotheismus als politisches Problem"*, in *Theologische Traktate*, Munich 1951, pp. 45–147.

[197] For Xenophanes see H. Diels and W. Kranze, *Die Fragmente der Vorsokratiker*, Vol. 1, 7th edition, Berlin 1954, frag. 23, p. 135. For the Orphics, see Otto Kern, *Orphicorum fragmenta*, Berlin 1922, frag. 21, 21a, 168, pp. 90–93 and 201–207; also Diels and Kranz as above, frag. 6, p. 8. For Cleanthes, see J. von Arnim,

Stoicorum veterum fragmenta, Vol. 1, Stuttgart 1964. For Marcus Aurelius, any edition of his *Meditations*, known also as the *Communings with Himself* or *Conversations with Himself*, 7,9,2; C. R. Haines' translation in the Loeb Library (1915); or better, A. S. L. Farquharson's critical edition of Marcus Aurelius in 2 volumes, Oxford 1944.

[198] This confession makes use of a formulation which came into Jewish Hellenism from Hellenistic mysticism; *cf.* Marcus Aurelius' much-quoted (4,23,2): "O nature, from you are all things, in you are all things, unto you are all things."

[199] Reflection within the New Testament continues on to an insight into the unity between Father, Son and Spirit (Matthew 28:19; 2 Cor. 13:13; Mark 1:10f.).

[200] *Einheit der Kirche? Ringvorlesung der Evangelisch-Theologischen Fakultät der Westfälischen Wilhelms-Universität Münster*, Witten 1964. S. Hanson, *The Unity of the Church in the New Testament*, Uppsala 1946. J. Scharbert (editor), *Zum Thema Eine Kirche — Eine Menscheit*, Stuttgart 1971. P. A. van Stempvoort, *Paulus und die Spaltungen zu Korinth*. H. Schlier, *"Die Einheit der Kirche nach dem Apostel Paulus"*, in M. Roesle and O. Cullmann, (editors), *Begegnung der Christen (Festschrift O. Karrer)*, Stuttgart and Frankfurt, 1959, pp. 83–113. J. Feiner and M. Löhrer (editors), *Mysterium salutis*, Vol. IV/1 (*Das Heilsgeschehen in der Gemeinde*), Einsiedeln 1972.

[201] The term and concept "body of Christ" will be taken up in the fourth volume of our present work. In the explanation supported by Rudolf Bultmann (*Theologie des Neuen Testaments*, 6th edition, Tübingen 1968, pp. 169f. and 298f.), H. Schlier (*Der Brief an die Epheser*, 6th edition, Düsseldorf 1968), and E. Käsemann (*Leib und Leib Christi*, Tübingen 1933), among others, the concept makes use of the Gnostic myth of the primordial man who gathers into himself those who are redeemed from out of the world. This view was for a long time regarded as exegetically valid; but more recently it is increasingly criticized or entirely rejected. Present day discussion would rather accept the idea that notions from Old Testament Jewish, Hellenistic, and New Testament Christian domains have been united in the concept "body of Christ." It must be remembered that the Gnostic texts that have come down to us were written later than the New Testament. See P. Benoit, *"L'Église corps du Christ"*, in *Miscellanea Alfredo Cardinale Ottaviani*, Vol. 2, Rome 1969, pp. 971–1027; J. Gnilka, *Der Epheserbrief*, Freiburg 1971, pp. 33–45.

[202] The theme of God as Creator is mentioned here only as occupying a place at this point in the continuity of the New Testament teaching about God. The biblical theology of creation was presented in some detail in our present *Theology of the New Testament*, Vol. 1, pp. 13–72.

[203] For a further treatment of this point, see Joachim Jeremias, *Abba*, Göttingen 1966, pp. 15–67; and also of Jeremias, *Neutestamentliche Theologie*, Vol. 1, Gütersloh 1971, pp. 67–73 and 174–196. Jeremias has repeatedly demonstrated that the address "Abba", originally an infant or child's word for father, like daddy or papa, carries with it the notion of the familiarity and trust that a child invests in

his father. To the contemporaries of Jesus, nevertheless, it must have seemed disrespectful to address God with such a term.

[204] O. Procksch and K. G. Kuhn, Art. ἅγιος, in *Theol. Dict. N. T.*, Vol. 1 (1964), pp. 88–115. G. Schrenk, Art. ἱερός, *ibid.*, Vol. 3 (1965), pp. 221–283. F. Hauck, Art. ὅσιος, *ibid.*, Vol. 5 (1967), pp. 489–493. H. Bietenhard, *Die himmlische Welt im Urchristentum und Spätjudentum*, Tübingen 1951. G. Kittel and G. von Rad, Art. δόξα, in *Theol. Dict. N. T.*, Vol. 2 (1964), pp. 232–255. See also our present *Theology of the New Testament*, Vol. 1, pp. 106–107, 115–126, 148–152; Vol. 3, pp. 171–178.

[205] H. Kleinknecht, O. Grether, O. Procksch, J. Fichtner, G. Stählin, and E. Sjöberg, Art. ὀργή, in *Theol. Dict. N. T.*, Vol. 5 (1967), pp. 382–447.

[206] In Mark 1:41 numerous manuscripts read σπλαγχνισθείς (He showed mercy) instead of ὀργισθείς (He was moved to anger). The more difficult reading, ὀργισθείς, will be preferred as the original reading. [*Translator's note*: This is the common rule of hermeneutics, based on the more or less obvious fact that it can easily be explained why a copyist or someone else would change a reading difficult to understand to one easy and more natural; whereas it is well-nigh impossible to give any rational explanation for the change of a perfectly understandable reading to a difficult one. Hence, everything else being equal, the difficult reading must be regarded as the more authentic]. Someone unable to tolerate the reading which depicts Jesus as experiencing anger has changed it so that it reflects the more common portrayal of his mercy.

[207] The whole of the Old Testament — Prophets, Psalms, Wisdom and Deuterocanonical writings — along with Philo, Josephus, and the Rabbinic writings, is concerned with the works of conversion and repentance. The performance of works of penance is laudable and has great efficacy, but that is all. And this is true also in the Judaism of the New Testament era. If there is a saying of the Rabbi Abbahu (*ca.* A. D. 300), that "on the step on which the truly contrite stand, the perfectly pious cannot stand," it would, nevertheless, be difficult to find another such statement in all the literature of Judaism. See Strack and Billerbeck, *op. cit.*, Vol. 1 (1922), pp. 162–172; Vol. 2 (1924), pp. 210–212. Also E. K. Dietrich, *Die Umkehr (Bekehrung und Busse) im Alten Testament und im Judentum*, Stuttgart 1936.

[208] H. Kleinknecht, F. Baumgärtel, W. Bieder, E. Sjöberg, and E. Schweizer, Art. πνεῦμα, in *Theol. Dict. N. T.*, Vol. 6 (1968), pp. 332–455. F. Nötscher, *Zur Terminologie der Qumrantexte, Bonn 1956*. R. Schnackenberg, *"Die 'Anbetung in Geist und Wahrheit' (Jo 4,23) im Lichte von Qumran-Texten"*, in *Bibl. Zeitschrift*, new series, Vol. 3 (1959), pp. 88–94.

[209] The Jewish biblical presuppositions of John 4:24 are found quite clearly represented in the writings of Qumran, where the concepts *truth* and *spirit* are likewise united. God will purify the works of men "through the Holy Spirit and the Spirit of Truth" (1 QS 4:21). The worshipper petitions: "to be strengthened through your Holy Spirit and to remain faithful to the truth of your covenant

and to serve you in truth and wholeheartedly and to love your Name" (1 QH 16:6f.).

[210] Thus Chrysippus, fragment 310; and Cleanthes, fragment 1009; in J. von Arnim, *Stoicorum veterum fragmenta*, Vol. 2, Stuttgart 1964, pp. 112 and 299. See also H. Kleinknecht, Art. πνεῦμα in *Theol. Dict. N. T.*, Vol 6 (1968), p. 356.

[211] A. Oepke, Art. λαμπάς, in *Theol. Dict. N. T.*, Vol. 4 (1967), pp. 16–28. W. Michaelis, Art. λύχνος, *ibid.*, pp. 324–327. H. Conzelmann, Art. σκότος, *ibid.*, Vol. 7 (1971), pp. 423–445; also of Conzelmann, Art. φῶς, *ibid.*, Vol. 9 (1974), pp. 310–358. S. Aalen, *Die Begriffe 'Licht' und 'Finsternis' im Alten Testament, im Spätjudentum und im Rabbinismus*, Oslo 1951. W. Beierwaltes, *Lux intelligibilis. Untersuchungen zur Lichtmetaphysik der Griechen*, dissertation, Munich 1957. Rudolf Bultmann, *"Zur Geschichte der Lichtsymbolik im Altertum"*, in *Exegetica*, Tübingen 1967, pp. 323–355. J. Chmiel, *Lumière et charité d'après la première Épître de Saint Jean*, Rome 1971.

[212] W. Grundmann, Art. ἀγαθός, in *Theol. Dict. N. T.*, Vol. 1 (1964), pp. 10–18. E. Stauffer, Art. ἀγάπη, *ibid.*, Vol. 1, pp. 21–55. K. Weiss, Art. χρηστός, *ibid.*, Vol. 9 (1974), pp. 483–492. J. Chmiel, *Lumière et charité d'après la première Épître de Saint Jean*, Rome 1971. K. Prenter, *"Der Gott, der Liebe ist"*, in *Theol. Literaturzeitg.*, Vol. 96 (1971), pp. 401–413. E. Schutz, *Die Vorgeschichte der johanneischen Formel ὁ θεὸς ἀγάπη ἐστίν*, dissertation, Göttingen 1917. Ceslaus Spicq, *Agapè dans le Nouveau Testament*, 3 vols., Paris 1958–1960 [translated by Sr. Marie Aquinas McNamara and Sr. Marie Honoria Richter under the title *Agape in the New Testament*, 3 vols., St. Louis, 1963–1966]. L. R. Stachowiak, *Chrestotes*, Freiburg in der Schweiz 1957. V. Warnach, *Agape*, Düsseldorf 1951.

[213] W. Bousset and H. Gressmann, edited by E. Lohse, *Die Religion des Judentums im späthellenistischen Zeitalter*, 4th edition, Tübingen 1966, pp. 302–320. G. Dellin, *Partizipale Gottesprädikationen in den Briefen des Neuen Testaments*, in *Studia theologica*, Vol. 17 (1963), pp. 1–59. M. P. Nilsson, *Geschichte der griechischen Religion*, Vol. 2, 2nd edition, Munich 1961, pp. 569–701. Wolfhart Pannenberg, *"Die Aufnahme des philosophischen Gottesbegriffes als dogmatisches Problem der frühchristlichen Theologie"*, in *Grundfragen systematischer Theologie*, Göttingen 1967, pp. 297–346.

[214] H. Sasse, Art. αἰών, in *Theol. Dict. N. T.*, Vol. 1 (1964), pp. 197–209. As to the plural formations, like "from the eons to the eons", probably there is an influence here of ritual or courtly acclamations. See the article of Theodor Klauser, *"Akklamation"*, in the *Reallexikon für Antike und Christentum*, Vol. 1 (1950), pp. 216–233.

[215] G. Kittel, Art. A Ω, in the *Theol. Dict. N.T.*, Vol. 1 (1964), pp. 1–3.

[216] F. Büchsel, Art. εἰμί, in the *Theol. Dict. N. T.*, Vol. 2 (1964), pp. 398–400.

[217] W. Michaelis, Art. ὁράω, in the *Theol. Dict. N. T.*, Vol. 5 (1967), pp. 315–382. R. Bultmann, *"Untersuchungen zum Johannesevangelium* (Joh 1,18)", in *Exegetica*, Tübingen 1967, pp. 174–197. E. Fascher, *"Deus invisibilis"*, in Marburger *theologische Studien*, Vol. 1, Gotha 1931, pp. 41–77.

[218] Hellenistic religious language is used in the other predicates of God, in 1 Tim. 1:17 and 6:15; see the comments to these passsages immediately below in § 20,3 and § 20,4.

[219] G. Harder, Art. φθείρω, in the *Theol. Dict. N. T.*, Vol. 9 (1974), pp. 93–106.

[220] Rudolf Bultmann, Art. ἀθανασία, in the *Theol. Dict. N. T.*, Vol. 3 (1965), pp. 22–25.

[221] A considerable number of the Fathers of the Church read John 1:3c and 4 together: "What was made was life in him." Nor is this interpretation excluded even in modern commentaries. See K. Aland, *"Eine Untersuchung zu Jo 1,3,4"*, in *Zeitschrift für die neutestamentliche Wissenschaft*, Vol. 59 (1968), pp. 174–209.

[222] G. Bertram and F. Hauck, Art. μακάριος, in the *Theol. Dict. N. T.*, Vol. 4 (1967) pp. 362–370.

[223] As the Blessed One, God has no needs (Act. 17:25). This thought too is familiar enough to the Greek world, and is found especially in the Stoa. It is known in the Greek Old Testament (2 Macc. 14:35 and 3 Macc. 2:9), as also in Philo (*De vita Mosis* 1,157: "The Godhead, to whom everything belongs, and who needs nothing").

[224] G. Bertram, ὕψιστος, in the *Theol. Dict. N. T.*, Vol. 8 (1972), pp. 614–620. F. Cumont, Art. ὕψιστος, in A. Pauly and G. Wissowa, *Realencyklopädie der klassischen Altertumswissenschaft*, Vol. 17 (1914), pp. 444–450.

[225] W. Michaelis, Art. παντοκράτωρ, in the *Theol. Dict. N. T.*, Vol. 3 (1965), pp. 914–915. F. Buri, *Der Pantokrator*, Hamburg-Bergstedt 1969.

[226] J. F. Fitzmyer, "Qumran and the Interpolated Paragraph in 2 Cor 6:14 — 7:1", in *Essays on the Semitic Background of the New Testament*, London 1971, pp. 205–217. J. Gnilka, 2 *"Kor 6:14 — 7:1 im Lichte der Qumranschriften und der Zwölf-Patriarchen-Testamente"*, in J. Blinzler *et al.*, editor, *Neutestamentliche Aufsätze (Festschrift J. Schmid)*, Regensburg 1963, pp. 86–99.

[227] G. Delling, Art. τρεῖς, in the *Theol. Dict. N. T.*, Vol. 8 (1972), pp. 216–225. R. Mehrlein, Art. *"Drei"*, in the *Reallexikon für Antike und Christentum*, Vol. 4 (1959), pp. 269–310. J. Feiner and M. Löhrer (editors), *Mysterium salutis*, Vol. 2, Einsiedeln 1967, pp. 15–401 (*Gott als Urgrund der Heilsgeschichte*). H. Geisser, *Die Trinitätslehre unter den Problemen und in den Prolegomena christlicher Theologie*, typed dissertation, Tübingen 1962; also of Geisser, *"Der Beitrag der Trinitätslehre zur Problematik des Redens von Gott"*, in *Zeitschrift für Theologie und Kirche*, Vol. 65 (1968), pp. 231–255. E. Jüngel, *Gottes Sein ist im Werden*, Tübingen 1965. L. Scheffczyk, *Der eine und dreifaltige Gott*, Mainz 1968. A. W. Wainwright, *The Trinity in the New Testament*, London 1962.

[228] It is a controversial point whether the third genitive κοινωνία τοῦ ἁγίου πνεύματος is to be understood as an objective or as a subjective genitive. Understood as an objective genitive it signifies a participation in the Holy Spirit. It would mean that God produces pneumatic existence in Christ. More frequently, however, the genitive is understood as subjective; and then it indicates that the Spirit operates just as personally as do God and Christ. This interpretation can appeal to the fact

that, with its acceptance, all three genitives of the passage are ordered grammatically and structurally alike. In Rom. 15:30, the phrase "love of the Spirit" is quite certainly a subjective genitive, *i.e.*, it is the love that goes out from the Spirit, not that which has the Spirit for its object. Dogmatics has a vested interest in the passage, in finding in it a testimonial to the personality of the Spirit.

[229] J. Knackstedt, *"Manifestatio Ss. Trinitatis in baptismo Domini"*, in *Verbum Domini*, Vol. 38 (1960), pp. 76–91. For further literature on the baptism of Jesus, see note 162 above.

[230] The *Didache* (7:1,3) employs the same trinitarian formula for baptism. It is questionable, however, whether the *Didache* was acquainted with any written Gospel. Apparently it drew only from oral tradition. But then the trinitarian formula of Matt. 28:19 is not a construction of the Evangelist; it arose in the tradition of the Church.

[231] K. B. Barth, *Die kirchliche Dogmatik*, Vol. 1/1, 5th edition, Zollikon-Zürich, 1947, pp. 311–404 [pp. 339–440 in the English edition referred to above in note 11].

[232] Karl Rahner hints very strongly at this problem in his *"Bemerkungen zum dogmatischen Traktat 'De Trinitate' "*, in *Schriften zur Theologie*, Vol. 4 Einsiedeln 1960, pp. 103–133 [in English translation by Kevin Smyth, "Remarks on the Dogmatic Treatise 'De Trinitate' ", in *Theological Investigations*, Vol. 4, Baltimore 1966, pp. 77–102]. Also of Rahner, *"Der dreifaltige Gott als transzendenter Urgrund der Heilsgeschichte"*, in J. Feiner and M. Löhrer (editors), *Mysterium salutis*, Vol. 2, Einsiedeln 1967, pp. 317–401; and Rahner's articles "Divine Trinity" and "Trinity in Theology", in *Sacramentum mundi* (English edition), Vol. 6, New York 1970, pp. 295–303 and 303–308 respectively. On the history and problematics of the concept of person in the dogma of the Trinity, see also Wolfhart Pannenberg, *Grundzüge der Christologie*, 2nd edition, Gütersloh 1966, pp. 182–189 and 351–356.

GENERAL INDEX

347